AF540688

HOW TO LEAD A TRANQUIL LIFE

Praise for the Book

'This luminous work is a soul-stirring reminder that tranquillity is not a retreat from life, but a quiet flowering within it. In a world increasingly swept by turbulence, noise, and avoidable velocity, the author recommends a pause and beckons us toward a luminous and profound inner realignment. For the earnest seeker, this book may well become a turning point—a sanctum, a mirror, and a mantra.'

—**C. S. Lodha**, Jurist and Independent Counsel

'This book is a rare gift—simple in its language yet profound in its message. In a world overwhelmed by speed, distractions, and constant striving, it offers a gentle reminder that true peace does not lie outside but within us. What makes the work remarkable is its practicality: it does not demand withdrawal from life, but teaches us how to live fully engaged in the world while remaining inwardly tranquil.'

—**Dr Vinay Nangia**, former Head,
Department of Management Studies, IIT Roorkee

'This book presents a rare and compelling invitation: to move beyond the material and to engage directly with the very foundation of awareness. It is at once profound and practical, free from ideology yet rich in timeless insight. I consider this book a significant contribution—not only for those seeking peace, but for anyone devoted to understanding that which endures beyond the ever-shifting currents of circumstance.'

—**R. N. Choubey**, former Secretary,
Ministry of Civil Aviation; former Member, UPSC

HOW TO LEAD A TRANQUIL LIFE

DISCOVER THE SECRETS TO SERENITY

SWAMI SHEKARANAND

ALEPH

ALEPH BOOK COMPANY
An independent publishing firm
promoted by ***Rupa Publications India***

First published in India in 2025
by Aleph Book Company
161-B/4, Gulmohar House,
Yusuf Sarai Community Centre,
New Delhi 110049

ISBN: 978-93-6523-905-8

1 3 5 7 9 10 8 6 4 2

Printed in India

CONTENTS

FOREWORD

Have you ever felt a stirring within—a subtle recognition that there's more to life than meets the eye? In spite of material comforts, do you feel uneasy and wonder what is missing? Consider this: amidst the daily hustle and bustle, do you truly feel aligned with your deepest aspirations or are you full of fears and worries? Do you know who you are? Do you sense a need for transformation, a yearning to navigate life's complexities with greater ease and fulfilment?

Then you have the right book in your hand.

Our materialistic world has shaped us so that if we cannot explain something, then it cannot be! In the journey of spiritual awakening, some moments serve as catalysts, propelling us into deeper realms of understanding and self-discovery. Serendipity often plays a profound role in our lives, orchestrating encounters that defy logical explanation. For me, that moment came in the form of an interaction with Swamiji in 2023, during his mind management training programme. Until then, I had believed myself to be spiritually aware, but it was through Swamiji's guidance that I realized the depth of my delusion. It was an acknowledgement that true wisdom begins with unlearning the toxic narratives and misconceptions of the modern world that cloud our perception of spirituality.

Swamiji's invitation to pen this foreword is both a joyous opportunity and a daunting challenge. How does one, a spiritual novice like myself, do justice to the profound interpretations encapsulated within this book? Despite lacking the literary prowess or spiritual clarity to encapsulate this book in just a few pages, I strive to honour Swamiji's faith in me.

This book isn't here to instruct, but to guide you while you ask questions, nudging you gently towards profound self-reflection and growth. It acknowledges the inherent conflicts we face within ourselves and in our interactions with others, which often manifest as stress and discord. How do we navigate this without fear of isolation in our societies? Well, you don't need to abandon your worldly duties to seek spiritual balance. This is exactly what this book offers—pathways to transform your relationship with yourself and others, fostering harmony, resilience, and a deeper sense of connection in your daily life.

In today's world, spirituality is often packaged for mass consumption, leaving us spiritually malnourished. We've adopted a shallow understanding of spirituality, influenced by a bias towards easily digestible content. Swamiji's writings bridge the gap between ancient wisdom and modern understanding, inviting us to reconnect with timeless truths. This book defies the need for a foreword or introduction; it demands to be read from start to finish. It won't provide comfort; instead, it will challenge your worldly beliefs, prompting you to question your knowledge, biases, and faith in modern spiritual trends.

Amidst the turmoil of life's tribulations, there exists a path to inner peace and liberation—a journey of self-discovery and enlightenment that transcends the limitations of ego-driven desires and attachments. Through understanding the inner workings of our minds and embracing the timeless wisdom of Vedanta, we can navigate the complexities of existence with clarity and compassion, ultimately finding solace in the eternal truth of our shared humanity. In a world inundated with superficial distractions and fleeting pleasures, true spiritual growth demands introspection, discipline, and a willingness to confront the uncomfortable truths that lie within.

Embark on a journey of profound self-discovery and spiritual awakening with this book, where ancient wisdom meets modern insight to illuminate the path to inner peace and fulfilment. In a world besieged by superficial distractions and the relentless pursuit of material success, there exists a longing within each of us—a yearning to reconnect with our true selves, to transcend the limitations of ego, and to discover the timeless truths that unite us all. Through the teachings of Advaita Vedanta (the non-dual Vedanta philosophy) and the guidance of spiritual luminaries, this book invites you to explore the depths of consciousness, unravel the mysteries of existence, and embark on a transformative odyssey towards a life of clarity, purpose, and spiritual abundance.

At its core, this book delves into the profound truths of Advaita Vedanta, unraveling the mysteries of Brahman, the karmic cycle, and the essence of consciousness. It compels us to confront our preconceived notions, and invites us to explore the depths of our spiritual heritage with renewed vigour. Life today, with its myriad stresses, often leaves us feeling unfulfilled. Yet, true fulfilment lies in mastering the mind and body through meditation—a journey of self-discovery and connection with the divine.

The topics it addresses—Brahman, the essence of human existence, death, and the karmic cycle—are profoundly fundamental yet often overlooked. It reminds us that the tangible world we perceive is but an illusion, while Consciousness constitutes the ultimate reality.

At the heart of this exploration lies the timeless wisdom of the Bhagavad Gita, which flows quietly yet profoundly through the pages of this book. More than just being a scripture, it offers a steady compass in the chaos, complexity, and quiet confusions of modern life. Its teachings protect the seeker from the relentless swings of life's dualities and illuminate the path towards living with resilience and grace. At its essence lies a simple yet transformative lesson: to act with full dedication, yet without attachment. After all, even our emails today come with attachments—how freeing it is to discover that our actions need not! It is this stillness in action that anchors us, helping us navigate the turbulence of daily living with clarity and inner balance.

Gunas refer to the three fundamental qualities of nature (Sattva, Rajas, and Tamas—Swamiji terms them the SRT factor) that shape thoughts, actions, and characteristics in individuals and the world. Understanding these qualities is essential for navigating life's challenges and achieving spiritual growth. Understanding SRT offers profound and practical insights into human behaviour and spiritual evolution. While the Bhagavad Gita touches upon these qualities, it often does so in passing, focusing more on action and duty. SRT, however, delves deeper into the intricacies of these qualities: Sattva, representing purity, harmony, and balance; Rajas, embodying passion, activity, and restlessness; and Tamas, symbolizing inertia, darkness, and ignorance. Understanding these gunas unveils the subtle interplay that dictates our mental states, motivations, and the quality of our interactions with the world. By recognizing and cultivating Sattva, mitigating the excesses of Rajas, and transcending the inertia of Tamas, individuals can harmonize their inner landscapes and progress towards spiritual clarity and fulfilment.

Karma, the law of cause and effect, governs our actions and experiences, driving us towards spiritual evolution. Karma operates akin to a cosmic system of points, where every action, thought, and intention contributes to our karmic balance—accumulating positive or negative points akin to a modern-day gaming score. Much like earning points for victories and penalties for missteps, our karmic balance determines the trajectory of our subsequent lives. Positive karma reflects virtuous actions that lead to favourable outcomes and spiritual growth, while negative karma results from harmful thoughts or deeds that perpetuate suffering and setbacks. Embracing humility and shedding ego are pivotal in navigating this karmic journey, as they pave the way for inner transformation and enlightenment.

Vedanta teaches us to transcend the gunas, and recognize the unity between the essence of human Consciousness that resides in individuals (Atman) and the universal reality (Brahman). Through meditation and self-inquiry, we can attain liberation from the cycle of birth and rebirth.

In embarking on a spiritual journey, one is confronted with the profound intricacies of existence, where the illusions of separateness and ego-driven desires veil the eternal truth that resides within. This journey is not merely a quest for enlightenment but a transformative odyssey of self-discovery, wherein the seeker confronts the depths of their own consciousness and navigates the labyrinth of their innermost thoughts and emotions. It is a journey that transcends the confines of time and space, leading the seeker to the realization that they are not separate from the boundless ocean of Consciousness but an integral part of its infinite expanse.

At its core, the spiritual journey is a pilgrimage of the soul—a sacred sojourn towards the realization of our true nature as an expression of the divine. It is a journey of surrender and acceptance, wherein the seeker relinquishes the illusion of control and embraces the flow of life with equanimity and grace. Through the teachings of Vedanta and the timeless wisdom of the ages, we are guided along this path of self-realization, shedding the layers of ignorance and delusion that obscure the radiance of our inner being. As we embark on this voyage, may we tread with reverence and humility, honouring the interconnectedness of all beings and the eternal presence of Consciousness that pervades the universe. Ultimately, this book gives us, with modern-day language and context, a beacon of wisdom in a world plagued by uncertainty and discontent.

This book is action in words. This is what I feel about this book. As you go deeper into its pages, you will encounter not just ideas but prodding—to question, to explore, and to embrace a deeper understanding of yourself and the universe. The wisdom within these chapters challenges you to transcend passive reading; it beckons you to apply its teachings actively in your life.

As you embark on your introspective path through the pages of this book, I encourage you to approach it with an open mind. Within these pages lies the key to unlocking a deeper understanding of the self and a profound sense of inner fulfilment. Embrace the journey, for it is through exploration and self-discovery that we truly awaken to the essence of our being.

Srinath Sridharan
Author, Corporate Advisor
Mumbai

AUTHOR'S NOTE

From Banker to Monk: A Transformational Journey

THE EPIC MOMENT

At 6.30 p.m. in late October 1998, I was in the middle of a conference call, explaining the intricate details of a complex financial proposal to a prestigious client, when a phone call from my father interrupted me. He informed me that my mother was scheduled for her first dialysis session the following day. A slight tremor coursed through me as I processed the news. While I trusted that she was in the hands of one of the country's top nephrologists, I couldn't shake off the worry about how she would endure the procedure, given her fragile health and other medical complications. My 65-year-old mother's kidneys were nearly non-functional due to polycystic kidney disease—a genetic disorder that causes cysts to develop within the kidneys, gradually enlarging them and impairing their function.

The following morning, I rushed to Vijaya Hospital in Chennai, a city in southern India. As I arrived, the scene outside the dialysis centre was heartwrenching. The pain etched on people's faces while waiting to receive medical attention ignited within me a spark of curiosity about the roots of human suffering. Yet, in that moment, the questions were fleeting and my focus remained on my mother.

Passing through the hospital's corridors, I reflected briefly on how I had strayed from my youthful ambition of pursuing medicine and found myself in the banking industry instead. My understanding of the human body's complexities—its intricate emotions and interplay between joy and sorrow, pain and pleasure—remained basic despite my curiosity.

I made my way to the dialysis centre, only to find the door closed. Glancing through a tiny window, my heart sank as I witnessed a row of beds, each cradling a child no older than eight. The sheer helplessness in their innocent eyes was gut-wrenching as they gazed at the bare ceiling. One arm was restricted by tubes hooked up to an AV fistula and a machine. At the end of the row, lay a girl in her early twenties who had been rushed in the day before due to sudden kidney failure, without any prior symptoms. Tragically, I learned that she was to be married the next day.

The scene caused utter shock and disbelief, leaving me grappling with the haunting question, 'What is unfolding here?' I struggled to process the distressing sight before me. It served as a stark and sobering reminder of the unforgiving truths confronting those who wage battles against a multitude of diseases. Witnessing this profound moment left an indelible mark on my heart, stirring a profound well of compassion, and concern for my mother's health and welfare.

As I entered the chamber, heavy with the air of despair and a nauseating aroma, I took cautious steps towards my mother's bed. She was lying there motionless with tubes tethered to the protruding veins of her neck, since the doctors couldn't find any in her arms. In her eyes, glistening orbs, sorrow and love converged, spilling forth tears of anguish. A smile, radiant yet frail, greeted me. But as our hands entwined, her attempt to hide her suffering with the joy of seeing me quickly turned into a quiet protest. In that moment, a whispering verse emerged from her lips amidst the vast silence of the room, as she pleaded, holding my hand, 'Take me away, Shekara, I don't want to endure this pain. I'd rather die.'

Later that afternoon, upon returning home, I was taken aback to find a distant cousin of mine opening the door. To my surprise, her purpose was not to offer assistance to my father but to seek solace from him. Soon, it became evident that she was battling depression and a severe mental condition, all rooted in the abrupt estrangement from her daughter.

As I listened to her, I felt that she wasn't being entirely truthful, and I decided not to prolong the conversation. Little did I know in the moment that she was ensnared by PORD (Position, Obsession, Relationship, Demand)—a form of mental ailment in which an individual, typically occupying a higher position within a relationship, persistently demands specific reactions and behaviours from the subordinate party to gratify their ego.

With time, their obsession with controlling everyone they interact with, regardless of the brevity of the interaction, becomes increasingly apparent. Such individuals become victims of their ignorance—ignorance of who they are, often manifested in the form of egoism. Trapped within the clutches of PORD, they firmly believe that the world revolves around their contributions alone, thus insisting on unwavering obedience to their commands.

This behavioural pattern is a recurrent phenomenon in various relationships, including those between parent and child, teacher and student, and employer and employee.

In the realm of parent–child dynamics, this phenomenon originates from the depths of a parent's subconscious mind, manifesting as an innate yearning for obedience from their offspring. Children, often guided by a blend of fear and innocence, traverse the path set before them—their compliance serving as a precious offering to satiate their parents' pride and ego.

Amid this intricate choreography, some parents take solace in offering constant guidance, even when unwarranted, finding reassurance in the glow of their self-perceived wisdom. Meanwhile, the more vigilant among them adopt an unyielding posture of perpetual watchfulness—a steadfast shield devoted to safeguarding their children's well-being with unwavering dedication.

'You constantly remove obstacles so that your kids don't have to deal with challenges and frustrations. This form of hyper-involvement disempowers children,' says Esther Wojcicki, educator and journalist, while discussing helicopter parenting.

As children outgrow the constraints of fear and cease catering to their parents' egos, a darker facet of this dynamic often emerges—parents may resort to aggression and abuse when their demands remain unfulfilled. In households marked by a parent's affliction with PORD, the children's lives are often imbued with a persistent sense of misery, compelling them to seek opportunities to distance themselves during tumultuous times.

My cousin's narrative mirrored this painful pattern; her yearning for respite from emotional torment was palpable, yet accepting her reality proved to be an agonizing journey.

As night descended, I couldn't help but reflect on the two situations, intertwined by the thread of pain. In those quiet moments, I grappled with the perplexing paradox that if life is indeed destined to be fraught with suffering, it casts a shadow upon the belief that being born as a human is nature's most profound gift.

Three days later, oblivious to her actions while under the sway of a potent sedative, my mother bid her farewell to this world, exhaling her final breath in solemn silence.

This grave experience left me grappling with lingering questions about the very essence of suffering—questions I had deemed irrelevant until that fateful night. In our capacity as intelligent beings, it struck me that we might be overlooking a crucial element—an equation that could unlock the intricate puzzle of cause and effect. I found myself wondering why, despite our ability to create the brilliance of daytime stars, we continue to endure physical, mental, and intellectual anguish. The challenge lies in our shared struggle to identify and eliminate the root causes of suffering, even as we acknowledge its constant presence and lasting effects.

As the CEO and country head of a prominent European bank in India, I thrived in my professional life, standing out from my peers. Blessed with what seemed like divine favour, I had achieved an enviable career trajectory at a young age, poised for continued ascent. Yet on that fateful night, doubts began to infiltrate my mind, casting a shadow over my belief in the fairness of a divine system that meted out rewards and punishments to humanity. Impatience swelled within me, and a fervent thirst for answers consumed my thoughts.

As I meditated on these thoughts, my perception of life began to shift—albeit subtly—igniting a cascade of questions about the essence of existence. Although I yearned for answers, I had not yet fully explored the underlying cause of suffering that pervades human life. Still, I pondered why the pursuit of peace often culminated in death, and why living beings seemed trapped in an endless cycle of birth and rebirth, much like the eternal connection between the earth and sky. These reflections, though abstract, hinted at deeper truths about existence—truths that eluded my understanding.

It wasn't until 2008, during a tumultuous fall from the heights of my banking career, that I began to grasp the profound pain of life's trials. Confusion consumed me as I struggled to comprehend the misfortunes that had befallen me. Despite consistently ranking among the top 5 per cent of performers globally at the institution, I was relentlessly haunted by doubts and plagued by questions of self-worth.

In this crucible of despair, my curiosity about human suffering evolved into a profound obsession. I became determined to uncover the root causes of pain and explore solutions to attain inner calm amidst life's adversities. In an unexpected twist, the notion of venturing into uncharted territory took hold—an ethereal realm that seemed to beckon me. It felt surreal, as though the gates to this spiritual domain had swung wide open, extending an eager invitation to take that bold step forward.

It dawned upon me that my journey into the spiritual realm was distinct from those who had trodden this path before. It felt as though nature held a mysterious code, bestowing a select few with a second chance at life—a rare opportunity to delve into the profound essence of existence. Such revelations often emerge in one's darkest moments—amid the sting of rejection and failure—when the soul, weary and wounded, longs for a spark to reignite its spirit. And I couldn't help but wonder: why must it take such suffering to awaken us? Yet, in my case, it was the poignant witnessing of others' suffering that ignited the spark of this inner journey.

I am no avatar graced with extraordinary innate capacity, yet, as I embarked upon my spiritual journey, I carried a unique advantage, a divine bonus bestowed upon me. In the serene space of my mind, I discovered the presence of a fair measure of the virtues that one cultivates through the sacred practices enshrined in the Vedas. Perhaps it was this treasure that initially drew me towards the Vedic scriptures, capturing my senses and compelling me to invest greater effort.

Thus began a new chapter in my life—a chapter driven by an unwavering mission, despite my lack of formal training in Vedic scriptures. I came to realize that these ancient texts contained invaluable insights into the metaphysical truths of existence, the nature of suffering, and the pathways to solace. In my quest for clarity, I resolved to bypass traditional routes, delving directly into profound metaphysical concepts that promised to unveil truths beyond the confines of physical science—a decision I deeply regret. And even though my beginnings were humble, I remained steadfast in my pursuit of understanding, even as I sought to reclaim my lost career.

This marked a pivotal moment in my life—a moment with which my mind grappled, struggling to fully comprehend its significance. The wisdom of the Vedas, often hailed as spiritual humanism, offered a grand design to uncover the very essence of our innate truth. Its brilliance lay in its universal accessibility, transcending boundaries of culture and creed. The Vedas extend an unbiased invitation, free from discrimination based on faith or social standing. Embedded within them is the philosophical treasure of Vedanta, forming the concluding portion of these sacred texts. Unlike doctrines rooted in conversion, Vedanta eschews imposing or altering beliefs. Instead, it offers potent truths that liberate the mind from narrow perspectives and restrictive thinking.

What fascinated me most was the realization that the sacred scriptures are not prescriptive commands but profound insights meant to be absorbed through the teachings of a guru. The guru's role is to present this wisdom in its purest form, leaving it to the seeker to engage in deep introspection and internalize the teachings. The journey to uncover the truth of one's being is inherently personal—unique to each individual—and impossible to share fully with others.

The Vedas, composed in poetic meters known as chhandas, are masterpieces of enigmatic artistry, crafted specifically for Vedic chanting. The rhythm and resonance woven into these verses create a binaural harmony, making them ideal for the foundational stages of meditation. Their melodious strains possess an enchanting quality that resonates deeply with the soul. Interestingly, the rhythmic patterns in contemporary rap ballads—such as 'Calm Down' by Divine Ikubor (Rema) and Selena Gomez—trace their roots back to the ancient craft of Vedic chanting, bridging millennia of artistic expression.

For me, encountering Vedic chanting was love at first hearing. It compelled me to explore this sacred tradition further, and I found immense relief by applying a few basic concepts from the Vedas. It was as if the fog of confusion clouding my intellect had lifted, enabling me to think more clearly and regain control over my life. As I delved deeper into Vedic wisdom, I felt an undeniable pull towards the Supreme Consciousness—the all-encompassing force that governs existence. With each step, my faith in this path deepened, as I diligently forged a foundation of values to fortify my spiritual quest. The concoction of bliss flowed within me—nectar that swelled with every new spiritual insight—and from that moment, there was no turning back.

Over the next six years, I embarked on an unwavering journey, dedicating countless sleepless nights to the study of Vedic philosophy—the ancient, sacred literature of India. Immersed in the works of eminent scholars and brilliant authors, I marvelled at their linguistic virtuosity and profound insights. Their words, imbued with wisdom, became guiding lights in my exploration of these age-old teachings. I humbly acknowledge these eloquent writers, whose influence shaped not only my expressions in this treatise but also my understanding of the Vedic doctrine.

Despite gaining fresh insights with every reading, grasping the central message of the doctrine proved to be a formidable challenge. It emphasized that ignorance of the self is the root of all suffering—and the remedy lies in discovering one's genuine self through personal experience. At first, this seemed deceptively straightforward, yet I was haunted by questions: how could one remain unaware of their true essence? Did we unknowingly harbour multiple identities? Bridging this gap between intellectual understanding and personal realization became a source of profound internal conflict, leaving me feeling increasingly adrift and disheartened.

In 2015, following a period of deep introspection and communion with the transcendent, I made a life-altering decision to become a Vedic monk. To my surprise, the Vedas do not mandate monkhood for the acquisition of their teachings. Instead, they emphasize that the profound knowledge they offer—designed to alleviate human suffering and guide one towards a tranquil life—is equally accessible to those living within the framework of family life.

Embracing monkhood allowed me to immerse myself in divine love and connect deeply with the sublime truth of Consciousness—the awareness principle. This transformation stands as the most auspicious event of my life. With my mind focused on the One—the indivisible essence from which all things emerge—I began perceiving the interconnectedness of the universe. Understanding the nature of non-dual Consciousness—the awareness that empowers our senses to perceive both the tangible and the intangible—initially seemed enigmatic. Yet, I discovered that this Consciousness, often veiled from ordinary perception, reveals its treasures to those who seek the truth with sincerity and pure intention.

Through a profound connection with the Supreme Consciousness—revered as Brahman in the Vedas—I embarked on a transformative journey that transcended intellectual comprehension, unveiling a path to liberation and clarity. This journey deepened my appreciation for the timeless wisdom embedded in the sacred scriptures and revealed a crucial void in my spiritual quest: the absence of a guru. My progress remained constrained without a guide to dispel entrenched preconceptions and biases.

Destiny, however, had other plans. A radiant soul of compassion and insight entered my life, embodying the role of a guru. The serendipity of this encounter felt far from coincidental; years later, I came to see it as an extraordinary gift of benevolent karma from the past.

Under my Guru's guidance, my faith in the divine deepened, leading to two pivotal realizations early in my journey. First, I came to understand that the combined force of intelligence and knowledge stands in true opposition to ignorance—forming one of the three authentic pairs of opposites. The other two are: pain and pleasure, which can be experienced simultaneously; and sound and silence, for sound can be perceived only against the backdrop of silence. All other so-called dualities are merely linguistic constructs used to describe contrasting features of two aspects of the same phenomenon. They do not exist simultaneously—day and night, for instance, alternate but never coexist. In contrast, knowledge and ignorance represent a true polarity: they can coexist, yet one inevitably dispels the other. Grasping this insight is crucial, since it determines the way our minds are shaped and how our choices unfold thereafter.

Second, I realized that egotism is the greatest obstacle to wisdom. It distorts perception, inflates self-importance, and obstructs the subtle inner unfolding of truth.

The guru's teachings illuminated the distinction between valuable knowledge and mere information, between truth and opinion, and between right and wrong.

In our spiritual voyage, a guru is like an exceptional leader guiding an organization towards its vision. Having traversed the path to inner peace, a guru accelerates our learning, inspiring us to shed misgivings and embrace the truth. As Adi Shankaracharya, a venerable sage of AD 8, the champion of Advaita Vedanta, proclaimed, 'Happy are they who come into thy sight even for a moment, for they become fit recipients of wisdom.' The guru's kindness, untainted by personal motives, fosters a relationship of trust and guidance, enabling students to progress steadily on the path to liberation.

With my guru's teachings, the intricate mysteries of the universe began to unravel. Through listening, contemplation, and meditation, I found that my experiences resonated with the Vedic teachings. This sacred knowledge, often referred to as the greatest open secret, is what I share in this treatise. It is not a new doctrine but a restoration of eternal truths passed down from master to disciple, as emphasized in chapter 4, verse 3 of the Bhagavad Gita.

Today, I treasure the transformative power of the Vedic scriptures which have reshaped my understanding of life and consciousness. I am inspired by the boundless wisdom and compassion they offer and sincerely hope that others may find peace, clarity, and fulfilment as they embark on their journeys into this eternal reservoir of knowledge.

A TRIBUTE TO SACRED GURUS

Mortal words can scarcely capture the essence of a true guru—an extraordinary being whose presence transforms the spiritual journey of a seeker. Figures such as the Buddha, Jesus, Prophet Mohammed, and Jagat Guru Shri Adi Shankaracharya stand as guiding lights to countless souls. These divine manifestations of Brahman walked among us, distinct from the rest of humanity; their brilliance illuminating the path to truth and bringing solace to innumerable hearts.

The deeds of such enlightened beings focused on alleviating human suffering, spreading knowledge, peace, and happiness. As the Bhagavad Gita 4.7 eloquently describes, they descended not to partake in worldly pleasures but as special emissaries of the divine, rising through sanctified spirituality to fulfil their divine mandate. Revered across time, these extraordinary manifestations are celebrated not for their supernatural attributes but for their unwavering commitment to relieving humanity's anguish. Their actions harmonized warring factions, comforted the suffering, and disseminated the highest knowledge—the knowledge of truth, peace, and happiness. Yet, the significance of their noble deeds often eludes the understanding of the common man.

The pursuit of spiritual understanding, I realized, is akin to a racehorse's course. Even the most adept horse requires the skill of a jockey to secure victory. The jockey orchestrates the course, sets the pace, and conserves energy for the final push towards the finish line. Similarly, a seeker needs the guidance of a wise and compassionate guru to illuminate the path through the intricate journey of metaphysics.

For me, the timely arrival of a guru in my spiritual journey has been nothing short of a priceless blessing. For years, I had sought solace in my religious beliefs, drawing strength from a personal God and immersing myself in the empirical world. Naively, I assumed these experiences sufficed to master the subject of metaphysics. However, life soon revealed the gravity of this path—a path that demanded more than solitary effort. Despite my best intentions, I struggled to navigate scepticism and ignorance, often stumbling on the profound truths I sought.

In my guru, I found not just a teacher but a wellspring of knowledge, grace, and kindness. His teachings, offered with no hidden agenda or personal interest, sought only to benefit humanity and posterity. Under his guidance, the misinterpretations and biases that had bent my understanding of sacred scriptures were straightened. He dispelled the darkness of ignorance, illuminating obscured paths and revealing profound truths firmly grounded in personal experience.

Through his grace, I came to see sacred knowledge not as abstract speculation but as a living reality that unfolded within me. This transformative power of sacred wisdom touched the very core of my existence, reshaping my understanding of life and the universe. Looking back, I humbly acknowledge that my guru's presence has been the guiding force behind my spiritual growth and self-discovery. It is through his benevolence that I now comprehend the vast expanse of metaphysical truths and the boundless potential for spiritual evolution.

Now, at the age of sixty-eight, I can genuinely assert that I no longer know the meaning of unhappiness. The inner peace and fulfilment I have discovered stand as a testament to the teachings of my guru, and the timeless wisdom of the Vedas.

Even as a Vedic monk, I carry one desire—not for material gains but for the spiritual awakening of others. My heartfelt aspiration is that everyone who reads this book may find the same inner peace and fulfilment that has transformed my life. May the wisdom I have gleaned from the sacred teachings of the Vedas illuminate your path, guiding you towards spiritual awakening and enduring contentment.

EMBRACING VEDIC WISDOM IN A SCIENTIFIC ERA

As I delved into the subject matter at hand, I found myself navigating beyond the confines of the physical sciences. As such, the presence of numerous references to physics within this text may prompt curiosity. My intention, however, is to shed light on the precarious situation we face, should the undecided intellectuals of the scientific world fail to reconcile their egos and bestow their endorsement upon the knowledge of 'truth'. This validation, unfortunately, holds immense significance for the millions who seek solace in an intricate doctrine, with scientific validation being a paramount prerequisite.

In this context, I recollect the words of wisdom voiced by Prof. Edwin Arthur Burtt, a quote that originally appeared in *Introduction to Vedanta* by Dr P. Nagaraja Rao (Bharatiya Vidya Bhavan, 1958):

> Philosophy has much in common, on the one hand, with naive reflections in which unsophisticated people engage; and on the other hand, with the abstract and exact inquiries of Science. It seeks essentially to transcend the limitations of science while respecting the fundamental standards of intellectual attainment upon which science has come to exist. It is a queer hybrid in the realm of reflective inquiry profound through the fertilization of the spontaneous speculations of common sense about ultimate things by the discipline of scientific logic. The philosopher is a child in his open-eyed wonderment at the world and a man of mature research in the critical and rigorous fashion in which that wonderment is satisfied.

Within the realm of science lies the noble pursuit of enhancing the quality of human life, much like the aspirations of philosophy, which seeks to elevate humanity towards the highest good. While their focus and methodologies differ, both are indispensable. Science aims at material progress and understanding the physical aspects, whereas philosophy ventures beyond these boundaries to address the emotional and mental well-being of humanity. It is not a matter of choice between the two. Both are essential components of our existence.

Regardless of whether the concepts expounded in this book are embraced as facts or rejected due to differing beliefs, I am aware that imposing my opinions upon others may not effectively alter the convictions rooted in deeply held beliefs. Yet, the universal truth remains: pain is an inevitable part of the human experience. My intent here is to allow readers to discern the potential benefits that this knowledge can bestow upon them.

The sole purpose of this book is to offer a solution that aids in overcoming physical ailments and mental disturbances. In presenting the principles of applied Vedanta in their purest form, I have attempted to untangle the misconceptions and mysticism that often shroud this cherished wisdom. To truly understand and transform its contents, one must be willing to open the metaphorical envelope and explore its merits.

The suggested remedy constitutes an intellectual endeavour, intentionally crafted to refine the mind's capacity to accept situations devoid of choice and resistance, all the while nurturing the equanimity necessary to navigate the vicissitudes of life. Its essence hinges on personal conviction, untainted by any form of coercion or conditioning.

Consequently, this treatise should not be approached as mere casual reading. In truth, it may compel some readers to revisit certain passages, perhaps even multiple times, as I did when I tried to comprehend the first text I read on Vedanta in the quest to fully grasp and integrate the profound concepts it presents, with the ultimate aim of deriving wisdom from its knowledge.

While I recognize that objections to the theories presented here may arise, addressing two key concerns is essential. Supra-rational knowledge, grounded in individual experience as the ultimate measure of validation, often shows variations from person to person. This contrasts sharply with scientific theories, which yield consistent results across numerous experiments. However, these variations in experience do not stem from the knowledge itself, which is fundamentally sound, but rather from the flawed understanding of the Vedic principles by individuals. Just as we do not question the efficacy of electricity when a faulty bulb fails to light, we should not doubt the validity of this knowledge due to imperfect comprehension.

On the other extreme there are astute individuals who, with complete disregard for the sanctity of the scriptures, adeptly assimilate the wisdom from the Vedas and craftily repackage it as their philosophy, garnering significant popularity as sought-after thinkers. To enhance their appeal, they boldly dismiss the wisdom embedded in the Vedas as impractical, questioning its efficacy and claiming that the concepts have not produced the promised results. Alas! Those graced with exceptional intelligence have opted for ignorance as their chariot—an ill-fated choice destined to steer them down a perilous path towards self-destruction. The consequences of such a decision may manifest in this present existence or subsequent lives, marked by an intensity that proves truly insufferable.

Amidst the modern world's technological wonders and rapid advancements, the urgency to pursue knowledge of Consciousness may be questioned. After all, science has revolutionized our society and uplifted humanity significantly, seemingly negating the need to discover esoteric truths. The prevailing sentiment demands instant gratification, and utility reigns supreme. Even truth must supplicate before the tutelary goddess of society to gain admission. 'Utility is the guardian angel of the society, the tutelary goddess at its gate, and even truth has to bend her knees before her and beg for admission,' wrote Rajam. He goes on to say, 'to trade liquors is certainly more profitable than reading the Upanishads, and to convert our temples into factories and workshops may be a useful reform'.[1] However, the missing point in this new world behaviour lies in the realization that science cannot pacify the troubled minds of millions, save through sedation accompanied by cruel side effects. It is a fallacy to believe that the progressive world of capitalism can compassionately address the plight of those suffering from hunger. While science can produce material goods, it falls short of supporting those who cannot afford to consume them. It lacks the profound understanding of why an individual may fail despite best efforts. What option does science give to one who is denied the consumption of goods scattered within his reach? In such circumstances, the knowledge of truth offers peace of mind at no cost, empowering individuals with a rigorous understanding and the courage to confront the heartbreaking realities of their actions, and to rise to challenge their fate.

In the forging of this opus, my expedition delves deeply into the wisdom procured chiefly from twin Vedanta scriptures.

The first of these volumes, the lesser-known Ashtavakra Gita, unfurls verity unapologetically, withholding clemency from those who persist in clutching suffering instead of dispelling the ignorance that lies beneath—to unearth ceaseless felicity from within. It is about attaining a state wherein the mind does not hanker for acquisitions to appease unwarranted desires. The contents of this scripture, I must confess, do not cloak themselves in saccharine veneers or foster false aspirations. They prepare an individual to confront the unbending realities of life directly. Such unflinching candour and unapologetically straightforward pedagogy might not resonate with the general populace, yet they cradle profound sagacity for those who seek authentic comprehension.

During my ongoing exploration, I found a consonance with the verses of the *Mundaka Upanishad*, which aptly state, 'In the midst of ignorant fools fancying themselves wise and learned, go round and round, oppressed by misery as blind people led by the blind. Fancying oblations and pious gifts to the highest, fools do not know anything good.' It does not take much to misconstrue ignorance as wisdom, and this text strives to dispel such illusions.

The second is the prominent text, the Bhagavad Gita, a comprehensive guide to an individual's true direction in life, helping one reach their rightful destination without compromising values based on personal culture and religion. The popularity of the Gita is said to be no less than that of the divine Lord, who imparts the essence of the Vedas to humanity through this text. It extends sympathy to those who are inherently unaware, and steers them towards their ultimate aspiration. The Bhagavad Gita is hailed as the 'Song of God', consisting of 700 verses across 18 chapters. It offers the recipe for a peaceful life, free from fear, bondage, anxiety, and mental anguish; all while making progress in the material world. The composition of this text can be readily comprehended as it weaves metaphysical truths with the everyday realities of an ordinary person. It encourages students not to simply accept the doctrine but to realize and substantiate the remedies proffered through personal experience. The Gita is an eternal spiritual power, which belongs to the very essence of humanity. It is for everyone—the good, bad, and ugly.

I have used analogies extensively within this text to shed light on complex metaphysical concepts. However, it is crucial to underscore that these analogies are entirely incidental, and bear no deliberate resemblance to any specific past or present personal experiences. My intention is not to offend any individual, whether living or deceased. Furthermore, I have interwoven actual events, including those from the lives of contemporary individuals, to further illuminate distinct ideas. To respect and preserve privacy, pseudonyms have been used for the characters in these accounts.

Within this text, you will come across terms used interchangeably, such as 'Brahman', 'Atman', 'Self', and 'Spirit', all of which converge upon the ultimate truth—Consciousness, the sublime 'I'. Moreover, you may observe certain concepts revisited in multiple sections. This repetition is not an inadvertent editorial oversight, but a deliberate strategy intended to underscore their profound importance in causing the transformative shift necessary for the attainment of enduring inner peace.

Upon engaging with this book, some of you might find certain ideas already resonating with familiarity. Indeed, the concepts elaborated here are not entirely novel; rather, they are intended to emphasize aspects that you may not have fully harnessed to your advantage. As we are aware, pure knowledge is a potential state; applied knowledge is the key to unlocking the potential for self-improvement.

In alignment with the pedagogical approach employed in learning metaphysics, I have arranged the various topics into eleven parts. The first nine parts provide the knowledge requisite to transcend suffering. Part ten serves as a means to internalize this knowledge through Vedic meditation, and by the time you arrive at the concluding part, you are poised to immerse yourself in bliss of a mysterious nature. Subsequently, no further action is necessary apart from maintaining a steadfast determination in upholding this knowledge.

In closing, I dedicate this work as a heartfelt tribute to my daughter, Shruti—her very name, bestowed with divine grace, echoes the Vedas themselves; and to those who, like her, carry within them the quiet reminder that truth is not created but revealed, not sought outside but heard within. In particular, to those who yearn to stretch their horizons, unburdened by the weight of stress, and to those who chase greatness not just in worldly endeavours, but also in tending to the blossoming garden of inner peace. May you embrace and bask in the profound serenity that dwells within.

INTRODUCTION

The Discovery that Resolves Fundamental Human Struggles

Human beings—unlike gods or subhuman entities—are uniquely endowed with the ability to attain true knowledge and achieve complete liberation through conscious, purposeful action while still alive. In contrast, gods and animals merely undergo the results of their past karmas, lacking the capacity to initiate new actions that lead to spiritual evolution. Why do people continue to suffer, then?

On 1 December 2014, Swathi, a twenty-four-year-old software engineer who had secured a coveted position at India's tech behemoth TCS, met a tragic end when a bomb concealed beneath seat number 23 detonated at Chennai's bustling railway station. Originally assigned seat number 9, Swathi made a fateful decision to switch her seat, adjacent to her roommate in the same coach. In a twist of fate, her companion had wandered away from the blast zone moments before the explosion tore through the air. Swathi had embarked on the ill-fated Bangalore–Guwahati Express, bound for her hometown Guntur in Andhra Pradesh, India.

Grim events such as these, commonplace as they are, often prompt us to dismiss them as mere games of chance.[2] In a world where the fragility of life is constantly exposed by relentless tragedies, we find ourselves grappling with unanswerable questions. How do we make sense of events that seem to defy reason? How do we find meaning amidst the chaos?

Swathi's story is not just a tale of untimely loss; it's a stark reminder of how, in the blink of an eye, the fabric of our existence can unravel at the hands of fate. Is it just fate—or something beyond?

Her decision to switch seats—an innocent, almost trivial choice—became the turning point of her destiny. Incidents like this, both shocking and recurring, force us to face the unsettling randomness that governs our lives. Whether it's finance, relationships, or health, it often feels like one aspect of life is always disrupting our tranquillity. As these stories unfold, they leave behind a trail of haunting, unanswered questions: are we mere players in a game of chance, or is there a greater design at work? And perhaps most importantly, how do we continue to live, love, and dream in a world where the next moment is never guaranteed?

Is death truly the release from physical and psychological pain, or is it merely an escape? Why do we fail to take the time to understand the root cause of our suffering, opting instead for the easy explanations—'everything happens for a reason', or 'it's karma'—without ever probing deeper? Are we incapable of understanding, or have we chosen to struggle as victims of our ignorance?

These reflections are not just philosophical musings; they are the very threads that weave our resilience, pushing us to search for clarity and purpose in a reality shaped by unpredictability.

THE ORIGIN AND END OF PAIN

A fundamental prerequisite for attaining peace is the recognition that all forms of pain can be eradicated, rather than accepting them as an unavoidable curse of human existence, as declared by the Vedas, one among the oldest repositories of philosophy known to humanity. The key lies in identifying the root cause of suffering and eliminating it through necessary individual transformation.

To this end, a basic yet serious inquiry into our very existence is the sole means to establish the necessary foundation. If we accept the notion that our destiny hangs in obscurity on either side of the grave, what can we aspire to comprehend once life's flame dims, if, during our earthly existence, we have not understood why a human soul was bestowed upon us?

The human race stands as a radiant gem adorning the celestial crown of evolution, not merely for the splendour of intellect capable of creating stars that shine in broad daylight, but owing to the divine decree that graces us with sacred privilege. The exclusive privilege to uncover the important truth about ourselves: the knowledge that we are immortal spirits, unchained and unbound, unaffected by the constantly changing world realities. This understanding, while recognizing the body–mind complex as a mortal vessel designed for functioning in the physical realm, brings an end to sorrow. It leads us to immerse ourselves in the infinite bliss of Brahman's embrace—the Supreme Consciousness.

Throughout history, remarkable individuals like Einstein, Newton, Sir Frederick Banting, Mozart, and Picasso have unwittingly accessed this Supreme Consciousness to make groundbreaking discoveries which eluded the grasp of ordinary minds.

However, this enlightenment escapes many, as they continue to chase lasting serenity in an external world filled with illusions. Despite the long-standing understanding that such pursuits will not bring true peace, resistance to change prevails. This reluctance often stems not from any form of fear or disinterest, but from a deep attachment to one's ego and self-image that one creates. With an unyielding belief in its infallibility and the assumed superiority of their chosen path to personal growth, individuals become ensnared in a cocoon of complacency. As a result, even when their efforts yield no meaningful outcomes, they cling to these convictions, rejecting alternative approaches and obstructing their path to genuine and lasting peace.

The obstacles extend beyond this. Our minds are trapped in a complex web of conditioning, shaped by words echoing from the ancient whispers of time immemorial. Words designed to denote variation in conditions are registered as opposing pairs within the language of communication, reinforcing the illusion of duality. Influenced by these words, we develop likes and dislikes, driving us to pursue what we desire and shun what we detest, thereby intensifying our entanglement in the endless cycle of dualistic perception.

Consider the example of touching a piece of wood. When you slide your palm over the wood, you may feel its uneven texture—parts that are smooth and parts that are rough. If the perceiver does not have preconditioned words to articulate these sensations as 'smooth' or 'rough', the experience remains neutral. The wood is simply accepted as it is, without forming judgements, aversions, or attractions.

However, the moment labels like 'smooth' or 'rough' come into play, they introduce duality. Smoothness might evoke a sense of comfort or pleasure, while roughness could trigger discomfort or aversion at a psychological level. These labels influence our perception, shaping how we interact with the object and our emotional response to it. The absence of such conditioned articulation allows the perceiver to experience the wood purely as a fact, free from bias or emotional attachment. Yet, disregarding the tactile distinctions is inappropriate at the physical level, particularly when the piece of wood is crafted into a commercial object.

This principle applies universally to all forms of perception where duality prevails. When we encounter sensations, sights, sounds, or other stimuli, our conditioned minds instinctively label these experiences—good or bad, pleasant or unpleasant, desirable or undesirable. Naturally, such an attitude inevitably leads to sorrow when faced with countless undesirable and unavoidable situations.

More importantly, our thoughts, shaped and constrained by the relentless march of time, limit our capacity to decipher the mystery that veils subtle emotions like fear, anxiety, and anger. As a result, we fail to experience emotions as pure and unfiltered facts. Instead, we direct our efforts towards superficially analysing the fragmented idea derived from external sources that can never lead us to the root cause of the problem. A great deal of energy is squandered when we attempt to resolve issues without truly understanding the negative emotions as a fact. Consequently, we either continue to endure the pain triggered by these emotional outbursts, or hastily turn to quick-fix solutions offered by a capitalist-driven world, thus allowing the cycle of pain to continue.

All emotions stem from the interplay of our thoughts and words, even though words are meant solely for communication. This interaction creates an illusory divide between the individual experiencing the emotion and the emotion itself, obscuring the underlying truth that dissolves this gap.

For instance, when recalling the word 'anxiety' in response to a condition we encountered in the past, we often perceive anxiety as an external force—something separate from our body–mind framework. This perception compels us to treat anxiety as an adversary to be overcome through various remedies. The mind immediately sets itself in motion, analysing the present state based on inputs from memories. However, this analysis tends to persist without resolution because we fail to recognize that, in the psychological realm, the analyser and the analysed are inherently the same. These efforts often fall short of addressing the root cause, leaving the cycle of recurrence unbroken. Understanding the illusory nature of this perceived separation is crucial for resolving emotional challenges at their core.

In truth, emotions are experiences of the mind, deeply intertwined with our ego. As such, the experiencer and the experienced emotion are never separate; no experience is possible in the absence of the individual who experiences it. When this unity is understood, the perceived division dissolves. Anxiety dissipates, ending our battle with it instantly because it is not distinct from the one who feels it.

Yet, when we view emotions through the lens of preconceived notions, the true essence of the experience becomes obscured, hidden within the recesses of our memories. This misunderstanding traps us in a false sense of duality—the root of psychological distress and anguish—and we become victims of misperceptions perpetuated by our ignorance.

To truly grasp the nature of anything, particularly in the psychological realm of our being, we must first clear our minds of preconceptions and memories associated with that subject. While it may be impossible to eliminate all thoughts or memories stored in our minds, allowing the specific thoughts tied to an experienced emotion to dissipate removes the illusion of division. In that moment, a profound realization occurs: the experiencer and the experienced are not separate but one unified entity. This understanding dissolves the troubling emotions born from duality, removing the need to 'overcome', and bringing lasting resolution to conflict.

On the phenomenal plane, too, the misperception, due to physical differences and distance between individuals, becomes the source of all conflict. In this fragmented perception, we engage in a dangerous interplay with the shadows of division, disrupting the unity of our existence—Brahman, the eternal spirit.

The toll of this duality, resembling a turbulent whirlpool of dire circumstances, awaits those brave individuals who are steadfast in embracing the illusion of duality, risking their lives in the pursuit of somehow uncovering the faintest traces of pleasure. Furthermore, those fixated on preserving their ego and individuality within a dualistic framework only amplify divisions, intensifying conflict and contradiction. The consequences ripple outward, leading to the disintegration of families, societies, and nations. Quite often, these divisions are manipulated to serve hidden agendas and futile quests for dominance, perpetuating cycles of destruction and disharmony.

Relationships, another aspect of our existence that plays a vital role in the pursuit of joy for many, oftentimes conclude in enigmatic circumstances, strife, sorrow, and disharmony: a glaring contradiction to the initial intentions that drive people into such unions. It is astonishing to note how people frequently underestimate this critical facet of life, permitting their self-serving desires to dictate the trajectory of their relationships.

Verily, all of these trials arise from misunderstandings of the intrinsic essence of the term 'relationship' and, consequently, the unrealistic expectations invested in each association that inexorably steer one towards disillusionment. In this vein, all relationships founded upon a vague comprehension of the term, and constructed upon ideas tainted by the principle of 'give and take' are bound to engender repercussions such as preferences and aversions, rendering the relationship destructive from its inception to its culmination. Rather than offering joy, these relationships often devolve into a relentless effort to mend fractures. Small wonder, then, that human beings seem to take their first genuine breath of freedom only within the stillness of a coffin.

We find ourselves in ceaseless battles with our mental state, attempting either to suppress it or to quell the turbulence within. But our misdirected efforts often bear no fruit, leading us only to the desolate fields of futility. What can one anticipate from the endeavour to resolve a conflict wherein the two antagonists find themselves trapped within the enchantment of misperceived status, as a result of thoughts infected by ignorance of the self?

Within the reverberating corridors of human experience, the answers to two fundamental questions—'What am I?', and 'Who am I?'—become essential in resolving human predicaments. As the vast realm of humanity unfurls, we are prompted to reflect on these inquiries, each directed towards two distinct aspects of our being: the finite self and the infinite Self. The former prompts us to explore the depths of our inner being and our emotional personality that shapes our thoughts, expressions, and actions. On the other hand, the answer to the latter bestows upon us the power to decipher life's intricate complexities, unveiling solutions for the challenges that besiege us.

Upon realizing the profound essence of life, the wise individual commits to focused practices designed to reduce the karmic ties of attachment and aversion. This intentional realignment of the diverse layers within one's personality is ideal for a highly coveted inner metamorphosis achieved through active engagement in Vedic meditation. A radical transformation in perspective follows suit, extending beyond the physical realm, and endowing wise persons with the capacity to maintain unwavering equanimity amidst the fluctuating tides of all circumstances. They become impervious to the allure of material possessions. This serenity is born of personal observation and the assimilation of the complete spectrum of facts, rather than mere analytical scrutiny.

The discerning mind observes existence as a whole, while considering the physical body as a lower reality taken on lease for an unknown period for functional use. This very recognition becomes the source of a deep sense of tranquillity, a state that cannot be conveyed through the shallow exchanges of social media. It remains an intensely personal experience—a sacred realm reserved for those who have attained such a state of transcendence.

TIME TO REFLECT: HUMAN BEINGS, A PARADOX IN MOTION

Life is a tapestry woven with betrayals, injustices, and wounds—both those we endure and those we inflict. It demands accountability, introspection, and the courage to confront not only the wrongs we've suffered but also the harm we've caused. Reflecting on the real-life situations outlined below may evoke memories of the undesirable disturbances that disrupted your efficiency and impacted your mood.

When was the last time you felt the deep, searing sting of betrayal from someone you cherished—a spouse who broke their vows, a child who dismissed your love and guidance as irrelevant, a parent whose words cut deeper than they knew, or a friend whose professed loyalty proved to be a façade? Perhaps it was waiting anxiously for a text from someone you loved, only to be met with silence, signalling the heartbreaking end of a once-promising relationship. These moments leave behind indelible scars, shattering the peace and stability you worked so hard to cultivate.

Even those with no close emotional connection—teachers, in-laws, colleagues, or bosses—can leave their mark. Recall the humiliation of being questioned by a cashier over a high-denomination bill, the disapproving stares of bystanders, or the indignity of pleading with an unyielding airline clerk over excess baggage fee. Perhaps you remember the sting of a university rejection letter, or being denied entry to an event because you arrived a moment too late. Such seemingly small slights can feel enormous in the moment, casting long shadows over our days and lives.

Then there are the greater injustices: watching an undeserving colleague rise through favouritism rather than merit, or hearing devastating news about your child's health. What about the ceaseless torment of negative thoughts that gnaw at your mind, becoming your most relentless adversary?

In such trials, what path did you choose? Did you succumb to the alluring pull of revenge, let anger consume you; or endure the suffering in silence, waiting for time to dull the pain? And do you truly believe time is the ultimate healer, capable of transforming even the most excruciating tribulations into distant memories?

Amid this reflection, consider the harm you might have caused others. Have you ever acted out of selfishness or pride? Perhaps you manipulated your children to satisfy your ego, disregarding their dreams. Have you guilted them into accepting gifts they didn't want, prioritizing your desires over their feelings? Think back to times when you maligned a colleague to gain favour with a superior, or denied your mother a simple request, deeming her needs irrelevant due to her age.

And what about moments of quiet apathy—like choosing to discard perfectly good food after a gathering instead of sharing it with those in need, justifying the act with the belief that they weren't deserving? Each of these actions, no matter how small, leaves a mark, shaping not only those you hurt but also the person you become.

The list of dilemmas we face in life would seem endless. Yet, when we reflect honestly on how often such moments arise in our daily lives, it becomes clear that these moral, emotional, and ethical conflicts are not isolated incidents. Rather, they are persistent undercurrents that disrupt our inner peace. Each unresolved conflict, no matter how minor, subtly erodes our mental and emotional well-being.

Furthermore, we often find ourselves reacting to life's circumstances, bewildered by the indifference of others, and sometimes acting against our conscience, fully aware that it may hurt someone in the process. We are perplexed by the adverse events that unfold in our own lives, with no clear reasons to explain them.

The deeper truth is that each of us operates within a unique framework, shaped by beliefs, rules, and patterns influenced by borrowed thoughts that our minds find acceptable. This intricate design, the framework of others, may not always align with the framework we consciously create for ourselves As a result, the actions and reactions of others may seem inconsistent with the patterns we expect. In general, no behaviour, action, or reaction can be inherently labelled as wrong; it is simply our lack of understanding of the motivations behind them at any given moment.

However, in our tireless endeavours to mitigate the tribulations that arise, we often embark on futile missions to reform the attitudes or behaviours of others, or we place blame on external forces for the vicissitudes of life, all of which can lead to inner turmoil. The key to emancipating ourselves from this anguish lies in understanding the inner workings of our minds, thereby reshaping our perspectives not only towards ourselves but also towards the people with whom we interact and the circumstances that influence us.

To lead a life of tranquillity, we must recognize these disturbances for what they truly are: signposts pointing to deeper issues that demand introspection and action. Addressing them requires more than casual acknowledgement—it calls for a serious commitment to confronting them with courage and clarity. When we face these challenges head-on, we begin the process of transforming chaos into understanding. We cannot hope to change the deceptive world, as its very nature is to constantly change. Instead, our focus should be on cultivating the wisdom and resilience needed to navigate its complexities with grace and integrity, enabling us to reclaim the inner peace that is inherently ours.

A closer examination of the dilemmas we encounter often reveals that they stem from a fundamental ignorance of our true selves. This ignorance perpetuates cycles of dissatisfaction, attachment, and misplaced priorities, leading to inner turmoil and disconnection from lasting peace.

The ancient wisdom of the Vedas offers insights to address the root cause. As timeless scriptures dedicated to exploring the nature of existence and the self, the Vedas guide us in discerning the transient from the eternal, helping us align with our higher purpose. They illuminate the interconnectedness of all life, urging us to transcend ego-driven desires and embrace a perspective rooted in unity and self-awareness.

By internalizing Vedic teachings, we gain clarity about the workings of our minds, the impermanence of worldly possessions, and the essence of true happiness. This knowledge enables us to break free from limiting beliefs and destructive patterns, replacing them with practices of mindfulness, compassion, and self-inquiry. In doing so, the wisdom of the Vedas becomes a transformative tool, addressing the root of human suffering—ignorance—and guiding us towards a life of balance, purpose, and enduring inner fulfilment.

In the timeless words of Alexander Pope from the early eighteenth century, he wrote, 'To err is human, to forgive is divine.' Sadly, we often misinterpret this saying, clinging to the naive hope that the divine will forgive our wrongdoings while we continue to repeat them. Unfortunately, this hope is destined to fail, as even the divine cannot override the unchanging laws of nature—laws that the divine itself set into motion. This leaves us with no recourse but to endure the repercussions of the mistakes we make.

In the earthly realm, action and consequence are inseparable companions, succinctly defining our existence as: 'Action, reaction.' The human spirit thrives on endeavour, leaving no idle moment in its wake. As Shankaracharya once articulated, this endeavour encompasses not only physical pursuits but also the restlessness of the body, mind, and senses. Until we transcend our inherent inclinations, we remain ensnared in various forms of bondage.

Yearning for freedom is universal; even an unborn child resists spending more than ten months within the dark, obscure confines of the womb, submerged in amniotic fluid. However, long before the appointed time arrives, the world is ready to welcome us, exposing us to a cascade of both joyful and unsettling revelations. These first steps into the external world are influenced by the cosmic sway of karma, which inevitably compels even the child to relinquish its cherished sense of freedom.

Thereafter in our journey through life, we often find ourselves caught in actions that paradoxically lead to outcomes contrary to our intentions, pulling us deeper into the relentless web of bondage. But we must continue with our actions, pushing forward until we achieve what we desire! The anticipation of a favourable result breeds anxiety, a feeling that lingers until the outcome is revealed. This result may or may not align with our desires. Yet, the yearning for more persists, prompting us to take new actions. Desire, by its very nature, is insatiable; remaining unfulfilled whether we attain or fail to attain the objectives we seek. It grows stronger, much like a fire that intensifies with every drop of fuel. As a result, the pursuit shifts to cultivating new desires. So, where does the fallacy lie in our quest for liberation through action?

This misunderstanding arises from our failure to acknowledge our true nature as Consciousness, the eternal and self-sustaining principle that underlies all existence, while the physical world—including our body and mind—is merely a projection of labels and forms, lacking independent existence, like shadows that depend on light.

Intellectually, we must comprehend that Consciousness alone is the unchanging essence from which everything arises, and nothing exists outside of it. True tranquillity emerges from this realization, as we align ourselves with the principle that sustains our existence, while releasing attachment to the body and mind.

This truth becomes most evident during deep sleep, where bliss emerges from the absence of duality–division between the subject (body and mind) and the objects of experience (external world). In this state:

- The mind, body, and external world fade into a dormant state.
- All experiences, thoughts, and knowledge temporarily dissolve.
- The individual self appears unconscious because there is no activity of the mind or senses.

There is neither the burden of past knowledge nor the pursuit of new learning—and more importantly, with no desires stirring within, as the self abides in stillness. Yet, the individual's life in sleep and the world's existence remain uninterrupted, sustained solely by this Consciousness even when the mind and body are inactive. When we awaken, the mind reactivates instantaneously, and the external world reappears, restoring the perceived division between subject and object and re-establishing the duality—the division between 'self' and 'other' that was absent during deep sleep.

The experience during deep sleep reveals an essential truth:

our existence is not dependent on the active participation of the body and mind, but on the self-sustaining, independent nature of Consciousness.

In this state, free from desires for action or acquisition, one experiences unshaken peace—a glimpse of the inherent tranquillity that emerges when the distractions of duality vanish. Aligned with the higher Self, the sleeping personality perceives the world as a unified whole, devoid of division, even though the mind appears unconscious. This deep harmony imparts a unique peace, characteristic of deep sleep, which is subtly registered even in the mind's dormant state and is consciously experienced as tranquillity upon waking.

Known as Advaita Shantam (non-dual peace), this state is not limited to deep sleep; it can also be experienced in waking moments, even amidst the superficial dualities of daily life. These dualities often fuel comparisons and a deep desire to elevate one's social standing through acquisition, triggering internal conflicts and anguish. To transcend this turmoil, we must dissolve the illusion of separation. When this happens, we no longer act out of compulsion, desire, or the need for external validation. Instead, actions arise naturally and effortlessly, free from attachment, and driven by an innate harmony with our true self . In this state, life flows effortlessly, and the individual embodies the pure essence of being.

Is this achievable for someone deeply entangled in the material world of duality?

For anyone earnestly seeking a life of tranquillity, this is not an unattainable feat. It is entirely possible for a conscious human being through awareness of the truth—a truth that every individual unconsciously experiences during the state of deep sleep! True liberation does not require abandoning the world; it requires transforming how we perceive it. When we align ourselves with Consciousness, we see the world not as a place of division but as a unified whole, and our actions become spontaneous, peaceful, and free.

This paradox urges us to acknowledge the Supreme Consciousness revered as Brahman, and essence of awareness as the sole force underlying all three states of human experience, namely, waking, dreaming, and deep sleep. However, until we reach this understanding, ignorance, like an all-encompassing fog, will obscure every aspect of our existence. It not only veils the boundless potential of human nature but also convinces us that our limited physical form is all that there is.

As long as ignorance persists, it breeds negative thoughts that result in harmful consequences, with the most profound being a misapprehension of the 'absolute truth'. Even the brightest minds are often ensnared by this ignorance, accepting a distorted version of reality as truth, which inevitably leads to suffering. Overcoming ignorance is a formidable challenge, akin to dispelling darkness. This complexity often shifts our focus to addressing its symptoms rather than confronting its root cause.

ACTION CANNOT LEAD TO FREEDOM

Security, peace, happiness, and freedom—these cherished aspirations are facets of a single universal yearning. Yet, their fulfilment does not arise from relentless activity but from a state of stillness and rest, free from the compulsion to act. How can restlessness, striving, and ceaseless effort genuinely bring about serenity? Each action, by its very nature, binds and confines the jivatma—the individual soul—preventing its intellectual and spiritual union with the paramatma, the supreme soul, which serves as the gateway to liberation, eternal peace, and everlasting bliss. Thus, it is a huge error to believe that such a state of fulfilment can be achieved through actions alone.

Should we then abandon all actions and efforts in our quest for liberation from the bondage that labour imposes? The Bhagavad Gita, one of the foundational texts of Vedanta, offers clarity: 'One does not attain freedom from action by merely refraining from work; nor does one achieve perfection by renunciation alone.' This teaching emphasizes that liberation is not achieved through inaction or renunciation but by performing one's duties with detachment and self-awareness, aligning actions with higher principles.

The seemingly contradictory idea presented here inevitably places one in a quandary: should we labour, or relinquish it altogether? Yet, the undeniable truth remains that absolute abstinence from action is unattainable.

Labour is inherent to the very nature of conscious beings, particularly humankind, as action serves as a vital vehicle for progress. Actions, in themselves, are harmless; they become binding only when tainted by the ego—the essence of the 'I'—that stamps them with the imprint of ownership.

When the ego intertwines with action, whether through affection or animosity, the expectation of favourable outcomes inevitably take hold, ensnaring us in attachment to results. Therefore, the Bhagavad Gita exalts the state of Naishkarmya—a mindset free from the natural law of expectation. This state entails relinquishing any craving for outcomes, abandoning complaints, and embracing complete detachment—not from actions themselves, but from their fruits.

This philosophy does not advocate purposeless or aimless deeds; instead, it emphasizes acknowledging that the results of actions depend on countless uncontrollable factors. By renouncing attachment to outcomes, one cultivates mental equilibrium. The Gita calls not for the cessation of deeds but for the renunciation of self-serving desires born of conviction. Outward restraint alone is insufficient; one must curb the mind's fixation on sensory objects, which inherently fail to provide lasting fulfilment. True renunciation involves shedding unnatural and artificial yearnings that compel action in the first place. This compulsion dissipates only when one realizes their unity with the infinite—a state achieved through dispelling ignorance.

In this context, Vedanta aims to impart yet another crucial facet of Karma. It elucidates that when we engage in karma, we are essentially planting the seed that we will harvest either in the present or across successive rounds of birth and rebirth. Inevitably, we find ourselves bound to confront the outcomes of each action we undertake, outcomes moulded by the dictates of our misguided ideals—a false standard we yearn to acquire and maintain, stemming from our lack of understanding.

Actions borne out of ignorance and coercion, irrespective of their apparent nobility, cannot attain absolute virtue. The judgement of whether an action is good or bad cannot be solely based on the intentions of the doer; it must consider the impact it has on other individuals. What's considered good for one person can be detrimental to someone else, similar to how a fruit good for a diabetic can be detrimental to one suffering from kidney disease. As a result, the outcomes of our efforts consistently include a mixture of both happiness and sorrow.

True freedom transcends all forms of earthly bondage, including the bondage of action. It is not about freedom from this or that; it is not something to be acquired, but something to be realized, for it always exists as an inherent part of our nature.

The wise, understanding this truth, act not for gain but for the sake of action itself. Their efforts, untainted by craving or attachment, transcend the pursuit of specific ends and instead manifest as acts of fulfilment. Even when working for the welfare of humanity, such actions are performed with detachment and in a spirit of dispassion, unshackled by ego or desire.

FROM IGNORANCE TO KNOWLEDGE: THE KEY TO LIBERATION

Ignorance of any kind is not bliss; incomplete knowledge can be perilous. Strangely, we've managed to thrive despite knowing less than 5 per cent of our physical world. Our global economy now stands at a staggering value of over US$100 trillion. It's the ignorance of the know-it-all, the awareness within us, that truly afflicts us. This ignorance not only prevents us from recognizing the eternally free Consciousness, our core reality, but instead projects the body–mind, our transient identity, as our true self, leading to a state of bondage. Attachment and aversion, the twin progenies of ignorance, ensnare us in a cycle of virtuous and harmful actions, or they drag us into apathy and inaction.

Attachment, in particular, gives birth to its malevolent companions: sorrow, delusion, anger, greed, desires, expectations, and jealousy. The man who loves freedom suffers from bondage because he does not know how to experience happiness without attachment. We become entangled in attachments to people for the right and wrong reasons, possessions, power, fame, and wealth. Ignorance can guide us towards self-deception and compel us to engage in unrighteous deeds, as witnessed in tragic narratives. Shocking events unfurl a labyrinth of deceit and fraud, unveiling the depths to which ignorance can plunge a person in such harrowing tales.

To grasp the destructive power of greed, a product of attachment, consider 'the riveting true story of the Stuart Murder Case which rocked Boston', as detailed in the book, *Deadly Greed* by Joe Sharkey (2017). Here is a brief, horrifying account of the Charles Stuart case, in which ambition drove a man to murder his pregnant wife and blame a fictitious African-American killer.

The murder of a 7 months-pregnant woman in the Mission Hill neighbourhood of Boston on October 23, 1989 incited huge uproar when her well-to-do husband, Charles Stuart reported them both being robbed and shot at by a black man. Amidst heavy racial tensions in the community, Willie Bennet—the black man who Stuart identified—was successfully convicted. It was only revealed later that Stuart was the actual murderer of his wife and child, who owing to his distress over the pregnancy, and romantic interest in a co-worker, managed to evade justice until he died of suicide.

Vedanta, the concluding portion of the Vedas and one of humanity's oldest philosophical systems, asserts that our ignorance stems from failing to recognize that all existence is, at its essence, part of the unified and boundless ocean of Consciousness—free from duality. This ignorance leads to the mistaken perception of non-dual Consciousness and the material world as separate entities, giving rise to duality and creating a false sense of detachment from the Truth. As the *Brihadaranyaka Upanishad* aptly states: 'And where there is duality, there one sees another thing, another smell, another taste, there hears another, there touches another thing.'[3]

The human mind, ever restless, perpetually seeks answers, striving to resolve every question that arises. As Chase and Dasu observe in their HBR article on applied behavioural science, people desperately want things to make sense. They want explanations, and they will make them up if they have to. It is the rationalization effect.[4]

Long before humanity's arrival, the inert world and the elements of nature existed undisturbed. Yet, with its boundless curiosity and heightened faculties, humankind embarked on a quest to unravel nature's magnificence. This journey has unveiled many of nature's treasures, marking one of humanity's most extraordinary achievements. However, the pursuit of answers to two fundamental questions—who shaped our origin, and to what end—remained dormant until humanity was forced to confront the dwindling diversity of the world and its unrelenting suffering.

Alas, the vast cosmos and its myriad forms continue to confound human understanding, leaving behind a web of questions and uncertainties with every attempt to decipher them. Faced with unanswered queries, humankind often turns to the belief in a divine architect—a supernatural force responsible for creation and the laws governing the physical realm. Similarly, life's unresolved mysteries are frequently attributed to the 'will of God', with both blessings and adversities viewed as divine intent. Yet, the enigma of creation persists, constrained by the limits of human faculties that cannot transcend reason.

Ultimately, it is ignorance entwined with the complexities of contemporary existence that veils the truth of human essence—within which lie the answers to these fundamental questions. The conviction in the reality of the manifold world is a profound fallacy, one that inflicts immeasurable emotional turmoil upon humankind. When seen through the lens of pure Consciousness, the world's existence dissolves into mere misperception. In truth, no world exists—only Consciousness endures, a singular reality untainted by duality.

Although this truth remains unchallenged, humanity often suppresses the realization that all existence is merely a radiant mental construct, confined within the bounds of individual Consciousness. To one aligned with pure Consciousness, the world becomes a mere illusion, devoid of creation, creator, or purpose. Only the Supreme Consciousness prevails, rendering space and time meaningless.

According to the Vedas, 'time' is but an illusion—a counterfeit relationship between ignorance and the knowledge of truth. When ignorance is dispelled, misperception dissolves, taking the illusion of time with it. Without the constraints of time, space loses significance, liberating individuals from the chains of bondage. It is in this freedom that one finds pure love, empathy, care, and lasting peace.

Yet, for those ensnared in the labyrinth of worldly multiplicity, reigning ignorance obstructs the acceptance of the world's illusory nature. They struggle with the intangible reality of pure Consciousness, which lies beyond the reach of the senses. As long as they perceive the world as a creation, doubts about its origins and purpose will persist, binding them to the cycle of uncertainty and misapprehension.

Vedanta, however, succinctly concludes—without unnecessary speculation—that the world eternally abides; both man and nature will always exist. It asserts that the world is not a creation but a misconception born of human ignorance. In the absence of intentional contemplation, questions regarding purpose find no footing. Just as the error of mistaking a rope for a serpent arises from ignorance rather than deliberate thought, so too does the misperception of the world. When ignorance is eradicated, the veil of Maya (illusion) is lifted, revealing the eternal truth.

This misperception compels individuals to engage in actions (karma), driven by desires and influenced by comparisons, inadequacies, and internal conflicts. The very concept of karma—rooted in desire—stems from the cosmic process of manifestation, metaphorically described as Brahman's outward breath, facilitated through its inherent power known as Maya.

Maya, the cosmic intelligence, transforms the unmanifest, undifferentiated Brahman into the manifest world of forms and names. Through this process, duality arises, creating distinctions such as subject and object, self and other. This sense of separation fuels desires, which in turn propel actions and their consequences, perpetuating the experience of plurality and the diversity of the manifested universe. While this plurality appears real, the universe, at its core, remains formless energy—a fact reflected in Einstein's principle of mass–energy equivalence, which reveals that matter and energy are fundamentally interchangeable.

At the individual level, ignorance rooted in Maya compels us to perceive ourselves as separate from the infinite Consciousness. This misperception confines our true boundless nature to the limitations of the ego, giving rise to narcissism, fears, and complexes, such as the fear of mortality and the need for self-preservation. Driven by this sense of separation, individuals oscillate between submission to external forces and arrogance fuelled by egotism, further entrenching their isolation from the whole.

The division of the indivisible Brahman into fragments fosters selfishness, jealousy, competition, and attachment. It perpetuates karma and bondage while distorting perception and concealing the consequences of unrighteous actions. The mind, ensnared by this illusion, seeks solace in external pursuits, perpetuating a fatal cycle of desire, attachment, and suffering. This ignorance becomes the driving force behind the endless cycle of birth, death, and the emergence of negative traits.

On a universal scale, this cosmic intelligence perceives itself as separate from Brahman, presenting the illusory world as real. Vedanta aptly describes this ignorance, both individual and cosmic, as Maya, meaning 'that which truly lacks existence'.

The realization that Atman—our inner essence—is identical to Brahman, the universal Consciousness, dissolves the illusion of separation. Just as ornaments made of gold appear different in form yet remain inseparable from the gold itself, so too are we inseparable from Brahman. This awareness liberates us from the constraints of finitude, elevating us beyond grief, contradictions, and comparisons.

In this ultimate state of realization, the individual aligns with Brahman, free from the conditions governing the material world. The ancient sages, upon attaining this understanding, declared with clarity:

'All this is born of Me (Brahman), all this exists in Me, and all this is absorbed in Me: I am all this wonderful world. Virtue and sin do not belong to Me. Destruction there is none for Me. Birth, body, senses, and intellect do not belong to Me. I am above the earth, water, fire, air, and space.'[5]

This proclamation underscores Brahman's boundless nature and the ultimate freedom available to those who transcend the illusion of Maya.

Our problem is that we can neither dismiss action nor the world as an illusion. If we need peace, it appears we have to accomplish a seemingly unattainable feat of disengaging from action and engaging with the world at the same time. Instead, we must discover our intrinsic truth to find peace amid the chaos. Destroying ignorance, contracting Vasnas (the impressions we form at every worldly interface with our senses), and reconfiguring the Sattva, Rajas, and Tamas (SRT) factors (energy propensities of the mind) hold the keys to solving human problems.

The Vedas offer knowledge that can liberate us from ignorance and guide us on this transformative journey. Understanding the real 'I' and recognizing its boundless glory is the path to salvation and ultimate peace. Only through this self-realization can we navigate the ever-changing world while remaining anchored in our intrinsic truth.

The first step is to acquire the knowledge of our real Self. As B. R. Rajam eloquently puts it in his book *Rambles in Vedanta*, we must transcend the superficial and delve deep into the vastness of our being to discover the essence of existence:

> You may remain a thousand feet below the ground and cities, railroads and temples might have risen upon you; but your fossil-like existence, discoverable only by geological enterprise, does not mean salvation for, at that rate, the tiny worms and insects which every stratum of earth exhibits on excavation should be better sages than you. You may live without food, but that is nothing, for dyspepsia does not mean Brahma Gyan (knowledge of Brahman). What is required of man is that he should know what the real "I" means and realize its boundless glory in which the suns and spheres, constellations and milky-ways are like drops which nature's mighty heart drives through thinnest veins.'

Step two involves embracing the practical application and reaping its rewards. Personal experience holds value and doesn't necessarily demand scientific evidence or external validation.

CONFRONTING THE SHIFTING TIDES OF EXISTENCE

Our grand entrance into this perceptive world often brings an anticipated thrill to both familiar and unfamiliar faces gathered around us, marking the start of an exhilarating yet daunting adventure. However, all apprehensions vanish in an instant when we recognize the soothing rhythm of our mother's heartbeat as she holds us close to her nurturing embrace.

In this warm sanctuary, we begin our uncertain journey through life, leaning on the external world to face fear—a deeply personal struggle rooted in the mind's primal nature. This reliance on the unpredictable, unreliable, and transient external realm for physical and especially psychological comfort continues unabated until our final breath, despite the many unpleasant experiences it often brings.

As we grow, we find joy in the love and emotional connections shared with those close to us. However, over time, these very connections can become the source of human affliction, known as bondage. Even our mothers, often revered as sacred figures, are not exempt from this reality. While a mother's love is undeniable and comforting, we must acknowledge that she is an individual with a fluctuating mind, influenced by her thoughts. Therefore, it should not surprise us when her attitude towards the very child she loves changes. True wisdom lies in embracing the ever-changing nature of existence and the pain that comes from such shifts.

Dependence on the outer world to resolve inner struggles, attachment, and the unpredictable behaviour of others are three challenges we encounter early in life. These challenges persist stubbornly, making them difficult to overcome.

Once we step onto the world's grand stage, we assume our roles alongside fellow actors in this epic drama, for which no one is furnished with a script. We do not comprehend our designated actions, yet everyone is engaged in some action in pursuit of the very same objectives for the sake of enjoying material happiness. Triumphs and setbacks alternate; nothing arrives effortlessly.[6]

We engage in diverse endeavours to continuously satiate the inner void we feel. This sense of incompleteness persists because we opt for ignorance concerning Consciousness—our innate reality, boundless, perpetually liberated, and brimming with bliss. Consequently, as long as we identify with our finite body and mind, which are subject to various limitations, we'll perpetually confront insufficiency, necessitating the fulfilment of gaps through karma.

Therefore, complete disillusionment with the idea of true bliss through the experience of finite material objects is necessary before one seeks liberation. Those who continue to cherish the faintest hope of achieving an ideal state of existence by clinging to the relative world will remain unprepared for the teachings of Vedanta. To such individuals, the teachings of Vedanta promise the opportunity for a life beyond death, enabling the refinement of the mind through each reincarnation, and ultimately leading to liberation from the cycle of birth and death through the attainment of truth.

William Shakespeare undeniably possessed a rare wisdom to encapsulate this life's secret in his literary masterpiece *As You Like It*, wherein he declares, 'All the world's a stage, and all the men and women merely players; they have their exits and their entrances; and one man in his time plays many parts.' Departure from the stage transpires according to one's turn. Such exits evoke sorrow in some and elation in others.

The endless efforts each individual makes to attain freedom from fear, eliminate all afflictions and torments, and avoid unhappiness affirm that the ultimate results of these endeavours lie beyond human understanding.

Mired in ignorance, we find ourselves caught in an unending conflict, constantly bombarded by trials and tribulations. Because we are born of ignorance and fail to properly diagnose the root cause of our predicament we remain trapped in a continuous cycle, attempting to eradicate the effect rather than erasing the root cause. As long as our true nature remains veiled by ignorance, the wisdom of Vedanta holds: genuine freedom remains out of reach. This ignorance clouds our perception of reality, allowing our minds to revel in transient joy, devoid of true wisdom.

Wisdom should not be mistaken for erudition or intellect; it is the possession of a precise understanding gained through discerning valid knowledge from invalid knowledge. It simply involves discovering the knowledge that leads to liberation—a state where we dwell in uninterrupted joy born from the complete absence of suffering. Wisdom is the ability to keep the knowledge of the past at bay, to end the betrayal of the present moment. Vedanta underscores that only the right knowledge can dispel ignorance of the Self and not the execution of any action or the pursuit of novel experiences. The realization of one's intrinsic self, upon its discovery, is not an experience in the conventional sense. It's crucial to understand that experiencing Brahman is impossible because we are Brahman.

Discovering Brahman, which is attaining the knowledge of our true Self through Vedic meditation, is the key to liberation. Vedic meditation stands as the sole path to building lasting psychological immunity. It enables us to navigate the full range of life's tribulations, which stem from our misconceptions and misdeeds. Through this practice, we can break free from the cycle of repeating the same errors of the past. It is simply the acquisition of the right knowledge: 'words of wisdom,' through a purified mind that is sufficient to dispel ignorance.

This transformative journey demands attentive listening and deep introspection, guiding one towards self-realization grounded in unwavering conviction, free from external influences. Accordingly, the Vedas—particularly their latter portion—intentionally refrain from prescribing explicit guidelines or processes for discovering and identifying with Brahman, the essence of one's true nature. Offering instructions would imply introducing a method, prompting the human mind to construct its interpretations and engage in analytical struggle.

This, in turn, would undermine the very purpose of the journey, veiling the truth it seeks to reveal.

The Vedas serve as a profound source of knowledge about the individual self, guiding seekers towards supreme wisdom through specific practices and disciplines. Their purpose is to purify the tainted mind, the sole instrument through which we perceive both the visible and the invisible realms. However, a mind veiled by ignorance of its true nature and preoccupied with material perceptions cannot comprehend the impermanence and limited significance of itself and the external world. Only by dispelling this ignorance through the knowledge imparted by the Vedas can the mind recognize its limited nature and acknowledge Consciousness as the absolute truth that underpins and sustains its very existence. This understanding is essential for bringing order to a chaotic mind, paving the way for a life of genuine tranquillity.

This is analogous to our innate identification with our body–mind, our incidental reality, requiring no external guidance for recognition. However, given the paramount importance of purifying the mind, necessary for assimilating knowledge, it prescribes a triad of practices: Karma Yoga, which emphasizes selfless action; Bhakti Yoga, that focuses on devotion; and Jnana Yoga, delving into the path of knowledge. Alongside these practices, a fourfold qualification is outlined to train the mind, enabling individuals to pursue spiritual goals without withdrawing from the ongoing progress in the material world. These disciplines together form a comprehensive approach to balancing the spiritual and material realms.

At this juncture, a brief introduction to the Sattva, Rajas, and Tamas (SRT) factors of the mind is essential, as they form the foundation of our inner personality, and influence our actions and interactions both internally and externally. These SRT factors represent three fundamental energy propensities known as gunas that shape an individual's thoughts, actions, behaviour, habits, and character.

The mind, a unique possession of every individual, governs behaviour in a distinct manner for each person. As a formation of cosmic energy, which inherently embodies these three ingredients, the mind naturally absorbs their distinct properties. The three gunas—Sattva, Rajas, and Tamas—exist in varying proportions in every individual and every object of experience in the world. Together, they shape the nature of our interactions and the essence of our existence.

Sattva (purity and harmony) is the sanguine and sanity factor that fosters goodness, nurturing positivity within us.

Rajas (activity and passion) is the rebelling factor, the quality of dynamism and passion that serves as the driving force for action, intermingled with both constructive and destructive tendencies.

Tamas (inertia and ignorance) is the toxic factor that embodies inertia and complete negativity.

The three factors function either independently or in unison, collectively shaping our thoughts, speech, actions, behaviour, and character. At any given moment, they may act in opposition or harmony with one another. The SRT factors form the essence of our individuality and inner personality. As a result, the change in behaviour we display is a direct reflection of the dominant energy (guna) influencing our mind at that specific moment.

Knowing about the SRT factors prompts us to explore the depths of our inner being and our emotional personality, while the revelation of our Self ushers in a transformative paradigm shift, altering our perception of ourselves, the world, and the divine. It proclaims unequivocally that the current focal point of our existence, the pursuit of material comforts, is simply a means and not the ultimate goal.

Three steps to attain knowledge of your real Self:

1. Revamp your thought framework based on a change of vision to align with Consciousness.
2. Shatter the shackles of religious dogma and misleading rituals.
3. Dissolve the fallacious self by intellectually claiming and assimilating it into the authentic Self through Vedic meditation—hear, introspect, and internalize by remembering the following expressions:
    a. Brahman, the universal essence, the absolute truth, is the only unchanging reality. Since my existence depends on Consciousness, I cannot claim an identity separate from that Self. (I am that truth.)
    b. The material world is illusory because it is not self-sustaining; its existence depends on me, the Consciousness. When seen through this perspective, the world's events, objects, and people, which rely on me, hold no power over me, just as the ocean remains undisturbed despite the surging and retreating waves.

c. I am always the non-dual Consciousness (the grand 'I'), the ultimate Truth, while I also experience the subordinate truth of my individuality (the small 'i'), playing roles in the unfolding drama of life. In this narrative, I enter the stage without prior knowledge of my role or its duration. Hence, I shall confront an array of trials and experiences during this brief period, engaging with circumstances either individually or in conjunction with fellow characters. My amalgamation of body and mind merely serves as the attire donned to suit the character I portray.
d. As long as I stay grounded in the awareness that my physical form and mind have no true substance from the perspective of my Consciousness, and remain an impartial observer of the drama, not attached to the illusions of the role I play, I will remain free, secure, tranquil, and content.

RELIEVING HUMAN SUFFERING THROUGH VEDIC MEDITATION

The contemporary world order, firmly anchored in the domains of science and technology, remains impervious to the cries of the numerous casualties of its unrelenting brutality. It fails to comprehend the immense burden it places on individuals, compelling them to meet stringent qualifications to stake a legitimate claim to economic prosperity. The timing could not be more opportune for selfish individuals to infiltrate human emotions, offering an array of meditation techniques as the sole escape from stress arising primarily from unfulfilled material desires, as well as the anguish resulting from financial instability or chronic health issues. The diverse array of meditation practices, each with its promise spanning from tranquillity, mind control, or a thought-free state, falls short of delivering comprehensive outcomes.

The mind's inherent function is to think and retain thoughts. Striving to render the mind thoughtless, and sustaining that state for a brief period seems feasible for yogis who have withdrawn to remote forests. Yet, even these accomplished practitioners cannot claim to maintain such a state indefinitely, a reality they might not readily concede. For those engaged in daily urban battles, this proves nothing short of a harsh suppression, intensifying internal conflicts rather than resolving them. Their circumstances demand constant, purposeful thinking. Attitude and conduct, the two principal catalysts of human deeds, hinge on the prevailing thoughts within the mind at any given juncture.

As long as one entertains unsavoury thoughts, inner calm eludes them, regardless of the form of meditation practised. 'It is possible to tie the mouth of a tiger, but it is impossible to quieten the mind,' as Rajam, a wise philosopher, asserted.

'Mind of a man,' said Jagat Guru Shankaracharya, 'is like a drunkard monkey bitten by a scorpion.' Thus, the endeavour to reshape the essence of the mind equates to attempting to make sugar taste like salt without adding a grain of salt. Such practices draw stern reproach from this Vedic exposition, for they do not truly address the core predicaments of humanity.

Meditation must play a pivotal role in addressing the challenges we face daily. It should delve into both the physical and psychological dimensions of human experience, particularly focusing on understanding why human behaviour often leads to a life riddled with conflicts. Relationships, as we know, are an inevitable aspect of life. However, without the ability to manage conflicts within these relationships, life can become burdensome and devoid of meaning. Meditation, in its truest sense, must serve as a powerful means to dissolve mental disturbances arising from both internal turmoil and external pressures. Before embarking on any form of meditation, it is vital to understand its true nature, purpose, and underlying motive. Meditation should not be approached as a superficial activity or a quick fix for life's complexities, but rather as a practice aimed at self-discovery and inner transformation. It is equally important to question why meditation is pursued if it fails to directly address the fundamental psychological challenges one faces daily, such as fear, attachment, or conflict, as these will interfere with the practice almost immediately.

We should not be afraid to question when instructions on how to meditate are given by a master with promises of spiritual growth and ultimate enlightenment while neglecting the resolution of the basic psychological issues.

Moreover, it reflects a form of spiritual corruption when meditation is taught within a framework of commercialization, where the sacred practice is reduced to a product for monetary gain rather than a tool for genuine enlightenment. Such an approach risks leading individuals further into illusion, offering temporary solace without addressing the root causes of suffering. True meditation must always aim to liberate the mind, guiding individuals to confront and transcend the psychological barriers that hinder clarity, peace, and authentic self-realization.

At the heart of most human quandaries lie conflicts born from the ego and the false self-image we construct. Each individual, in some form, becomes entangled in maintaining an identity shaped by external validation, societal expectations, or personal ambition. Considerable energy is spent in protecting or embellishing this image—often through the pursuit of material success, ideological rigidity, or relentless self-justification. This illusion of self, when threatened, breeds inner conflict and separation from our true nature. To achieve true tranquillity and lead a life free from both inner and outer conflict, one must release the false self-image and relinquish the ego. Is this possible?

The ego, or 'I', consists of the body, mind, and reflected consciousness. While eliminating the mind is impractical, eradicating its ego-constructing thoughts is achievable. The ego forms through self-images like 'I am intelligent' or 'I am right', creating division, comparison, and conflict. To protect this image, individuals often engage in self-deception, wasting energy on futile pursuits.

Some philosophers advocate for instant ego dissolution, contrasting with gradual religious methods, which are hindered by the mind's constant influx of thoughts. Thoughts stem from Vasnas—unprocessed impressions from interactions and past lives—making their complete eradication unfeasible.

Instead, the Vedas suggest aligning our true reality with Consciousness. Identifying with Consciousness automatically dissolves the ego, revealing the Self as a unified, universal essence. This realization brings profound tranquillity, and freedom from desire and aversion.[7]

Meditation serves as a powerful tool, enabling us to understand and transcend this detrimental aspect of human nature by addressing the root of conflict, which is a universal challenge faced by all. By questioning the need to preserve the ego and the false image at a psychological level, both during and beyond meditation, one can gradually transcend these limitations, paving the way to genuine inner peace. Unfortunately, this vital insight is seldom emphasized. Yet, it is only through such meditative inquiry that the journey towards harmony and self-realization can truly unfold.

In a confluence of acquisitiveness and resourcefulness, astute entrepreneurs, unwavering in their pursuits, have forged a multi-billion-dollar industry. They have ingeniously repackaged a simple notion, adorning it with linguistic flair. Simultaneously, the convergence of thought brought about by technological advancement shares some of the blame. Our lives have been rendered so effortless by science and innovation that independent thinking has become an inconvenience, and yet our minds are burdened by stress.

In the meantime, we continue to read reports, published articles and write-ups extolling the virtues of meditation, particularly those of mindfulness practices which resonate globally. The more their echoes reverberate, the more swiftly the idea solidifies as an unassailable truth. In the realm of meditation, the cash registers chime ceaselessly for proprietors, regardless of whether individuals fully grasp the purported advantages. The common person is easily enticed into engaging with these practices, lured by the perceived benefits of the lesser variants of meditation. Thus, we remain oblivious to the authentic benefits that could be achieved by adhering to meditation's precise definition.

A simple act of unwinding, wrapped up and presented as the practice of meditation, adorned with multiple layers of deception, becomes the unique selling point. The human mind readily embraces these deceptions if they offer sensory satisfaction. Discovering the profound truth and genuine essence of humanity requires a deliberate shift in perspective from the individual 'self' and its associates to the higher 'Self', the spirit, achieved through focused meditation. This transformation offers the ultimate solution to all human dilemmas, yet can be challenging for minds shaped by different conditioning.

At this point, I am compelled to talk about the age-old Vedic scripture known as the Ashtavakra Gita, a vade mecum that endures the most rigorous trials of human logic. For the seekers of enduring tranquillity amidst the capricious existence in the new world order, embracing its counsel shall undoubtedly yield great benefits.

The text emphasizes adopting Vedic meditation, encompassing attentive listening, introspection, and contemplation, as the enchanting formula. In this practice, the subconscious mind absorbs thoughts that possess the capacity not only to acknowledge the law of cause and effect with impartiality and serenity but also to transcend mentally. At this pivotal moment of Vedic meditation, one attunes with Consciousness, wherein the individual 'self', the lower plane of reality, seamlessly merges with the true 'Self', the higher plane of reality—both intellectually and mystically, in harmony.

The primary focus of Vedic meditation, a potent tool, centres on dispelling a threefold misapprehension born of ignorance—the root cause of human suffering—and elucidates how an individual can counteract tribulations stemming from their karmic history:

- Erroneously attributing qualities such as consciousness and bliss to the non-self, the individual 'self'—comprising the body–mind complex, which is inherently inert and unconscious–results from a fundamental misunderstanding. This confusion stems from the mistaken perception of the eternally free Supreme Consciousness as a personal possession, confined within the physical framework of the body, mind, senses, and breath. As a result, identifying oneself as a limited individual renders the world and its events overwhelmingly intimidating. This perspective breeds feelings of insecurity, fear, anguish, and dependence on external support. Consequently, selective attachment to and aversion towards people, objects, and circumstances in the world come to dominate and direct one's actions.
- Harbouring the belief in the multiplicity of entities within the cosmos, while perceiving and treating fellow beings as separate and distinct objects, disconnected from oneself.
- Failing to realize the true 'Self' as Pure Consciousness—eternally free, indivisible, undifferentiated, self-sufficient, and the untainted witness of the phenomenal world.

Those who ascend beyond the confines of body and mind, recognizing their oneness with the supreme 'Self', discover profound solace, untouched by the concepts of virtue and vice. Shifting thought patterns and resolutely adopting a fresh perspective stand as the paramount remedy to humanity's enduring dilemmas. It is essential to clarify that when we speak of 'shift', we don't mean mere change, for change implies moving from one preconceived state to another, where both states are constructs of the same mind. There's no genuine change in this process. 'If we change according to a pre-established pattern, it's not true change; it's simply a modified continuation of the same. Therefore, the genuine meaning of change is the cessation of the old patterns and not a mere modification of existing ideas,' as succinctly articulated by the philosopher J. Krishnamurti during one of his lectures in California.

This process requires regenerating a tainted mind, leading to genuine transformation. It demands complete detachment from identification with the physical body and finite mind, alongside a sincere awakening to our true Self—the Supreme Consciousness.

This shift should not be merely a superficial adjustment of thought patterns; rather it must be deeply rooted in the unwavering conviction that every thought—whether stemming from personal experiences or borrowed from external influences, especially those that tie us to the body–mind complex—can persist only when we actively bring them into conscious awareness through the inherent principle of ever-present Consciousness itself. Nothing works without it.

Simultaneously, liberating ourselves from the shackles of the body–mind complex demands a deep understanding of how this identification comes to be. Fundamentally, it stems from the thoughts we cultivate, moulded by the language we use to define ourselves, such as 'I am this and that', conspicuously affirming the limited nature of the individual self. These thoughts, grounded in the past, are limited, as they were constructed based on the knowledge which is never truly comprehensive at any given moment, since knowledge is in a perpetual state of evolution.

It is imperative to note that anything other than the Consciousness principle is inherently finite and destined to perish someday. As a result, the ego—the self, as we perceive it, can only operate as a restricted entity chained by the constraints of thoughts, time, and physical boundaries. In stark contrast, words fall short of describing the Supreme Consciousness, rendering it beyond the grasp of thoughts or notions. This Consciousness residing both within and beyond the scope of our mental constructs can only be comprehended through its nature: existence, awareness, and bliss.

As the awareness principle, It always remains the 'real subject' and not an object to be experienced by the individual who is merely a 'pseudo subject' perceiving all things solely within Its eternal presence.

Thus, it is emphasized that nothing can create any division

when we fathom Consciousness, which is beyond the confines of words, thoughts, imaginations, time, space, and sensory perceptions. The Supreme Consciousness is boundless, existing as the sole infinite reality—completely free, and therefore eternally in a state of bliss. No mental constructs or ideas can interfere when we align with Consciousness—the unchanging awareness principle that underpins the very foundation of our existence. Our identification with the Supreme Consciousness—our real Self—is thus, truly boundless.

Considering that all human struggles sprout from the soil of ignorance, their resolutions can be solely accomplished through the cultivation of precise knowledge rather than through any goal-oriented action or the pursuit of groundbreaking theories through experimentation. Thus, though formal training may not be a mandatory gateway to wisdom, a profound willingness to immerse oneself in hands-on, rigorous exercises becomes the fertile ground for its growth.

YOUR PATH TO A TRANQUIL LIFE

While it is an undeniable truth that life confronts us with adversity, yet the greater truth lies in our inherent strength as humans to overcome these challenges, whether just or unjust. We have the power to endure the twists and turns shaped by our fate, which is influenced by the karmic consequences of our past actions.

We are human beings, and that is the difference. We stand apart from the silent tree witnessing its leaves wither without protest, not knowing they will sprout anew; distinct from the bird struggling in harsh and unfamiliar conditions only to succumb, and unlike an animal yielding to a mightier predator when its strength fails. We are fortified with unyielding tenacity and abundant resilience to face life's ebbs and flows. Empowered with intellect and free will, we can take new actions even when all else seems to fail, persevering until we catch a glimpse of the blue skies at the end of the dark tunnel, regardless of the journey's length.

All of these accomplishments become possible when we begin to shift our perspective and reshape our thoughts. By utilizing our capacity to release unwanted memories that bind and hinder us, we free ourselves to take new actions that can ease the burdens of past karmas. We have the power to draw strength from the divine presence within, a constant source of guidance that leads us towards relief as we face the consequences of our past misdeeds in this life. At the same time, this inner strength prepares us for a brighter future, both in this life and the next.

Notwithstanding the above-mentioned truths, it is crucial to avoid repeating the same mistakes by remembering the chief tenets of this text, which can be summarized as follows:

- **Self-Realization**: The path to true wisdom lies in understanding the nature of the Self, which transcends the body and mind. The essence of our being is Consciousness, and acknowledging this truth leads to freedom from suffering and ignorance.
  The root of all human predicaments lies in a lack of awareness of one's true identity. At its core, humanity is nothing less than the transcendental deity. Jesus exemplified this divine state through his willing submission to the divine, as evidenced by his declaration, 'I and the Father are one.' These words encapsulate the same fundamental truth. Isolation emerges only when individuals perceive themselves as separate from their true essence. With this separation arises the need to defend the various beliefs formed through life experiences and the attachments to possessions, ultimately succumbing to fear and suffering.
- **Detachment from Material Illusions**: The pursuit of worldly desires and attachments only leads to suffering. By detaching from the transient, we can find peace and inner contentment, realizing that external circumstances cannot provide lasting happiness.
- **Embrace of Impermanence**: Everything in the material world is temporary, including our bodies and minds. Acknowledging this impermanence allows us to transcend the fleeting and focus on what is eternal—the Consciousness within.
  The tangible world, as perceived by the conscious soul, serves primarily functional purposes. However, its lack of ultimate reality remains a metaphysical certainty. This perspective does not deny the physical existence of the world but emphasizes its lack of intrinsic, self-sustained existence.
- **Transformation of the Mind**: The mind, often clouded by ignorance and desires, must be purified through knowledge

and self-discipline. Only a clear and disciplined mind can recognize the truth and attain liberation.

Aligning one's mind with the principles inherent in the subjective realm emerges as the only reliable and enduring source of security, serenity, and joy. This truth stems from the finite nature of all entities bound by time and space, which are ultimately destined to fade away.

- **The Role of the Vedas:** The Vedas serve as a guide, offering wisdom to dispel ignorance and lead the seeker towards spiritual awakening. Their teachings help us realize our true nature and align with the divine principles of life.

Those who consistently engage in the proper practice of Vedic meditation will dissolve misconceptions and conflicting ideas about their true Self. Through this disciplined process, they will harmonize their thoughts with the principle of Supreme Consciousness, allowing their minds to flow smoothly, like a tranquil stream.

SECTION ONE

HEAR AND INTROSPECT—THE SECRET TO ENDING THE BATTLE WITH SUFFERING

Chapter 1

IT'S YOUR CHOICE

A man's mind is in constant turmoil, perpetually caught in the struggle to discern between choices, as he seeks to elevate his existence. In this state, he must deliberate wisely, choosing between a life plagued by inner turmoil and one of tranquillity; between the restless workings of a conscious mind and the stillness of pure Consciousness; between being tossed by the shifting tides of reality and navigating life's challenges with balance and equanimity.

Such a feat is impossible without the practice of meditation. The choice is not between some practice and no practice; it must, without a doubt, be the choice between the genuine and the illusory.

The fundamental dilemmas of human existence remain unresolved, even amid the extraordinary economic growth of the past century. We have now arrived at a critical juncture where reliance on nature's support is no longer viable. It should come as no surprise, then, that technology continues to weave itself deeper into our lives, for such is the trajectory of the modern world. The shift from 'privacy protection' to 'privacy invasion' is a direct consequence of the so-called digital revolution, though its undeniable benefits to humanity cannot be overlooked.

The contemporary man has distanced himself from self-reliance, instead leaning heavily upon science and technology even for the most mundane of daily tasks; yet, paradoxically, respite for his self remains elusive, when, in truth, it ought to be the reverse. Despite relying less on instincts, today's individual faces greater stress than ever before. Artificial intelligence has so deeply permeated human life that genuine emotions are now filtered through devices and machines.

Tolerance and patience—the twin pillars underpinning human harmony—stand among the gravest casualties of this technological eruption. It is not the passage of time that consumes man, but rather the inexorable march of technology. Man has, in his acquiescence, permitted technology—and its companion, capitalism—to infiltrate every facet of existence and to dictate even the realm of medicine.

The field of advanced medical science produces medicines through rigorous research protocols and multiple phases of clinical trials, all driven by the noble aim of alleviating human suffering. Yet, it remains imperfect, as every remedy carries the duality of benefits and side effects. Given that death is an inescapable covenant of existence, the decision to introduce new medicines is undertaken only when the benefits vastly outweigh the risks.

The pioneers of modern medicine, adept at harnessing the advancements of our age, have developed two primary approaches to treating ailments. Their primary focus lies in delivering rapid relief from physical pain and acute conditions. However, a closer examination reveals a profound purpose: these treatments, designed for immediate and temporary alleviation, aim to provide the body's immune system sufficient time to generate the necessary antibodies for restoring health.

The approach shifts significantly when addressing chronic ailments, the persistent and less glamorous counterparts of diseases. Those afflicted with long-lasting conditions are often subjected to ongoing management, their fate ultimately deferred to death's inevitable verdict. In truth, it is a matter of commerce. While the increased life expectancy achieved over the past century is a notable statistical triumph, for the many who endure prolonged physical pain from emerging illnesses and the psychological toll of unaffordable healthcare, such longevity offers little solace.

A report by the World Health Organization (2019) suggests that a large number of people in the world will be affected by mental or neurological disorders at some point in their lives. Around 450 million people currently suffer from such conditions, placing mental disorders among the leading causes of ill-health and disability worldwide.

Perhaps, this is nature's gentle manner of voicing her discontentment over mankind's haughty presumption; to remind us that intellect is different from wisdom. Fuelled by malice, man delights in revelling in his unjustified arrogance. And when he oversteps his limits whilst tampering with the harmonious environs designed to bestow tranquillity, he—nay, the entire human race—is fated to confront the repercussions.

Nature, from which both corporeal frame and psyche of humans are fashioned, hastens to summon forth one of her five constituents, be it an earthquake, a tsunami, a tempest, a deluge, or a drought, to assert her power, a power that man has perpetually underestimated. Even a modest avian creature can induce the entire world to reel in trepidation. It is a dread-filled occurrence. Regrettably, man's hubris continues to swell unabated, even as he is encircled by the haunting ghosts that shroud his surroundings.

Throughout the globe, societies persist in their collective swagger, progressing upon the path of skewed economic growth. They neither have the time nor the inclination to heed the wisdom of philosophers who offer valuable insights and practical solutions to humanity's challenges. Instead, they are often unfairly labelled as useless individuals who constantly discourage the pursuit of joy as a means to attain happiness.

However, the undeniable reality is that those who are more affluent tend to prioritize their interests over helping their less fortunate peers. Thus, the responsibility lies squarely on humans to take swift action, to pause and bridge the dissonance between their intellectual impetus and the plaintive cry of their heart for change.

Thus, abdicating the modern way of existence is their foremost recourse for extricating themselves from their woeful state.

CAPITALISM: THE ILLUSION OF PROSPERITY

Capitalism, the growth formula that emerged in the eighteenth century, has led a significant portion of the population into delusional existence. Individuals with limited financial means find their minds in constant turmoil, caught between unfavourable alternatives. They struggle to adapt to the recurring void left behind by fulfilled or unmet desires, trapped in an unending cycle of yearning.

Having succumbed to the allure of the tech-driven world and having unwittingly surrendered the key aspect of their true nature without hesitation, these hapless individuals stand bewildered. Their stance remains paradoxical: they claim contentment in life's modest joys even amid considerable hardship, deferring profound philosophical contemplation to life's end.

Human propensity to endure considerable discomfort for fleeting pleasures derived from sensory gratification is remarkable. In their relentless quest to emulate others, they push themselves not out of necessity but driven by an obsession with conformity, mistaking it for the comfort of familiarity. The added fear of isolation when straying from conventional norms further anchors them to the path followed by the majority. Regrettably, they have forsaken their autonomy to think independently, opting instead to align with the actions of individuals from far-flung lands.

Ultimately, whether one attains complete contentment through the accumulation of an undefined quantity of material possessions or not, what everyone truly seeks is relief from pain, whether mental or physical. Innately, the quest for solutions takes a non-rational course, swayed by a misguided understanding of the predicament. Symptoms rather than causes command attention, resulting in an unending pursuit of remedies.

It's hardly surprising that modern meditation practices, which are essentially simple forms of relaxation techniques masquerading as authentic meditation, have gained tremendous popularity. Their appeal doesn't stem from their effectiveness in addressing profound issues but rather from their convenient alignment with the mindset of the modern individual.

Unsurprisingly, in today's world, instant gratification—the desire to experience pleasure or fulfilment without delay—and the pursuit of 'quick fixes' have become increasingly commonplace. Nevertheless, whether this yearning for instant satisfaction is solely a product of our technology-driven world or a deeply ingrained and inherent human trait is a question that warrants thoughtful consideration.

A well-known experiment that offers insight into this inquiry is the Stanford Marshmallow Test, originally conducted by psychologist Walter Mischel in 1972. In the experiment, each child was allowed to choose a piece of candy, which was then placed on a table in front of them. The child was told that they would receive a second treat if they could wait for fifteen minutes without eating the first one. The child was then left alone in the room.

The results of the experiment showed that children who were able to wait for the second treat didn't just distract themselves—they used strategies to ignore or avoid thinking about the candy to handle the discomfort of waiting.

The root of human problems lies in ignorance, as demonstrated by both mental and physical suffering. The man struggles to identify 'ignorance' as the underlying issue, a seemingly straightforward concept for two reasons. Firstly, it's essential to acknowledge the humbling reality that an individual's intellect deflated by ego frequently hesitates to accept this truth due to its lack of awareness regarding a deep-seated ignorance. This ignorance resides at the far end of the complex eight-layer cause-and-effect sequence explained in greater detail later in this treatise. Secondly, the urgency to swiftly alleviate pain prevents deep introspection to identify the real cause.

The oft-repeated solution in this text lies in dispelling ignorance by knowledge—particularly the awareness of the Supreme Consciousness. Attaining this knowledge necessitates establishing Consciousness as the foundational element for contemplation and then validating this understanding through personal experience. Paradoxically, both of these pursuits are hindered by our highly conceited reliance on the very Consciousness that enables all action through the mind. This reliance obscures our ability to recognize the Supreme Consciousness as the true knower, while undeservedly crediting the mind with achievements it has not earned. For the ordinary person, entangled in ignorance, this presents a profound challenge: to realize that the true knower of all is not the body–mind complex, but the Self—the Supreme Consciousness itself. What is this knowledge? Where is it? How can one attain this knowledge?

Ignorance does not signify the absence of scholastic knowledge but relates to man's lack of knowledge about his intrinsic nature, and his real identity.[8] The universally applicable supra-rational knowledge is available in the texts of the Vedas. It pertains to the spirit, the driving force of all existence. It transcends everything that a man can conceive, including material objects, people, birth, disease, death, time, space, nation, boundaries, religion, and God.

This profound knowledge can be acquired and assimilated through Vedic meditation, which is based on the doctrine of Vedanta. Vedic meditation serves as a reliable means to revive and protect man against the shocks of the deceptive world of consumerism. English writer and philosopher Aldous Huxley described the Gita (one of the triple texts of Vedanta) as 'one of the clearest and most comprehensive summaries of the perennial philosophy ever to have been created. Therefore, its enduring value extends not only to Indians but to all of mankind.'

Arthur Schopenhauer, the German philosopher, upon reading the Upanishads—which cover the end portions of the Vedas, and are also known as Vedanta—exclaimed, 'And oh, how thoroughly is the mind here washed clean? In the whole world, there is no study so beneficial and elevating as that of the Upanishads. It has been the solace of my life; it will be the solace of my death.'

In the trinity encompassing Jiva (all embodied beings, including humans), Jagat (the inert world), and the immanent deity (who is worshiped and revered through rituals, offerings, and sacrifices for personal gains), the human form is deemed most fitting for enacting the deeds requisite to acquire the invaluable wisdom that leads to liberation—the ultimate state of existence wherein agony is no longer known.

This knowledge, which is deeply rooted in the wisdom found within the Vedas, can be attained by delving into the teachings of Vedanta through the practice of Vedic meditation. It is a path of introspection and contemplation that unveils the nature of reality and the essence of one's being. By exploring these ancient texts and engaging in the practices they advocate, individuals can gain insights into their true nature and the fundamental principles governing existence.

The central objective of this treatise is the elimination of ignorance, serving as the antidote to humanity's afflictions. The remedy is readily available for those who seek it.

Chapter 2

ACCOMPLISHING THE COMMON GOAL

Solely two desires stir within every soul in this vast expanse of existence: one, liberation from suffering, and two, uninterrupted experience of joy. This exalted state can be realized by all through the acquisition of Self-knowledge, facilitated by the practice of Vedic meditation.

In this context, it is crucial to recognize that relaxation and meditation are fundamentally distinct concepts, each addressing different needs and desires, and cannot be reasonably substituted for one another. The essence of meditation hinges on the foundation of thought. To meditate is to 'think, contemplate, and reflect'. This is a distinctive human faculty that reveals itself with each unearthing of truth in the phenomenal realm. It is the same faculty that the ancient sages cultivated, harnessing it in concert with their elevated faculties to plumb the depths of supra-rational truths.

Regrettably, human beings, a complex interplay of virtue and vice, spare no occasion to harness this faculty for self-serving aims. The concept of meditation, too, has suffered at the hands of such a criminal disposition.

Contemporary meditation practice, peddled as a commodity, manifests as a weakened iteration, proffering a few transitory indulgences—pleasant and advantageous, yet transient and bereft of transformative might.

What gain shall man derive from embracing any meditation form if it fails to usher tranquillity into a perturbed mind, permitting him to bask in that serenity long after the cessation of the practice? The pursuit of physical or mental prowess through activity-based meditation may extend immediate respite, yet it often metamorphoses into a burden.

Liberation sprouts from the kernel of knowledge. Any prescribed regimen bereft of the knowledge requisite for severing the fetters of the mind shall transmute into mere mechanical manoeuvring. It shall soon find itself relegated to the realm of mundane tasks, susceptible to evaluation vis-à-vis the allotment of time. This rationale frequently leads many to prematurely discontinue their practice. Meditation, at its core, must serve as the catalyst for the eradication of all obstructions to the conversion of lofty philosophical insights into direct spiritual apprehension of transcendent truths, a realm distinct from the objective world.

Indeed, Vedic meditation, meticulously tailored to reshape the patterns of thought, stands equipped to fulfil this lofty purpose, all the while endowing boundless benefits upon all, often at minimal or no expense. The shift in thought patterns not only retains its steadfast purpose but also enriches one's endeavours to achieve material goals, as it fosters a deeper understanding and brings about a transformative perspective on both oneself and the world.

The primary gains encompass enhanced concentration of mind and increased clarity of thought, along with better governance of the tendencies—the SRT factors—the energy propensities nesting within the mind, which wield direct influence over our thoughts, actions, and inclinations. Designed with the intent that its rewards permeate beyond the confines of candlelit meditation chambers or the ambience punctuated by melodies, this practice negates the necessity for such prerequisites, a requirement that should never be.

Its potency lies in its unwavering promise to sculpt the mind, paving way for the spiritual realization of higher, more profound truths.

SCIENCE IS NOT THE ANSWER TO ALL HUMAN STRUGGLES

The trials that plague humanity endure unabated, despite the relentless efforts of medical science to harness technological advancements in the fight against suffering. Yet, these endeavours often reach an impasse. The root of human dilemmas lies deeply embedded in the subtle realms, beyond the grasp of conventional reasoning. With senses as his primary tool of perception, the average individual remains tethered to the tangible world of sensory objects, stumbling in his pursuits. Science, for all its remarkable achievements, reveals its limitations when it attempts to venture beyond the boundaries of the physical domain.

'Science examines the world with frantic eagerness but does not get to the bottom; it furiously knocks itself against a barrier beyond which it cannot go,' proclaimed Rajam in his treatise, *Rambles in Vedanta*. It is an acknowledged truth that while science is firmly rooted in empirical evidence, its assertions are constructed upon a substrate of conditions that may transform over time, perhaps spanning several millennia, owing to the inherent nature of change in the world. As a result, the eternal validity of scientific principles cannot be unequivocally guaranteed. Faced with such unpredictability, science frequently encounters constraints, rendering it incapable of proactively addressing the challenges of humanity until they manifest overtly.

Furthermore, scientific theories, in their very essence, bear flaws that erode their reliability. The data, culled by instruments, finds its ultimate interpretation within human minds, inherently flawed in numerous aspects. This very aspect finds eloquent elucidation in Kenneth Chan's article, 'Why Relativity Exists' (2016) his blog *Physics & the Observer Effect*, where he remarks, 'While scientific theories are based on data obtained from scientific experiments, the key point is this: We need to observe these experiments. Even the use of scientific measuring apparatus does not obviate this requirement; ultimately, we have to retrieve the data from the scientific equipment, and this means observation by humans. This is the crucial point. Sooner or later, our human sensory apparatus and our consciousness come into play. It is unavoidable.'

Nevertheless, in the broader context, discontent with existence remains relatively rare, as modern humanity has secured the essentials for survival. The core issue lies in man's inability to accept the fair distribution of outcomes resulting from his actions. He perceives it as unjust, struggling to understand why competence and success manifest so differently across individual destinies.

Why doesn't the cultivation of ethical virtues always yield prosperity? Life, by its very nature, is interlocked in idiocy. Irrespective of one's societal or economic status, apprehensions about the future invariably clutch at us all.

A mind preoccupied with reflections on the past or the nebulous future can never stand as a haven for serenity. 'The rage of the lion, the rancour of the elephant, the ferocity of the tiger, the venom of the serpent, the low cunning of the fox, the ugly instincts of the boar, the vileness of the rat have all their counterparts in the mind of man,' asserts Rajam (*Rambles in Vedanta*, 1946).

Hence, meditation aimed at mollifying the mind often merely furnishes fleeting solace as thoughts weave pathways in disparate directions. Simultaneously, endeavours aimed at achieving a state of thoughtlessness prove equally impracticable for a man entwined deeply within the web of material existence.

The second verse of sage Patanjali's *Yoga Sutras* elucidates the purpose of yogic practice as 'Yogas chitta vritti nirodhah'—yoga is the stilling or controlling of the modifications or fluctuations of the mind—thus signifying the subjugation of mental fluctuations. However, relinquishing false identification with the surging waves of thought, alongside other prescribed techniques for governing thought waves, although captivating, scarcely stands as a substitute.

Practitioners of contemporary meditation regimens may indeed cultivate myriad desirable attributes at both the physical and mental strata. Yet, as long as they remain oblivious to their authentic identity, the tempest of their minds persists, fuelled by thoughts born from adverse experiences during the meditative pursuit, rendering their efforts counterproductive.

Humanity stands at the edge, threatened by the unchecked intrusion upon nature, driven by man's relentless pursuits. How prepared are we to face the inevitable changes ahead? Is there a strategy to shield us from the mental stagnation that will inevitably accompany this transformation?

THE SOLUTION

Acquiring self-knowledge and harmonizing with it emerges as the exclusive remedy for extirpating human predicaments. This journey through four distinct phases comprises the progression of becoming qualified to seek knowledge, acquiring knowledge, embracing knowledge, and ultimately reaping the benefits it bestows. Aligning with Consciousness, far from being an abstract concept, stands as the sole recourse to liberate the beleaguered corporeal vessel. A concise comprehension suffices to validate the aforementioned assertion.

All material entities, including the corporeal and mental domains of humanity, reside as insentient substances unless enlivened by sentience infused by the all-pervading Consciousness principle. Ergo, their very existence hinges upon Consciousness, and their capacities, too, assume qualification. Entities bereft of independent selfhood possess no intrinsic identity; they are but mere labels and forms. The genuine identity, in truth, resides within the realm of Consciousness.

This philosophical contention does not obfuscate the tangible experience of the physicality, mentality, and other constituents of the world, and the empirical reality they constitute. Rather, its intent lies in underlining the imperative to recognize and concede the foundational distinction that shall eternally endure. Manifesting as the realm of multiplicity, Consciousness encompasses the human form, the human psyche, and the world at large. Yet, they stand as insentient constructs, susceptible to alteration and circumscribed by finite potentialities, relegating them to a lower stratum of reality. Conversely, as a distinct and unblemished essence, Consciousness boasts boundless dimensions—ceaselessly sentient, eternally existing, and thereby residing within a higher realm of reality. Consciousness serves as the fundamental essence to validate or dismiss the existence or non-existence of anything, encapsulating Consciousness within itself. Consequently, it stands as the only self-evident substance with eternal existence.

Insentient objects rely on the all-knowing entity, Consciousness, for their very existence. Regardless of the presence or absence of the physical world, the supremacy of Consciousness persists. It remains untouched as physical entities come into existence and, in the same way, fade into its embrace.

Aligning with Consciousness signifies a harmonious connection with our higher Self, the source of life, and the fount of all existence. It denotes that individuals understand their true nature and live in alignment with it. This pursuit involves letting go of the connection between the physical and mental aspects of existence, which are like superficial layers imposed on the fundamental substrate, much like the waves that are merely distinct labels for identification purposes, with their true destiny being a natural reunion with the underlying water.

This endeavour entails relinquishing the corporeal–mental entwinement, mere overlays of names and forms upon its foundational substrate. The paramount lesson garnered from Vedic meditation rests in the comprehension of the elevated nature characterizing Consciousness. It stands as the progenitor of all knowledge, for, devoid of it, no cognition can transpire. The corporeal vessel and the conscious mind stand impotent sans the presence of Consciousness.

Simultaneously, though endowed with sublime nature, Consciousness resembles a phantom in the absence of an entity capable of harnessing its potential. To secure life's continuum, a physical form buoyed by Consciousness stands as a prerequisite. Amidst its role as the bedrock of awareness and all experiences, it remains impervious to emotions—be it love, hate, pleasure, or pain that saturate human existence.

Consciousness must precede any volitional or cognitive endeavour. It serves as the parent of actions and the bedrock of cognition, thereby substantiating the notion that all that is known or yet to be fathomed resides inherently within its cosmic embrace. Every occurrence takes place within its sphere and emanates from it, yet it remains unscathed by the vicissitudes of existence much like the principle of light, which imparts illumination to objects but is not affected by the alterations transpiring within the objects it graces.

It can also be thought of as the catalyst in a chemical reaction, which is not affected while actively expediting the process. The sense of security and contentment arising from the possession of material wealth finds its footing through the lens of Consciousness. Nevertheless, material possessions, grounded within the confines of time and space, march towards eventual dissolution, rendering them a capricious bastion of security. Within its nature—the triad of existence, awareness, and bliss, Consciousness emerges as the sole enduring source of security, tranquillity, and felicity.

It stands as the fount of all knowledge, the throne of universal awareness. In its absence, knowledge finds no foothold for it is the cosmic principle that unveils the expanse of the universe and its enigmatic beyond. It stands as the substratum, the quintessence permeating all facets of being. That said, 'the infinite is not an abstract principle but an active universal consciousness. It is the unity of the finite and the infinite', pointed Dr Radhakrishnan when describing the spirit. It is the force behind life, which science calls 'the energy' found in all objects.

COMPREHENDING CONSCIOUSNESS—IN AND BEYOND THE UNIVERSE

Consciousness, often called the awareness principle, saturates the very essence of every entity, rendering it all-encompassing and ever-present. It stands as the ultimate life force without which life would cease to exist, even if all other essential forms of energy required for bodily functions persist. This luminary force illuminates the subtle workings of the mind and body, and bestows awareness upon all sentient beings. It stands fundamentally apart from the scientifically proven forms of energy that propel motion and power the myriad functions in our material world, including the intricate mechanisms of our bodies.

Understanding that Consciousness, as the ultimate force, maintains its independent existence is a matter of paramount significance. In contrast, the diverse forms of energy acknowledged by science are deemed to exist within the realm of Consciousness, for nothing—whether tangible or intangible—can find existence beyond the dominion of Consciousness. It is, therefore, imperative to acknowledge and embrace the lucid distinction between these two fundamental principles aforesaid. The phrase, 'It is different yet it is in and through the entire material world,' offers a distinctive perspective on the relationship between Consciousness and the entirety of existence. It underscores the role of Consciousness as the eternal observer of all unfolding events in the world, thereby accentuating its inherent connection to the totality of existence.

The notion of a non-material dimension to existence, it is argued, harmonizes with the domain of physical science. The journey of unveiling the universe's origins, particularly over the past half century, has marked a revelation: observable matter—or baryonic matter—constitutes a mere 5 per cent of the universe. Another 27 per cent is ascribed to the theoretical construct of dark matter, awaiting conclusive definition. The remaining 68 per cent resides in the realm of speculation, labelled as enigmatic dark energy. The epithet 'dark' alludes to a latent presence yet to be unearthed—an existence possibly existing in subtler or even transcendent forms beyond the corporeal.

Einstein's iconic Mass–Energy equivalence is another captivating facet within this discussion. This principle reveals the remarkable interconvertibility of matter and energy, each serving as a mutable manifestation of the other. This principle also resonates with a universe that reflects the 'something from nothing' archetype, where the essence of 'something' materializes in both tangible and ethereal forms, encompassing mass and energy.

The spiritual legacies of India, spanning millennia, have consistently elucidated the concept of the 'nothing'—the unmanifest—that gives birth to the 'something', the manifest. In this context, 'nothing' doesn't mean emptiness, but rather 'not a thing' that can be measured or seen. It refers to a source that cannot be perceived by our senses, yet it is the foundation of everything in existence—from physical space and time to the unseen forces of energy that shape the universe.

This essence predates everything that can be sensed, serving as a foundational backdrop for both the perceivable and the imperceptible. As it precedes anything the human intellect can conceive, the unseen substratum is postulated to reside intrinsically within all forms of matter and ethereal energy, including humanity. It functions as an omnipresent, universal essence—flowing through the very veins of creation, present in all that is seen and unseen.

The animating force within sentient beings equally emerges as the fruit of its presence. The spark of life extinguishes with the cessation of sentience, a spark kindled by this spiritual essence. It stands as the primordial Principle of Knowing, transcending the confines of logic. It rests as the residual essence beyond the limits of conceptual thought—a realm far removed from our cognitive faculties, thus immune to contradiction.

Comprehending the veracity of Consciousness requires no herculean effort, yet humanity remains shrouded in ignorance or ceaseless pursuit. 'The impediment to self-realization and freedom is due to our preoccupation with the objective world, which invariably leads to conflict of interests and consequently to feud, jealousy, revenge, and moral depravity. The result is the erection of barriers between man and man,' opined S. Mukerji, a venerated philosopher.

Verily, three formidable impediments obstruct humanity's grasp of the aforesaid philosophical verities. These obstacles, firmly rooted in the soil of ignorance, cast a shadow upon understanding. The first and most significant is the strong belief people place in the physical world around them. Because this belief is shaped by direct sensory experiences, individuals come to see themselves not just as playing roles in the world, but as real and permanent entities within it. Thus ensnared, they find themselves entirely enveloped by this perspective, rendering it nigh impossible for them to envisage an identity apart from their physical forms. Their minds stand impervious to any truth that contradicts beliefs born of personal encounters. This tenacious adherence bears semblance to persistently citing the sun's rising and setting, notwithstanding the existence of profound truths that lie beyond immediate observation. Moreover, the mind—bound by the limits of matter—mistakenly identifies itself as Consciousness. This misunderstanding clouds the recognition of true Consciousness, leaving individuals unaware of the ultimate reality. The second hurdle takes form in an errant understanding of the unidirectional relationship between the complex of body and mind, and the Supreme Consciousness. By its very essence, Consciousness stands as an autonomous, unattached entity, disentangled from the human collection. At the moment of birth, the body's swift sentience is channelled through the medium of the mind, a reflecting vessel for the ceaselessly illuminating Consciousness. This process impels humans to conceive of the body and mind as conscious entities, despite their intrinsic state as insentient amalgams of the five elemental constituents.

Thirdly, owing to the absence of clear demarcation between body, mind, and Consciousness, the notion of an independent Consciousness detached from corporeal bonds eludes human contemplation. Philosophers aptly liken this singular association to the mirage and the desert, wherein the mirage, though illusory, draws sustenance from the desert beneath, which remains untouched and aloof. Likewise, the Consciousness dwelling within all beings remains unsullied by the world's afflictions, akin to the sun's imperviousness to the frailties of the eyes or the external objects it unveils.

'As the sun which helps all eyes to see is not affected by the blemishes of the eyes or the external things revealed by it, so also to Consciousness dwelling in all beings is never contaminated by the misery of the world being outside it.'[9] Just as the mirage assumes a semblance of reality while remaining illusory, the material reality of the body–mind complex assumes significance only when perceived through the lens of Consciousness.[10]

The all-sentient Consciousness and the utterly insentient matter bear inherently contradictory natures and therefore cannot form a binding alliance. Within the vast expanse of the universe—wherein each entity, including the mortal coil of man, relies upon Consciousness to grant legitimacy to its being—a fallacy ensues. We treat the body, mind, and the world as real, and perceive Consciousness as just one more part of that system. But this is a mistake. In reality, Consciousness is the subject, the knower—and everything else, including the body and mind, are objects—it is what is known. Consciousness gives meaning to all experiences but is not itself an object of experience. It cannot be a part of the body or mind, because those are things we are aware of. The subject (Consciousness) can never be reduced to the object (body or mind).

It eternally stands as the subject, the illuminator of the world, unmasking everything to man through his mind adorned with its constraining adjuncts. This facet becomes paramount in our endeavours to fathom the nature of Consciousness. It is the one that reveals every aspect of the world and all that lies within it, yet remains separate and untouched by any of it. Within its boundless presence, all dualities—light and dark, cause and effect—arise and play out. Still, it is unaffected by either the cause or its consequence. Without it, neither conflict nor resolution could exist, for it is the silent witness, the unchanging foundation behind all change. It bears no affiliation whatsoever with the palpable or the abstract within this world, even as it forms the bedrock for the embrace or dismissal of any notion. Yet the benighted man, ensnared by his perceptions, observes it contrarily. He fails to recognize its autonomous existence, simply because it eludes sensory perception. Supreme Consciousness—immutable and eternally free—is wrongly perceived by the ignorant as migratory: believed to journey through realms, confined within the human form in this life, only to be reborn into another body after death.

Moreover, the incorrect belief of ownership over the Supreme Consciousness is a deceptive notion that fosters the illusion of duality, within which man continues to nurture his ignorance. The true soul, or pure Consciousness, is an indivisible essence, transcending both the confines of the universe and individual existence. Yet, swayed by the deep-rooted delusion, Consciousness, encased in the physical form, is mistakenly perceived as fragmented, scattered among individual beings. It resembles how the concept of 'space' appears partitioned among empty pots of diverse sizes, despite space itself being one and undivided.

The space within and outside the pot cannot be construed as distinct units of space. This verity becomes evident when the pot shatters. Amidst this realm of duality, the initial consequence in the chain of cause and effect, stemming from man's ignorance, culminates in suffering. Subsequently, the identification with the mind, illuminated by the reflection of Consciousness, which man mistakenly takes as his consciousness, births the ego of individuality. Both of these phenomena mark the genesis of all tribulations. Man perceives himself as distinct from fellow beings. When he gazes upon the world through this lens of differentiation, his inclinations, aversions, attractions, and repulsions take shape, profoundly influencing his thoughts, conduct, and deeds.

However, this illusion dissolves upon realization that the world comprises solely of two constituents: Consciousness and the remaining realm of inert matter. When contemplated from the vantage point of Consciousness, the world, lacking self-independent existence, is akin to non-existence. The world experienced in the waking state vanishes during profound slumber. Likewise, objects encountered in dreams fade upon awakening. Any object, animate or inanimate, devoid of intrinsic, self-contained existence, is effectively non-existent.

The entire world, dependent upon Consciousness for its being, essentially belongs to Consciousness when viewed from the empirical standpoint. Conversely, from the perspective of Consciousness, nothing belongs to it as nothing can exist apart from it. Consciousness is all that exists; and from this perspective, everything is but the Consciousness. Hence, for an individual harmoniously attuned to their genuine essence, it becomes impossible to perceive anything or anyone distinctively, for the very notion of difference vanishes. In this state, inflicting pain upon another is not possible, given the absence of dual entities. Likewise, placing blame becomes an untenable notion in the absence of differentiation. Similar to abstaining from assigning blame to one's teeth or tongue when inadvertently biting the latter, the prospect of differentiation loses its viability.

Consciousness stands as an essential prerequisite for all forms of knowledge. In fact, being the awareness principle, it is knowledge itself. It is through the self-contained Consciousness, existing amidst the confines of his corporeal form and beyond, that man gains access to knowledge. This Consciousness aligns itself with the intellect of man, thus seemingly engaged in the process of thought. Alas, comprehending this truth eludes him, as the sole instrument at his disposal for grasping the concept of Supreme Consciousness is the mind (intellect), nourished by material influences. Paradoxically, this very intellect, the instrument of his pursuit, is itself a creation of ignorance.

RELEVANCE OF RELIGION

Can religion guide humanity towards understanding the absolute truth—Consciousness?

Throughout history, religion has attempted to serve as a bridge between the visible world and the unseen essence that underlies it. At its highest expression, religion must point beyond rituals and dogma towards a deeper recognition of the Self, as not merely a body or mind, but as Consciousness itself—eternal, formless, and unchanging.

An examination of religion's role in shaping humanity's pursuit of the highest good often reveals a paradox—it appears more often to obstruct rather than illuminate the path.

The role of religion in deepening the ignorance of individuals is a notable phenomenon. Religion originally entered the realm of human existence with the noble aspiration of shaping the human mind and fostering a curiosity that would eventually lead to the understanding of one's intrinsic nature. Each religion offered a unique path towards comprehending the divine, catering to the varied perceptions of mankind. The emergence of numerous religions, each tailored to human spiritual needs, was seen as a positive development in the quest for higher understanding.

However, a pivotal shift occurred when religions began to alter their fundamental purpose. Instead of guiding individuals towards the unified consciousness of 'One God', many religions started promoting the worship of personal deities. This transformation, which took place centuries ago, has significantly influenced the deepening of ignorance. While religious practices may have initially channelled faith and brought individuals closer to their chosen deities, the focus gradually shifted towards seeking absolution for sins or pursuing material gains.

This fixation on personal Gods has had a detrimental effect, distorting the minds of many, and fostering animosity towards adherents of other faiths. As these personal deities obstruct the pursuit of truth, ignorance assumes an even more potent form. Dr P. Nagaraja Rao aptly underscores the tragic consequences of this shift in his *Introduction to Vedanta* (1958): 'In the face of the unfair exploitation by religious impostors, religion unsurprisingly is not an acceptable vehicle for realizing the higher Self to many. That's why the practical results of religion have been horrendous. They have defended class interests and at times have tried to justify social injustice in terms of the will of God.'

Driven by selfish motives, religion has often failed to help humanity discover its true Self. Perpetually estranged from the profound knowledge of his true place within himself and the vast expanse of existence, man finds himself trapped in the body–mind complex, as Vedanta explains. With misplaced faith and over-reliance on the body–mind complex, man becomes endlessly absorbed in worldly pursuits and religious rituals, hoping to attain material gains. Yet, every action—whether rooted in love or hate—remains subject to the immutable law of cause and effect. Nothing happens by accident or outside the governing principles of the universe. Each deed inevitably leads to a reaction or consequence—a truth encapsulated in the adage, 'We reap what we sow.'

Thus, man becomes enmeshed in a cycle of opposing experiences, each one an outcome of his actions. Sadly, it is only after enduring the pangs of suffering for a time that he awakens to the fundamental truth: actions bound by time and space cannot yield lasting happiness. At this point, known as 'yatamana', he begins to recognize the futility of striving for enduring tranquillity through endless toil.

Unreservedly, Vedic meditation stands as an unequivocal practice, yielding enduring benefits. It does not burgeon from any religious lineage; rather, it extends its embrace to all souls. It exists as a cerebral pursuit, a means to assimilate the transcendental wisdom bestowed by an enlightened guru and the sacred scriptures, the two pillars of authentic knowledge. As the *Niralamba Upanishad* avers, 'Knowledge (Jnana) involves first a clear intellectual grasp of the nature of Self through the most searching inquiry, and secondly realizing for oneself the truth through the blessings of a Guru.'

Drawing on the wisdom of sage Suresvara as articulated in the *Naishkarmya Siddhi*, a treatise on Advaita Vedanta authored by him as one of the direct disciples of Adi Shankara, it elaborates on the significance of scriptural knowledge. According to this text, the role of a Guru involves the liberation of the Supreme Consciousness, which humans have mistakenly intertwined with the inert body–mind. The endeavour to unify two elements of diametrically opposite natures is deemed impossible through any means of agreement. Such liberation is considered as one of the forms of emancipation.

Even from its inception, when Vedic meditation was first conceptualized, the seers harboured concerns regarding the human mind, understanding its natural inclination to align with concepts grounded in scientific validation. Therefore, Vedic meditation doesn't demand the pursuit of mystical visions as many seers did, but instead encourages the integration of supra-rational knowledge with reason, despite the inherent limitations of reason in grasping and concluding matters related to the subjective realm. It enjoins the exclusion of hypotheses untested by direct, personal experience. Therein lies a total absence of conjecture or speculation.

The seeker of truth is explicitly counselled not to embrace the seers' insights without subjecting them to the rigours of logic (yukti). Much like these teachings, which were originally inscribed by seers drawing from their personal experiences and revelations, seekers must similarly engage in introspection and thoroughly immerse in the vast knowledge, arriving at conviction through personal exploration rather than partaking in debates that could inadvertently allow the teacher to influence the students' thoughts.

The towering figure of Advaita Vedanta, Shankaracharya himself withheld an unwavering endorsement of scriptures as the ultimate authority. 'The life of contemplation is not easy for those who are unregenerate. It is not the result of learning and systematic philosophizing that brings experience. Spiritual realization is a matter of experience. It is self-certifying and beyond reason. Experience is the ultimate authority. The final acceptance is not based on second-hand reports or inherited authority but on direct experience', aptly stated Dr P. Nagaraja Rao.

THE BEGINNING AND END OF TROUBLE

Trouble arises when an individual attributes autonomous power to the body–mind complex, to function independent of their true source, which is Consciousness. Consequently, when one confers actuality upon the mind, it inadvertently lends substance to the realm of diversity. Inevitably, the individual associates himself closely with this perceived separate self, and accredits the mind with all faculties, all the while remaining oblivious to the underlying verity. This ignorance exacts a steep toll when he finds himself submerged in the tumultuous sea of worldly existence.

Continuously enslaved by the pendulum swing of contrasting encounters, the man endures the weight of these dualities as long as he acknowledges the dichotomous nature of the world and the insubstantiality inherent in every facet of existence—animate or inanimate. As he clings to the insubstantial mind, the regal ego emerges, accompanied by its entourage of influences. Only those who attain self-knowledge escape the grasp of this colossal ignorance. This is why man is likened to a tree, where ignorance forms the root, and ego stands as the trunk, while attraction and aversion sprawl like branches. Above all, there is an unspoken desire to live, driven by the fear of death causing distress to all save for those who have gleaned the wisdom of the Self.

WRIGGLING OUT OF THE QUANDARY

Self-realization stands as the timeless remedy according to the philosophy of Advaita Vedanta. Its doctrine intricately unravels the connections between life (Jivas), the inanimate world (Jagat), and the immanent God (Ishwara), within the phenomenal realm. It lays bare the causes of human constraints and, in its culmination, proclaims methods to transcend these limitations, securing an unshackled existence from all forms of suffering. Vedanta proclaims with unwavering conviction that liberation is attainable only when one discerns the genuine from the illusory and subsequently aligns oneself with the genuine. It proclaims the omnipresent spirit, characterized by 'existence, knowledge, and bliss', as the absolute 'truth', deeming everything else relative truth (Mithya). The precepts enshrined in this doctrine underscore the significance of contemplating this truth for Self-realization, guiding the seeker towards the ultimate destination where individuality unites with the supreme spirit to experience boundless freedom, akin to the experience during deep sleep.

It affirms that anyone can attain this state called 'turiyam', a realm of existence manifesting absolute bliss. An individual who, after traversing through distinct stages, attains the culminating stage of meditation known as Nirvikalpa, resides in the silence of the absolute observer. For them, neither the mind nor thoughts hold relevance, as perpetual bliss becomes their perpetual experience.

The process of Self-realization, characterized by five stages, is elucidated as follows:

1. Recognize the necessity to purify the mind.
2. Engage in virtuous actions (Karma Yoga) exclusively.
3. Harmonize thought, speech, and action through concentration.
4. Shape and refine the mind, quelling tumult and instilling tranquillity through meditation (Upasana Yoga).
5. Attain mastery over the mind by first controlling thoughts, and ultimately merging them with Self-knowledge (Jnana Yoga).

A multitude of individuals across the globe, grappling with stressful lives, turn to various forms of meditation for solace. However, these methods merely offer transient relief, at best providing a momentary respite for the mind. Thus, they fall short of authentic meditation. The verity of meditation eludes many. The inquiries remain: why should we meditate? How can one extract maximal benefits?

SECTION TWO

THE FINAL MESSAGE

Chapter 3

THE RISE AND FALL OF ELIZABETH HOLMES

MAN PROPOSES, MAN DISPOSES

As I reflected on the news that broke on 18 November 2022, my thoughts were drawn to Elizabeth Holmes, the once-promising founder and CEO of Theranos, whose ambitious dreams of revolutionizing healthcare came crashing down as she was sentenced to eleven years and three months in prison for committing wire fraud. As a Vedic monk, I couldn't help but feel a pang of sympathy for Ms Holmes, not in disagreement with the law, but acknowledging the undeniable principle of karma that governs our lives. Regardless of the scale of transgressions or the shrewdness employed to evade the law's reach, the cosmic mind meticulously documents every action we undertake, leaving no room for anyone to escape the repercussions of their deeds. Be it a minor misdeed or a grand offence, a crime is a crime—whether manifested through thoughts, words, or actions—even if the offender manages to pull the wool over the eyes of earthly law.

In the ultimate reckoning, no one can manipulate the painstaking record-keeping and the unfaltering enforcement of the law of karma by providential governance. From the pious saint plagued by a deadly disease for past wrongdoings to the thirsty buffalo struggling in silent protest inside the jaws of a famished crocodile, every living being is justly ordained by the cosmic mind governed by the immutable law of nature. The sinners walking freely in the open today should therefore not be jubilant over the miraculous escape from impeachment. After all, in the grand scheme of things, both the sinners and saints must reckon with the enduring consequences of their karmic actions across numerous lifetimes.

Ms Holmes's journey is a poignant reminder of how swiftly fortunes can shift. Once touted as the world's youngest self-made female billionaire, she embarked on the path of a precocious child to a Stanford dropout, determined to change the face of healthcare with her startup. However, her progress took a dark turn, leading her towards an embattled position in the face of legal proceedings that ultimately found her guilty of wire fraud. Her ambition and pursuit of immense wealth clouded her judgement. The very idea of revolutionizing healthcare was not flawed, but her means of achieving it were tainted by deceit. Driven by the insidious force of greed, she encountered hurdle after hurdle until she met her inevitable destiny, much like a moth irresistibly drawn to destructive light.

Why did a talented young woman, who had earned admission to Stanford based on her merits, involve herself in such questionable endeavours? What drove her to follow in the footsteps of luminaries such as Steve Jobs and Mark Zuckerberg, who chose to forsake their college education, yet succeeded in accumulating immense wealth?

Imprisoning her will not deter new offenders from emerging, for we are aware that the fear of punishment alone cannot dissuade malevolent minds from indulging in nefarious acts. After all, 'life is nothing but a competition to be the criminal rather than the victim'.[11] Until large-scale spiritual refining of the minds happens, the coexistence of good and evil is inevitable.

As a society, we must grapple with the deeper questions raised by Ms Holmes's downfall. How can we ensure that the ambitious aspirations of both the young and the old are subjected to unwavering scrutiny, thereby averting such catastrophic outcomes? What led the astute minds at prominent corporations, renowned for their discerning investment decisions, to overlook the deception concealed within her gaze? They failed to delve deep into Ms Holmes's utopian vision statement, a mere hollow assertion; a mere conjecture woven by a charismatic woman in the absence of substantiating proof.

Given our past encounters with large-scale financial frauds like Bernie Madoff's Ponzi Scheme, one would have anticipated such discrepancies to surface much earlier. It prompts one to ponder why it necessitated millions of dollars in investments to distinguish between fraud and mistake, an outcome ultimately shaped by the avarice inherent in human decision-making. Alas, akin to countless other news narratives, the saga of Ms Holmes shall fade into obscurity—a testament to the perennial presence of greed, an age-old narrative.

We have witnessed kingdoms fall, nations falter, and families torn apart because of greed. The insatiable desire for more than is needed has been at the heart of countless calamities throughout history.

Greed, manifesting as political corruption, economic exploitation, and the relentless pursuit of wealth and power, played a significant role in the fall of the Roman Empire. Countries like Zimbabwe and Venezuela stand as examples of economic decline fuelled by greed. Similarly, the decline of prominent families such as the Medici, the Rothschilds, the Onassis family, and the Bonanno family can largely be attributed to their relentless pursuit of power and wealth. Their downfalls were often marked by internal strife, betrayals, and even murders—all driven by greed.

Sadly, the people of modern society are no wiser than their peers of the erstwhile era. They are too arrogant to learn from the tragedies born of the presumption that avarice is part of human nature and that such catastrophes are inevitable. Greed is not inherent; it is a destructive force that can be avoided.

Ms Holmes's actions centred around her company, Theranos, and her audacious claims of revolutionizing healthcare with a wearable medical device. The device was meant to monitor patients' blood and administer medication with a simple finger pinprick, promising accurate and reliable results for various medical conditions. 'The tests would be able to detect medical conditions like cancer and high cholesterol, it was said. Holmes and Ramesh Balwani, Theranos's former president and COO, used advertisements and solicitations to encourage and induce doctors and patients to use Theranos's blood testing laboratory services, even though the defendants knew Theranos was not capable of consistently producing accurate and reliable results for certain blood tests.'[12]

Ambition and audacity are a bad combination for those who are not lucky. The time-tested formula for success becomes a recipe for disaster for those who do not have karma by their side. Certainly, it was the case for Ms Holmes, who dressed in black turtlenecks like her Silicon Valley hero, former Apple CEO Steve Jobs, and even changed the tone of her voice to sound like a successful veteran of the tech world. Her trajectory deviated drastically off-course, ending up in a place she could never have imagined during her childhood days with aspirations of becoming a billionaire.

With the jury's verdict rendered, Ms Holmes is destined to spend the next decade or less in a minimum-security Federal Prison, Camp Bryan in Texas with three other cellmates in a tight, concrete space—

a far cry from the grandiose world she once inhabited; one that boasted of bay windows, marble-topped credenza, hardwood floors, in-unit laundry, alabaster entryway, an outdoor garden, and more. The austere realities of prison life, devoid of luxuries and adoration, will challenge her to confront her true Self and the consequences of her actions. The prison room buried in the noise of unfamiliar voices, with no one to admire her charm may be choking for some time, until she gets accustomed to a different set of routines, especially the demand to end self-deception.

Eleven years is a lot of time—to mull over the errors of omission and commission of the past; to get inside Elizabeth (her real Self) to understand hard truths about human beings, about the unreality of this world: a counterfeit body–mind complex, and its arbitrary demands; to question why we find ourselves entangled in the ever-changing phenomenal world of good and evil, pleasure and pain, praise and criticism—often without a clue.

Society may perceive her incarceration as a manifestation of retribution, but her destiny ought to stand as a poignant reminder of a more profound truth—that we are eternally trapped within the vast prison which the world itself represents. Within this realm, we partake in actions both virtuous and malevolent, traversing the spectrum of pain and pleasure amid the clamour of the concrete jungle, the expansive vistas, the pollution, and the web of mass deceit.

As we ponder on the tale of Ms Holmes and the trail of deceit she left in her wake, we must seriously reflect on our collective responsibility to seek knowledge, understanding, and liberation from the self-deceptions which may lead any one of us down similar paths. In this reflection lies the gateway to a brighter and more harmonious future for all of humanity.

'You are not free the day you walk out of prison; you are free the day you walk out of ignorance,' said Matshona Dhliwayo, a Zimbabwean-born Canadian Philosopher. Whether inside prison walls or not, the spectre of recurring mistakes shall haunt those who remain oblivious to their innermost essence. It is solely through emancipating ourselves from ignorance and dispelling delusions that we can endeavour to avert such grievous occurrences in the days to come, steering our course towards a realm suffused with enlightenment and compassion.

TRACKING THE SRT (ENERGY PROPENSITIES) PLAY

Even though the story of Ms Holmes may be contentious, we need bright and bold people who make a difference in the world; people consumed by the mission of bettering lives of the countless souls who are born to struggle, and struggle to die. Nevertheless, individuals blessed with unique capabilities must possess wisdom and a resolute mind akin to tungsten, unyielding to fleeting fantasies of the relative world. Their minds should radiate serenity and harmony, driven by an innate inclination to contribute, encapsulating the quintessence of 'S' dominant energy propensity—one of the three fundamental attributes of our mind, collectively known as the SRT factors or gunas, which was briefly mentioned earlier.

Indeed, the precise translation of the term 'guna' proves elusive. In essence, this energy encompasses three fundamental attributes—Sattva, Rajas, and Tamas—existing in varying proportions within all of creation, consolidating to form a comprehensive whole. Much like strings controlling marionettes, we are subject to the influence of these three energetic threads, shaping our thoughts, words, deeds, habits, and ultimately, our distinctive character and overall personality. It constitutes the very bedrock of our inner essence, and even alterations in our physical form throughout our life's span are derived from the intricate interplay of these three factors. Yet, they do not disrupt the matrix of our fully developed character, much like a triangle sustaining its shape through the harmony of its complementary forces.

Before I describe the features of SRT in some detail, serving as a contextual reminder, it is important to mention that the inclusion of Ms Holmes's saga is not intended for Hollywood storytelling but to serve as a conduit to elucidate the profound Vedic concept that guides us in our spiritual journey.

- 'S' energy embodies purity and positivity, an indispensable force for generating ideas and bringing them to fruition.
- 'R' is impure, but it is the driving force that fuels desires for material comforts, worldly pursuits, and restlessness. It is the energy that transforms dreams into reality.
- 'T' energy embodies qualities of dullness, inertia, confusion, and negativity, all of which can impede the realization of ideas and, at times, even steer individuals towards ill-advised actions

> in the pursuit of their dreams. When an individual's 'T' levels are elevated, weight gain becomes more likely. The inclination towards inertia drives one to overindulge in eating when the body remains inactive. This potent energy, particularly in moments of profound frustration, may prompt individuals to consider drastic measures. In essence, 'T' is not just bad; it's profoundly detrimental.

The interplay of these energies becomes more profound when we explore the motivations behind the ideas. When an idea is born from the intention of benefiting the world and serving the greater good, it is guided by the pure essence of 'S' energy. Such ideas are characterized by a stress-free approach and actions that align with the inherent goodness of the soul. When endeavours are supported by the 'S' factor, there is no room for failure. Each action taken leads to some degree of fulfilment, with 'S' energy at the forefront and 'R' energy playing a secondary role. It aligns with Blaise Pascal's concept of taking a leap of faith, where he splendidly stated, 'If you win, you win everything; if you lose, you lose nothing.'

Conversely, when an idea is driven by personal desires, such as wealth, fame, or power, 'R' energy dominates. This leads to a blend of hubris, narcissism, and oppression, as the pursuit of the goal becomes more significant than the goal itself. For 'R'-dominant individuals, the end goal often justifies any means, even if it means bending the truth or resorting to unethical practices, particularly when honest attempts fail to produce timely gains and the prospect of failure begins to daunt. It is often the challenges and failures encountered along the way that provoke the onset of negative thoughts. To use Benjamin Disraeli's words, they use lies, damned lies, and statistics to sustain despite failure, just to remain in the game as long as they can stall the sinking hopes of success.

In the most concerning scenario, when the idea becomes a means of personal gain at the expense of harming others or the world, 'T' energy takes the lead, while 'R' energy obediently follows. The purity of 'S' energy is likely to remain dormant in such instances. A dominant 'T' energy can profoundly influence a person, leading an activity-seeking individual to embrace lethargy; transforming a positive mind into complete negativity, and clouding the ability to discern right from wrong, and truth from falsehood. Large-scale corporate frauds often find their roots in 'R'-dominant individuals who, unbeknownst to them, unconsciously encourage 'T' energy to fulfil their selfish motives. Frauds committed at Wirecard Germany, Luckin Coffee China, Enron USA, WorldCom USA, and ZZZZ Best are a few in that bracket.

In this complex interplay of energies, understanding their dynamics can help us channel our thoughts, actions, and intentions in a manner that aligns with higher spiritual principles, fostering a path of growth, compassion, and harmony with the world around us.

In the pursuit of changing the medical world through disruptive technology and making healthcare affordable, the noble ambition of Ms Holmes was likely driven by the dominance of the 'S' factor within her constitution. Yet, only she possesses the veracity to attest whether the conception was spurred by the impetus of 'R' or 'T' energies. Deciphering the precise core SRT configuration of any individual is nearly impossible due to the significant influence of the floating component, which governs how most people generally act, react, and behave. This instinctive behaviour seldom rests upon reason but is rather impelled by its own volition. However, it may be feasible to evaluate a person's core SRT through vigilant observation of their behaviour over an extended period to ascertain consistency. A comprehensive exploration of this theme awaits in the subsequent sections of this text.

For now, in extending the benefit of doubt to Ms Holmes, it is reasonable to posit that during her formative years, she likely did not formulate deceptive methods to realize her childhood aspiration of amassing substantial wealth. Nevertheless, it remains imperative to contemplate the notion that the acumen for perpetrating fraud seldom emerges abruptly. Rather, it tends to develop from a pre-existing inclination towards deception encoded within one's Vasna, manifesting when circumstances align under the principles of Karma Phalam. In the final analysis, the onus of judgement is bestowed upon the readers of this tome.

Another vital Vedic concept pertinent to this narrative is the notion that the ambition of Ms Holmes to transmute into a billionaire was not an abrupt caprice but was entrenched in a seedling state, possibly from a preceding existence, biding its time to burgeon in her current life. This yearning links with the Vedic tenets of Vasna (deep impressions) and Ruchi (footprints of strong inclinations and tendencies), two pivotal constructs expounded upon subsequently. The notion to reshape the world ensues as a ramification of these very concepts in action.

Verily, Ms Holmes did profit from the remarkable support of the benevolent karma of yore interwoven into the very tapestry of her present existence. The propitious karmic outcomes did grant her triumph in sundry undertakings, from excelling in her studies at high school to securing entry into Stanford's esteemed halls, and winning the hearts of political heavyweights to sit on the board of her startup company. Seasoned venture capitalists, too, were enticed to invest in her lofty endeavour.

Her steadfast determination and tireless exertions did propel her forth, bringing delight at each stride. Indeed, her prosperity was verily guided by the attribute of 'R'. She did stretch her limits, toil diligently until her likeness graced the cover pages of *Fortune* and *Forbes* publications, and rubbed shoulders with illustrious magnates of business and politics such as George Shultz, Henry Kissinger, Rupert Murdoch, Bill Clinton, Joe Biden, Larry Ellison, and even attained the status of a Fellow of the Board at Harvard Medical School. She couldn't have asked for more from a compelling idea packed into an electronic contraption that struggled to fulfil the mendacious pledges she had made.

Yet, this did not thwart her from claiming the mantle of the youngest female billionaire, for her favourable karma had bolstered her deeds all along. Whether she pondered upon the potential aftermath of her stratagems to overhaul the healthcare domain through dubious methods remains unknown. Ms Holmes followed the dictates of her mind.

No one exactly knows the inner workings of karma: the precise juncture at which providential and adverse circumstances unfurl their tendrils. The span of their sway remains an enigma. Those enmeshed in the dominion of 'R' are likely to transgress righteous bounds, in near synchrony with the advent of adverse karmic aftermath. And as these occurrences transpire in stealth, many among us might be drawn into the noose of unethical comportment, entangled by a similar destiny—particularly when avarice displaces morality in our feverish quest to attain unbridled desires, as fate's wheel turns against us.

At this juncture, it is crucial to briefly explore the understanding of morality: what defines it? What truly constitutes right and wrong?

Morality is commonly understood as adherence to established codes or principles of right and wrong, reflecting the fundamental values of a community. While this definition is widely accepted, a pressing question arises: who holds the authority—community, culture, society, or the prevailing laws—to determine what is morally right or wrong? The fluid nature of morality becomes evident when actions once deemed immoral gradually gain acceptance as evolving perspectives reshape societal norms.

In light of this, one might argue for a more universal definition of morality: any action that causes harm or could potentially harm oneself or others is inherently immoral, whereas actions that promote well-being and happiness are moral. It is important to note that actions encompass thoughts, speech, and deeds. This perspective aligns with a consequentialist view, emphasizing the outcomes of actions as the primary measure of their moral value.

Even adherents of the faith with a dominant 'R' have not refrained from exploiting the frailties of the innocent, cunningly misinterpreting holy texts to rationalize their exploits and amass vast riches. 'Beseech the divine with fervent supplication so that wrongdoings might be absolved,' they proffer, though prayer's true intent lies in purifying the soul to eschew transgression. And they often propose elaborate sacrifices and tributes, purportedly to invert the fruit of karma or to amass material bounty, though neither claim holds water.

In our so-called grand existence, karma assumes a paramount mantle, shaping our destinies with meticulous care. It extends its influence even over the choices we make and aspirations we nurture throughout our journey in this mortal coil. The journey of Ms Holmes, along with other real-life events, serves as a powerful example and a clear reminder of the complex interplay between spiritual forces. In this intricate dance, our actions create ripples, and their karmic consequences reverberate through time.

Karma, the ethereal judge, weaves its threads of fortune and misfortune with an impartial hand. Today you are a rooster, tomorrow a feather duster, as the ancient Chinese adage proclaims.

As Ms Holmes ventured into action, her life's path shifted dramatically. The once benevolent karma that had blessed her with joy faded, making way for a tide of misfortune. A shadowy era of darkness and despondency descended upon her. The resolute 'R', representative of her fortitude, ceded dominion unto the ascendant 'T', as the waves of fortune ebbed and flowed.

When 'T' energy takes control, a person's mindset veers far from divinity and recedes towards darker, unholy realms. In this shadowy state, self-deception becomes paramount, and empathy for others fades into a distant memory. Mental landscape tainted by this descent becomes so corrupt that deceiving and exploiting innocent people for personal gain lose their stigma of sin. Morality becomes twisted and contorted, incubating wicked musings within its fold.

This never-ending journey often moves from the darkness of Tamas ('T') to the restless pursuit of material desires symbolized by Rajas ('R'), eventually reaching the sanctuary of virtue embodied in Sattva ('S')—only to descend back into the gloom of 'T' all too soon. This cycle mirrors the arc of human life: from a sluggish beginning in early years, we progress through phases filled with hopes and ambitions, experiencing fleeting joy through their fulfillment—yet all of it fundamentally driven by ignorance at the core. Rarely do we find the time or inclination to develop and sustain the state of Sattva before falling once more into inertia. This is why our journey through life is marked by recurring sorrow and discontent, interrupted only by brief flashes of joy.

In the anguish of these trials, it assumes paramount importance for each of us to embark upon a quest for wisdom and keen insight, steering away from the treacherous pitfalls constructed by the dominance of 'T'.

Thus, the earnest endeavour lies in achieving a harmonious equilibrium amid the triad of energies— 'S', 'R', and 'T'. By tending to the noble facets inherent in the 'S' energy, and skilfully directing its currents towards deeds of benevolence, one may seamlessly harmonize with a loftier intent, thus illuminating the path to a life replete with purpose and gratification. This expedition into self cognizance and spiritual maturation emerges as a key that unfastens the bonds of ignorance, endowing individuals with the authority to conscientiously craft compassionate choices, both for their welfare and that of their fellow beings.

WHEN THE DEVIL BECOMES GOD

As I delved into the events that shaped Ms Holmes's life through a Vedic lens, I could see the harmonious interplay of three essential aspects within us: Karma, Ruchi, and Vasnas.

Karma, derived from Sanskrit, refers to the application of the law of cause and effect, encompassing broader dimensions beyond the physical sciences. It includes both the actions we take and the consequences that may unfold immediately or in future, perhaps even long after the action is performed. Often referred to as 'luck' in the moral world, it persists as a mysterious concept with many layers yet to be unveiled.

Ruchi, which I have briefly defined earlier, in its essence, embodies our fervent desires and ambitions, propelling us to chase dreams, often within impractical time frames or with limited resources. Its potency is such that it can coax our thoughts towards yearning for things deemed taboo, and drive us into practices detrimental to our well-being, sometimes blinding us to the extent of our involvement in unethical or unscrupulous pursuits devoid of integrity. Often, it renders us so vulnerable that we become easily swayed by shallow gestures of kindness from people who embody malevolence; their support for our unethical endeavours seeming like divine approval. Their sinister intentions, cloaked in cunning persuasion, may appear irresistibly sweet, akin to honey-dipped candy. In such situations, poison masquerades as nectar, and we find ourselves drawn into the web of evil minds when the devil becomes God.

Vasnas, often referred to as thought waves, make their appearance as impressions in every instance of our interaction with the external world. These thought waves traverse the layers of the mind, reaching the intellectual zone where they undergo evaluation. It is in this phase that we categorize these impressions, separating those which we believe enhance our status from those that could potentially diminish it, based on ideas about an object we have gathered through our experiences or the external appearance or behaviour of a person. Following this categorization, the Ego takes centre stage as the evaluated Vasnas in the form of our thoughts become integrated into memory. Our attractions and aversions to various objects originate in this very process. Vasnas find a deep-seated abode within the recesses of our subconscious, akin to robust sandbanks at the bottom of a lake. They hold a significant sway, directly influencing our behaviour.

The role of memory cannot be underestimated in the execution of day-to-day functions at the physical level. However, when we create unpleasant Vasnas through our psychological interactions with others, they become a breeding ground for self-deception and hatred. Given that eliminating Vasnas demands herculean efforts, it is exceedingly beneficial for humans, endowed with intellectual capacities, to proactively thwart the formation of negative Vasnas.

Even though pure Consciousness unfailingly reveals the good, the bad, and the ugly to all individuals, the comprehension and interpretation of this revelation is a task entrusted to the mind—the reflected Consciousness. Consequently, if the mind is saturated with negative Vasnas innately present or newly acquired through interaction with other individuals, it will inevitably manifest negativity through thought, speech, and action.

These facets of Karma, Ruchi, and Vasnas extend beyond a single lifetime, moulding our behaviour and tendencies. They compel us to engage in particular actions during our current existence and can persist through subsequent incarnations. According to this principle, it is posited that Ms Holmes's aspiration to attain billionaire status was the continuation of an unfulfilled burning desire from a previous life. The deceitful methods she employed to achieve her objective might have been a necessary path leading to the anguish of imprisonment—a consequence of adverse karma accrued in a former life.

To the rational mind, this equation might appear irrational, groundless, or even nonsensical, as the unexpected outcomes of karma are not immediately apparent. It is known as Adrishya Phalam—the unseen consequences of our actions, even when no action is taken. This equation comprises three embedded components: the present action or inaction; the hidden force behind it (PK) which includes actions from past and present lives, the results of which have not yet appeared; and the outcome—Karma Phalam, the joy or sorrow one is destined to experience from those past actions. Notably, Karma Phalam can influence an individual's choices, prompting actions that align with the concealed repercussions of karma, which may manifest through external force or one's internal circumstances.

For instance, if an individual is destined to experience joy according to Karma Phalam, they might receive a lottery ticket as a gift for rendering exceptional service. If that ticket turns out to be the winning one, particularly when that individual holds no belief in gaining wealth through such means, the outcome is said to be propelled by an enigmatic and previously unknown factor—the result of past karma shaping their predestined fate. Comprehending the interplay of these forces provides valuable insights into the of existence and the profound influence that our intentions and deeds can exert on our fate.

What could have been the SRT configuration of Ms Holmes? The response to this query, at best, remains speculative, for no degree of imagination can convert speculation into certainty. Nevertheless, for the sake of concluding this aspect of the discussion, one might surmise that she embodied a blend of 'R'—reflecting her self-confidence—and 'T'—indicative of her ambition. This, perhaps, stands as the most plausible inference within reach of reality. Drawing inspiration from Vedanta, I feel compelled to reiterate the significance of the concept of karma, which, if misunderstood, could lead one to erroneously refrain from engaging in future actions. According to this teaching, the virtuous and evil tendencies we manifest, and the happiness and suffering we experience in this lifetime through our interactions with the external world, are intricately connected to the repercussions of our actions in prior incarnations. Nevertheless, the doctrine of Karma is not meant to imply the cessation of all prospects for growth; instead, it functions as an encouragement to cultivate a proper perspective and a harmonious approach to life and the world.

It accentuates that an individual's ascent or descent is not solely dictated by external circumstances or the caprices of a temperamental deity; instead, it is moulded by one's actions. This insight beckons us to assume responsibility for our thoughts, decisions, and actions—acknowledging that what we do today can exert a profound influence on our spiritual odyssey.

Chapter 4

THE HAPLESS HUMAN: A VICTIM OF THE KARMA GAME

Nature's unwavering principles consistently warn of impending danger, a fact that we, as the recipients of its myriad impacts, should not ignore. Yet humanity, perched at the pinnacle of evolution, astonishingly persists in repeating its mistakes. At the root of this self-perpetuating cycle lies ignorance—the fundamental source of life's vicissitudes. This ignorance distorts our actions (karma), disrupts the delicate balance of our gunas (Sattva, Rajas, and Tamas), and leaves behind unexamined tendencies, or Vasnas, which profoundly shape our essence and behaviour.

These three elemental forces orchestrate the symphony of our existence, influencing every thought, action, and reaction. Resolving 80 per cent of human dilemmas begins with understanding and harmonizing these powerful forces, aligning them with higher awareness and conscious intent. For the remaining 20 per cent, the strategic exercise of free will—an inexhaustible resource akin to an ever-replenished tool—becomes the pivotal factor in navigating life's complexities and steering our journey towards fulfilment and balance.

In the chapters that follow, we will delve into the interplay of these three forces—the 'musketeers' that wield significant influence over the span and quality of our lives.

DECODING KARMA: THE PERPETUITY OF CAUSE AND EFFECT

'Buddhi Karma Anusara' is a Sanskrit phrase that encapsulates the profound concept of the mind operating in harmony with karma. Here, karma takes on a more expansive meaning, denoting Karma Phalam, an imperceptible yet potent force. It represents the ecstasy or anguish that unfurl as the outcomes of our preceding deeds, a tapestry woven by actions of yore.

Actions of past and present lives that have failed to manifest as consequences until now are christened as Prarabdha Karmas (PK) in the teachings of the Vedanta. Predominantly, they reside among the countless webs of positive and negative karmas of the past, woven through the threads of our thoughts, conversations, and actions. Correlating our present experiences with their precise causal actions remains an insurmountable feat, nudging us to simply declare: 'Every event unfolds for a purpose.' These karmas defy reversibility, for their purpose lies in being gradually depleted as the fruits of bygone actions.

It might sound strange, but every single action we undertake churns out results in proportion to the energy we put in. Some of these outcomes yield immediate joy or sorrow, while others bide their time. Importantly, they don't just vanish into thin air; rather, they remain credited to our account. Strangely, the consequences of actions that haven't unfolded yet get stacked up in our minds in a random sequence, unrelated to the chronological order of their performance. These concealed outcomes sway our thinking and even muddle our rationality, guiding us towards specific actions that set the stage for pleasurable or painful events, which we perceive as our fate.

This cosmic cause and effect, referred to as 'Karma Phalam', doesn't dictate the exact events that bring joy or sorrow into our lives. Instead, it charts out the periods when we're destined to experience delight or despair. Individuals typically seek joy from specific events in different stages of life, but Karma Phalam holds the potential to either entirely deny that pleasure or subject individuals to prolonged delays in experiencing such joy, while Prarabdha Karma creates the events through which Karma Phalam is manifested.

For instance, an ambitious scholar might face the disheartening reality of being denied admission to a respected institution, despite possessing the most fitting qualifications. This situation is labelled as educational sorrow (Vidhya Dukkham). A young woman in her early thirties, fervently aspiring to settle into matrimony, may find no suitable partner in a world with a population surpassing 8 billion, resulting in the denial of the joy of marriage (Vivaha Sukham). Similarly, a fledgling startup could secure substantial funding approval from an angel investor just as it receives a rejection letter for a bank loan on the very day it urgently needs financial support to execute timely actions. This juxtaposition of PK creates a situation that extends the much-desired joy derived from career progression.

PK holds its influence over our thoughts and prompts us to

take the necessary steps that align with the karmic outcomes. It also masterminds the circumstances, timing, and geographical coordinates of our birth and eventual passing. In the grand opera of existence, PK is the unseen maestro—directing a mesmerizing spectacle that may conclude in joy or sorrow, as destined. The widespread scourge of Covid-19 wreaked havoc on a global scale. We witnessed the lifeless strewn in the open, lying unattended, long lines of those who had succumbed, and grieving relatives scrambling to secure a place in the overcrowded crematoriums even before the final moments of their loved ones arrived. Nevertheless, the passing of my father during the peak of the pandemic's onslaught did not obstruct a tranquil and dignified farewell. This extraordinary event unfolded through the divine intervention of his PK within two hours of his departure, a poignant moment chiselled in the annals of June 2020.

On 2 May 2015, two infants entered the world with contrasting destinies. In one corner, the air was abuzz with festivity as Her Royal Highness Princess Charlotte of Cambridge made her debut. Meanwhile, in a distant corner, another child took her first breath in the open, burdened with a heart ailment known as 'atrial septal defect'—a hole in the heart's wall. The disparity is stark: jubilation in one corner, despondency in the other. Both embarked on disparate journeys, weaving threads of joy and sorrow through the fabric of their lives, all rooted in some past karma.

What's intriguing is that these infants were still too young to perform any conscious actions. So, how can this paradox exist? Vedanta has an answer: it's the influence of PK—the karmic ripples of past lives shaping their current experiences.

Think about it this way: PK operates as the master plan for our current existence, dutifully following the directives laid out by Karma Phalam. It's akin to a meticulous supervisor overseeing all the components within our body, both tangible and intangible. From the delightful to the distressing, and even the downright unsightly encounters we face—PK orchestrates them all. Now, if this concept holds, are we, as beings of intelligence, condemned to a state of utter passivity? Does our life amount to nothing more than preordained destiny? Is there no glimmer of hope to be found? The tenets of Karma theory offer clarity on this matter.

While the grand narrative of our existence adheres to the principles elucidated earlier, we possess a potent tool known as free will, which remains constantly at our disposal. This free will empowers us to counteract the adverse effects of PK and embark on fresh endeavours aimed at enhancing our circumstances. It's crucial to grasp that 'fatalism' signifies an irreversible state of bondage, whereas 'karma' hinges upon the freedom of our volition. In essence, PK should be regarded as a catalyst, propelling us towards novel actions, particularly those which align with goodness and virtue.

TRANSMIGRATION OF KARMIC FOOTPRINTS

As human beings, we engage in a myriad of actions throughout our lives, some virtuous and others less so. Yet, the ledger of deeds that yield no immediate consequences often escapes our attention. Forgotten, it lies dormant in the shadows of memory. However, as long as we navigate existence and embrace the world as a real entity with an independent existence, we remain beholden to the universal law of cause and effect—an unwavering principle that unfailingly begets reactions from each action, regardless of its nature. This mirrors the essence of karma's doctrine. Eventually, the ripples of our actions lap at the shores of time, bearing repercussions.

A single lifetime proves insufficient to bear witness to the myriad karma we perform through thoughts, speech, and action. Vedanta posits that these ripples may extend their reach into future lives, a notion sometimes grasped as life after death, akin to rebirth, though not in the literal sense. The term 'reincarnation', more aptly aligned with this understanding, substantiates its scientific foundation. Upon the demise of the corporeal vessel—the gross body, the vital and mental sheaths of the conscious self embark on migration, seeking new embodiment to facilitate the exhaustion of karmic consequences not experienced, while preserving an objective continuum between various past and present manifestations.

Referring to the ripples of our past actions, Adi Shankara believed, 'Without these impressions, no action can be done, for organs are not skilful in unaccustomed work. But when the organs are prompted by impressions of past experiences, they can acquire the skill even without experience in this life. It is observed that some are clever in certain kinds of work, such as painting, from their very birth, even without experience in the present life, while others are not skilful even in elementary tasks. All this is due to the revival or non-revival of past experiences.'

In essence, the individual soul traverses different corporeal vessels at the start and end of each life, like shedding old attire for fresh vestments. As aptly captured in the Bhagavad Gita, chapter 2, verse 22: 'Just as a person casts off worn-out clothes and takes up new ones, so does the jivatma, the embodied soul, acquire a new body after casting off worn-out bodies.'

Given the inherent challenge of tracing actions from bygone lives to their manifestations in the present, the symphony of past deeds, orchestrating our current reality and shaping our future, emerges as an enigmatic overture, a mesmerizing, unforeseen melody that captivates and mystifies in equal measure.

An article on Business Insider India dated 29 August 2023, which features a conversation with Jeffrey Long, a radiation oncologist in Kentucky, serves as a contemporary affirmation of principles embedded within the Vedic scriptures. In the article, Dr Long states, 'I initiated the Near-Death Experience Research Foundation. I began gathering accounts from individuals who had undergone NDEs and analysed them through the lens of a scientist and physician. I formed conclusions grounded in evidence and initially approached this subject as a sceptic. However, confronted with the overwhelming body of evidence, I have now come to believe that there is undoubtedly an afterlife.'

The news of Malala Yousafzai's Nobel Prize triumph in 2014, when she was merely seventeen, and of Sundar Pichai's appointment as Google's CEO in 2015 could easily have ignited torrents of critique or stirred envy among millions across the globe. This reaction springs from a world that only knows of the most recent feat that propelled them to the limelight, leading to a perception that these accomplishments lack the magnitude for the grand accolades bestowed on them. To deduce that their triumphs rested on celestial alignment, tied to the birthdates of global luminaries, would concede to a discreet homage to superstition.

The heart of the matter, indeed, lies in our inability to recognize the reservoir of virtuous deeds they planted in days long past. These are deeds whose effects appear with time. I, for one, wasn't surprised because no one achieves worldwide eminence without the push of an inexplicable force. This force isn't rooted in mysticism or mere speculation.

The wealth of fortune doesn't overflow solely from the intellect and labour invested over two to four decades. True greatness follows a different path—often marked by a single idea that paves the way to influencing billions, but this is a privilege granted only to a few. Who can better vouch for this truth than the billionaires themselves? These exceptional individuals have sown seeds of benevolence that have been reaped across epochs, and my convictions in this regard grow stronger.

'The possibility that anyone with the right idea at the right time can have an impact on others is no longer limited to a single place. It's possible everywhere. Great ideas in technology no longer come from Silicon Valley. They can and do come from anywhere. And now they can quickly reach scale,' articulated Pichai in one of his speeches. It is ideas that truly matter, and their significance is not necessarily related to their place of origin. However, two specific phrases in his speech warrant special attention: 'the right ideas' and 'the right time'.

While every idea possesses intrinsic value, not all ascend to the zenith of global recognition and impact. Does this then imply that ideas failing to attain global acclaim are inherently flawed?

What often eludes our notice is the pivotal role played by PK in propelling seemingly unassuming ideas towards the lofty realm of global recognition, or conversely, in steering ideas away from the limelight. The legitimacy of ideas is earned when they secure the endorsement of one's personal PK. As for the temporal aspect, it operates organically, for ordinary notions metamorphose into extraordinary ones when they synchronize with the maturation of one's formidable PK.

In the hallowed halls of Google, a place often lauded as fertile soil for nurturing ideas, not every conception burgeons into a global sensation. Moreover, the enduring prosperity of a corporate entity does not solely hinge on the sagacity of its leadership. Rather, it is profoundly shaped by personal characteristics and prowess, which is a fusion of SRT and PK of the leader in question. After all, an enterprise is, at its core, a manifestation of its people. This reality holds whether we consider the fortunes of a family, a society, or an entire nation. It becomes evident that their prosperity hinges on the

PK of the individual who assumes a position of leadership.

It is worth noting that 70 per cent of corporate calamities can be ascribed to the failure of the person at the helm, whose SRT and PK wield the power to either make or mar the fortunes of the company. A concrete illustration of this phenomenon can be discerned in the case of General Electric. Once venerated as the epitome of corporate triumph under the leadership of Jack Welch, the firm relinquished its claim to the throne of the largest company by market capitalization, while Apple has tenaciously retained its preeminent position for multiple consecutive years. Even as we acknowledge the evolving landscape driven by contemporary preferences favouring technology-driven enterprises, a discernible shift away from the conventional brick-and-mortar giants of yesteryears, it is no exaggeration to assert that Apple's exceptional capacity to retain its top position is unequivocally linked to the PK of its leader.

The same holds for nations as well. For the better part of three years, Lebanon found itself besieged by a catastrophic and multifaceted crisis of unprecedented proportions in its modern history. The unfolding economic and financial turmoil, which initially reared its head in October 2019, was further compounded by the dual economic blows inflicted by the onset of the Covid-19 pandemic and the colossal explosion that rocked the Port of Beirut in August 2020.

Among these three crises, it is the economic debacle that undeniably exacted the most substantial and enduring toll. The nominal Gross Domestic Product (GDP), which stood at nearly US$ 52 billion in 2019, plummeted to a staggering estimated figure of US$ 20.3 billion in 2023. This protracted economic contraction caused a precipitous drop in disposable income, with GDP per capita registering a stark decline of 36.5 per cent between 2019 and 2023. In sum, it is reasonable to infer that the PK of those steering the ship of the nation's leadership may well be at the root of the current crisis.

THE KARMIC LEASH

In the contemporary global landscape, we're well aware of the imperative to transcend the ordinary if we aspire to savour extraordinary delights. Yet, the extent to which our endeavours are commensurately rewarded remains an open inquiry. Encouraging words from motivational orators resonate deeply, guiding us as we navigate the shadows that shroud our existence. However, what solace can we extend to the countless souls ensnared in the clutches of destitution? And what of the exceptional, diligent scholars adorned with perfect scores, who receive rejection letters from the apex of educational institutions they fervently pursued?

Within our world, many individuals exhibit unwavering resolve, toiling ceaselessly; yet the gleam of triumph often eludes their grasp. These valiant souls endure prolonged tribulations, shackled by karmic debts immune to reconfiguration or renegotiation. No one embarks upon the path of karma with the intent of courting sorrow, not even the most misguided among us. Nonetheless, every being, to varying degrees, encounters the presence of adversity. To assert exemption from this cosmic dance would mirror the folly of a child emboldened to frolic with a scorpion, presuming exemption from its sting due to their status as a minor.

Conversely, the tide of prosperity bestows disproportionate rewards, a boon attributable to virtuous deeds performed in times bygone. Life, inherently capricious, dutifully bestows a medley of surprises. Strangely, the question 'Why me?' seldom reverberates through our psyche during moments of abundance. Yet, it is precisely this query that wields the potency to forestall the repetition of historical blunders. It is in those moments of experiencing favourable karmic outcomes, no matter how brief, that individuals tend to cast aside the lessons of the law of Karma. Consequently, they engage in fresh acts of speech and thought steeped in arrogance and pride, unwittingly sowing the seeds of future misfortunes to be reaped either in this present life or in the times yet to come.

Hence, relying solely on scientific intervention to untangle the web of human predicaments is an exercise in futility, for we are both architects and recipients of our trials. Thus, the mantle of responsibility rests upon us to mend the fractures we've wrought, knowing that our capacity for transformation far outweighs the inertia of stagnation.

PK wields immense power within the framework of our existence. Through PK, the fabric of fate unfolds effortlessly, orchestrating the outcomes of our actions in a seamless choreography, often before we are even aware of it. Our experience of PK manifests as joy or sorrow, depending on the ripening of our karma (Karma Phalam).

Like puppets in the hands of a skilled puppeteer whose movements are guided by the script, we experience life's peaks and troughs—moments of maximum joy or sorrow. The key distinction in our actions lies in being guided by our Prarabdha Karma, SRT, and other influences, rather than following a clean, predetermined script. The reins governing these movements are firmly held by karma, ultimately determining the measure of joy or suffering one will experience in a lifetime.

The example below illustrates this concept: people across the globe—whether rich, famous, notorious, or impoverished—all experience their share of peak joy or deep sorrow during their lifetimes. Upon death, they disappear along with these experiences, leaving behind only the imprints of their actions and the consequences shaped by karma.

In the annals of April 2008, a pivotal juncture emerged, painting the bleak narrative of Chris Wang, a stalwart within the upper echelons of a prominent British banking institution. Chris, who was my mentor during our tenure when we worked as colleagues at another bank based in Singapore, was summoned by his head of HR for an urgent meeting.

Famed for his prowess, Chris was feted with a princely bonus of $150,000 in early January, a resounding tribute to his superlative contributions in the year prior. A sense of anticipation swelled within him as he approached the meeting, his heart aflutter, yearning to glean news of his ascension to the venerated realm of global leadership.

Gathered within the bustling embrace of a downtown Singapore coffee haven, the meeting unfolded like an ethereal dance, a mere fifteen minutes shaping destinies. The front man gave a brief idea of how the division was expected to be revamped to align with new strategies, following the takeover of another bank. Abruptly, as though scripted by some cosmic playwright, the course of fate shifted as the HR man delivered an unanticipated decree: 'You have three months to embark on a quest for new horizons, for no role befits you in the forthcoming chapters of our growth odyssey.'

As the sands of time sifted through the hourglass, three swift months passed by in a blink. Yet, Chris, a paragon of banking erudition and loads of experience, found himself trapped within a quagmire of the unemployed. At our reunion, he narrated his tale, his voice coloured with notes of disbelief. Enlisted by a board member who bore an enduring aversion for Chris's direct superior, the die was cast from inception; this odium (negative Vasna) swathed in veils of diplomatic veneer.

But it was a single nocturnal episode that set ablaze the unravelling of his fortune. Chris requested a female colleague, his project coordinator at the Indonesian branch of the bank to come to his hotel room to discuss the details of the agenda for the next day's meeting. It was past 1.00 a.m. and they were still discussing. The midnight rendezvous, borne of professionalism, crystallized into whispers of misconduct. A passing mention of her late-night engagement as the reason for late arrival to next day's meeting snowballed into a symphony of slander, notes reaching the ears of Chris's superiors. An exhaustive inquiry was conducted to disproportionately amplify the magnitude of the incident.

Soon, yet another tempest brewed; one kindled by the flames of corporate politics and Chris's anxieties about an uncertain tomorrow. This chapter portrayed him as an unbearable teammate, further tarnishing his reputation. The pivotal moment of destiny arrived—the time to greet the takeover of another bank. Amidst the various clauses of the deal lay a mandate, compelling the extension of employment to a substantial cadre of personnel hailing from the acquired bank. The stage was set for Chris's superiors to offer him an unexpected option to leave the bank. The imperative to employ those displaced by the recently acquired bank served as a convenient excuse to remove Chris from his position in the upper echelons of his professional sphere.

September 2008 unfurled a tragic postscript—the financial market's collapse dealt the final blow to Chris's vocational voyage. An eerie silence met his earnest endeavours, his 135 job applications evoking a lone response, a telephonic encounter that left an indelible psychological scar. A pronouncement of unsuitability due to seniority extinguished the flicker of hope, forever sealing Chris's professional fate.

His annual earnings, once surpassing the $300,000 mark, now lay buried beneath the rubble of unemployment, a chapter closed prematurely. Chris, a man of astute intellect and worldly sagacity, narrated his misfortune with a sense of disbelief, grappling with the incongruity of his actions.

The questions hung like a spectre—how could a man of his calibre stumble into such inconceivable follies? Why did foresight elude him, shielding him from the consequences of his choices? How could he not think about the possible repercussions of the actions he was taking? What was forcing him not to look for opportunities outside the banking industry? Truly, no one questions the actions that land one in trouble until after one begins to experience the pain. These reflections nestled in the heart of his narration, a testament to the enigmatic ballet of existence.

In retrospect, the parade of events unfolded in a remorseless sequence, a symphony of mishaps and misjudgements, orchestrating a requiem for Chris's grand aspirations and their demise. 'Everyone comes into this world wearing a karmic cap,' a phrase crystallized in my mind, summing up the culmination of Chris's destiny, a testament to the inexorable currents of Karma Phalam—the harvest of deeds.

VASNA—SUBTLE IMPRESSIONS

Every day, we witness peculiar incidents unfolding across the world. These events are not random; they are set into motion by the deliberate manifestations of the three fundamental forces we have previously explored: PK, Vasnas, and the SRT factors. In the preceding pages, we explored the concept of PK, a direct outcome of the ignorance of our inner truth, and the interference of SRT factors directing our actions.

To complete the circle and fully comprehend the intricate dynamics shaping human experiences, it is essential to revisit the salient features of Vasnas and their profound impact on our lives.

Vasnas, the subtle impressions formed by our past actions, thoughts, and experiences, are deeply embedded in our psyche. They shape our tendencies, preferences, and behaviours, often without our conscious awareness. At their core, Vasnas are rooted in self-deception—a pervasive human trait that distorts our perception of reality, and disrupts relationships. This distortion clouds our judgement, fuels unexamined desires, and perpetuates endless cycles of action and reaction, preventing us from perceiving the intrinsic SRT factors that define others' true nature.

Vasnas—both evaluated and unevaluated—are etched into our subconscious and are formed during the first and subsequent interfaces of life. These interfaces include interactions with familiar and unfamiliar people, environments, emotions, and even the choices we make daily. Each interaction leaves behind a solid imprint, shaping our tendencies, preferences, and responses, often unconsciously driving our future behaviour. Over time, these accumulated impressions weave a fabric that defines our character, influencing our decision-making and the trajectory of our karmic journey.

Vasnas are akin to the bedrock beneath a lake—deeply embedded and exceedingly challenging to eradicate. Hence, total eradication of Vasnas is unfeasible. Therefore, it is imperative to cultivate positive Vasnas and avoid forming negative ones, particularly at the onset of an interaction or relationship. Vasnas directly contribute to self-deception, and reducing negative Vasnas helps in fostering the 'S' factor, or positive energy. This requires conscious effort to prevent the reinforcement of existing negative Vasnas. Key steps to reducing and avoiding the formation of negative Vasnas include:

- Stop complaining
- End expectations
- Stop talking behind the back
- Stop finding faults in other beings

Verily, the possession of these four qualities alone defines a true monk.

Depending on whether an individual is destined to experience joy or sorrow, PK, Vasnas, or SRT factors take the lead role in ensuring the flawless realization of Karma Phalam (the results of actions). These factors nudge individuals towards making right or wrong choices, or even choosing inaction. When PK is on our side, every action we take yields positive outcomes automatically. Conversely, when PK takes an unfavourable stance, Vasnas and SRT factors form a partnership that clouds our judgement, convincing us to commit errors either through omission or commission.

This is how we often find ourselves engaging in forbidden actions, repeating them while neglecting our responsibilities. These missteps render us susceptible to the triad of ecological adversaries, which can strike us without warning. These three adversaries are:

1. (Adhyatmika) Disruptions within our bodies, causing psychological and physical distress at a personal level.
2. (Adhibautika) Tribulations arising from interactions with

fellow humans, animals, and other species in the world.

3. (Adhideivika) Adversities originating from supernatural forces orchestrated by nature.

As long as we remain entangled by ignorance, fail to diminish Vasnas, and remain trapped in the influence of SRT factors, it is impossible to escape from the vicious cycle of becoming. The fundamental aspirations of humanity—peace, happiness, and security—will remain distant goals. The harsh truth: PK cannot be reversed, transferred, or bargained away. We can't simply absolve ourselves from the mess we create.

But here's a glimmer of hope: Vasnas can be diminished, and SRT can be reshaped. Ignorance, the root cause of all suffering, can be eradicated. We possess the capacity to mitigate the impact of life's ups and downs. This is achieved through intellectual exercises that reshape the emotional aspect of our personalities, enabling us to maintain equanimity in both favourable and challenging circumstances. While PK exerts its influence over various aspects of our lives, it spares our free will and SRT in general—the precious tools we can employ to alleviate the adverse effects of PK.

Only by recognizing the aforementioned points can we truly embrace and face the painful aspects of reality. This shift allows us to relinquish the habit of assigning blame to the external world, let go of past grievances, and channel our efforts towards shaping a future through the deliberate exercise of our free will.

Chapter 5

COMING TO TERMS WITH REALITY

HARMONIZING MATERIAL LIFE WITH SPIRITUAL WISDOM

Having gained some understanding of how our past actions shape the course of our lives, this is not the time to venture into uncharted territories in pursuit of serenity. Instead, it is a moment to make a decisive and meaningful choice. As we stand at this crossroads, we must deliberate on whether to strive for a lasting resolution in our pursuit of peace or persist in an unending, melancholic cycle, bearing the weight of recurring errors.

Our prolonged suffering has endured far too long, its burden amplified by our chronic scepticism and reluctance to embrace metaphysical truths, often discarded due to their lack of tangible proof.

Nevertheless, let us not hastily disregard the enormous benefits that countless souls worldwide have reaped upon unravelling the enigmatic 'secret truth'. Instead of relegating it to the realm of mystical reverie or dismissing it as the ecstatic declarations of spiritual yogis, who are often considered inconsequential to our material progress, we should discern its boundless potential.

In making this assertion, I do not suggest that humanity is eternally mired in misery, held captive by forces beyond our influence. Neither do I deny the intermittent moments of serenity that grace us all. Yet, we cannot afford to bury our heads in the sand, evading the unvarnished truths of existence that have arisen from our actions. We should not waste our lives yearning for a miraculous reversal of fortune, oscillating between a harsh world and a forgiving deity each time the unexpected befalls us. Rather, we must promptly confront the reality that unfolds before us.

I do not seek to impose my personal beliefs; instead, my purpose is to advocate for the profound 'reality' that resides at the core of every element in creation, an essence some might liken to the 'city of God'. This truth serves as the foundation of survival for all existence, whether we acknowledge it or not. Attaining enduring peace through the recognition of this truth doesn't demand grandiose actions, for it dwells within each of us, inseparable from 'us' as a whole. A modest shift in our perspective, both towards ourselves and the world, holds the potential for miraculous transformation, unleashing profound wonders.

It begins with the sober recognition that the quest to end man's tribulations through reasoning, guided by thoughts, has thus far borne no true fruit. Should we not then reason one final time—to see that the security, happiness, and tranquillity so ardently sought by every soul can never be found in the fleeting images fashioned by thoughts? For thought is but the child of experience, and experience is bound fast to memory, which itself is but the dust of the past.

Human beings often anchor their sense of security in beliefs shaped by favorable experiences—whether with an activity, a person, or an ideology. These beliefs create a comfort zone, and once people are settled within it, they rarely welcome a shift in mindset. Yet, such comfort is often illusory. Even if the belief appears well-reasoned, it is still built on thoughts, which are inherently limited by past experiences and memory. Besides, thoughts belong to the matter principle, ever shifting and eventually fading. As a result, the security it offers is fragile and fleeting, providing a false sense of security. In essence, we create a belief through thought, feed it with further thought, and then cling desperately to the illusion of safety it provides.

But this is a self-made refuge that crumbles the moment reality no longer conforms to the fragile framework that sustains it. To seek lasting peace in the ruins of a failed yesterday is as futile as declaring, 'I shall never stumble, for I have read of falling.'

When this truth is grasped, the clinging to the perishable body, the unreliable mind and the restless surge of its unpredictable contents, shall lose all hold upon us. The veil is lifted, and the resplendent, ever-present truth of our boundless being stands revealed. In that holy instant, what we think ourselves to be shall melt into who we truly are, and the long tyranny of our inner trials shall meet its end.

Thus, by altering our thought patterns and harmonizing them with Supreme Consciousness—our inherent essence—our actions will inevitably mirror this alignment. Yet, comprehending the essence of Consciousness proves no simple task; it transcends all conventional boundaries. Words, regardless of their abundance, falter in their attempt to encapsulate Consciousness fully, for there exists nothing beyond or contrary to it. Its authentic nature eludes expression through mere comparisons or conceptualizations, and attempting to apprehend it via the senses or reason proves fruitless, as it resides beyond the realms of physical sciences.

Now, do not misconstrue my perspective as a denigration of logic and reason. They undeniably hold their utility, but they are not devoid of limitations. When delving into the realm of metaphysical truths, a distinct approach becomes necessary. This journey commences with the acquisition of knowledge from diverse texts that expound upon the experiences of seers who have traversed this path before us. Crucially, it should be undertaken under the wise guidance of a capable mentor.

However, accepting these teachings without personally experiencing them renders this knowledge pallid, much like second-hand information. In imparting sacred metaphysical knowledge, the guru does not entertain debates with students, as any discussion has the potential to direct or condition the mind, either partially or entirely. Thus, the guru refrains from becoming an obstacle for individuals who need to introspect and achieve conviction in the concepts through personal realization. Instead, the guru's role is to offer clarifications in response to questions, to make the knowledge as free from doubt as possible. Reason is never dismissed; rather, it is employed to elucidate and enhance our understanding of what we have gleaned through our spiritual encounters.

Epistemology assumes a pivotal role in deciphering supra-rational knowledge, guiding us through a process of self-certification to arrive at reasoned conclusions. Physics and metaphysics, these twin realms of understanding, diverge distinctly—one delving into the material realm and the other into the spiritual. The acquisition of knowledge in physics unfolds through the meticulous application of logic and reason, while metaphysics embarks on the opposite journey—proceeding from knowledge to logical constructs.

Therefore, we must grant science the space to unravel the marvels of the natural world, propelling human advancement, while spirituality stands as an indispensable guide in humanity's quest for inner peace, irrespective of the presence or absence of these worldly wonders.

Embarking upon the quest for truth is undeniably a formidable journey, but not one beyond our reach. The road to truth necessitates a recalibration of our daily rhythms, a reshaping of our ingrained thought patterns, and a redirection of our gaze. For any seeker, these shifts can prove a daunting undertaking. As we venture along the spiritual path, what initially appears as a modest obstacle may loom before us like an endless ocean, and moments of anguish might seem to perpetuate themselves. Triumphs can swiftly morph into frustration, urging us to confront Consciousness—an abstract truth that demands personal revelation rather than mere intellectual grasp. This journey, though challenging, unveils its rewards to those who persist.

It beckons us to contemplate how we can perceive the entire cosmos through our eyes while remaining challenged to perceive our own eyes. The wisdom it imparts underscores the imperative to release our relentless pursuit of material aspirations, liberating us from the barriers that obstruct our pilgrimage towards the intrinsic truth.

It necessitates an essential realization: the need to nurture focus and allocate the necessary time, a challenge that emerges when our fixation remains steadfastly affixed to the trappings of the material realm. And then, a revelation dawns upon us: comprehending the truth mirrors recognizing the presence of Brahman within us, an acknowledgment that being alive converges with this profound realization. In this realization, any discourse concerning the hurdles along the spiritual path dissolves like a doll crafted of salt immersed in boundless sea.

Spiritual growth doesn't require renouncing material pursuits, but rather understanding that true fulfilment comes from balancing both material and spiritual aspects of life. Embrace the spiritual truths while actively engaging with the world, allowing wisdom from both realms to guide your actions.

However, we must remember that the feelings of inadequacy that often beset us are firmly rooted in the limitations of the finite, objective world. The true fulfilment of our being can only be realized by transcending these confines and delving into the boundless expanse of the spiritual realm, a journey that necessitates the dispelling of ignorance which veils our inner vision. This profound insight empowers us to forge a harmonious union between our earthly pursuits and the ascent of our spiritual selves, thus embracing both facets of our existence in a symphonic and enriching equilibrium.

MANAGING THE TWISTS AND TURNS OF LIFE

No one seems to have any quarrel in acknowledging the ubiquitous truth that life resembles a rollercoaster—a wild ride oscillating between the peaks of fortune and the depths of adversity. One moment, we revel in the radiant glow of happiness; the next, we are enveloped by the sombre shadows of despair. And sometimes, the future shrouds itself in an enigmatic veil. Each moment stands as a unique canvas, just like the ever-shifting landscape of the sky, where clouds may, at times, obscure the sun, casting a melancholic hue, while at other times, the canvas remains clear and blue. The ebb and flow of these clouds elude our grasp, their comings and goings a mystery we cannot decipher, much like an unpredictable visitor to the vast expanse of space between the earth and the sky.

The uncertainty of life follows a mysterious pattern, impervious to any endeavour of foretelling or comprehension. No algorithm can unravel its capricious nature. It remains a captivating enigma, simultaneously bewildering, as it impartially bestows its gifts of joy and sorrow upon all, irrespective of their social standing, whether wealthy or destitute, renowned or obscure, powerful or humble. It remains an impartial arbiter, ready to surprise even disparate individuals like Mike Tyson and Marie Curie, with its unpredictable twists and turns.

At times, it becomes nearly tempting to envision a celestial emissary, handpicked by the divine, tasked with meting out justice and apportioning rewards and penalties that unfold as our daily encounters. Typically, no one examines or challenges the experience of joy, but it is the looming shadow of sorrow that piques our curiosity. The question isn't about how much or what the rationale is behind our encounters with sorrow, but rather, it centres on our responses when we stand in its melancholic embrace. Amid these moments, our actions often appear as mere placeholders, marking time until the pendulum of existence swings once more in its eternal rhythm.

Having gleaned that the domain of physical sciences stands powerless in taming the unruly cadence of life, we have made the conscious choice to enfold struggles as an inherent aspect of our being. In our daily pursuits, we journey through the terrain of fleeting joys nestled between the realms of pain and sorrow, charting a course through the undulating waves of emotion that accompany us. The venerable teachings of the ancient Vedas resound with a timeless message, guiding us to harness our intellect in the pursuit of righteous actions, thereby savouring the essence of joy, and guarding our threshold against the encroachments of sorrow.

In our insatiable quest for happiness, we find ourselves entangled in ceaseless activity with the external world, as we engage in both virtuous, and sometimes less-than-virtuous and evil actions. Yet, we often fail to recognize that this pursuit remains inherently unfulfilling, forever intermingled with shades of unhappiness and cultivating inclinations towards addiction. In this misguided chase for happiness, we inadvertently sow the seeds within ourselves for the flourishing of sorrow. Those who remain unenlightened, unburdened by the fear of transgressing moral boundaries in their pursuit of unnatural desires and artificial needs, often become the architects of their misfortunes.

The inevitability of human suffering, encompassing both sorrow and pain, stands as an indisputable fact. An exploration into human suffering unveils startling facts, leading to the imperative need to trace and eliminate its root causes. Suffering is not inherent to human nature; otherwise, individuals would be in a perpetual state of agony, devoid of motivation to overcome it. Therefore, sorrow and pain are acquired phenomena experienced by the human body, and must, therefore, have a cause.

Our tribulations do not solely emanate from an external force with a mere secondary role in the pervasive experience of sorrow. Instead, they unfold as immediate consequences of our actions, 'karma', echoing the principles of cause and effect as declared by the Vedas. The doctrine of karma, encompassing various harsh realities often challenging to comprehend, discourages the renunciation of karma and underscores the importance of considering karma as an incentive to engage in more righteous deeds when facing its consequences. It is not intended as a means of escaping or rationalizing sorrow, as some individuals with a shallow understanding of the doctrine of karma may misconstrue it.

A clear understanding of the framework surrounding pain and sorrow establishes a direct link between the compulsion to engage in karma due to ignorance and the inevitability of suffering as an inherent feature of karma. This understanding affirms that ignorance is the root cause within the framework of karma's cause-and-effect cycle, where ignorance gives rise to actions that ultimately lead to suffering. This analysis can be found under the topic, 'Tracing the cause of pain'.

However, the intricate threads connecting cause to effect often confound even the most astute minds. The saint of today may have once assumed the mantle of a villain, a fact that frequently eludes human comprehension. This emergence of profound pain, an intangible burden in the subtle depths of the heart when ambitions shatter, transcends the physical realm to manifest as emotional anguish. This experience, though intangible, remains undeniably real. The doctrine of karma serves as a stark reminder that effects invariably spring from causes, whether tangible or intangible. Therefore, dismissing the existence of a cause that isn't immediately perceptible would be folly. We must be prepared to grapple with the consequences of our actions, both seen and unseen, as they weave the intricate fabric of our lives.

Happiness and unhappiness represent facets of human existence that lie beyond the domain of science. Science meticulously scrutinizes the present, yet its gaze does not extend into the past or project into the future. While it wrestles with the enigma of human emotions in all earnestness, it ultimately falls short of completely unravelling the intricate web woven within us. Consequently, we find ourselves compelled to explore alternative avenues for comprehending the origins of these complex states.

The techniques employed by ancient sages to unveil the subtle truths of our essence can be said to closely mirror the very methods that conscious or unconscious minds like Einstein and Newton wielded to unveil the verities of physical science, truths that have always existed. New discovery does not emerge from instinct, reasoning, or through shallow intuition. Rather, it demands the construction of a pathway using an elevated faculty to access the source of yet-to-be-unravelled knowledge. Deep within Consciousness lies the wellspring of all knowledge, both its origin and the process through which remarkable individuals unlock profound insights.

As Arthur Koestler, the author of *The Sleepwalkers* (Hutchinson & Co., 1959), posits, 'The individual discoveries are not a purely rational process, a continuous curve. It is sometimes the result of an unexpected by-product of a chase after quite different hares. We cannot say scientific discoveries are confined to the deliverances of sense and reason.'

At the heart of this process lies unyielding inquiry, wherein individuals relentlessly probe until nature reveals hidden verities to those endowed with extraordinary acumen. The scientist then interprets these revelations, ultimately bequeathing their practical applications for the greater good. As Leslie Stephen astutely observed in *Hours in a Library* (Smith, Elder, & Co., 1874), 'Genius begins where intellect ends; or takes by storm where intellect has to make elaborate approaches according to rules of scientific strategy. One sees truth and another demonstrates.' It seizes its prize like a tempest, unfettered by the measured strides of scientific strategy.

Typically, individuals who opt to remain uninformed seek instinctive relief from the numerous available options to alleviate their pain. Life continues its course, albeit temporarily, until another predator readies itself for an assault. And so, the narrative persists. Some argue, 'We exist in this world with an unalterable body–mind complex; thus, we should channel our efforts into maximizing the material benefits of our present state.'

Ensnared by Maya, the ancient veil of ignorance, this perspective is characteristic of those who endure suffering by perpetuating their errors. The majority willingly endure suffering as an inescapable affliction upon humanity, convinced that all human predicaments can be resolved solely through the all-encompassing power of science. While we mustn't disregard science's remarkable contributions to human advancement, we must also acknowledge its inability to shield us from emotional distress. Matters of the heart cannot be rectified through objective scientific means.

Human beings are intricately composed of both physical (the tangible body) and metaphysical (the intangible essence) elements by intentional design. Consequently, it becomes imperative to consider the transcendent and ethereal aspects of human nature to address challenges that stem from both realms. This entails exploring the credibility of answers provided by esoteric wisdom to myriad enigmatic queries with an open and receptive mindset. Meanwhile, embarking on a spiritual journey guided by a competent guru stands as a viable option worth contemplating for a holistic transformation in life, as it personally did for me.

Chapter 6

A ONCE-IN-A-LIFETIME JOURNEY

ATTAINING SPIRITUAL FREEDOM

One might wonder why human beings—spiritual entities merely passing through a physical experience—must labor to attain spiritual freedom. After all, the very essence of spirit is freedom itself. In truth, liberation requires nothing more than a reversal of identification: shifting our sense of self from the body and mind to the eternal Self. Yet, this simple truth remains hidden under layers of ignorance.

Engulfed in avidya (ignorance), the soul forgets its true nature and becomes entangled in the illusion of separateness, bondage, and ego. Thus, despite being inherently free, each soul must undertake a journey of Self-discovery—a process of cleansing the mind, quieting the ego, and awakening to the light of inner wisdom. This path is not about gaining something new, but about removing the veils that obscure what has always been present: our divine, unbound nature.

The spiritual journey revolves around gaining a pearl of profound wisdom that unveils the metaphysical truths of our inner reality. This pursuit is crucial but is reserved for a select few destined to embark on this pilgrimage with genuine purpose, and only they manage to reach the ultimate destination. Vedas elucidate that this is due to ignorance, a hereditary legacy passed down from the mind's source, Maya—the illusory force. Nonetheless, we mustn't berate those who opt to centre their lives on the material realm or perceive no compulsion to tread the spiritual path, whether due to a lack of awareness or personal convictions.

Until my encounter with the suffering of men, women, and children at the hospital—an experience I recounted at the beginning of this book—I mistakenly regarded a journey into the spiritual domain as a pursuit reserved for the less fortunate. But hindsight has illuminated my understanding. I eventually grasped that inner spiritual fortitude is the very force that bolsters one's resolve to confront challenges head-on when nothing works. I misconstrued my father's honourable intentions at times, misinterpreting his gentle encouragement to explore an unfamiliar realm as veiled attempts to sway me. On other occasions, I suspected him of diverting my attention, perhaps driven by envy of my accomplishments in the material sphere—or so my imagination conjured.

How could the mere acquisition of abstruse knowledge, as encapsulated in the Vedas, wield the potential to bestow an unbroken stream of bliss? This question gained prominence amidst countless creature comforts of the material world persistently faltering, despite continuous enhancements and remarkable innovations.

In the initial phase of my spiritual journey, I learned that the Vedas represent knowledge—not just any knowledge, but the spiritual wisdom that embodies the divine commands. These teachings revolve around the ultimate truths, particularly the metaphysical reality of Consciousness itself. Think of it as an expansive reservoir of wisdom, encompassing the essence of arts, science, philosophy, insights from ancient seers, and much more.

It is neither a theological dogma nor a mystic object of experience for the Yogis. It is the knowledge (the awareness principle), and also the means to obtain knowledge. Its authenticity stands as a testament to its truth, self-evident and self-affirming. The philosophy of the Vedas elaborates extensively on a 'way of life' aimed at delivering the much sought-after inner peace craved by every individual across the globe.

It achieves this by focusing on commonalities, steering clear of the divisive points that self-serving religious leaders, self-proclaimed spiritual gurus, and opportunistic politicians often exploit for personal gain, knowing well the historical toll such divisions have exacted through human conflict. Vedic knowledge, bereft of contention, avoids opposition to any school of thought or religion. Instead, it urges us not merely to embrace, but to truly respect people from all corners of the world, diverse in their nationalities, faiths, races, and beliefs.

Much like a thread woven to create a garland of flowers, each boasting distinct colours, fragrances, and beauty, all harmoniously united to adorn the divine, Vedic philosophy serves as the common thread upon which any religion can be built. Just as religions might diverge in rituals, dispositions, emphases, and methodologies, they all share a singular objective: guiding their followers towards higher virtues.

History has shown that faith in religions crumbles when their tenets aren't interwoven with a foundation of philosophically sound principles. It's akin to the blood that binds flesh and bone together, an inseparable and vital connection.

Aldous Huxley, who drew inspiration from Swami Vivekananda, sums it up neatly in his book, *The Perennial Philosophy* (1945). Speaking of the timeless philosophy that threads through all religions, he explains, 'It is the denial of the final reality of the visible world; the affirmation of a higher Reality, with which the true Self of each human being is identical; and, above all, the attempt, through the elimination of the personal ego, to establish in the life of the individual his identity with the "That" which is the "Ground" of everything. The chief point is that the individual "Who" should turn into the universal "That"—that man should become God.' In his 1944 essay in *Vedanta and the West*, he describes 'The Minimum Working Hypothesis', the basic outline of the Perennial Philosophy found in all the mystic branches of the religions of the world: that there is a Godhead or Ground, which is the unmanifested principle of all manifestation.

- That the Ground is transcendent and immanent.
- That it is possible for human beings to love, know, and become the Ground.
- That to achieve this unitive knowledge, to realize this supreme identity, is the end and purpose of human existence.
- That there is a Law (Dharma), or Way (Tao), that must be followed in order to reach this realization.

Furthermore, as Huxley pointed out, the Perennial Philosophy finds its most concise expression in the ancient Sanskrit axiom 'tat tvam asi' ('That thou art'), a concept we will delve into later. In this framework, the *Atman*—the eternal Self residing within every being—remains ever united with *Brahman*, the all-encompassing Absolute Principle. A human's ultimate purpose is to personally uncover this truth—to unearth their authentic Self. This clarifies the significance of the Vedas, which encompass knowledge of the boundless Brahman, the ultimate reality, standing in contrast to the empirical sciences' focus on the finite and ever-changing world. Establishing an unshakable faith and a precise comprehension of the Vedas serves as a prerequisite for embarking upon the spiritual expedition I am discussing.

Verily, this knowledge blazes through ignorance, bestowing the coveted freedom sought by every individual. It grants liberation from the manifold tribulations stemming from our attachments to people, objects, and external circumstances. It liberates us from the grip of a predetermined outcome of an action, releasing us from the shackles of preferences and aversions that drive us into ceaseless actions (karmas). Above all, it bestows paramount freedom from the paralyzing fear of mortality.

This instantaneous transformation occurs as the knowledge catalyses the fusion of the experiencer and all elements of experience. The observed phenomena seamlessly meld into the observer, forging a singular entity. The journey requires no arduous or painful physical trials; it hinges on the faculties of intellectual discernment. It begins with the recognition and embrace of Brahman, our innate reality, and culminates in the relinquishment and detachment from the body and mind, which are transient.

The process happens in three steps:

1. Go beyond the idea of individuals, the world, and cosmic intelligence (Immanent God), seeing them as one, non-different from Brahman.
2. Divide the world into two basic constituents: yourself as Consciousness, the essence, and everything else as objects of experience.
3. Dissolve the diversity of the world in you because everything in existence originates from the Consciousness that defines your core.

With this intellectual integration comes the termination of all associations with the corporeal and mental domains—birth, death, the sensations of hunger and thirst, the constraints of bondage, the dynamics of action and inaction, and the emotions of sorrow and happiness. The individual who has nurtured this realization through unwavering conviction, unburdened by coercion, stands as a sage (sthita pragya). He comprehends his role in the grand theatre of life without becoming ensnared by the diverse characters he portrays. He leads a life infused with sagacity and departs in tranquillity.

FROM BONDAGE TO BLISS: THE PROMISE OF A SPIRITUAL JOURNEY

The Vedantic ideal emphasizes harmony amidst the differences present within individuals and society, recognizing the unavoidable reliance of each upon the other. Reigning angels know that they cannot control the religious rebels nor influence the rich and the poor to desist from evil deeds, except through tolerance and empathy, which are deeply embedded in the Vedic philosophy.

The approach outlines merely three steps to gain and apply this wisdom: first, the study of scriptures (shruti) under the guidance of a proficient guru; second, introspection driven by logical reasoning (yukti); and finally, the actualization of truth through firsthand experience (anubhuti).

This realization, achieved by the enlightened, instantaneously liberates the individual soul (jivatma) from all temporal bondage, allowing it to ascend into the realm of boundless Brahman. Here, a ceaseless wellspring of joy flows from unparalleled freedom, as it abides within the rediscovered Self—a realm that remains elusive to the unenlightened, tethered as they are to their corporeal forms. This bliss parallels the euphoria a prisoner feels upon freeing legs bound by iron shackles.

Amidst life's most trying ordeals that elude none, undisturbed tranquillity reigns within these enlightened souls. Their presence in the world is marked not by an indifferent mindset but by a compassionate heart that resonates with the struggles of those trapped in ignorance and insensitivity. Now, this can be likened to a grand banquet for a lifetime. Of course, acquiring this knowledge demands a certain price, yet it comes at no monetary cost. It remains crucial to remember that the rewards of dwelling in sacred knowledge are intangible and necessitate unwavering patience. Indeed, devotion and determination stand as indispensable prerequisites.

It's a source of comfort to believe that the path of spirituality is free from mental obstacles, challenges, rivalry, and disappointments. Nevertheless, anyone venturing into the realm of spirituality is bound to encounter difficulties along the way due to the incessant workings of our rational mind. It becomes imperative, then, to reshape our thought patterns as we step into the spiritual domain.

The journey of mind refinement, a prerequisite for true understanding, commences with the recognition of the necessity to transform one's emotional disposition. The subsequent process is not left to chance, but is the result of dedicated engagement in the demanding disciplines outlined briefly below, culminating in the eventual manifestation of this profound transformation.

1. The quartet of practices referred to as sadhana chatushtaya (discussed in detail in chapter 25 of this text) is designed to facilitate a profound shift in one's inner and outer perspectives, founded upon sincere belief rather than mere obligation.
2. Karma Yoga, aimed at instilling desirable virtues; diminishing the influence of malevolent forces within; purging the mind of profane impressions (Vasnas) which cling like stubborn boulders; and reshaping SRT—the emotional fabric to withstand the ebb and flow of contrasting life experiences.
3. Upasana Yoga, a practice adopted to tranquillize the tempestuous mind, fostering the invaluable trait of humility, and nurturing the capacity to unwaveringly embrace truth through devotion.
4. Jnana Yoga is a practice that unfolds as a tripartite process—acquiring, introspecting, and securing the grasp of Self-knowledge acquired under the guidance of a competent guru.

The pursuit of one's endeavours yields favourable outcomes in due course, yet the realization dawns only upon the willingness to surrender ego to the all-encompassing force, through unwavering devotion and a connection to the divine essence (Bhakti Yoga), throughout the various stages of the aforementioned yogic disciplines. Crucially, we must recognize that the time span necessary to harvest the abundant fruits of our endeavours shall mirror the intensity of the dedication we invest. Yet, of even greater import is the unwavering faith we bestow upon an ethereal yet potent entity, hidden from the grasp of our senses, but capable of unravelling the knots of all human tribulations.

In the realm of Vedanta, the exercise of our free will is paramount, leaving no room for complacency or resignation to the caprices of fate, whether we aspire for material advancement or seek to traverse the spiritual path and reap its profound rewards. However, it is imperative to recognize that even the most accomplished of teachers, no matter how skilled they may be, will falter in their efficacy unless we possess an unwavering resolve to break free from the shackles of worldly bondage. Simultaneously, a fervent yearning for transformation and emancipation from life's entanglements must blaze within us like an unquenchable fire.

For those dominated by 'R' or 'T', inner transformation remains elusive. True metamorphosis is achieved solely by embracing the 'S' factor, fostering an unwavering devotion to the divine with a pure heart. This sacred alignment brings one closer to the truth, the source of love and serenity, ultimately elevating us to a divine plane, as professed by the Vedas. Subsequently, each act of surrender driven by a profound love for the divine bestows a taste of immortality. The only remaining yearning is to seek the divine's blessings—to abide in constant remembrance, forsaking all past grievances and cherished attachments to the material realm.

The man of wisdom understands that even a momentary lapse in awareness of the divine could lead back to enslavement by the illusory world. And once inside, it is difficult to resist falling in love again and again with the sense objects, only to experience fleeting pleasures stuffed in between sorrow and misery. It's not surprising that someone seeking liberation paradoxically finds joy in the confines of illusory existence.

The spiritual realm, we must earnestly acknowledge, commences precisely where the realms of religion, rituals, disputes, and the manifold distinctions of the functional world reach their limit. Importantly, it does not preclude those who aspire to fathom the depths of the absolute from concurrently traversing the spiritual path while pursuing their material objectives. This harmonious duality represents the quintessential approach to living a balanced life, responding to the demands of the intellect while simultaneously nurturing the essence of the heart.

To flourish in the material world, the intellect must be honed and employed to its fullest, while inner serenity and peace are sought through spiritual pursuits that nourish the heart. These dual paths, akin to two sides of a single coin, each have their rightful place, and there should be no conflict between them, much like the eyes and ears that coexist harmoniously in a person's perception of the world.

As Rajam eloquently states in his extraordinary work *Rambles in Vedanta*, 'Each should know its place and there should be no conflict between the two.'

Noteworthy luminaries in the realms of philosophy and physics, including Max Mueller, Gottfried Leibniz, Schopenhauer, Immanuel Kant, former NASA scientist Dr Tom Campbell, and former Indian President Dr S. Radhakrishnan, deliberately delved into the realm of spirituality, driven by a purposeful quest rather than mere happenstance.

Nevertheless, if one ventures into this realm of purity and peace for misguided motives, a sense of suffocation is bound to ensue. The pristine, flawless domain stands worlds apart from the chaotic, experiential realm we're familiar with. The liberation born from mastering one's thoughts, coupled with the ability to dispel self-deception with ease, can be an awe-inspiring encounter. For many, taming the austerity of silence and confronting the absence of empirical grandeur might prove to be a daunting experience.

If the voyager's objective is to engineer a remarkable turnaround in material pursuits through spiritual quests, it is not possible to escape from the sorrow of becoming. Furthermore, embarking on the spiritual path led by charlatans cloaked in orange robes, armed with hollow promises, can lead to catastrophic consequences. Greed has no abode in the spiritual sphere, which lacks both the inclination and resources to appease the insatiable appetites of the human senses.

For those disenchanted by the absence of tangible rewards or disheartened by the often-harsh realities of life, the gateway to the spiritual realm remains firmly closed. However, those who persist and persevere come to a startling revelation that they are spiritual beings, untethered by birth and death, undergoing a temporary human experience.

Chapter 7

FASCINATING REVELATIONS OF EXISTENCE

As the root cause of all human predicaments, ignorance is an omnipresent riddle, showing no mercy in its sway over every individual on this planet. Its effects are as diverse as the multitude it affects.

To some, it violently pulls the foundation from beneath their aspirations, abruptly halting the voyage towards life's envisioned dreams. To others, it spreads a magic carpet, allowing them to soar boundlessly through the realm of fantasy. People, distinct in their essence, harbour varying thoughts and actions, sculpted by their unique SRT configurations. Yet, each is a performer on life's grand stage, ceaselessly enacting desires that leave a mark on the psyche, entitling them to revel or endure in accordance with their deeds. The outcomes may differ between individuals, but they are effects of one cause—ignorance of one's intrinsic truth.

To unravel this profound metaphysical verity, I embarked upon a voyage of self-exploration. The findings that unfolded were absurd and astounding. The absurdity arose from the realization that I often reaped lavish rewards without deserving, while also enduring harsh retribution devoid of justification. The startling revelation was that I couldn't discern why I experienced greater bliss compared to my siblings. A cryptic element seemed absent from the equation, defying my attempts at reconciliation. My faith in religion stood resilient, safeguarding my conviction that divinity was not to blame for this inequality. I came to fathom that God's role lay solely in dispensing the fruits of action without partiality, as humans played out their roles in the eternal opera of existence through the law of nature.

I kept wondering why my conduct diverged from that of my siblings, despite sharing the same parental lineage. I refrained from futile debates; a path preferred by others. Such discrepancies, not limited to behaviour but spanning intellect, academic prowess, career trajectories, and beyond, are commonplace within families. Yet, the quest to unravel these mysteries remains dormant. My path wasn't one of sainthood, for I had my share of entanglements with less-than-moral pursuits. Yet, an innate awareness would guide me away from indulgence, a sign that something distinct was at play. The seed of curiosity sprouted within, urging me to uncover the factors that governed my unique journey. A realization dawned that some unknown forces orchestrated events, much like the uneven distribution of genetic mutations among siblings sharing the same flawed genes.

This realization propelled me to delve deeper, akin to the fervour of scientists probing the birth of the sun. My commitment translated into months of dedicated introspection, ending in the ancient meditative practice of Dahara Kash.

Amidst this contemplative voyage, four pivotal metaphysical truths about our existence gradually unfurled, laying the foundation for the remedy to human tribulations.

The significant role played by our mind as a bridge between the physical body and the ever-present realm of pure Consciousness was the first revelation.

ROLE OF THE MIND IN DEATH, BIRTH, AND LIFE

To truly grasp the role of the mind, we must begin our exploration at the point of death, where the mind—or the conscious essence, known as jivatma—separates from the physical body.

The journey after death...

The entire unfolding of this process resembles scenes from a fantastical movie, appearing implausible to the rational mind. Death, in this context, is marked by the departure of the mind (a subtle part of our body) at the predestined moment when the individual has fully expended the PK allocated for their current life.

The human physical body originates from the five fundamental elements of nature: space, air, fire, water, and earth. At the cessation of life, the body returns to its elemental essence, often symbolized by fire (or earth in certain faiths). This transition reflects the cyclical nature of existence, wherein the corporeal form emerges through a sequence of sacred processes—offerings and libations involving faith, the moon's influence, the blessings of rain, sustenance derived from food, and the transmission of semen. This profound cycle mirrors the principle of energy conservation, underscoring the eternal flow and transformation of life's essence.

Once the conscious mind, or jivatma, departs from the physical body, it embarks on a journey through the vast cosmos, guided by the momentum of past actions and aligned with the divine plan for its next incarnation. It is vital to remember that the jivatma, or individual soul, is inherently the mind—a subtle substance that attains awareness solely through the illumination granted by Brahman, the Supreme Consciousness.

This is why the conscious mind is referred to as the jivatma or the individual soul. Its consciousness remains unwavering, as it is eternally connected with Atman while residing within the physical body, and with Brahman (both terms representing the Supreme Consciousness) when transitioning through space in search of its next embodiment. This continuity can be likened to the technology of a cell phone, which enables seamless switching from a home Wi-Fi network to mobile data provided by a service provider when outdoors, all according to the user's plan. It is also vital to acknowledge that the mind perpetually retains its material nature and thus, can never merge with the eternally sentient Consciousness. Contingent upon the deeds carried out in their earthly existence, the jivatma may take leave either during the six months when the sun moves northward or during the six months of its southward journey.

In the former circumstance, it is widely held that the jivatma after spending some divine period unites with the cosmic mind, achieving spiritual elevation, eventually breaking free from the relentless cycle of rebirth. In the latter scenario, following a sojourn within the realm of cosmic energy, the jivatma embarks on a transformative journey, progressing through various phases: from the ethereal expanse to the realm of air, from air to wisps of smoke, from smoke to mist, from mist to cloud, and ultimately merging with the essence of rainwater.

Subsequently, these souls are reborn as various forms of sustenance such as rice, barley, herbs, trees, sesame plants, and animals. When a person capable of procreation consumes food containing the jivatma, the soul enters that individual and becomes incorporated into their semen. This semen is later deposited into a mother's womb at the appropriate moment, giving rise to the formation of a foetus that inherits the characteristics of the father.

'Those who have led virtuous lives on Earth swiftly attain a favourable human birth, while those who have indulged in malevolence are relegated to lower forms of existence. Those who neglect rituals for the divine cosmic intelligence find themselves as insignificant beings. Those who engage in sinful deeds are reborn as grains and similar entities, and after experiencing the consequences of their karma, are once again reborn as humans.

However, those who are exceedingly wicked are reborn as insects, destined to be consumed by birds through repeated pecking. Only a select few who have realized the essence of Brahman in their present existence transcend the cycle of birth and death, attaining liberation from the eternal cycle of existence.'[13]

In a publication from 2017, Johns Hopkins Medicine offered a clear definition of brain death: the irreversible halt of all brain functions, encompassing the brain stem. According to Vedanta's perspective, this marks the mind's departure from the body, a point of no return for the brain. The entire gross body, including the brain, loses its sentiency once the mind—the official agent that renders the body conscious—has departed from the physical frame.

Before the beginning of life...

The mind, a unique facet inherent to each individual, comes into play long before the very formation of the foetus itself. It doesn't stem from our DNA; rather, it collaborates with parental physiology under the guidance of PK, as declared by the Vedas, in the intricate creation of the foetus.

Emerging from cosmic energy, the mind exists as a subtle entity—insentient matter. Verily, this mind, like a miniature rendition of the cosmic mind, is enriched with an array of energies that empower its functions.[14] In perfect harmony with nature's design, the mind maintains constant awareness due to its unbroken connection with the undivided Consciousness. Nestled within the realm of the developing foetus, the mind swiftly mirrors the Consciousness, infusing it into the evolving physical framework.

We acknowledge that Consciousness stands as a fundamental prerequisite for enlivening any entity. In its absence, comprehension stumbles, animation wanes, and both growth and decay grind to a halt. This emphasizes that every organ, every cell, including the brain within our body would relinquish their functions if their sentience fades, a consequence of failing to receive reflections from the conscious mind.

Within Vedanta philosophy, this conscious mind, a conduit of reflection, assumes the name 'reflected consciousness' (RC). It embodies the jivatma, the individual soul, frequently misconceived as the non-dual pure Consciousness that pervades every human being, every object spanning the immense expanses of the universe and beyond. To distinguish it from the individual soul—the reflected consciousness—and to bestow the reverence it merits as the wellspring of our perceptual reality, the term 'pure Consciousness' is often graced with a capital 'C'. For this reason, the jivatma—the amalgamation of the body and the conscious mind—is referred to as the individual self, the small 'i', while the Supreme Consciousness is known as the big 'I', the real Self.

From the beginning of Life to Death...

Upon reincarnation and the acquisition of a new body, the mind takes charge of the subtle body's functions, and orchestrates the harmony of the physical form. In collaboration with PK and other governing elements, the mind serves as the catalyst that drives human actions or inactions. Depending on the strength and nature of these influences, it adopts suitable stances, enabling the newly acquired body to undergo its destined experiences.

Certainly, we've all felt the vulnerability of our mind when it barely opposes or doesn't oppose at all as events unfold per our fate, especially when PK is unfavourable and intensely dominant. There are instances when it might even hasten the process. Equally, we've encountered moments when our mind staunchly battles and ultimately conquers anguish.

An enlightening article released by the Cleveland Clinic provides us with a comprehensive grasp of gene mutation, and this holds significant contextual relevance—the silent intervention of PK is evident in the mutations that occur and in their impact.

> A genetic mutation is a change in a sequence of your DNA. Your DNA sequence gives your cells the information they need to perform their functions. If part of your DNA sequence is in the wrong place, isn't complete, or is damaged, you might experience symptoms of a genetic condition. Genetic mutations occur during cell division. When your cells divide, they hand-write your body's instruction manual by copying the original document word for word. *There's a lot of room for error*

during cell division because your cells might substitute (replace), delete (remove), or insert (add) letters while they're copying. If you have an error (genetic mutation), your genetic instruction manual for your cells may not be readable by the cells, may have missing parts, or unnecessary parts added. All of this can mean that your cells can't function as they normally should.

A genetic mutation changes the information your cells need to form and function. Your genes are responsible for making proteins that tell your body what physical characteristics you should have. If you have a genetic mutation, you could experience symptoms of a genetic condition because your cells are doing a different job than they should be.

Symptoms of genetic conditions depend on which gene has a mutation. There are many different diseases and conditions caused by mutations. Not all genetic mutations lead to genetic disorders. Some genetic mutations don't have any effect on your health and well-being. This is because the change in the DNA sequence doesn't change how your cell functions.

Your body also has enzymes, which are a substance that creates chemical reactions in your body. These enzymes help your body protect itself from disease. Enzymes can repair a variety of genetic mutations before they affect how a cell functions.

Some genetic mutations even have a positive effect on humans. Changes in how cells work can sometimes improve the proteins that your cells produce and allow them to adapt to changes in your environment. An example of a positive genetic mutation is one that can protect a person from acquiring heart disease or diabetes, even with a history of smoking or being overweight.

While some genetic mutations can lead to genetic conditions, most mutations don't cause symptoms in humans. It's difficult to prevent mutations from happening, especially as genetic mutations can occur randomly, some without being present in your family history.[15]

The mind is often likened to a commander-in-chief, exerting direct or indirect control over both subtle and physical bodies.

Functioning as the reflected consciousness, it is the primary observer of all internal occurrences. Armed with comprehensive knowledge of PK, it can strategically intervene in the brain's two-way communication with various organs. This intervention provides the crucial bolster to the functioning of the physical body or selectively triggers malfunctions, all under the guidance of PK.

For those deeply rooted in scientific realms, this concept may initially appear as absurd: the idea that the mind, the experiencer of all emotions, in collaboration with our physical form and external pressures, can influence the brain to trigger the release of dopamine, often referred to as the 'pleasure hormone', through the endocrine system, ultimately resulting in a sense of pleasure. However, it is crucial to underscore that the mind possesses the authority to supersede brain functions, for it serves as the direct physiological catalyst for the brain and heart to function. The mind provides both of these vital organs with the necessary awareness to carry out their functions.

Its pivotal role in orchestrating pleasure is undeniable. Often, the mind's fixation on negative thoughts or anxiety about future outcomes dulls our ability to enjoy even the most joyful experiences—such as watching a favorite comedy show—by either blocking the release of pleasure-inducing hormones or rendering that release ineffective.

THREE DISTINCT BODIES OF HUMAN BEINGS

The second revelation took on an even more captivating hue when I came to grasp that humans consist of three distinct bodies: the physical (or gross) body, the subtle body (mind stuff), and the causal body. These three bodies are interwoven with the pure essence of Consciousness, which acts as the underlying substratum for the mind and the body. *Tattva Bodha*, a respected text in Vedanta philosophy, intricately details the unfolding of the universe, depicting its emergence from the cosmic energy of the universal mind into the threefold body of human beings, mirroring the cosmic triad. This doctrine proclaims the unity of the macrocosm (the universal realm), and microcosm (the individual realm).

Consciousness, the human mind, and the corporeal form maintain their autonomy yet share an intimate connection, like the facets of a three-sided coin. While the mind and the body without an independent existence are merely extensions of Consciousness, it is imperative to understand their status at the physical level. The brain, a component of the physical body, should not be confused with the mind, which belongs to the subtle body; therefore, the two cannot be interchanged. Remarkably, while there exists no physical distance between these aspects, they retain their distinctiveness and divergent lifespans. The physical body, transient in nature, possesses the briefest existence, followed by the expansive span of the mind, while Consciousness endures eternally. Despite its intangibility, Consciousness is the bedrock of all perception, an absolute existence necessary for comprehending the material world.

The body becomes insentient when the mind departs from its frame, marking the death of the individual. Yet, the remains of the body continue to serve as a reflecting medium for the ever-present Consciousness. While Consciousness with eternal existence pervades all creation, it remains physically unattached. Only the embodiments through which it is expressed undergo constant transformation within the Spirit—from the physical body when the individual is alive, to ashes when the body is cremated, to water as the ashes are immersed in holy rivers during rituals, and finally to the atmosphere as the water evaporates.

Just as a mirage relies on the desert to appear, the universe depends on Consciousness to exist from an individual's perspective. This doesn't mean the universe and its objects aren't real, but it emphasizes that their existence and relationships are only understood through our conscious awareness. Recognizing this is a choice—if someone refuses to acknowledge it, the world, for them, effectively disappears.

In simpler terms, the mind shapes what we perceive, but its power is ultimately guided by Consciousness. Since the mind's existence depends on pure Consciousness, only this deeper foundation can validate or reject what we experience. This illustrates how everything we see and experience originates from Consciousness—just as all furniture owes its existence to the wood from which it is crafted.

This understanding, rooted in the teachings of the Vedic scriptures, stands in stark contrast to the emerging theories presented by neuroscience. The divergence lies in how the body, mind, and Consciousness are conceptualized, revealing a significant gap between spiritual insights and scientific frameworks. This difference creates a formidable challenge for science in addressing metaphysical truths.

The difficulty does not stem from a lack of effort on the part of science but rather from its inherent limitations. Science is confined to the realm of the tangible and physical, making it ill-equipped to explore the intricacies of the mind, and the exceedingly subtle nature of Consciousness. Its tools and methods are unable to venture into the ethereal dimensions where these truths reside.

'Blaise Pascal, a seventeenth century French mathematician, physicist, and inventor, acknowledged this reality through his philosophical inquiries. He discovered that there were inherent limits to human knowledge. For him, neither the scientific method nor reason in a broader sense could provide individuals with the meaning of life or guidance on how to lead a righteous life.

Pascal also delved into how humans often sought to evade contemplation of their mortality, the extent of their ignorance, and their propensity for error. Nonetheless, he firmly believed that nothing was of greater importance for individuals to ponder than their authentic human essence. From his perspective, comprehending who we are is an essential step towards grasping how we should lead our lives.

According to Pascal, gaining self-awareness represented a vital phase in the journey towards recognizing one's necessity for living with faith and a sense of purpose in something greater than oneself.'[16]

Within the body, mind, and Consciousness equation, Consciousness stands as the self-independent entity with eternal existence. 'The Self (pure Consciousness) is unmoving, indivisible; it is swifter than thought. The senses never reach it, as it is ever ahead of them. Though standing still, it outstrips those who run. And in it does the moving spirit support the activities of man.'[17]

Therefore, my perspective asserts that science approaches this realm by diligently mapping and recording the effects of changes in the intangible mind, which are revealed within the tangible brain. It is through this method that science strives to progress towards the realm of Consciousness.

In my understanding, this process mirrors the approach of physics, which utilized mathematical measurements to uncover the quantifiable value of energy transference to objects or bodies by observing their effects. Just as energy eludes direct sensory perception, so does the mind, which is an outcome of primordial energy. This mystery amplifies within the human body because the mind's behaviour varies across individuals. Thus, the mind and Consciousness are often bundled as one unit of the brain, for tracing the changes they cause inside our brain. This is perhaps the only option science has when it deals with metaphysical truths.

The *Tattva Bodha*, in further revelation, unveils that the imperceptible mind and the perceivable physical body are both manifestations of the same energy. Einstein's revelation—articulating mass and energy as distinct expressions of the same entity, and that all masses at rest will have energy inherent to them ($E=mc^2$)—echoes the Vedic proclamation, scientifically validating this connection. Invariably, the cause must always be present within the effect, albeit in some form.

It is, however, crucial to distinguish that the inherent energy mentioned isn't synonymous with pure Consciousness. This Supreme Consciousness permeates all entities, both manifest and unmanifest forms of energy, earning its distinct epithet as the ultimate reality, surpassing both known and yet-to-be-unveiled truths. The dynamic interconversion of energy and mass, as expounded in Einstein's mass–energy equivalence theory, is a perpetually shifting phenomenon within the objective world. However, this flux does not impinge upon Consciousness—the unwavering truth and observer of the ever-evolving objective realm.

This timeless awareness principle suffuses the cosmos, animating the entities duly ordained by the divine, yet retaining its autonomy. This knowledge gains validation from the fact that Consciousness is imperative to perceive presence or absence, activity or transformations within the universe. As the foundational pillar of existence—past, present, and future—it cannot die. Regardless of the world's existence or dissolution, Consciousness remains the confirming constant. Its essence remains distinct from matter, as the two by nature stand inherently opposed—one mutable, the other immutable.

UNRAVELLING THE GENESIS OF THE CREATIVE CYCLE

The third realization shattered my misconceptions about the immensely intricate macrocosm and microcosm realities. Grasping this understanding is vital to embracing the solution presented in this text, a solution that aims to eradicate all human predicaments stemming from our lack of awareness.

Macrocosm realities: Zooming out to the macro level, our misguided perception leads us to believe that the world and its myriad objects are a creation, whereas in truth, what we perceive are intricate alterations of entities that have always existed. In line with the philosophy of Vedanta, Consciousness stands as the primal existence predating the inception of the universe, before the very concept of time, even preceding the cosmic explosion known as the big bang. This epoch is termed 'singularity', a concept popularized by futurist Ray Kurzweil. Cosmic singularity denotes a point in space and time where the principles of conventional physics lose their grip.

It is imperative to note that Consciousness doesn't emanate from any identifiable source, nor is it a product of divine creation, for the genesis of anything necessitates a temporal moment—a concept inapplicable to Consciousness. It embodies the 'transcendental God', surpassing the confines of time and space. It's not an enigmatic entity secluded in some uncharted realm; rather, it's an intimate presence, closer to us than the dearest lover to the beloved.

Every element, including the cosmos itself, emanates from Consciousness. This designation holds because Consciousness antecedes everything conceived by the senses. Hence, Vedanta doesn't espouse the notion of creation but employs the term 'shrishti'—projecting the subtle into the tangible. This doesn't signify bringing something into existence from something non-existent; rather, it's a transformation from the subtle to the manifest state.

Before the inception of the creative cycle, the potency of Consciousness, known as 'Maya' in Vedanta, existed eternally as cosmic energy, along with living entities and other entities in their latent causal or seed state. None of these emerge abruptly in a fleeting instant, conjured by some phantom; rather, they emanate from Consciousness when due. In Vedanta, the creation of the universe is called shrishti, which is like the phase when everything unfolds and becomes diverse. Its dissolution is referred to as 'pralayam', which marks the end of this cycle when the entire universe, along with everything in its subtle form, returns to its original seed or latent state.

The perpetuity of matter and energy preservation stand as significant teachings within the Vedas. While the Vedic cosmological perspective bestowed by the ancient Indo-Aryan seers of the Indus Valley might lack empirical validation according to contemporary physics, it is worth noting that physicists recognize the harmony between Vedantic knowledge and rational thought. Encouragingly, the chasm between the understanding of the physics of the subject and the metaphysical truths enunciated in the Vedas is progressively narrowing.

This convergence is evidenced in the YouTube video, 'Who Created "Nothing" Our Universe Formed From'.[18]

The video elaborates on this concept, stating, 'According to the big bang theory, our universe once began to expand, inflating like a balloon. However, it is also theorized that, at some point, this expansion will reverse, causing the universe to contract and ultimately return to a state of cosmic singularity. And then, intriguingly, the cycle repeats itself, another big bang emerges seemingly from nothing and eventually disappears into nothing. According to Bucha Walt's theory, the birth of each universe marks the end of the previous one. Our universe is neither the first nor the last; countless similar universes have existed before us, and countless more will exist after us.'

MAYA'S PLACE IN THE COSMIC DESIGN

In the genesis of the creative cycle, Maya, the imperceptible cosmic energy, due to perturbations in its attributes, initially manifests itself much like a spark emerging from a fire's depths. Subsequently, it engages in the process of evolution, which ushers forth the twenty-four categories of manifestations, encompassing a spectrum of energies, culminating in the material world. This phenomenon aligns with the concept in physics known as 'everything comes from nothing', wherein the concealed energy takes centre stage.

It's essential to note that the term 'nothing' could lead one astray into believing that an absolute void preceded the big bang. This notion is erroneous, as even within nothingness, Consciousness persists, for it is Consciousness that grants us the cognizance of the nothingness we experience.

What fundamentally defines us as individuals aligns with the universe in every aspect, as previously mentioned. However, a deeper reality unfolds as part of our daily experience, known as the 'small bang reality'. Just before the onset of deep sleep, the three inherent energy propensities—Sattva, Rajas, and Tamas (SRT)—return to a state of equilibrium, and our mind and body transition into a latent mode.

In this state, the mind is only marginally capable of absorbing the illumination of the Atman, which remains ever-present. As a result, the reflected consciousness—the jivatma or conscious mind—briefly recedes. We become fully disconnected from the external world and all its experiences. Everything related to worldly identity and perception ceases to exist for the individual during this phase of deep sleep, a state referred to as 'layam', or dissolution.

After a short interlude, due to the restoration of disruption in the SRT configuration induced by the force of PK, we awaken with a gentle resurgence—a phenomenon I would refer to as the 'small bang'—when everything left behind before the beginning of deep sleep miraculously falls back into place. This reality stands unquestioned, much like the reality of a dream, an intricate creation of the mind during the dream state of human experience.

In this intriguing phase of human experience, while the individual, encompassing both body and mind, enters a dormant state resembling a seed in deep sleep, the everlasting presence of Consciousness continues to radiate through the latent potential of the individual's body and mind, thus upholding its existence. The conscious mind, devoid of any experiences, immerses itself in a state often characterized as pure ignorance, frequently likened to a sense of bliss, as both the subject and object of experience, all memories, and all the accumulated knowledge temporarily dissolve into Consciousness during this phase.

Regrettably, the Western world disregards this phase, dismissing it as a 'nil experience zone' in their pursuit of understanding physical realities. Yet, it is during this phase that everyone across the universe uniformly experiences their most cherished psychological desire: happiness.

Expanding this concept of deep sleep experience to the broader universe, which mirrors the individual on a grander scale, the universe dissolves into Consciousness in its potential state. This dissolution marks the transition from the manifest form of the physical world to an unmanifest form, occurring after each creative cycle, known as 'pralayam'.

On the individual level, deep sleep, or 'layam', represents dissolution. Similar to how, at the end of deep sleep, the same individual who had metaphorically dissolved re-emerges with a 'small bang', affirming the existence of the individual in a potential form and its return upon waking, the entire universe undergoes a parallel process.

Consequently, the entire universe, along with everything within it, re-emerges through a 'big bang' at the beginning of a new creative cycle.

While the manifestation (shrishti), preservation during the waking and dream states (sthithi) of an individual, and the individual's dissolution (layam) at the onset of deep sleep occur daily within a twenty-four-hour cycle, the comprehensive process at the universal level unfolds over an extensive period, spanning 4,320,000,000 years—referred to as one kalpaka.

Maya's (cosmic energy) attributes, also termed the Sattva, Rajas, and Tamas gunas in Vedanta, correspond to what I earlier denoted as the SRT factors in this discourse. Modern physics clarifies that everything we experience, at the deepest level, is made up of mysterious entities, fluid-like substances called quantum fields. These invisible fields sometimes act like particles, sometimes like waves. They can interact with one another; vibrate, and experience; even flow right through us.

Assuredly, human beings and other entities of this world can engage in actions solely within the encompassing presence of Consciousness. Maya, the fundamental energy, at the cosmic scale, assumes the identity of the cosmic mind. This cosmic mind gives rise to diverse energy forms and evolves into the realm of multiplicity, deriving its vitality solely from the Consciousness it obtains. Hence, deeming creation solely as an outcome of insentient cosmic energy's evolution reflects a profound lack of understanding. Maya, emblematic of our cosmic-level ignorance, contributes to presenting the singular Supreme Consciousness as a multitude.

From a philosophical vantage point, all the objects we perceive possess an illusory and transitory nature—mere designations and shapes, lacking inherent, self-standing existence. The world is not real and not unreal at the same time. It's not genuinely real, as it holds finite and dependent existence bereft of substantiality, unlike the self-sufficient, everlasting Consciousness. Yet, it isn't unreal, for its presence is discernible through our senses.

Microcosm realities: Similarly, at the micro level too, the situation mirrors these patterns precisely as in the macrocosm. It is ignorance that leads us to construct an ego, convincing ourselves of our prowess in all matters owing to our intellect, oblivious to the fact that the intellect itself lacks sentience and remains impotent without the vigour it gains in the presence of the omnipresent Consciousness.

If Consciousness uniformly pervades all objects within the world, why do we see disparities in capabilities amongst different living species, and particularly among different individuals?

Disparities in animating capacity, levels of intelligence, or even complete incapacity arise due to variations in the conditions or limiting adjuncts, known as upadhi, formed within the mind—the medium that absorbs and reflects Consciousness. It is essential to recognize that the inherent characteristics—PK in living beings and SRT in non-living beings—of each object play a crucial role as limiting factors, shaping how they manifest and interact within the world.

These limitations or conditions often influence the extent to which an object can absorb and reflect the energy or essence of Consciousness. The level of intelligence, the capacity to think and act, and even the inability to animate are all determined by these intrinsic traits, which ultimately shape their role in the larger scheme of existence. Upadhis act as distortions within this reflective medium, influencing and altering the reflection that emanates from the source, thereby ensuring the accomplishment of the dictates of PK.

When considering objects with animating abilities, it's important to understand that each object's characteristics act as limiting factors. Consciousness shines most brightly through life, especially through the mind, which includes the intellect (or antahkarana—the aggregate of mental faculties). This phenomenon is more evident in living beings than in the material world. The distinction helps explain why we perceive the world in a hierarchy, with living and non-living things arranged according to their ability to absorb and reflect Consciousness, and the capacity to animate from it.

Regarding the purpose behind the extensive exposition concerning creation and its associated matters within this text, my perspective aligns closely with Swami Nikhilananda's assertion in his English rendition of Shankaracharya's *Atmabodha* (*Self-Knowledge*, (Ramakrishna–Vivekananda Center, 1946), 'In connection with the Vedantic cosmology, it should always be borne in mind that its purpose is not to explain the universe and its origin but to establish, through it, the ultimate reality of Brahman (Consciousness). Apart from Brahman, the universe is unimportant, whether from the standpoint of reality or the standpoint of value. It is found to be non-existent in the deepest spiritual experience. Its value is transitory. But the reality of

Brahman, which exists independent of creation, is self-evident and is revealed in the innermost experience of man.'

Human beings uniquely cling to the limited constructs of body and mind. This attachment, driven by ignorance, traps us in a cycle of illusion, obscuring the finite nature and inherent limitations of these constructs. This attachment prevents us from recognizing and embracing the infinite, boundless Consciousness that is our true essence. As a result, ignorance, both at the macrocosmic and microcosmic levels, emerges as the fundamental cause of all human challenges and sufferings. These challenges manifest as Karma Phalam—the fruits of past actions—that must be experienced and resolved by individuals in their journey of existence.

THE DISCONNECT BETWEEN OBJECTIVE SCIENCE AND THE SUBJECTIVE BEING

Our current understanding of human anatomy is truly remarkable. Undoubtedly, the advancements made by medical science for the betterment of humanity are extraordinary. Yet, the enigmatic influence of Karma Phalam, which hinders the success of medical interventions, remains a puzzle that continues to elude scientific comprehension. At the forefront is the unpredictable nature of the human body's responses, presenting a perplexing challenge for the medical community while casting a discouraging shadow over patients.

For a deeper understanding of the effect of Karma Phalam (the fruits of one's actions), let us consider the case of a life-threatening medical condition called sepsis. This condition, marked by the body's extreme response to infection, serves as a powerful metaphor for how accumulated actions and their consequences can impact an individual's existence, often tipping the delicate balance of life itself.

A September 2019 article published by the National Institute of General Medicine elucidates: 'Sepsis is caused by an overwhelming immune reaction to an infection. The body releases immune molecules into the blood to combat the infection. These chemicals trigger widespread inflammation, which leads to blood clots and leaky blood vessels. As a result, blood flow is impaired, depriving the organs of nutrients and oxygen, which leads to organ damage. In severe cases, one or more organs fail. In the worst cases, blood pressure drops, the heart weakens, and the patient spirals towards septic shock. Once this happens, multiple organs—lungs, kidneys, liver—may swiftly fail, and the patient may die.' It adds that sepsis occurs unpredictably and can progress rapidly.

Not everyone experiences an overwhelming immune response to infection. This is a crucial aspect that warrants serious contemplation. Frequently, we hear doctors remark, 'Despite timely medical intervention, the patient's condition remains unresponsive.' Incidents have also been recounted where two individuals afflicted with similar medical conditions undergo treatment, yet only one recovers. Medical science often attributes this divergence to variations in immune levels. What led to the diminished immunity, and what were the underlying causes? Why was one person exposed to circumstances that compromised their immunity?

As our inquiries deepen, we approach a juncture where further questioning becomes implausible. It is the moment to acknowledge Karma Phalam. The realm of Karma Phalam is accessible solely to the mind, which in advance, initiates disruptions within the internal system, ushering in consequences that culminate in an individual's untimely demise or facilitate the restoration of the body to its previous state.

Below is a selection of a few actual events sourced from the internet that lend credibility to the aforementioned theory:

April 1937: Wallace Hume Carothers, the American chemist renowned for creating nylon, battled depression and tragically took his own life through poisoning at the age of forty-one.

June 1954: Alan Turing, an English scientist celebrated as a pioneer in computer science, mathematics, logic, and cryptography, died by suicide after consuming a cyanide-laced apple. His torment stemmed from the humiliation and anguish of his punishment. In 1952, Turing was convicted for 'Acts of Gross Indecency', due to his admission of a homosexual relationship. Given a choice between eighteen months of imprisonment and chemical castration, bringing about side effects like breast enlargement, he chose the latter. Had this incident occurred thirteen years later, following the decriminalization of homosexuality in Britain, he might have lived a peaceful life for a longer period.

Both Carothers and Turing, remarkable intellects, left an indelible mark on humanity. What inner turmoil drove them to embrace death?

July 2005: Bernard Ebbers (Berney), a key executive at WorldCom, orchestrated a colossal accounting fraud that led to his sentencing of for 25 years in prison. The scheme, aimed at inflating earnings to maintain the company's stock price, ultimately pushed WorldCom—the second-largest long-distance telephone company in the USA at the time—into bankruptcy in 2002. What motivated Berney to distort his intellect and engage in such egregious deception?

2010: An earthquake lasting a mere thirty seconds claimed approximately 200,000 lives and caused $8 billion in damages. The catastrophe's origins trace back to blind thrust faults[19] associated with the Enriquillo–Plantain Garden fault system. How did such a grave oversight occur?

2011: Dominique Strauss-Kahn faced arrest amid charges of sexual assault and attempted rape against a thirty-two-year-old hotel housekeeper named Nafissatou Diallo at the Sofitel New York. Though the judge eventually dropped all charges due to the complainant's perceived lack of credibility, the incident significantly marred Strauss-Kahn's reputation. At the time, he held a prestigious position as the head of the International Monetary Fund (IMF), and was a prominent contender for the 2012 French presidential election. Just four days after his arrest, he voluntarily resigned from his role at the IMF. What unforeseen force compelled a man of his stature to confront such humiliation and forfeit his chance at the French presidency?

From the likes of Robin Williams to Marilyn Monroe, from struggling farmers in India to accomplished engineering students ending their lives, the true narratives behind their tragic destinies remain elusive. The more we delve into these stories, the more enigmatic they become. Interestingly, during times of prosperity, few raise questions; yet when confronted with adversity—experiences all of us encounter at some point—few seek answers. Some attribute these events to fate, others believe there's a purpose, and then there are those who are indifferent to unravelling the underlying causes. Regardless of the reasons, the pain is undeniable.

SECTION THREE

WHAT AM I?

Chapter 8

UNFOLDING THE MYSTERY OF THE KNOWN

TORN BETWEEN A TEAR AND A SMILE—THE SECOND PERSON IMPACT

The sagely words of the late Shri Chandrasekara Swami of the Kanchi Mutt in southern India resonate with profound wisdom. In a discourse that now graces the treasury of *Deivathin Kural (Voice of God)*, a compendium of the sage's enlightening discourses, he cogently elaborates on the notion of the 'second person', attributing to it the genesis of insurmountable hindrances in every individual's journey.

Amid the light of day, during the waking state, our senses extend towards diverse external objects, orchestrated by the subtleties of the mind. Within the span of the external world resides the provocateur—the second person—who could be someone you love. The mind, when endeavouring to bestow benevolence upon a cherished one, is caught in a tussle. Often, this cherished individual occupies a familial position or holds a place within our inner sanctum. Closer scrutiny, however, discloses that love for the second person is essentially a yearning for self-love veiled under the guise of benevolence. The compulsion to extend goodwill to the second person stems from the pleasure garnered in return, even if these beloved individuals frequently serve as sources of anguish.

Conversely, when the second person does not inhabit our inner circle, the sentiment generally tends towards aversion or rivalry. While actions fuelled by our affection towards the second person may yield delight, those tainted by animosity and rivalry bear the fruit of wrath and disillusionment. The sting of such interactions can be so enduring that the echoes of their impact reverberate throughout the day, and sometimes weeks beyond.

Remarkably, the second person who extends happiness, distress, grief, anxiety, apprehension, and dread during wakefulness may reappear within dreams with even greater fervour. In the dream state, even as our senses repose, we continue to perceive mental projections, conjured by Vasnas stored in the subconscious. The dream reality feels tangibly authentic during its course, engendering significant distress.

A stark contrast emerges in the realm of deep slumber. Here, perception wanes and tranquillity reigns. In this state, the mind adopts a passive demeanour, and serenity blankets the realm. Curiously, our composite entity (the body–mind complex) remains sentient despite the mind's dormancy, for it is sustained by the ever-luminous Consciousness, the source of its sensibility. The bliss universally encountered during this phase retains an unwavering purity, impervious to the nuances of daily experiences.

However, this tranquil harmony dissipates upon awakening, as the second person of the external world once again comes into our purview through the conduit of senses and the mind. Indeed, all tribulations sprout from the presence of the second person. Hence, a logical inquiry ensues: can liberation be found through the annihilation of the second person? Yet, even if, hypothetically, all living entities were eradicated, the inert world's existence would persist.

Even if the entire cosmic kingdom were obliterated, pangs of hunger and thirst would torment, fear and anger would assail, resounding from the deepest hiatus of the self from action. Such sentiments surge forth from within each sentient being. When faced with these internal upheavals, what remedy can solitary contemplation provide? What then is the essence of advocating the abandonment of the second person to attain inner peace? Can such a feat be accomplished?

The mind, a tool of perception and connection, bridges people with the external world in wakefulness and the inner realm during dreams. Yet, in the depths of slumber, when the mind lies dormant, nothing is perceived. There is no world, no second entity; though their existence persists in distinct forms and places. Herein lies profound tranquillity. This serenity, born from the world's absence and the cessation of affliction, finds its roots solely in our stilled state of mind. Thus, the universe in its entirety, encompassing both the animate and inanimate, is but states of mind. As the mind recedes into latency, the universe's diverse entities dissolve from perception. Sufferings, distress, and pain linger only in tandem with the mind's presence.

Anaesthesia serves as an exemplar—under its influence, pain recedes even as physicians probe our very essence. Each night's slumber sustains the world, yet its impact remains insubstantial. The body alone becomes the vessel for pain, pleasure, and hunger; sensations roused solely when the mind awakens. Therefore, the second entity is neither another living being nor the world—it is the mind itself. Fear stems assuredly from this second entity. To fathom this truth, the assistance of the mind is requisite; paradoxically, to render it redundant, the mind's cooperation is indispensable—a paradox that is both philosophical verity and its jest.

Thus, by dissolving that mind, the second entity fades, yielding the non-dual state. With the second entity gone, actions cease, speech is stilled, wandering halts, obstructions vanish, and fatigue departs. In the absence of the mind, thoughts dissipate. With the mind's dissolution, the world's directional pulls and pushes wane. For you, the world fades into oblivion. Alone, you remain, untouched by varying emotions and urges, immersed in boundless serenity—an undisturbed peace. No voices shall bark to disrupt your equanimity. Full absorption of the mind into the Supreme Consciousness signifies attainment—'Samadhi' or 'Turiya' in Vedantic terms. In its embrace, you submerge in the tranquil ocean of bliss.

Unfortunately, the mind cannot grasp this blissful state achieved only in its absence.

DEEP DIVE INTO THE MIND

A recapitulation of the pivotal constituents of the mind is deemed imperative at this cross-roads. We must plumb the depths of the mind's structure, thereby gleaning the utmost bounty from our contemplative endeavours.

The mind, which springs forth from nature's loom, assumes a delicate mantle within the human form, holding sway as the pre-eminent player.

It functions as the junction where thoughts are intricately woven, mainly from the unevaluated impressions (Vasnas) arising from the sensory perception of worldly phenomena, seamlessly interlaced with linguistic expression. Following this fusion, the amalgamation undergoes meticulous scrutiny within the cognitive domain, where the discerning faculties of the mind come into play. In the subsequent stage, the ego factor, personified by the 'I' element, becomes interlinked, and the composite impression finds its abode in the repository of memory, crystallizing into a firm thought.

The potency of these Vasnas depends on the duration of their interaction with sensory objects. Their nature—virtuous or vicious—hinges on the character of the individual. When the mind is swayed by the restlessness and turmoil of Rajas or the darkness and inertia of Tamas during its engagement with the external world, negative Vasnas often arise. Conversely, the clarity of Sattva fosters positive imprints. Once kindled, these Vasnas give rise to desire, which transforms into thoughts before any action (karma) is undertaken to fulfil the yearning. The nature of karma—whether righteous (sattvic), ambitious (rajasic), or indolent (tamasic)—aligns with the thoughts that drive it.

An influential adjunct known as Ruchi resides within the mind, manifesting as an intense craving that reinforces desire and drives actions towards sensory gratification, irrespective of harmful consequences. The vice of smoking is a striking example of endeavours steered by Ruchi. Vasnas and Ruchi, inseparable companions, remain entrenched in the mind until they evolve into thoughts and relinquish their hold only after the corresponding action has been executed. Furthermore, these Vasnas play a pivotal role in shaping the structure of one's subtle reality—essentially, one's emotional personality.

The Karmas ensconced in the inner sanctum of the mind merit contemplation at this juncture. Dubbed as Prarabdha Karma or PK, we have already seen the actions heretofore executed, biding their time before the agent reaps their consequences. The twists of fate woven into these outcomes, as well as the broader mosaic encompassing life's joyful and melancholic phases, find root in PK. A force of great clout, it stands as the veritable progenitor of triumphs and tribulations encountered in life's sojourn. It wields dominion over intellect, as its influence is capable of mellowing the mind's acumen and diluting its volition. Prarabdha Karma ensures that one reaps the just rewards or consequences of actions performed in the past.

The mind houses all requisites for human function, except for the elixir of bliss. Hence, man's hunt often leads him to chase material ephemera in pursuit of happiness—a sentiment experiential in nature, conjured by the union of intellect and object.

The visible consequence of any action within the objective realm, over which one might boast, is only as valuable as the delight it brings—a delight formulated entirely within the mind's precincts.

Contentment emerges solely in moments of mental tranquillity; conversely, disquiet arises when the mind is perturbed by adverse circumstances. Objects, events, or entities in the external world act merely as catalysts rather than causative agents. All emotions, fundamentally, are internal experiences.

Reflection upon two key aspects of emotional encounters is warranted. Firstly, joy does not inherently reside within any animate or inanimate entity of the external milieu, unlike the innate sweetness of sugar. If such were the case, these entities would never result in unhappiness.

The second facet pertains to the ability to experience elation and sorrow even in solitude. For instance, in the context of music, if happiness were the inherent trait of music, anyone listening to it at any moment should invariably experience joy. However, the reality diverges from this notion.

When we listen to favourite music, the mind momentarily attains a tranquil state—a state conducive to assimilating an increased measure of reflection of the primal Consciousness, characterized by existence, consciousness, and bliss. This state activates the 'S' factor, triggering the release of pleasure-inducing hormones within the brain. This intricate orchestration unfolds within the subtle body, invisible to the eye. Regrettably, we erroneously ascribe the resultant pleasure to the music perceived by the sense organ. Similar processes unfold when seeking pleasure through other sensory avenues.

This truth is analogous to a dog savouring a bone for the satisfaction it derives from licking its blood, drawn from its gums due to friction. The dog remains unaware of the marrow's nutritional value in raw bones, particularly beneficial for glucosamine and chondroitin. The dog's delight in chewing the bone emanates from the erroneous identification of its blood as that of another creature, a fallacious attribution.

Conversely, in moments of mental turbulence, the 'T' factor or negativity predominates. The mind, then unsettled, fails to absorb the pristine reflection of blissful Consciousness, leading to feelings of sadness. Both joy and sorrow, it becomes evident, reside within us, and not in the external realm.

The human mind is endowed with exceptional potential and capabilities compared to the 'mind-like aspect' present in other sentient creatures. This remarkable attribute often fosters a belief in the all-encompassing power of the mind, despite it being the source of the suffering and anguish we encounter. Therefore, the elimination of the mind seems a plausible recourse to extinguish all distress. Alas, eradicating the mind stands as an infeasible proposition, as it would entail the cessation of our awareness of self (individual consciousness), signifying, in essence, the cessation of life itself.

THE MIND'S CRUCIAL ROLE

Knowledge or awareness assumes an illuminating role. However, the awareness manifesting within sentient beings is indirect; it manifests as a reflection. Within the human frame, it is solely the mind (a reflecting medium) that becomes sentient, propelled by the mere presence of Consciousness. Other constituents of the body (all but reflecting mediums) acquire sentience due to their connection with the mind. It is essential to note that the mind and body, along with all the objects within this universe, function as reflecting media. This fundamental concept is the very reason we can perceive them.

At this point, two key considerations warrant our thoughtful reflection. The first pertains to our understanding of the singular principle of awareness, referred to as Consciousness. This radiant essence directs its illuminating gaze upon everything, whether it be the objects bathed in light or the profound darkness that surrounds itself. Every manifestation, whether currently present or not within the tapestry of creation, serves as a medium or conduit for the sole reflection of Consciousness.

The second aspect concerns the power that animates these forms, endowing them with their vitality. This life force is sustained only when Consciousness reflects through the intellect, situated within the contemplative mind's recesses. The potency of this impartial reflection of Consciousness, instilled within the constituents, varies from the abyss of nothingness to its zenith. This range of potential is dictated by the nature and extent of the limiting adjuncts that enshroud the mind's core.

In truth, the extent of this variance, the expanse of animating potential, is governed by the Karma Phalam, intricately interwoven into the very fabric of sentient beings, and by the intricate architecture of SRT (Sattva—Rajas—Tamas), etched into the countenance of the inert world.

Thus, in an entity with a dense physical form, where the light of intellect does not shine, the possibility of life and movement remains dormant, like a sleeping ember.

The functional, small 'i', comprising pure matter, erroneously identifies the reflected consciousness as real and appropriates attributes to itself such as agency, experience, birth, growth, decay, and death while the changeless 'I', the Supreme Self or Consciousness, stands as a distinct, superior echelon of reality. It predates all actions and cognition. No bodily action can transpire without the underpinning of the authentic 'I', the big 'I'. It serves as an essential prerequisite to existence. (Chapter 28 explains this feature in greater detail.)

Knowledge emerges in the objective world of physical science as humanity employs sensory faculties to gather information, later confirmed through empirical evidence. This form of understanding evolves, shaped by reason, which can be challenged and refined by superior reasoning. Millennia ago, ancient sages, through the elevated faculties of their minds, discovered the transcendental wisdom of Supreme Consciousness—the singular, immutable reality. This all-encompassing essence stands unrivalled as the sole witness to all events within the universe and beyond. Immersed in this sacred realization, the sages experienced an enduring state of unbroken and infinite bliss.

Vedic meditation serves as a guiding beacon for spiritual seekers striving to comprehend and embody this profound truth. Yet, the essence of this meditation lies beyond the reach of sensory perception. The realm of the spirit unveils itself only to those who diligently prepare through the fourfold discipline (sadhana chatushtaya), as meticulously prescribed in Vedantic scriptures. This preparatory practice purifies the mind from attachments to the material world. Over time, the restless mind comes to recognize its limited role within the interplay of body, mind, and Consciousness.

This transformative journey unfolds in a structured sequence, encompassing three interconnected components: Shravanam (attentive listening), Mananam (thoughtful contemplation), and Nidhidhyasanam (deep meditation). Shravanam and Mananam facilitate the conscious acquisition and intellectual grasp of knowledge, while Nidhidhyasanam fosters the profound absorption of this understanding into the subconscious mind. Through this meditative process, negative emotions rooted in the subconscious dissipate, easing the oscillation between joy and sorrow. The practice continues until unwavering conviction arises, revealing one's true essence as inseparable from the eternally free and serene Consciousness.

At this point, a transformative realization takes hold. Intriguingly, it is by embracing this very principle—coupled with sustained focus—that many luminaries in the material world have attained their goals. This latent potential resides within everyone. Once an individual recognizes their authentic nature through meditation, the practice itself becomes unnecessary, as its purpose has been fulfilled. Continuing it would only create a distraction, and spark a new struggle. The enlightened being transcends the need for meditation, forever dwelling in the ecstasy of pure Consciousness.

SRT FACTORS—ENERGY PROPENSITIES

We have grasped how the SRT factors impact the moulding of our inner personality, guiding our thoughts, desires, and actions. Unfulfilled desires and repeated failures directly contribute to heightened average stress levels. It is crucial to grasp the intricacies of SRT, as merely attempting to alleviate the effects without reconfiguring these factors will render our efforts futile.

The acronym SRT defines the three inherent energy propensities within every object of creation, and serves as the key to developing the inner personality or inner strength of both animate and inanimate entities. Similar to how genes are passed down from parents, these propensities naturally find their place within manifest objects. As we have already explored, the interplay of these propensities is responsible for all the internal changes we experience, and these transformations are mirrored in the external characteristics of all objects without exception.

The perpetual friction between Rajas and Tamas is the root cause of the contradictions and ever-shifting behaviours observed in human beings. Sattva, with its harmonizing nature, acts as the sole mediator to reconcile these conflicts. However, when the arbitration activity dominated by Sattva continues indefinitely, the Sattva factor weakens over the course of an object's life.

In lower species, Tamas, followed by Rajas, typically holds sway. Interestingly, in certain species displaying calm and kind behaviour, a higher proportion of Sattva is evident. This indicates that they have nearly exhausted the consequences of their past actions (karmas) performed as sub-humans, and are once again poised to attain human status in future births. Generally, they are born as herbivores. This possibility is not available to inanimate objects, which are predominantly Tamas-dominant. At the end of their life cycles, they integrate with one of the elements of nature and either return in a new form or eternally merge with the element itself.

Sattva—'S' Factor

Sattva embodies harmony and peace. Typically, God's energy (cosmic forces—the sun, the moon, and the universal energies) is predominantly the 'S' energy, evident in its vast benevolent acts, all working in harmony for the benefit of nature and every living being.

It's the energy associated with virtues such as self-control, compassion, contentment, positivity, and spirituality, which are evident in people. Innovation and the inclination to contribute positively to humanity through creative ideas stem from this energy. Whether found at the core or in its floating form, Sattva embodies virtue and positivity. It doesn't matter where it resides; it's a force for good. Qualities like empathy and tolerance, which naturally attract people and open doors to favour, emanate from Sattva. This energy also serves as a defence against self-deception and the detrimental outcomes it brings. It's worth noting that self-deception is a significant factor contributing to failed marriages and the underperformance of teams within organizations.

Regrettably, many individuals struggle to cultivate this crucial energy, often being predominantly influenced by either Tamas or Rajas. When life takes a downturn due to the effects of past actions (karma), having an abundance of Sattva becomes essential, but it is not something that can be acquired overnight. This highlights the ongoing need for us to remain conscious of nurturing and preserving Sattva in our lives.

Rajas—'R' Factor

Rajas serves as the primary force of activity in the universe. It's the driving energy behind turning ideas into reality. However, when Rajas dominates, it often brings along negative traits like jealousy, pride, egotism, and anger, among others.

Tamas—'T' Factor

Tamas, on the other hand, is characterized by lethargy and negativity. Individuals dominated by Tamas can display toxic attitudes and behaviours. They tend to be lazy and lack the drive to work or achieve their goals. A person may be dominantly influenced by Tamas at a physical or psychological level, or both.

At the beginning of life, every human being exhibits dominance of T energy, as seen in the two primary activities of a child: sleeping (lethargy) and crying or displaying resentment (negative behavior). Tamas is gradually reduced as the influence of rajas grows. With the maturation of the child, the drive to achieve and derive pleasure from accomplishments further boosts Rajas. However, as individuals confront the challenges of the world and encounter karmic obstacles in the pursuit of their desires, Tamas may resurface, flooding them with negative energy.

Throughout this life journey, without an understanding of the SRT factors, people often neglect the development of Sattva, which is crucial for regaining the motivation to work and experience even small moments of joy.

It is important to note that for those enjoying a favourable PK, the play of SRT factors has little significance.

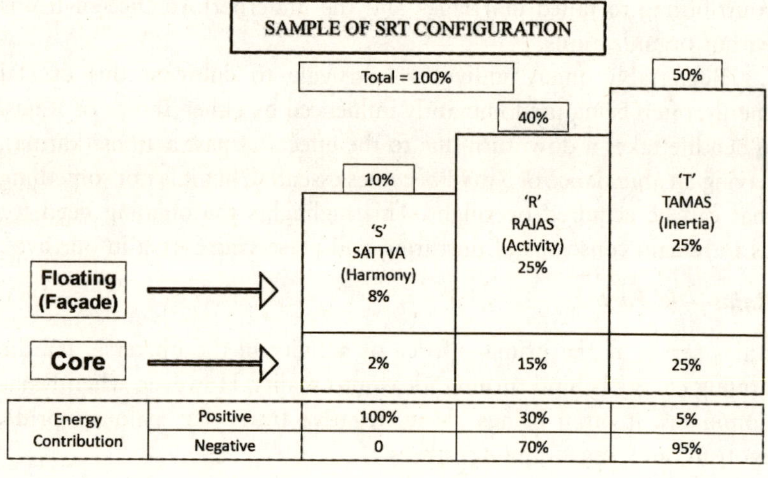

Energy Contribution		S	R	T
	Positive	100%	30%	5%
	Negative	0	70%	95%

A few key points to remember about SRT:

1. The total sum of SRT always adds up to 100 per cent.
2. Each propensity can be broken down into core and floating components. Core SRT represents an individual's inner character, whereas floating SRT shapes the external personality that an individual utilizes to navigate and influence, or even manipulate various situations.
3. The floating portion is highly reactive to experiences and situations. Often, we tend to judge individuals based solely on their floating SRT. For instance, we might say, 'He appears angry, but deep down, there's a softer side,' which signifies the presence of floating Rajas and core Sattva.
4. Cultivating Sattva can be challenging in a society driven by competition and greed, as it is the energy most needed, yet also the most fragile—and it can diminish easily.
5. To thrive in life, the optimal combination would be to have 60 per cent Rajas, 25 per cent Sattva, and 15 per cent Tamas energy.

ENGINEERING SUCCESS THROUGH SRT MANAGEMENT

It is easier said than done. Four facets beckon acknowledgement if we earnestly harbour to prosper in the material world. Karma Phalam, SRT configuration, Vasna, and the latitude of free will stand as the quartet. The fruit of karma is immutable and inconvertible which allows neither reversal, negotiation, nor transfer. The conquest of Vasnas proves formidable. Thus, SRT and free will remain in contention.

The essence of SRT governance rests in adeptly mastering the following. It is aimed at deliberately enhancing the 'S' factor at every opportunity to preserve the equanimity of the mind:

1. **Renounce ego:** The ego, or the small 'i' is a construct composed of the body, mind, and reflected consciousness (RC)—a reflection of the Supreme Consciousness upon the mind, which acts as a mirror. We acquire the body to experience the results of past actions and perform new deeds. This gives the body the role of the doer. However, a closer examination reveals that the body

cannot act on its own. It requires the mind to become conscious, and the mind, in turn, relies on Consciousness to function. How, then, can the body or the mind be considered the true doer? At best, they are instruments designed to perceive and engage with the world.

As such, the body and mind cannot claim the identity of the true 'I'—the subject—which essentially is the ego. These entities are merely pseudo-egos, temporary agents destined to perish. The true 'I', or authentic Ego, is none other than the Supreme Consciousness. From the perspective of Consciousness, the body–mind complex is a false entity. However, the mistaken belief that this complex constitutes the ego is the source of all human suffering.

This misunderstanding—the coexistence of knowledge about the body and ignorance of its inability to act independently—creates the division between the false self and the false world. It gives rise to egoism, where we see ourselves as independent entities, and egotism, where we claim superiority over others. Consequently, the ego takes a central role among the negative traits in an individual, fuelling harmful behaviours and diminishing life's quality. Despite its damaging influence, humans remain closely attached to the ego, often resisting the idea of letting it go.

2. **End self-deception:** Self-deception manifests in the engagement or disengagement from actions contrary to the dictates of our conscience. This quality takes root in the negative Vasnas we foster and nurture over time, abetted by the dominant presence of the 'I' factor. In addition, the emotional bonds we forge, coupled with the expectations they bear and their subsequent non-fulfilment, cultivate a sentiment of aversion that, with time, metamorphoses into animosity.

   At a certain juncture, the burgeoning aversion or, dare we say, hatred towards another individual or object compels actions contrary to our conscience, precipitating self-betrayal. It stands as the primary cause of relationship breakdowns and the dissemination of negative vibes within teams, resulting in underperformance in both corporate and social spheres.

   The practice of Karma Yoga proffers a remedy for the cessation of self-deception, entailing:

- cultivating a habit to generate positive Vasnas, and thereafter,
- abandoning lamentation and refraining from uttering disparaging words about any individual in their absence, as well as abstaining from futile disputes, for such endeavours yield no meaningful transformation.

It is imperative to remind oneself that to complain is to resist the ordained state, and argumentation strives to alter another's perspective on a given matter. Resistance to circumstances bereft of choice elevates average stress levels (ASL). The triumph of argumentation seldom alters the deeply held convictions of those entrenched in their beliefs. Nevertheless, the impulse to impose our views upon others persists unabated.

Individual convictions, forged in the crucible of personal experiences and beliefs, render them with a sense of justification for their perspectives. A conscious exploration of these facets can diminish the inclination to brood, thereby reducing the animosity and agony that begets self-betrayal or deception.

3. **Be kind:** Manifesting kindness, even if feigned, promptly soothes the perturbed mind of the other in a relationship. For karma-yogis, this flows effortlessly, as they have disciplined their mind through the fourfold qualification. They extend empathy towards those who exhibit unkindness, readily pardoning them and recognizing them as victims of their own ignorance.
4. **Accept situations with limited choice:** For well over two-thirds of our existence, individuals encounter situations devoid of choice. A third of their existence is irretrievably ensnared by the past, and another third is inexorably absorbed by the present, the very moment it unfolds. The limited control over the future is not difficult to anticipate.

A venerable sage once imparted that the acceptance of choiceless situations, devoid of resistance, stands as the optimal means to keep the mind from succumbing to agitation.

Much like the expanse of space, permit your mind to ascend above those who orchestrate choiceless predicaments, which can be both exasperating and odious. Observe how space accommodates all transgressions committed by humanity. Yet, at no instance, does it suffer harm or disturbance; it does not beckon them to depart, for it knows, in due course, they shall depart of their own accord, without prompting. It embraces reconciliation instead of retaliation. This mirrors the interaction of fire with air (wind), and water with earth. It is truly remarkable, and this is what a karma-yogi, who has heightened the 'S' factor through deliberate effort, wholeheartedly embraces.

5. **Accept the laws of nature and karma, and be prepared to act anew:** As long as we dwell within the confines of the physical world, the laws of nature and karma remain in force—unaffected by our beliefs about whether the world is real or illusory. Whether one is pious or cruel, religious or atheist, these laws operate impartially, binding all without exception. In each action we undertake, the outcome shall deviate from our expectations, contingent upon numerous extraneous factors over which we exert no control. Changes in the SRT factors of those individuals influencing the results of our actions can dramatically alter the outcome. Similarly, the Karma Phalam to be endured by an individual influences the consequences of an action.

   Accepting this reality is a paramount virtue of the wise who prepare to embark on the next endeavour without being unduly affected by the negative repercussions of the previous action. Here, the synergistic interplay of the 'R' and 'S' factors works marvellously to rebound from the psychological setbacks induced by failures.

6. **Engage in Upasana Yoga (meditation):** The significance of Upasana Yoga practice through diverse meditative techniques cannot be underestimated in the management of SRT configuration for success. It stands as the most potent tool at our disposal to elevate the core level 'S' factor. When genuine devotion to the divine is expressed, be it through Japa-mantra chanting or praying in silence, the 'R' and 'T' factors are contained throughout the entire period of engaging in such activities, automatically allowing the 'S' factor to momentarily increase. Over time, this leads to a gradual ascent in the core 'S'. Furthermore, Upasana Yoga pacifies the turbulence in the SRT factors, thereby calming the individual. It is imperative to acknowledge that Upasana Yoga is an active pursuit that demands an investment of time and effort, a challenge for individuals dominated by the 'T' and 'R' factors. Indeed, it is worthwhile to engage in this practice before an interview or an important meeting.

SECTION FOUR

WHO AM I?

Chapter 9

UNFOLDING THE MYSTERY OF THE UNKNOWN

SUPREME REALITY BEYOND PERCEPTION

Throughout this text, a consistent emphasis is placed on the core teachings of Vedanta, which unequivocally assert that ignorance (avidya) lies at the very heart of all human suffering. It is not external circumstances, but our fundamental misapprehension of reality—mistaking the transient for the eternal, the body for the Self—that breeds pain, fear, and bondage.

In this endeavor, it is important to understand that acquiring knowledge is only the penultimate step; it must ultimately culminate in the direct discovery of truth. Throughout the process of learning, one must remember that intellectual understanding alone is not sufficient. What is essential is the direct realization of our true nature—an essence inseparable from the Supreme Consciousness (Brahman), the boundless, ever-free, and blissful reality underlying all existence.

The role of the guru in this journey is to impart knowledge and point the way. However, the actual realization must arise from within. No external force or individual can bestow liberation. Ultimately, it must be self-realization—a truth discovered in the silent depths of one's being.

It is therefore imperative to inquire into the nature of this Supreme Consciousness. What is it that animates all life, yet remains changeless? What is the substratum of all experience, yet beyond it? To know *That*—to know the self—is to be free.

To know this truth is to awaken spiritually. This awakening is not about becoming something new, but about remembering what we are; the unchanging witness, the eternal Self—untouched by birth, death, or limitation.

Nothing can come into being without its presence. Every object of perception, whether seen or unseen, is revealed only through the light of Consciousness, the foundation upon which all existence rests. Thus, our ultimate and true identity as sentient beings is inseparable from this underlying Consciousness.

Every aspect of our experience, including our body and mind, manifests as diverse expressions of the one, indivisible Consciousness. Even within the realm of physical science, it is awe-inspiring to observe that everything in existence—from the tiniest duckweeds to the majestic blue whales, and the intricate human body and mind—acts as a mirror, reflecting the wonder of creation, all unified by the single principle of 'awareness'. Therefore, we are not separate from the world; we are the world, and the world is us.

Indeed, everything that breathes into existence must invariably arise within the cradle of Consciousness, for it predates every act of perception. From this perspective, a diminutive blade of grass, an imposing behemoth like an elephant, a soul steeped in sanctity, or even an individual draped in the guise of infamy, all emerge from the womb of Consciousness. When examined through the lens of intellect, they reveal their transient nature, devoid of independent existence beyond the realm of Consciousness, much like the waves that are inseparable from the ocean itself.

Yet when we observe the countless facets of the cosmos, we are often inclined to perceive them as separate entities, influenced by two key factors. First, we associate them with their name and form, and second, the object under observation exists physically detached from us. Our awareness, whether limited or expansive, colours the canvas of our mind, obscuring the true essence of the object and its inherent authenticity.

Thoughts intertwined with the object of knowledge saturate our minds, creating a barrier as we move across the mental gap between ourselves and the object, no matter how small that gap may be. However, in moments of profound revelation, we realize that nothing in the cosmos, not even the cosmos itself, can exist outside the observer's Consciousness. With this insight, thoughts about the object, distance, and time fade away. The object's very existence dissolves as the Consciousness of the observer rejects its separate identity. Space and time vanish, and the structure of thoughts unravels, merging the observer and the observed into a unified whole. This, indeed, is the realm of intellectual actuality.

This sacred Consciousness, the formless spirit, eludes the grasp of conventional instruments of understanding. Its true essence reveals itself only through the negation of all objects of experience, leaving Consciousness as the solitary witness in the void. Its singularity, unmatched and unrepeatable, arises from its complete divergence from any element in the cosmos, defying all comparisons. Our only path lies in comprehending Consciousness through its intrinsic nature, encapsulated in the triad of 'existence, knowledge, and bliss'. As the infinite spirit, it transcends the boundaries of time, space, and the material world. Indeed, all transformations occur within the realm of space and time, leaving Consciousness as the sole embodiment of changelessness. Awakening to the realization that this is the singular, absolute, and unchanging reality, simultaneously interlacing our past, present, and future moments, unfolds as a revelation of profound significance.

Consciousness serves as the source of all knowledge, offering deep insights into every facet of existence, and revealing an array of emotions. It is the all-pervading, eternal Supreme Self of both manifest and unmanifest objects perceptible to keen minds and discernible in every aspect of reality; even that which is imagined. Consciousness is present in all, whether it is the expanse of space, the gentle breeze of air, the fierce blaze of fire, the flowing currents of water, the solid stability of earth, the intricate beings of humans and animals, or even the steadfast demeanour of rocks. Thus, the wise, attuned to this divine presence, may stand alone—yet never experience loneliness.

This act of visualizing the entire universe within the Consciousness, the divine essence residing inside the individual body and uniting with it, is termed as 'Vishwa Roopa Darshanam', or the universal form of God. Its description in the Bhagavad Gita (chapter 11) offers a profound understanding of the interconnectedness of all beings and the eternal companionship found in divine union.

Take a moment to reflect: all phenomena, including you and me, are diverse manifestations; each tethered to unique identities, and characterized by distinct names and forms on the surface. Through introspection, a deeper wisdom emerges, revealing the fundamental truth that the external reality we perceive exists solely within the realm of our Consciousness. The countless objects and forms around us lack independent existence; their sustenance and motion are inseparably linked to the Brahman (Consciousness). Without Consciousness, nothing can be understood, experienced, or acted upon—not our actions, decisions, or even the deeds of others. In this realization, we uncover that our true Self, our identity is the Consciousness, which in essence is uniform for all the diverse manifestations in the universe.

However, until we shed the veil of ignorance that obscures the truth of our authentic Self—inseparable from Consciousness and reflecting the essence of others and all creation—we remain blind to the unity that underlies all existence. This fundamental essence, the inner reality, and the all-encompassing Consciousness that flows through every fragment of the universe, and even transcends it, is identified as the Supreme Self, known as Brahman in Vedanta philosophy.

One should not mistake Brahman for a name in the conventional sense, as doing so risks reducing it to the realm of names and forms—the ever-changing world of diversity. Brahman is not a personal deity or an object among other objects; it is not a thing with attributes, but the formless, unchanging essence of all.

The word Brahman is derived from the Sanskrit root 'b.rh', which simply means 'vastness'. It signifies that which is boundless and beyond limitation.

In the *Taittiriya Upanishad*, Brahman is described as 'Satyam jnanam anantam brahma' ('Brahman is Truth, Knowledge, and Infinity'). This description affirms that Brahman is the absolute reality, limitless and indivisible, beyond all dualities and distinctions.

The true identity of the individual is not other than the Supreme Self; they are the same. To apprehend Brahman is to understand the cosmos and all that lies beyond, as the differences we perceive among diverse entities are merely surface-level distinctions arising from conditions, names, and forms.

Yet, recognizing the distinctions among phenomena is vital for navigating the functional world. Treating a man and a woman, a lion and a sparrow, or a towering mountain and a flowing river as identical would be impractical, given their clear differences. Indeed, such differences are necessary for order and coherence in our daily interactions; without them, chaos would ensue. However, while acknowledging these differences, it is equally important to reflect on a deeper truth: all these varied entities are expressions of one Consciousness, each manifesting in its unique form, structure, and capacity.

Consider this analogy: a stone, a tree, a piece of glass, and a body of water—all reflect light differently, shaped by their distinct properties. Despite these differences, the essence of the light remains unchanged. Similarly, the variations we observe in living and non-living beings do not alter their intrinsic essence, which is Consciousness itself.

The *Aitreya Upanishad* beautifully illuminates this truth, asserting that Consciousness is the very medium through which we see forms, hear sounds, detect aromas, articulate speech, and discern what is pleasing or displeasing.[20]

Could it be that the vast diversity we observe in the world is merely a multitude of expressions arising from one underlying essence? If we truly understood this, how might it transform our perception of the world—and our place within it?

THE UNITY IN EXISTENCE

The significance of understanding Brahman, which reveals that the observer (you) and the observed (the world) are inherently one, much like the ocean and its waves, cannot be underestimated. By grasping this unity that connects all of existence, we gain the ability to engage with reality, take action or respond, without getting caught in thoughts that create barriers between us and the world.

As long as we view the world as separate from ourselves and focus only on the external traits of the objects we encounter, we remain vulnerable to being influenced by attraction or aversion. These emotional reactions are a reflection of the duality that shapes our experience. Moreover, as long as we identify with the workings of our body and mind, seeing apparent distinctions as reality, we continue to be swayed by forces that will inevitably lead us off course.

Living in a world of apparent duality, it is human nature to feel inadequate or distressed when we notice disparities in societal status, driven by factors like reputation and material possessions, even though we recognize that these things are temporary and come with their costs.

Indeed, the false belief that worldly riches can improve our quality of life, elevate our social standing, and bring peace and security drives people to take any measure necessary to imitate others. It is much like the absurd desire of a golden bracelet, wishing to hang from the earlobe of a beautiful maiden, hoping to receive the same attention as a finely crafted earring. Though both are made of gold, they are distinct in form and purpose.

All perceived disparities between individuals are merely superficial, for at our core, we are fundamentally made of the same spirit and matter. While we share this essential similarity—a combination of oxygen, hydrogen, carbon, nitrogen, water, phosphorus, and sulphur—we, during our existence, shall only receive what is destined for us and nothing more, as stated by the doctrine of Karma. Therefore, if we regard surface-level differences as reality, contradictions, comparisons, and internal and external conflicts are bound to arise.

We are bound to pursue actions beyond what is needed for physical survival, driven by unnecessary desires and unnatural cravings that may or may not be fulfilled, depending on each individual's unique karmic disposition. When the virtuous actions of individuals in their current lives do not yield the desired results, the six negative forces of yearning, anger, greed, illusion, envy, and unhealthy competition are stirred within the mind.

The virtuous may transform into the malevolent, first deceiving themselves, and then resorting to unlawful and unethical actions in pursuit of fleeting desires.

Striving to improve our social standing involves navigating a vast world full of deceptive forces, a challenge even for those with a strong will. We must remain vigilant, guarding against harmful intentions and the unpredictability of the external world, which can be overwhelming and difficult to counter without the necessary resources. The need to avoid evil and find contentment through both noble and less honourable actions seems to be the only option unless one chooses to serve the demands of society as a subordinate.

When even the pursuit of mundane desires falters, we are overwhelmed by a sense of disorientation and paralysis. Our limitations as finite beings become apparent, leaving us helpless when we lose sight of our true essence and become trapped in the distractions of body, mind, and ego. In these moments, we unconsciously begin to rely on the external world and a personal deity for support, driven by attachment and expectations.

The individual is enmeshed in dependence, as Immanuel Kant espoused—'Man holds a structural bond with three entities—God, the world, and the soul.' Man remains bound, incapable of escaping the triad composed of man (the pseudo-experiencer), object (the world), and the Lord (personal deity), all of which find their foundation in the supreme Brahman, untouched by the vagaries of phenomena, as expounded in the *Svetasvatara Upanishad*.

Relentlessly, we search for happiness in the wrong places, only to suffer as we navigate the difficult and uncertain paths of the material world, until we eventually reach Brahman—the true source of wisdom. In conclusion, we are none other than the Supreme Consciousness, regardless of the body we inhabit. The wise recognize this truth and claim their real identity when they declare: Aham Brahmasmi—I am Brahman.

Chapter 10

BEYOND THE BOUNDARIES OF THE MATERIAL WORLD

CONSCIOUSNESS IS A METAPHYSICAL TRUTH

In earlier sections, we delved into how individuals, despite being connected as children of the same divine source, often face struggles stemming from ignorance of their true nature—Consciousness, the foundation of existence, and our connection to the universe and one another. Vedanta emphasizes that the divine plays no role in the varied experiences humans undergo; these are consequences of their actions. Furthermore, it highlights how our attachment to the body and mind serves as the root cause of our trials and tribulations. The mind, caught in the web of ignorance and unaware of its limitations, perpetuates this turmoil. Vedanta teaches that understanding Consciousness is crucial, as only by recognizing it as our true essence can we overcome these human challenges.

Far from being just a religious belief, Vedanta is a philosophical guide revealing the universal truth that underlies all existence and illuminates everything in creation. The ancient Indo-Aryans discovered this knowledge, which became the spiritual cornerstone of India by divine coincidence, though it is not confined to any religion, race, or nation.

Like other great discoveries, the knowledge of Brahman is accessible to all. As the *Chandogya Upanishad* states, 'He who knows the Self overcomes grief.' By realizing Consciousness as one's true Self, a person also recognizes it as the essence of all beings.

Aldous Huxley extolled Vedanta as a singular and timeless philosophy—not merely a treasure of Indian thought, but a universal beacon of wisdom, offering guidance to all of humanity in its search for truth, harmony, and liberation. For those who are stable like a house of cards, Vedanta imparts the wisdom to accept the inevitable vicissitudes of life without resistance, much like majestic rocks that silently cradle the ceaseless waves of the ocean, which persistently caress them with a purpose. Mountains know that they emerge from the ocean and erode over time to return to it—a natural design and an irreversible blueprint which the enlightened mountains embrace with grace.

Over the past century, science has attempted to understand Consciousness—the singular, eternally still essence that underlies the restless world. Yet, the profound mysteries of life, deeply rooted in every human heart, have resisted full scientific understanding. Consciousness, being indivisible, cannot be dissected or analysed. All living forms exist unmanifest within Consciousness before coming into being, much like yoghurt, butter, and purified butter are forms of milk that always existed within it.

From this perspective, Brahman may appear as the cause of creation, but within Brahman, cause and effect do not coexist. Unlike other creations where the cause dissolves into the effect, Consciousness remains unchanged and independent even after the universe arises from it.

Vedanta, therefore, asserts that there is no real creation; what we perceive is merely an illusion. On the physical level, the energy within Brahman manifests as the universe, but analyzing this illusion cannot reveal the foundation of all existence as this foundation transcends the realm of cause and effect, and remains beyond the grasp of scientific inquiry.

Furthermore, Consciousness cannot be understood through our senses because it is not an object of empirical study. Consciousness alone can explain what Consciousness is. Scientists need to perform the impossible task of experimenting on the infinite Consciousness, which is our nature, our real Self, and the Self of every living and non-living being, whether we realize this truth or not. 'In the unique case of Consciousness, the thing to be explained cannot be observed. We know that Consciousness exists not through experiments but through our immediate awareness of our feelings and experiences. We should not be surprised that our standard scientific method struggles to deal with Consciousness', writes Philip Goff of Durham University.

This is why scientists struggle to formulate a definitive theory about Consciousness. The challenge does not stem from their shortcomings but from the limitations of human faculty itself. While science excels at unravelling the physical universe, it falters when faced with subtle, unmanifest phenomena. However, we cannot dismiss science entirely, as we live in an age where its practical applications and technological advances shape our daily lives—it works if it works.

All beings and objects follow the cycle of being unmanifest at the beginning, manifest in the middle, and returning to the unmanifest at the end. Science, despite its sophistication, can only engage with matter in its manifest state, leaving untouched what lies before or after. Dr P. Nagaraja Rao aptly explains this limitation in *Introduction to Vedanta* (1966): 'For concepts to work, scientists abstract a simplified private universe from the entire Reality, arbitrarily selecting qualities their methods can successfully address. This technique leads to astonishing success.'

Consciousness, however, is an eternal, independent entity, too subtle to be perceived by the senses or measured by scientific instruments. Even energy, a subtler form of inert matter in its unmanifest state, eluded scientific understanding for a long time. Its potential was only indirectly uncovered through the effects it produces when manifest. Consciousness, transcending even energy in subtlety, remains beyond the reach of empirical methods.

The doctrine of Vedanta proclaims that ignorance is dispelled when one attains the correct understanding of one's true Self which is Consciousness. And this can be comprehended through the knowledge bestowed by the scriptures and a capable guru. Consciousness stands as a metaphysical truth beyond the realm of direct experience, eternally occupying the role of the subject and never that of the object of knowledge.

As a result, it remains beyond the scope of any scientific experiment, regardless of how many aeons pass. The fundamental subject–object conundrum presents an insurmountable challenge for physical science in its pursuit to understand Consciousness. This is because science tends to treat Consciousness as an object of experience and endeavours to grasp it through experimental means. However, for a deeper understanding of our true Self, we must turn to a specialized instrument: the wisdom found in the Vedas.

Even when examining the physical world, the use of appropriate sense organs is essential to perceive corresponding sense objects. Just as we cannot expect our ears to affirm what our eyes have not observed, science finds itself lacking the necessary tools to engage with the intrinsic nature of Consciousness.

The Yogic method of attaining direct experience of Consciousness through Ashtanga Yoga, renowned for its demanding and methodical approach, might not be a sustainable solution. After all, Consciousness constitutes our inherent reality, and we naturally take on the role of the experiencer, the subject, when we engage with any objects of experience. The conundrum lies in how we can attempt to experience Consciousness when, in truth, we are the Consciousness itself. The paradox deepens as we ponder how we can simultaneously occupy the positions of both the observer and the observed. Not until we harmonize with our authentic nature, transcending the dualities where both subject and object dissolve into the singular essence of Brahman, can we truly understand our undifferentiated existence.

The philosophy of Vedanta is large-hearted, capable of embracing the diverse genetic heterogeneity of the universe with empathy and compassion. It refrains from mocking the limitations of other disciplines or philosophies concerning transcendental knowledge. For a Vedantist, it would be a crime to assail the intellect of physics or dismiss the wisdom of metaphysics. Instead, the essence lies in learning from both. As Dr S. Radhakrishnan aptly puts it, 'The partial truths of science differ from the whole truth of the spirit. Scientific knowledge is beneficial as it dispels the darkness that clouds the mind, reveals the incompleteness of its world, and prepares the mind for something beyond it.'[21]

If, as Vedanta boldly asserts, there is ultimately no creation in the absolute sense, then the very notion of a creator becomes redundant. This proposition—radical though it may appear—strikes at the core of long-standing beliefs held by vast segments of humanity, who place an omnipotent, external God at the helm of creation and cosmic order. And yet, it is conspicuous that no religion—each a product of human thought—has ever provided a clear, consistent, and universally accepted definition of who or what this God is. Can the finite mind, limited by time and space, ever hope to define the Infinite? How can thought, which is itself conditioned and bounded, presume to comprehend or articulate that which lies beyond all limits? No one has seen God; no definitive form, name, or nature has ever been witnessed—only imagined.

This leads us to a profound and unsettling reflection: what if God, as popularly conceived, is not the creator of humankind, but rather a creation of the human mind—an archetype born of fear, longing, and the desire for security in a world fraught with suffering and uncertainty? A being projected outward—endowed with boundless power and compassion—capable of absolving sins and granting protection. In constructing such a figure, humanity has sought solace and moral order, but in doing so, may have veiled the deeper truth of existence.

Vedanta gently dismisses the outward projection of divinity by turning the inquiry inward. It posits that the ultimate reality—Brahman—is not a personal God who creates, rewards, or punishes, but the impersonal, all-pervading Consciousness that underlies all appearances. In this view, the world of names and forms is not created in the way we imagine, but is a superimposition upon the eternal Self, much like a dream mistaken for reality. The error lies in our ignorance (avidya), which gives rise to duality, separateness, and the notion of a creator distinct from creation.

Thus, rather than seeking salvation through a deity external to ourselves, Vedanta urges us to awaken to our true nature—pure, non-dual awareness—beyond body, mind, and belief. The quest is not for a God in the sky, but for the realization of the divine Self within, which neither creates nor is created, but simply *is*—timeless, infinite, and free.

VEDIC WISDOM: THE ETERNAL GUIDE

Discovering Consciousness may seem difficult, but it is not impossible for anyone, irrespective of their circumstances. Vedanta treats everyone with compassion, from a criminal chained to the silence of a steel cage suffocating inside a high-security prison to a pious monk, who moves about freely, breathing fresh air amidst the serenity of the Himalayas. What is stopping us from knowing about our real Self, when 'It', as the *Chandogya Upanishad* says, 'extends from above, from behind, from before, from south, and from north of a truth. Consciousness is all this.'

The obstacle to this profound realization lies within the very means employed, which is both complementary and contradictory. To reach the boundless realm of Consciousness, we must journey through our inner world solely with the aid of our mind, even though this very mind, due to its inherent ignorance, erroneously believes itself to be independently conscious. This ignorance serves as a veil, concealing the unchanging reality, the knower of all from knowing. Consciousness stands ever-ready to embrace and reveal itself to all, yet it can only be realized through deliberate introspection into the truth of one's inner Self, guided by a purified intuition, rather than through the study of physical world objects, as emphasized earlier. 'Self (Consciousness) cannot be attained by instruction, nor even by much learning. It is attained by one whom the Self chooses'—*Katha Upanishad*, chapter 1.

The wisdom of Consciousness rests unveiled within the Vedas, the greatest treasure bequeathed by the divine energy upon the ancient sages. Its presence at the inception of the creative cycle is not merely a synchronous reality but an intrinsic part of the cosmic design. The annihilation of the Vedas remains an inconceivable notion, even in the realm of dreams, as it would signify the extinction of the sole instrument granted to humanity to explore the realms of Consciousness, a manifestation of the divine will. The Vedas provide access to the knowledge of an inner essence referred to as the noumenon, distinct from the knowledge of external phenomena.

This sacred wisdom is the key to unlocking our understanding of Consciousness, encompassing some common traits and several exceptional qualities. Swami Vivekananda underscored this insight, stating:

> Vedas are without beginning and end. It may sound ludicrous how a book can be without a beginning or end. But by Vedas, no books are meant. They mean the accumulated treasure of spiritual laws discovered by different persons at different times. Just as the law of gravitation existed before its discovery and would exist if all humanity forgot it, so it is with the laws that govern the spiritual world; the moral, ethical, and spiritual relation between soul and soul, and between individual spirits and the Father of all spirits were there before their discovery and will remain even if we forget them.

For this very reason, the teachings within the Vedas have remained unaltered since their inception. They are impervious to the shifting mountains, diminishing rivers, blazing forests, and disappearing species. They remain unaffected even by the passing of men, women, and children due to illness, old age, and bitter wars, enduring through the dissolution of the world after this and all future creative cycles. Their essence remains untarnished, undisturbed by the passage of time and the diverse perspectives of philologists, scientists, religious scholars, and philosophers alike.

Time, the great equalizer, spares no one. Renowned scientists whose discoveries shaped the world, ruthless dictators whose actions claimed countless lives, virtuous saints who protected the righteous, and brilliant composers whose music echoes through history—all are eventually claimed by time. Yet, amidst this unyielding march, the timeless wisdom of the Vedas remains untouched, standing forever beyond the reach of temporal decay.

In its dialogue with humanity, Time reveals its ceaseless motion and the tranquil pause it finds between cycles of creation—a period of introspection, where it recognizes its limitations within the boundless realm of Supreme Consciousness. The power it seems to wield in the phenomenal world is but an illusion, for its sway over creation and its ability to shape destinies cannot confine the infinite expanse of Supreme Consciousness. Yet, by divine decree and in alignment with its inherent nature, time continues its journey through the silent depths of the non-dual Brahman, resonating with the eternal melodies of the Vedas.

The Vedas do not postulate anything, nor do they present anything that cannot be substantiated. The insights they offer to the contemporary world remain unshakeable. Their resounding influence spans from the shores of the Indian Ocean to those of the Pacific. Impervious to missiles or silence, they stand as a beacon, a steadfast guide in the face of the oscillating human intellect swayed by the allure of technology-driven progress, gently urging it to recall the illusory nature of the deceitful world.

The Vedas bestow invaluable wisdom to the humble and the conceited, and guide them away from repeating egotistical errors. Their timeless fragrance intoxicates countless individuals, transcending boundaries of class and age, revealing an eternal reality that even the poetic imaginations of Shakespeare, Byron, and Yeats fall short of grasping.

Having unearthed the inner truth, the wise, amidst their engagement with the ever-shifting world, make inner adjustments which leave them unscathed. They remain undisturbed by the consequences of their deeds, liberating themselves from the relentless wheel of karma that shunts all from one life to another. They do not clutch onto happiness, recognizing its transient nature and the inevitable arrival of sorrow in its wake. They comprehend that true awareness of joy and every emotion that traverses the mind springs from Consciousness itself, and thus, they admit neither fleeting moments of triumph nor the pangs of failure to disturb their tranquil minds. Even celestial entities envy the profound tranquillity that these individuals attain while abiding in self-awareness.

It should come as no surprise that Vedic knowledge provides insights into perplexing questions surrounding inequalities and the seemingly unjust experiences of individuals across the globe, much like the inquiry posed by Angelina Jolie in her thought-provoking video where she says, 'I have never understood why some people are lucky enough to be born with the chance that I had to have this path in life. And why across the world, there's a woman just like me with the same abilities, and same desires, the same work ethic, and love for her family, who would most likely make better films and better speeches; only she sits in a refugee camp, and she has no voice. She worries about what her children will eat, how to keep them safe, and if they'll ever be allowed to return home. I don't know why this is my life. And that's hers.'

It's Karma Phalam, say the Vedas.

The Vedas serve as a comprehensive guide, leading everyone from darkness to light. The formula of the three A's—acknowledging reality, accepting oneself, and acting with renewed vigour to stay in the present—is encapsulated in their teachings, is unfailing when one struggles to overcome the sorrowful experience of one's karma. It offers both immediate relief and long-term transformation without imposing haste.

The wisdom of the Vedas is all encompassing, offering guidance to people from all walks of life. It reminds the fame-struck celebrity of humility, the struggling fisherman of perseverance, and the destitute beggar of hope. It teaches calm composure to the suffering saint and reveals the significance of a spiritual journey to those yet to explore deeper reality.

Two metaphysical truths have been emphasized in Vedanta:

First, all that exists is Brahman, and everything else is simply an illusion caused by ignorance. Maya, the energy of Brahman, manifests diverse conditions, names, and forms through which Brahman shines. Brahman is the all-pervading life force energy, the absolute truth. It is the basis of all existence and the essence of God within us. There is no life; nay, there is no existence without Brahman, the Supreme Consciousness, no life without God. Referring to Brahman, the transcendental phenomenon, by a name would be inherently inadequate. The supreme being cannot be identified as an exclusive individual, for it exists beyond the scope of any description that the human mind can conceive. Nevertheless, the term 'God' is employed primarily to provide a reference point for the restless human intellect, serving as a means of common understanding and communication. Hence, Brahman is often referred to as God. To me, Brahman—the Supreme—is the Lord of all lords. In the sacred text of the Quran, the term 'Allah' is indicative of the Supreme Consciousness as I perceive it. The omniscient, formless God who possesses knowledge of all that comes into being, whether it be of universal or particular nature; the One who comprehends all things, even before the creation of the world.

The understanding articulated above reinforces the notion of God as a singular, imperceptible phenomenon enveloping the entirety of the world. This remains true regardless of the diverse approaches and practices embraced by different segments of humanity, each shaped by its unique beliefs and viewpoints, all expressing their oneness with the same God. The apparent distinctions that surface within the realm of the phenomenal world between each entity and belief are merely outcomes of diverse mindsets, influenced by varying levels of ignorance, and thus necessitate distinct methods for comprehending God, the Supreme Consciousness.

Yet, their intrinsic unity remains undeniable, as every being and every belief originates from the same divine source. Indeed, ultimately, all paths converge towards the one Whole, and therefore, there should be no place for animosity among individuals, much like rivers of varying lengths that flow harmoniously from diverse origins before uniting into the boundless ocean. Alas, the spread of evil cannot be halted as long as individuals concentrate on the means and remain oblivious to the ultimate goal.

To know God is to know Consciousness. Consciousness is inseparable from life and God; they are the same. God, being infinite, transcends growth, decay, and extinction. Meanwhile, Maya, the cosmic energy that manifests as the human mind, governs every action we undertake, and ultimately heralds the end of every life.

Vedanta states that cosmic energy, a matter principle, is an essential facet of the unchanging Brahman. It abides in unwavering constancy, untouched by the passage of growth or decay. In that aspect, it is of the nature of eternal existence, though dependent on Brahman for existence. As a result, the universe, which is a harmonious blend of Brahman and Maya, neither truly extends nor contracts. Within the vast expanse of this cosmos, objects undergo nothing more than shifts in their conditions.

A humble seed sprouts into a mighty tree, then transforms into furniture, ultimately merging back into the nurturing bosom of nature. Under the expansive sky, true acts of creation and destruction remain conspicuously absent from nature's narrative. Instead, the transformations in conditions and forms perceived at each juncture are given different names to serve the purpose of identification. No process of expansion or diminishment unfolds. Fundamentally, the ever-changing conditions and forms of objects exist solely as constructs of the mind. As Shankaracharya remarked, 'The name and form of the pot are not in the clay but in your mind.'

The world's apparent improvements and advancements across all objects through science and technology are, in reality, alterations of conditions, names, and forms measured by the price paid for changing the condition, the name, and the form. With this profound understanding, an array of intriguing questions surface: who truly orchestrates the ebb and flow of human existence? Why does the shadow of widespread injustice loom over every race?

Even as existence finds its bedrock in the intricate blend of Consciousness and energy (God and Maya), why must individuals endure physical and mental anguish whenever the tides of circumstances shift? Who is God? Is He a sovereign ruler, a betrayer, a saviour, or a mere figment conjured by vulnerable human minds trying to fathom the enigmatic Spirit beyond sight?

The foregoing reflections invite a re-examination of conventional beliefs—not with the intention to hurt the sentiments of billions or undermine their faith, but to offer an alternative perspective. It is important to emphasize that this view is presented with utmost respect for all traditions, leaving it to each reader to discern what resonates as true for them.

Who is God, and does God exist? What is the Grace of God?

To address this inquiry, one must possess consciousness—an awakened mind—and the energy necessary to comprehend and engage with the question, irrespective of its complexity.

The question of God's existence and nature stems from a modern conflict between traditional portrayals of God and the scientific mind's demand for empirical evidence of this abstract concept. God, as an entity beyond physical experience, has been defined by noble qualities and virtues often absent in human behaviour. Elevated to a superhuman status, God becomes a relatable figure—a source of solace during grief, and reassurance amid insecurity. However, as this concept originates in human thought, God is fundamentally a construct of human imagination.

According to the Oxford Dictionary, God is described as the creator and ruler of the universe, the source of moral authority, and a supreme being or spirit worshipped for dominion over nature and human fortunes. Yet, the quest to understand the universe's origins and mysteries endures. Questions about creation, disparities within species, and the persistence of human suffering demand deeper exploration.

Some religious definitions assert that God created everything, including all matter and energy. Thus, God cannot be synonymous with the universe or any of its components, since energy is part of the created realm. However, contrary to such interpretations, energy—an eternal principle of matter—has always existed within the spirit. Energy manifests objects in their unmanifest state at the beginning of a creative cycle and facilitates the transformation of existing materials into new forms and names. This aligns with the Law of Conservation of Matter, emphasizing that matter cannot be created or destroyed, only transformed.

In this context, the world and its objects existed in potential form at the outset of creation. Cosmic intelligence, endowed with energy, enables the transformation of unmanifest substances into tangible forms and sustains the universe through deliberate interventions and energy releases. Human life, too, operates through the chemical energy derived from nature, primarily from food. These principles, reflected in Vedic scriptures, challenge the notion of creation as an illusion or misperception.

Given this understanding, redefining God as the force sustaining life—encompassing both consciousness (spirit) and energy (matter)—becomes essential. This entity must be omniscient, omnipresent, and omnipotent. Within this framework, only Consciousness alone can be considered God, eternally embodying all three qualifying components. Consciousness operates independently, is eternal and unchanging, providing the awareness essential to life and cosmic energy.

It is essential to recognize that human existence depends on both Consciousness (the Father) and Energy (the Mother) for its sustenance and functionality. Additionally, the five elements—space, air, fire, water, and earth—are vital expressions of energy and manifestations of the cosmic mind. Alongside the sun and moon, which play crucial roles in sustaining life, these elements are revered as gods. However, they are considered secondary gods, as they do not possess the attributes of omnipresence or omniscience.

All other entities, including the idols we worship in alignment with this understanding, are best viewed as imaginary gods of convenience—transient, situational, and bound by time and space. Importantly, every such entity must eventually dissolve at the end of the cosmic cycle, with energy returning to its latent state within the eternal spirit, awaiting the dawn of the next cycle of creation.

Despite this, we must never lose sight of the one eternal truth: nothing can exist without Consciousness. As the Supreme God, Consciousness is not only the origin but also the essence that permeates all existence. Accordingly, we are called to see the presence of the Supreme in every object—within this universe and beyond as stated in the Vedas.

The Rig Veda, the oldest of the Vedas, acknowledges this cosmic energy, paying homage to fire in its opening verse. Yet, the primary God remains Consciousness, the immutable force that illuminates all, including cosmic energy and all its variants.

Thus, a nuanced understanding of God unites traditional reverence with scientific awareness, emphasizing the profound interplay of Consciousness and energy.

The grace of God is the manifestation of cosmic free will, representing the same cosmic energy that sustains the universe. This process involves an individual uniting with cosmic energy through devotion and sincere supplication, which results in the creation of capacity within the mind to amplify positive energy, denoted as the 'S' factor, while reducing negative energy, referred to as the 'T' factor. By consciously cultivating 'S' energy, individuals revitalize their inner selves, achieving balance within the SRT (Sattva–Rajas–Tamas) configuration, and calming the turbulence caused by negativity.

The grace of God serves as a guiding force, enabling individuals to stay calm and overcome setbacks and karmic challenges. It acts as a catalyst for progress, offering strength and clarity amid life's trials, and nurturing growth on the path to ultimate realization.

Vedanta illuminates the enigma, asserting that Brahman, as the ultimate witness and knower, remains aloof from the theatrics of human roles, not subject to the sway of emotions, unbound by the shackles of birth, growth, ageing, sickness, or death. Brahman assumes the mantle of an impartial observer, embracing the entirety of existence with equanimity, of thoughts and thoughtlessness, pain and pleasure, cacophony and silence, all at the same time, all in perfect harmony. It neither incites human predicaments nor partakes as an actor in any capacity. While this understanding may absolve Brahman, the Supreme Lord, from blame in the realm of human trials, it reveals two profound and enduring mysteries.

PEACE IS AN EVER-PRESENT TRUTH

What is the genesis of human suffering, and how might we unearth tranquillity amidst life's ever-shifting uncertainties?

Why did a highly esteemed high court judge of a certain country suddenly collapse and die on a busy roundabout in June 2016, despite usually being accompanied by assistants and orderlies? And how was it that no one was present to administer CPR—even with two reputed hospitals located nearby? In contrast, in November 2022, a hepatologist came to the rescue of a fellow passenger who collapsed in the aisle of an aeroplane during a ten-hour flight from the UK to India, after he had suffered two cardiac arrests, even though the man had no prior medical history. Despite limited supplies, the doctor managed to resuscitate him. He survived. It makes you wonder, who or what is causing such peculiar twists in our lives? Some believe it's the result of our karma, which we perform endlessly because of our ignorance—a sentiment echoed in Vedanta and repeatedly restated at the cost of redundancy.

Here arises the necessity to transcend the confines of traditional logic, a step we might deem indispensable, even if it seems paradoxical to our logical minds that continue to endure various forms of suffering in the absence of a solution. We need physics and metaphysics for existence and making unqualified progress in life; not one or the other. They are like the two parallel tracks of a train, with the engine of progress propelling us forward. Otherwise, we can be sure of not reaching the destination, as Swami Vivekananda once remarked, 'Intellect has been cultured with the result that hundreds of sciences have been discovered, and their effect has been that the few have made slaves of the many—that is all the good that has been done. Artificial wants have been created; and every poor man, whether he has money or not, desires to have those wants satisfied, and when he cannot, he struggles, and dies in the struggle. This is the result. Through the intellect is not the way to solve the problem of misery, but through the heart. If all this vast amount of effort had been spent in making men purer, gentler, more forbearing, this world would have a thousandfold more happiness than it has today.' The world needs spiritual nourishment alongside economic progress.

Vedanta reveals a profound truth: our common belief that we function solely through the body and mind is a fundamental misconception. In reality, it is Consciousness that animates both; making thought, emotion, and action possible. In this sense, Consciousness is not a passive observer—it is the very essence that operates through the body–mind complex.

While human beings are composed of both matter (the body and mind) and spirit (Consciousness), Vedanta grants us the unique privilege of recognizing Consciousness as our true, higher nature. It is essential, however, not to confuse the perishable body–mind apparatus with the imperishable spirit. The former is a tool, the latter the source.

However, the mind, which by nature is unconscious and inert, is quick to proclaim that it is, in fact, the ultimate power behind every action which humans perform when it is not. Sadly, it remains unaware that the pride with which it declares its imperial status is a result of the generosity of the spirit radiating from within, illuminating the mind and bringing awareness to it, despite its false vanity. Thus, it is a grave error to confuse the non-self (matter) with the Self (Spirit) out of ignorance. Amidst the hustle of the contemporary world, people often find little time to explore Consciousness as their minds are preoccupied with thoughts related to material progress.

Vedanta does not oppose material pursuits but emphasizes the importance of achieving economic well-being and experiencing pleasures while simultaneously contemplating the spiritual journey. However, when material pursuits become the sole purpose of existence, we are bound to miss what we seek in the endless chase: security, peace, and happiness.

In our tireless pursuit of happiness, we work relentlessly to satisfy both legitimate and illegitimate desires. Yet, true and uninterrupted happiness remains elusive, even amidst material wealth. Insecurity, distress, and unhappiness persist, stemming from our lack of self-awareness and a clear understanding of our true nature. We only grasp a fragment of our being, while the profound truth lies concealed beneath.[22]

COMPREHENDING CONSCIOUSNESS: OBSTACLES AND CHALLENGES

What lies at the heart of this pervasive apathy towards unravelling the profound mysteries of Consciousness, which undeniably constitutes the very essence of our existence?

An incisive examination of our present circumstances lays bare a stark reality. The tapestry of indifference is intricately woven from two enduring threads of ancient practices, steadfastly intertwined.

There exists a striking void in our educational endeavours when it comes to imparting the wisdom of Consciousness. Even concerning the intricate matrix (SRT) that sculpts our personality, our understanding barely scratches the surface, a shallow pool bereft of profound depth. The dearth of attention during our formative years thus leaves our personalities marred, often bearing a burden of negative proclivities, primarily 'T' and 'R'. Within the confines of academia, there is an alarming absence of fervent advocacy for the imperative task of knowing about Brahman or the need for recalibrating the constituent elements of our inner selves, a task crucial for preserving the equipoise of our minds as they navigate the relentless tempests of this callous world.

Furthermore, some argue that the comprehension of such abstruse knowledge is a labyrinthine endeavour, a daunting pilgrimage for young minds that are still in the process of development. Yet, if non-French nationals can embrace a foreign tongue at any age, why should the luminous realm of Consciousness be an insurmountable peak? We, as humans, are adorned with a unique mantle, for we possess the innate capacity to absorb not merely a language but also the profound disciplines of geology, mathematics, physiology, biology, and more, concurrently, should the torch-bearers of wisdom guide us adeptly.

So, it's time we embrace the significance of Consciousness within our collective bosom, instead of relegating it to the dusty archives of indifference, treating it as another word among the myriad slumbering in the uncharted pages of the lexicon.

As the saying goes, familiarity breeds contempt, but it also hinders our curiosity to learn more. We become complacent with the people and objects we encounter regularly, taking them for granted. We know little about our loving parents, the earth we tread upon daily, the vast sky above us, or the mysteries of life and death. 'The child stares with surprise at a stranger but never so at its own mother. What do we know of the man? Nothing. He comes and goes, and we do not know where. One man is a poet and another a warrior, we hardly know why. Man breathes while he lives, but at the moment of death, breath fails: no human physiology can tell us satisfactorily enough what it is that lies breathless, and what that which—was breathing, why we came, and where we go if the life we lived ends with death, and whether we are matter, or spirit, or soul, or mind, or the senses, or everything, or nothing. The great and profound mystery that encircles us all around baffles our feeble attempt to unravel it' (B. R. Rajam, *Rambles in Vedanta*). As we strive to comprehend the profound mystery surrounding us, we find ourselves bewildered, as Goethe once said, '...man is a confused creature; he knows not whence he comes or whither he goes, he knows little of the world, and above all, he knows little of himself.'

This is perhaps the reason why the quest to understand Consciousness, our closest companion, poses a profound challenge. Ignorance regarding the oneness of individual souls and universal Consciousness results in suffering and a mistaken identification with the body–mind complex, creating a bondage that obscures our path to liberation. The journey necessitates deep introspection and the interpretation of the revelations of ancient sages, guided by the wisdom and compassion of a guru.

SECTION FIVE

BURNING DOWN IGNORANCE—3, 2, 1, STOP!

Chapter 11

UNCOVERING IGNORANCE

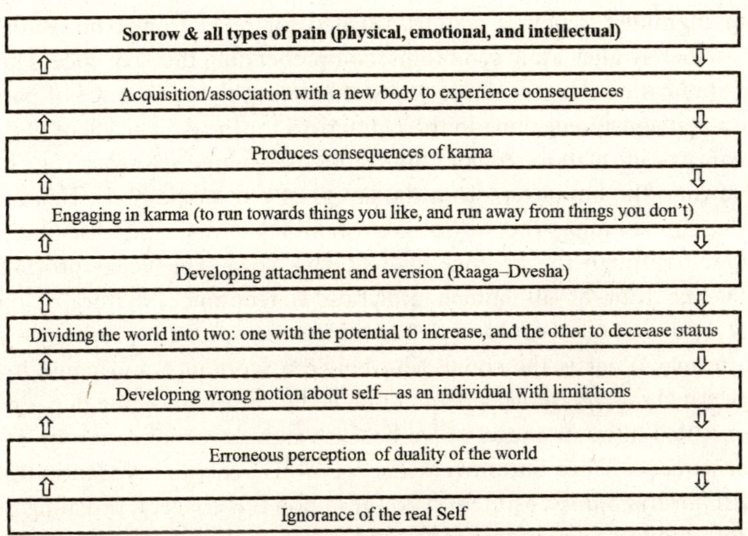

The fundamental goals of every human being encompass relief from all forms of pain, and improvement in the quality of life. In general, people instinctively seek relief by turning to medical aid or adopting the escapist's path to fulfil the former goal; and tirelessly engage in various karmas seeking security, peace, and happiness from the ever-changing external world in pursuit of the latter.

Affliction—and indeed, every manifestation of pain—resides within the individual, permeating both body and mind throughout the span of life. Suffering, in its various forms, becomes an inseparable companion of human existence. In this context, death is often viewed not with fear, but as a release—a final cessation of all suffering. The thought of death, then, becomes a quiet refuge, a distant horizon that offers hope of peace. Though it may not solve suffering in the moment, this hope acts as a balm, momentarily soothing the wounded heart and giving the weary mind something to hold on to amid life's relentless tribulations. Yet, the fear of death, purportedly a liberator from agony, is experienced universally by everyone at some juncture. Death is not panacea for terminating suffering; rather, it serves as the herald of a new embodiment, necessary to undergo the repercussions of past karma when the present corporeal form succumbs to physical incapacitation.

Discerning the intricate sequence of cause and effect, which traces back to ignorance, becomes imperative for the cessation of our ingrained, reflexive actions pursued for relief from pain. Rather than merely alleviating symptoms, comprehending this sequence is key to eradicating the root cause and pre-empting the recurrence of pain. Simultaneously, engaging in three practices for the enhancement of the quality of life elaborated later in this treatise—namely, Karma Yoga for cleansing the impurities from the layers of our subtle body, Upasana Yoga for calming the turbulence of SRT factors, and disciplining oneself through the practice of Ashtanga Yoga. The Vedas proclaim that the root of all human affliction is ignorance. Naturally, one may ponder how could such ignorance serve as the progenitor of suffering. What is the connection between ignorance and pain? It is discerned that ignorance operates not as the immediate cause but as the concealed ultimate cause, veiled beneath eight layers of causation and consequence. Sage Sureshwaracharya, in his venerable Vedantic text, *Nishkarmya Siddhi*, astutely expounds upon this concept, revealing the profound interplay of ignorance and its impact on human experience.

At its core, ignorance reveals itself as the erroneous perception that the world and the diverse entities within creation exist independently of their source—Consciousness. This misapprehension prompts us to erroneously ascribe reality to entities, mere names attached to various forms devoid of substantial existence, for all that exists is the self-independent Brahman, the pure intelligence. A division materializes between the source and diverse entities, as well as among the entities themselves. Due to this singular cause of misguided separateness from the source, multiple adversities emerge.

Furthermore, identification with our body and mind, which are merely instruments for use in the functional world rather than our intrinsic reality—Consciousness, leads us to perceive ourselves as finite individuals subject to the limitations of time and space. This perception persists when evaluating other individuals, a compelling exercise that we cannot evade, having embraced duality. It ends up in our judging them based on external attributes like appearance, as well as forming perceptions about their wealth, well-being, and more. A legion of afflictions follows suit: desire to imitate, contradiction of thoughts, conflicts, mental agitation, jealousy, likes and dislikes, and other forms of malevolence. The impulse to dichotomize the world based on the façade of name and form emerges, categorizing the world into segments perceived as enhancing one's false status and those potentially diminishing it. Natural attachments to the positive, and aversions to the negative inevitably develop.

The sense of inadequacy experienced by us as limited individuals acts as a catalyst for the emergence of desires that propel both moral and immoral actions. While the ceaseless pursuit to fulfil these desires encompasses the craving for things we find favourable and the avoidance of those we disdain, the persistent yearning to acquire additional material possessions or experiences serves as a poignant confirmation of our perceived state of incompleteness.

In some parts of the world, jealousy is commonly understood as the act of casting an 'evil eye'. This behaviour stems from the inherent tendency to compare oneself with others and aspire to attain a similar status. However, when these aspirations are obstructed by the outcomes of Karma Phalam, jealousy can arise, sometimes culminating in the act of casting an 'evil eye'. While this phenomenon has a basis in reality, its influence is limited to those who dwell excessively on it, allowing their minds to remain entangled in such thoughts.

The endless action one performs to satisfy the demand of one's ego necessitates the acquisition or association with a new corporal vessel for the subsequent experience of consequences. When actions yield results contrary to expectations, grief and mental anguish ensue. Physical pain, too, manifests as a repercussion of Karma Phalam, as does intellectual distress when one falls short in the pursuit of knowledge—a consequence of Karma Phalam as well.

In discerning the mystery enveloping the human experience, we recognize it as the progeny of profound ignorance, a riddle that can only be eliminated through the illumination bestowed by the knowledge of the 'One that unfolded into many'.

CHAPTER 12

THREE STEPS TO ENDING SUFFERING

The solution to secure relief from all pains lies in the formula detailed below. It entails transitioning from the triputi-triangular (Dvaita) mode to the Binary (Vishishtadvaita), and ultimately reaching the Singular (Advaita) state to become independent. Dvaita (dual), Vishishtadvaita (qualified non-dual), and Advaita (non-dual) are the three schools of Vedanta philosophy, explained in detail later in this treatise.

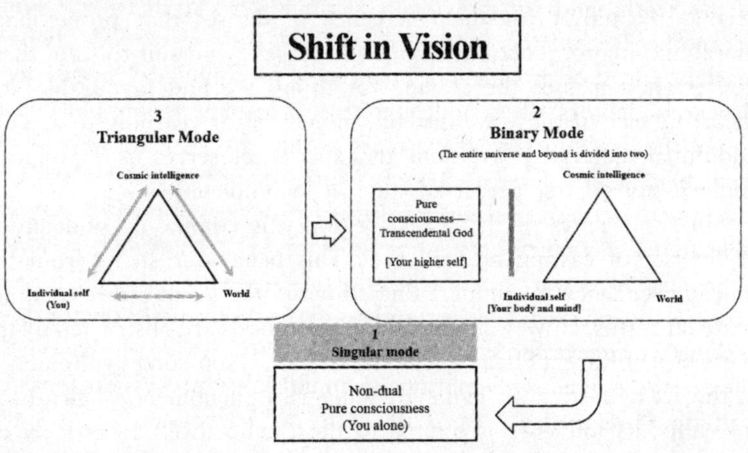

THE MISERY OF THE TRIANGULAR MODE

The triad encompasses the restless souls (jivatma), the world (inclusive of other conscious beings and the entire inert objects of creation), and the gods dwelling in places of worship. Some identify gods as the cosmic intelligence, or as the force steering all the natural forces of physical science and the laws governing the physical world. All these entities interact while remaining within the sphere of Brahman.

The crux of this state lies in the physical or psychological interdependence of the three bodies. Given that each of these entities is endowed with ever-changing energy propensities (SRT factors) and resides within the domain of the phenomenal world, they prove undependable, unsustainable, and unpredictable.

Even the gods within this triad, with a dominant 'S', depend on individuals for sustenance through the sacrifices and oblations offered by these individuals. If the jivatma decides not to visit a church or a temple, the gods of worship become insignificant. Hence, the *Brihadaranyaka Upanishad* states, 'they (the gods) do not desire the jivatmas to pursue the knowledge of Brahman, for they will cease to propitiate the gods. Thus, they are deemed hurdles in the way of attaining knowledge of the Self.' With the realization of the inner self as Brahman, the jivatma attains liberation from the need to depend on an external source, for it becomes the universe. Unaware of this truth, ignorant individuals attribute life's trials to one entity or another within the triad. Alternatively, they serve gods, human masters, gurus, or providers of financial or psychological support as if they were debtors, often under the fear of losing ongoing patronage.

In the vast tapestry of existence within the intricate web of the triangular mode, all entities from celestial deities to industrious ants are bound by desires. They fulfil diverse yearnings through mutual obligations, exchanging tangible and ethereal favours, whether real or imagined. As long as contentment prevails within this established order where interdependence stands as the linchpin, especially for those seeking worldly progress in pursuit of security, peace, and happiness, the cycle of reliance will continue in an unbroken procession, weaving patterns of dependence from one entity to the next.

At this juncture, it is crucial to understand why individuals lean on the external world to make progress in the material world, fully aware of its limited capacity to provide a sustainable solution. Essentially, it is because human intelligence, constrained by inherent limitations, often falls short of the requirements for success in the physical domain. Our functionality relies on the body and mind, which attain consciousness through the illumination derived from the all-pervasive Consciousness. While absolute Consciousness can bring awareness of the universe and beyond to the mind, the mind's limiting conditions significantly restrict the scope of awareness, much like how clouds impact the illuminating rays of the sun.

The constraints of the mind stem from Karma Phalam, affecting intellectual or physical capacities, or both. Remarkably, this framework doesn't diminish the fervour for progress in the material world and the pursuit of material wealth. Consequently, individuals immerse themselves in tireless endeavours, utilizing limited intelligence to fulfil their unending desires.

If we set aside the idea that Karma Phalam influences the conditioning of the mind, it's crucial to acknowledge that the intelligence we use to pursue our material goals, free from such karmic influence, is closely tied to our thoughts. These thoughts, in turn, are shaped by the reservoir of knowledge and experiences we accumulate. This highlights the importance of our intellectual faculties, driven by acquired wisdom and lived moments, as a powerful force in navigating the path towards our material aspirations.

However, since knowledge is an ever-evolving entity with inherent limitations, it always lags behind ignorance in the physical world. Consequently, our thoughts and the intelligence derived from them are confined and ever-changing. The sole exception to this phenomenon is the knowledge of truth, which cannot evolve, for it would lose its immutable status if it did. Thus, the knowledge of Brahman alone is considered unchanging and is the absolute truth.

When our finite intellect falls short of realizing our aspirations, a natural inclination arises, urging us to seek support from either fellow human beings or divine entities. The unrelenting pursuit of material abundance fuels a perpetual cycle of dependence, fuelled by seemingly insatiable desires. Any form of reliance is an acknowledgement of vulnerability, making individuals susceptible to exploitation by both the world and forces beyond.

If we accept the sobering truth that the world is not inherently just—and that while the gods are not unjust, they do not intervene directly or orchestrate grand solutions to life's challenges—it becomes clear that individuals must ultimately depend on their own inner strength.

Throughout history, humans have confronted life's trials by relying on their resilience, steadily overcoming inner weaknesses. Yet, it is equally true that many undertake the journey of life with a lingering hope—that divine intervention might one day miraculously unfold. Any support or breakthrough from outside is often seen as a providential gift. In truth, however, every genuine solution arises when we confront a problem as it is—stripped of mental distortions—

and engage with it through the silent clarity of pure Consciousness within us. Unfortunately, we remain unaware of this reality, as these transformations occur quietly within the depths of our own being.

The Vedas emphasize that the only dependable source is the infinite Brahman—an embodiment of pure intelligence and the true essence of every being. Consequently, the Vedas advocate for a transition from the intricate dynamics of the triad to a more straightforward binary understanding and, ultimately, to a singular mode of consciousness. This transition is deemed essential for those who seek to attain security, peace, and happiness.

THE BINARY MODE

Having unveiled our authentic Self as Consciousness, we must shift to the binary mode, in which we identify ourselves as Brahman, dividing the world into Atma (Consciousness) and Anatma (the insentient, inert world), encompassing the objects of experience, including our body and mind. From the standpoint of Consciousness, this partition serves as the termination of the division which we perceive in a triangular mode between the world and the various objects in creation. It involves reframing them not as entities with independent existence but as interconnected facets of the whole. It is like the dream world, dream people, and dream objects projected by an individual in a dream, eventually dissolving as the individual transitions into deep sleep.

Instantaneously, our perspective of the world and ourselves undergoes a radical shift as we step into the role of the observer, untethered by events unfolding in the phenomenal realm. The evident dependence of the non-self (Anatma) on the Self (Atma) becomes vividly clear, leading us to embrace every entity in the world with compassion and empathy, from a humble blade of grass to the mighty sun; a peace-loving cow to an aggressive lion; from a saint to sinner, all as mere reflection of ourselves; as harmless names and forms devoid of independent existence, much akin to how we treat every part of our body without any favouritism.

This profound realization aligns with the teachings of Vishishtadvaita, a distinct school of thought within the Vedanta philosophy. According to this philosophy, Brahman is not only the ultimate reality but it also encompasses the entire universe, with individual souls constituting His body and Him serving as their soul. In this conceptualization, Brahman is both the cause and the effect, transcending conventional boundaries. Importantly, embracing this perspective liberates individuals from the incessant tendency to judge others based on superficial attributes and behaviours. It facilitates the dissolution of negative traits such as the inclination to imitate, conflicting thoughts, internal strife, mental unrest, jealousy, preferences, and aversions—manifestations of malevolence that often arise within the confines of a triangular mindset.

THE SINGULAR MODE

The shift in vision reaches its pinnacle when we exist as a singular entity, encompassing the entire universe within us. This state mirrors our experience of dreamless sleep, where the entire universe, along with our body and mind, returns to its potential state. In this profound moment, all desires, conflicts, negative emotions, and the division between subject and object dissolve, bringing an instantaneous end to all adversities.

During this ephemeral period, the only existence is the Supreme Consciousness—a state defined as the non-dual bliss of Advaita Shantam. Individuals who have attained the knowledge of Brahman encounter this unique state, experiencing a bliss of an esoteric nature even in the awakened state. Such individuals continually abide in the silence of Brahman while navigating the tumultuous world around them. Such an individual is recognized as a 'sthita prajna', the wise one.

SUMMARY OF THE STEPS FOR SHIFTING THE VISION

Step 1:

Consider yourself as the consciousness principle, acknowledging that your intrinsic Self is Consciousness, not the body–mind complex, which is merely our incidental reality. This shift in perspective involves recognizing that Consciousness, with its supreme power, does not directly engage in the activities required for us to navigate life in the phenomenal world. It is so because Brahman is a principle, not the principal or an agent who can engage as a doer. This understanding allows individuals, the small 'i', to perform actions for action's sake, obfuscating the need to experience the consequence as a non-doer. Here, the individual is both the doer (small 'i'), and non-doer (the big 'I'). Although the benefits of embracing this higher truth have been emphasized upon throughout this book, it is understandable that one may find it challenging to easily shift gears and sustain this perspective elucidated above while using one's body and mind to carry out daily transactions.

A firm commitment to disavow the body–mind complex becomes paramount for the transformative shift facilitated by a correct understanding of the inherent limitations of the body and an assessment of the inadequacy of gains derived from its utilization in individual, familial, societal, national, and global contexts.

The analogy of electricity powering a bulb helps elucidate this intricate relationship. Similar to the reliance of a light bulb on electricity for illumination, the functioning of our body–mind is contingent upon Consciousness. Just as electricity remains unaffected when the bulb fuses, Consciousness endures even after the body's demise. Just like a single source of electricity adapts to diverse purposes—producing heat or cold air, fuelling a motor, facilitating rotation, and more, depending on the specifics of the machine—different living and non-living entities attain awareness through the illumination of a constant and unchanging Consciousness. This occurs in tandem with the distinct purposes of each entity, emerging with diverse features and characteristics that constrain their abilities according to their role in the phenomenal world, shaped by past karma.

Furthermore, the analogy underscores that the bulb is rendered useless without electricity, mirroring the nature of the body and mind without consciousness. Just as electricity, unconnected to a bulb, is energy dissipating aimlessly, Consciousness persists eternally as a witness to everything, revealing everything through its nature in the presence or absence of a perceiver.

Without grasping the highlighted reality and by wrongly attributing undue significance to our body–mind complex, which is deemed necessary for engaging in life's activities, we become entangled in attachment to it. This attachment leads to development of a notion of the individual self, the 'I' factor, the 'ego', known as Ahankara, and a strong affinity towards its belongings and associates, the 'mine' factor known as Mamakara, causing the most dangerous partition amongst humanity. This division manifests as 'my beliefs, my community, my religion, my deities, my state, my nation', and more.

An examination of this attachment reveals its contribution as nothing beyond dividing the immutable spirit and giving rise to egotism, contradictions, various forms of grief, emotional stress, and bitterness among individuals and families. On a broader scale, it manifests in wars, large-scale destruction, and the displacement of humanity globally, all for fleeting pleasures derived from creature comforts. Whether one struggles to accept this truth or not, aligning with Consciousness emerges as the only pathway out of the affliction that universally affects people around the world.

Step 2:

Divide the entire world into two categories—Anatma and Atma. Categorize all objects of knowledge and experience, including your own body and mind, as Anatma, and identify yourself as the Atma, the big 'I', or Supreme Consciousness.

Step 3:

Dismiss everything associated with Anatma, a relative reality lacking independent existence and thus regarded as unreal or non-existent. This understanding should be grounded in the recognition that ultimately, every object, whether in manifest or unmanifest form in the world of multiplicity, will disintegrate and return to its source in an unmanifest state.

It is important to note that the word *shift* does not imply a physical or linear movement from one mode to another. Rather, it refers to a shift in intellectual perspective. Speaking of a 'movement' from one to another suggests a division. However, since the triangular and binary modes are ultimately non-existent, no such division truly exists. Thus in reality, there is no path to traverse to reach the singular mode—for that alone is, and has always been.

SECTION SIX

PURE VEDAS (A COMPENDIUM)

Chapter 13

WHAT ARE THE VEDAS?

Truly, the term 'Vedas' finds its essence in knowledge itself. The dictates set forth by the Vedas, embraced by the ancient settlers in the fertile Indus valley, stood as their guiding light in those times. In this present age, the universal principles enshrined within have become the impetus behind a burgeoning desire among people hailing from all parts of the earth, seeking to apprehend and put into practice the authoritative counsel they proffer for peaceful existence.

The singular intent of the Vedas is to aid mankind in its quest to uncover the Truth—the pinnacle of all that is virtuous—thereby quelling all grief and achieving a state of liberation. Within its sacred verses, one encounters an ecstasy surpassing the known. It offers liberation from fear, from the shackles of bondage, from sorrow's clutches, and from the ensnarement of illusions.

Vedanta, the latter portion of this scripture, is a beacon with a clear, attainable goal. Engaging in a discourse to weigh the merits of Vedantic scholarship would indeed be an insult to its fundamental doctrine, which seeks nothing but individual realization of the Truth and consequent eternal felicity, gained through a personal odyssey.

Thus, a concise elucidation on the Vedas shall serve as an introduction to the philosophy of Vedanta and, with particularity, to the comprehension of the oft-invoked term in this treatise—Vedic meditation.

Termed also as Sruti, the Vedas stand as the primordial texts bestowing direct spiritual insight. They emerge as a fount of knowledge unaided by further authentication, a wellspring known as 'shastra chakshuhu' or 'pratyaksham', as designated in the *Brahma Sutra*, a part of the tripartite Vedantic canon. A comprehensive compendium, they delineate the means and ends of human existence. These scriptures, a philosophical foundation, serve as an authoritative repository, granting the wisdom of irrefutable universal truths, transcending race and creed alike.

The core import of 'Veda' is cognition that outshines rationality, dwelling beyond the precincts of human intellect. The Vedas were revealed to the ancient sages (risis), those who, in deep meditation attained awakening to the Supreme Consciousness. Knowledge gleaned from what they had heard, acquired through an extraordinary practice—a withdrawal of the senses from perishable sense objects, focusing intently upon the imperishable truth emanating from the cosmic vibrations that echoed inside their heart, the abode of the Supreme Consciousness. Thus, these scriptures are regarded as Apauruseya, far removed from human authorship or composition. The sacred divinity enshrined herein is the reason why both the risis of yore and humans today hold this knowledge in utmost sanctity. A peculiarity that has not only captivated but also swayed prominent figures from the West, such as Arthur Schopenhauer, Aldous Huxley, John Keats, Ralph Weldo Emerson, Max Mueller, and W. Somerset Maugham, among others. Curiously, the vast expanse of the Vedas, sprawling across numerous pages, was propagated for aeons primarily through the traditional method of disciples listening intently as the master intoned the verses of the Vedas on numerous occasions. The composition of the Vedas cannot be precisely dated, but the period approximately spanning from 1500 to 1200 BCE is widely accepted by most scholars.

The Vedas, by division, unfold into two segments: Veda Poorva, the threshold of knowledge meant for the common folk, and Vedanta, the end segment for attaining the highest knowledge. Krishna Dvaipaayana, popularly known as sage Veda Vyas, whose hand bore the task of compiling and ordering the Vedas, carved them into four broad categories—Rik, Yajur, Sama, and Atharva. Each of these branches, in turn, nestles into two major subdivisions.[23] His tasks are limited solely to the compilation of the Vedas, which have existed from time immemorial (Anadi Kala), without a discernible beginning.

The first portion is the Veda Poorva section, also hailed as Karma Kanda, which takes its stance in terrestrial matter, the field of actions, rituals, offerings, and sacrifices prescribed for the pursuit of three shared goals: enhancement of self (bodily well-being), augmentation and refinement of possessions (prosperity, repute), and betterment of the milieu. The channels demarcated for such achievements are: physical exertion and restraint (Kayika Sadnani—rites and sacrifices), linguistic propriety (Vachika Sadnani—prayers and recitations), and mental cultivation (Manasa Sadnani—meditation).

While the Vedas caution about the inherent limitations concealed within the aforementioned aspirations, the majority proceed down this path, blind to the pitfalls.[24] The ignorant soul, mistakenly perceiving itself as a finite entity, tirelessly engages in orchestrating numerous deeds to fulfil its desires. Consequently, in modern times, there is a compulsion to pursue security, serenity, and happiness through various endeavours. Even the wise often find themselves ensnared in the relentless pursuit of worldly gains, undeterred by the fleeting rewards that such pursuits may yield.

VEDANTA AND THE QUEST FOR LIBERATION

The common pursuits outlined in the Veda Poorva portion lose their grip of the one who unearths this truth, for his contentment is not tethered to possession or lack thereof. With this knowledge, the presence of companions or their absence neither burden nor empty him, as he is replete, anchored in the awareness of truth.

The texts of Vedanta resonate with pragmatism, grounded in the seeker's experiential faith rather than mechanical scriptural learning. According to Shankara Bhagavatpada, a scripture holds authority only when it resonates with personal meaning. Vedanta confers the understanding of the Self, of Consciousness, which is intangible and not subject to direct experience. Yet, each Vedantin is astounded by an enigmatic delight while studying these sacred scriptures under an adept mentor. The mere act of hearing the Vedas stirs a joy that is esoteric. This pursuit arouses curiosity and sparks an appetite for knowledge, uncovering the fruits of wisdom with each step in this sacred pilgrimage. It transforms a mere collection of words into a profound realization.

Engulfed in suffering, misery, and affliction, man struggles to derive genuine value from his human existence. Often, as life appears desolate, the spark of a spiritual journey ignites. While this odyssey commences against a backdrop of life's pessimism, the revelation of man's authentic Self, unveiled in Vedanta, grants him a much-desired optimism.

The knowledge garnered from the Vedas earns the designation of 'para vidya', an awareness that dwells beyond the dominion of the senses. To utter that no cognition can extend past the grasp of sensory perception would be a folly of the highest order. If it were true, humankind would have long terminated all tribulations without questing beyond the apparent. The attainment of wisdom, it proclaims, necessitates the employment of a tripartite process and a meticulous scrutiny of teachings gleaned from the master. The accentuation of introspection upon the Self and contemplation for self-validation stands as the hallmarks distinguishing the Vedanta scripture. 'In Vedanta, there is progressive discovery of truth,' articulated Dr Radhakrishnan. Yet, it does not culminate there. 'The dialectical method of Vedanta compels it to deal with the tenets of all other schools; it makes it a compendium of the entire range of Indian philosophy,' as Dr P. Nagaraja Rao accurately observes.

VEDANTA IS VERBOSE

The words of Vedanta cannot reveal Brahman, because it is not an object of knowledge, say the scriptures. God is that phenomenon which words cannot describe and the mind cannot fathom ('Yatho vacho nivartante apraapya manasaa saha'—*Taittiriya Upanishad*). Nevertheless, the scriptures are upheld as authoritative.

A word can assume the role of a revealer for an object only when it meets one of the five prescribed conditions ('Shabda pravrutti nimittaani'):

1. **Roodihi:** The object must be available for direct perception, and the word representing it should possess the inherent ability to instantly reveal the object to an individual whenever employed in the future.
2. **Jaathihi:** The word must be associated with a species previously encountered, and this association should empower the word to unveil the object, as in the case of a tree.
3. **Gunaha:** The word should unveil the object by signifying a property or a distinct attribute of the object, such as its colour or weight.
4. **Kriya** or **Karma:** The object should be revealed through a word that denotes its function or profession, as exemplified by terms like 'driver' or 'wind that moves'.
5. **Sambandha:** The word, when used to indicate a relationship, must expose a person through that relationship, as evident in terms like 'father' or 'brother'.

The aforementioned conditions delineate the permissible avenues through which a word may rightfully serve as the revealer of an object, embodying a set of criteria rooted in the intricate interplay between language and perception.

Brahman, the principle of knowing, is not an object. It transcends; exists in a realm above and beyond mere words, eluding the fulfilment of any amongst the aforementioned conditions. As a consequence, the definition of Brahman through the utterances of the Vedantic scriptures remains an endeavour deemed unattainable by its critics.

The critics' assertion underscores the ineffable nature of Brahman, a concept that stands beyond the boundaries of conventional linguistic description. However, this objection finds its resolution within Vedanta through the subsequent elucidation:

Words possess a remarkable capacity to unveil that which may not conform to the anticipated conditions.

Apparent Attribute: Frequently, the term 'blue sky' incorporates the adjective 'blue', indicating a semblance of an attribute. Similarly, references to the 'sunrise' and 'sunset' refer to the Sun. In the case of Brahman, often described as witness Consciousness, the apparent attribute is that of a 'witness' to the objective world, as both the presence and absence of objects manifest exclusively within the sphere of Consciousness.

Incidental Attribute: This attribute is not inherent but rather incidental. Just as a particular house within a cluster is identified by mentioning it as the house with a crow, not always present, Consciousness, too, is realized through the body's connection to it. Consciousness is not a product or possession of the body; it remains distinct. However, its omnipresence and its presence within the body render the body sentient. Despite the non-intrinsic relationship between the body and Consciousness (as evidenced by the body's dissolution upon death), a conscious body serves to reveal the presence of Consciousness.

Absence of Attributes: Among various glasses containing water or other fluids, one can discern the empty one. Emptiness is not a positive attribute of the glass; rather, it unveils the absence of attributes. This negative attribute, capable of revealing the glass, underscores the role of absence rather than presence. Similarly, Consciousness is termed 'limitless' to signify the absence of attributes, particularly the limitations experienced by individuals.

Indirect Implication: The conveyance of information about one thing through indirect discussion of another is plausible. When one of three individuals within a group affirms water consumption while the other two are absent, it implies their non-consumption. Similarly, Mauna Valkyana (silent statements) relay the presence of Brahman. The Upanishads, through the negation of everything within the universe as non-Brahman, delineate Brahman. By negating all entities, they ultimately reveal the unassailable subject—Consciousness. The *Kena Upanishad* declares: 'Neither known nor unknown, it is the knower principle, beyond these two.'

Critics argue that even if one concedes that words can convey knowledge, true understanding finds its ultimate fulfilment only through direct, intimate experience. In essence, knowledge must culminate in personal experience. Words, however, fall short in initiating direct experience and, as a result, remain incomplete. Vedanta, in its extensive discourse, imparts knowledge of Brahman that may not cultivate intimacy, as Brahman exists beyond the domain of direct experiential reach. Critics argue that this incompleteness renders the knowledge inadequate.

Indeed, it holds true that knowledge derived from Vedanta does not readily bestow direct experiential encounters. However, Vedanta does not aim to provide any specific form of experience, for its primary concern pertains not to the absence of experience, but to the absence of right knowledge itself. Every individual's experience can be categorized into two fundamental dimensions: Dvaita (dual) and Advaita (non-dual). Without exception, every human traverses both these dimensions throughout life.

During the waking and dreaming states, individuals encounter Dvaita experiences, wherein they perceive themselves as the experiencer—the subject—distinct from the objects in the world or dreams. This state of subject–object duality, known as savikalpa experience, creates a division between the subject and the object. Within this framework, individuals perceive themselves as unique entities, existing at specific places and times, and distinguishable from others. This recognition of separateness anchors their experiences in well-defined temporal and spatial contexts, reinforcing their sense of individuality.

Through this individual-centric perspective, individuals come to conceive of themselves as finite entities—an 'I' confined within the vastness of the world. This viewpoint entrenches the notion, 'I am a finite individual, and my world is intertwined with this individuality.' It is this perception that perpetuates the illusion of separation, obscuring the underlying unity and interconnectedness of existence. The subject's finite identity thus becomes central to their experience, shaping their interactions with the world and reinforcing the dualistic paradigm.

Conversely, during deep sleep, individuals do not experience this division between subject and object. This state, known as nirvikalpa, ushers in an experience that can loosely be referred to as 'nothingness'. In this state, all semblance of knowledge, division, time, space, and the world evaporate. Within this realm, non-dual Consciousness, the indivisible essence, reveals to the sleeper the sensation of nothingness, an experience that gains clarity upon awakening.

In the state of deep sleep, individuals are unable to realize their selves or the external world, resulting in the absence of individuality and localization. Consequently, the constraints of limitation elude them as well. This unbounded 'I' experienced during deep slumber is referred to as the Advaita experience. No other experiences lie beyond the boundaries of these dual and non-dual encounters. Vedanta does not offer new experiences, as human experience remains constrained by the triad of states—waking, dreaming, and deep sleep (avastratryam).

THE PREDICAMENT

It is one entrenched in perplexity. In the sheer of Dvaita, a person perceives himself as a confined 'I', whereas within Advaita, this very individual confronts no limitations. An individual cannot simultaneously be finite and infinite. Therefore, it can be posited that one of these states constitutes his authentic essence while the other assumes the guise of an incidental attribute. One must encompass his intrinsic nature (swabawika dharma), while the other is relegated to incidental attributes (aagantuka dharma). Either he truly embodies the intrinsic and incidentally assumes the veneer of limitation, or he genuinely embodies limitation and merely projects the illusion of limitlessness. The essence of the matter lies in comprehending this authentic nature as gleaned from the gamut of experiences at one's disposal.

Before engaging with the teachings of Vedanta, humanity adhered to the misconception that their authentic Self was the constrained 'i' while the boundless 'I' experienced during sleep was a transient deviation. Thus, the predicament stems from erroneous conclusions grounded in the prism of available experiences. The intent of Vedanta does not revolve around introducing a fresh experience or altering one's current experience. Instead, its purpose is to incite contemplation, urging individuals to question their conclusions and rectify them. 'The constraints experienced in the human journey are merely incidental.'

As articulated by the French philosopher Pierre Teilhard de Chardin, 'You are not a human being yearning for a spiritual experience or accumulating spiritual experiences; you are, in fact, a spiritual being, or the spirit itself, temporarily undergoing a human experience.' Vedanta aids human beings in arriving at accurate knowledge, a knowledge sufficient for claiming liberation. The predicament resides in the lack of knowledge, not in the absence of experience, and it is this very knowledge that Vedanta bestows.

From the foregoing, two conclusions crystallize with clarity, much like polished gemstones: firstly, the body and mind, though elevated to the status of intrinsic realities within the boundaries of Dvaita experiences, must relinquish their claim to the exalted domain of genuine intrinsic reality. This contention is grounded in the understanding that the body–mind amalgam is a possession temporarily held by the individual, inevitably fated for dissolution at a predetermined juncture. That which arrives and departs ought to be classified as incidental and fleeting in nature.

Secondly, in moments of slumber, the lack of conscious awareness about the presence of our body and mind unveils a profound truth: the essential role of the body and mind throughout our living existence becomes a subject of inquiry. The core of our existence lies solely within Consciousness—an essence that effortlessly leads our reconnection with all that existed before the depths of sleep, promptly upon the emergence into wakefulness. Therefore, one can assert with unwavering conviction that Consciousness stands as our quintessential intrinsic reality—an unbounded, unrestrained essence that transcends all limitations.

Chapter 14

THE THREE DISTINCT VEDANTA PHILOSOPHIES

The interpretation of Vedanta by venerable sages has given rise to three principal categories of beliefs, namely Advaita, Dvaita, and Vishishtadvaita. A brief understanding of these and their implications is crucial before delving into Vedic meditation. Equally important is a clear comprehension of the term 'soul' to form a well-informed perspective on the subject.

Brahman, the Supreme Consciousness, is the universal soul, the inner essence of all beings. Atman, not distinct from Brahman, is a term used only to signify Consciousness encapsulated within the human body as it were. They are identical, pure, and omnipresent. The individual soul, or jivatma, is the conscious mind, different from Atman. It becomes conscious due to the illumination it receives from Atman. In the absence of this illumination, the mind would resemble other inert objects in the world.

ADVAITA

Adi Shankaracharya is revered as the proponent of this philosophy, which is regarded as the oldest school of Vedanta. According to this perspective, Brahman is the sole reality and the world is deemed illusory (Maya). Suffering arises from ignorance of this reality, and liberation is attainable only through true knowledge of Brahman. The philosophy asserts that the real Self of an individual (Atman), the inner essence of all beings (distinct from the individual soul or conscious mind), and Brahman are identical. Liberation occurs when this realization dawns.

The crux of Shankara's philosophy is encapsulated in the aphorism 'Brahma satya jagat mithya, jivo Brahmaiva na aparah,' meaning Brahman (the absolute) alone is real; this world is unreal, and the inner essence of jivatma and God within the phenomenal world are non-different from Brahman. The individual identifies with the body–

mind complex due to Avidya (ignorance). The individuality persists as long as the reflection (awareness principle) of Atman, identifying itself with the mind—a reflecting medium—is mistakenly perceived by the individual as real consciousness.

The moment the jivatma grasps Atman as an independent entity within the body–mind–consciousness equation, acknowledging it as its true Self through jnana (knowledge), it sheds its individuality and recognizes its inherent nature, its infinite essence. The act of merging Atman (the inner essence of the individual) with Brahman (the Supreme Consciousness) is an intellectual exercise that unfolds only during the human lifespan.

DVAITA

Sage Madhvacharya propounded this school of thought.

This philosophy regards Brahman and Atman as distinct entities, and sees bhakti as the path to eternal salvation. Jivatma, the conscious mind, is considered Atman. Consequently, attributes such as birth, death, decay, and individuality, inherent to human beings, are ascribed to Atman. Due to variations in SRT, Karma, and Vasna, no two souls are alike and are different from Brahman.

Jivatma, the individual soul, which is essentially the conscious mind (matter), is being equated to Atman, the Supreme Consciousness (spirit). The jivatma naturally sheds its pseudo status upon uniting with Atman/Brahman, leading to liberation. Until liberation is achieved, the jivatma remains inferior to Brahman.

VISHISHTADVAITA

This philosophical school was initiated by Ramanujacharya in the eleventh century and is known as Vishishtadvaita, meaning 'qualified Advaita', signifying Advaita with certain modifications. While acknowledging Brahman as the unified whole, it posits that Brahman is characterized by multiple forms. According to Ramanujacharya, souls share an intrinsic sameness, aligning with the proclamation of Advaita.

In Vishishtadvaita, Brahman or God represents the entire universe, with matter and souls constituting Brahman's body while simultaneously being their soul. God is perceived as both the cause and the effect. This philosophy asserts that Brahman is the sole existence but allows for a plurality of souls. It occupies a middle ground between Advaita and Dvaita. God and individual souls are deemed inseparable, likened to the relationship between fire and spark. In liberation, the jivatma comprehends paramatma but does not merge with paramatma as it deems individual souls inferior to Brahman.

In the ultimate analysis, the aforementioned three philosophies represent distinct stages of spiritual evolution—from Dvaita to Vishishtadvaita, with Advaita as the culmination. It's crucial to note that no philosophy is deemed inferior to the others. The majority of Hindus typically align with the triangular mode, as elucidated earlier in this text, following the Dvaita philosophy, which maintains division among individuals with clear distinction between subject and object. In this perspective, they perceive God as the controller of their lives, distinctly separate from themselves.

Advaita philosophy is considered to precisely convey the essence of the Upanishads, the *Brahma Sutra*, and Bhagavad Gita. However, it finds popularity primarily among those who are spiritually highly evolved. Regarding individual belief, Advaita advocates adherence to the philosophy that resonates with the individual, allowing for a transition based solely on their understanding and conviction.

ADVAITA PHILOSOPHY—FURTHER ELUCIDATION

The notion of non-duality calls for further explication, although the term 'Advaita' was coined exclusively to dispel a misconception intertwined with the physical reality, a field deeply rooted in duality. This misconception arises from the failure to recognize the profound truth that the world, in essence, holds nothing; rather, the world itself resides within the singular and Supreme Consciousness. Everything as iterated ceaselessly within this text exists merely as name and form, devoid of independent substance. Duality evaporates in the radiant light of this realization.

Advaita philosophy, steadfast in its contrarian stance, refutes the concept of creation and, to a lesser extent, manifestation. It posits that the world, perceived as a manifold manifestation, is, in truth, but Brahman appearing like the world, akin to gold taking on diverse forms as ornaments. Sage Gaudapada, hailing from centuries past, boldly asserted that Brahman has never transformed into the universe, thus challenging the logic of causation. 'No one can prove the apparent enigma of the one becoming the many, for the many lacks genuine existence.' Advaita, however, does not dismiss the manifested world, for it constitutes an authentic experience.

Duality serves as a functional necessity within the phenomenal world. Nevertheless, it is incumbent upon seekers to unveil the truth, comprehending that duality and causality find no foothold within the non-dual Brahman. Those lacking the faculty of discrimination generally find solace in their experiences, deeming them real and eschewing inquiry. The undiscriminating mind remains trapped by life's theatrics, perceiving each experience as genuine and its outcomes as rewards or punishment.

Verily, the objects of the world subsist solely through belief in their existence. Mere belief, however, fails to validate reality. No object can subsist independently beyond the conscious mind of the perceiver. This revelation may, at some point, dawn upon anyone's life—a realization that we, like all other objects, coexist as mere apparitions. Advaita Vedanta aims to unveil the verity that duality is illusory. This wisdom shall extinguish the yearning for unreal objects.

In this context, numerous philosophers, capitalists, and critics argue that Advaita dissuades fervent individuals from actively pursuing aspirations, from transforming dreams into reality; instead, it promotes contentment within the space of dreams. Vedanta, on the contrary, never advises retreating from the bustling world to seek solace within uninhabited caves. Its decree is quite the opposite: be in the world, uplift humanity through the dissemination of knowledge, and the execution of virtuous deeds. The gravest misfortune, therefore, would be to deem progress unattainable without duality, without the subject-object relationship, and the 'I' factor—the sense of a doer. In truth, the most significant contributions to transform and save humanity have arisen from the absence of ego in noble souls who flourished in their altruism.

Aisha Ali, a resident of the UAE, is a highly accomplished woman in her early forties. Armed with a master's degree in Law and a wealth of experience in the banking sector, she appeared to have a promising future ahead of her. However, her life took an unexpected turn when she encountered a series of formidable challenges.

Her world was abruptly shaken by her PK. The unrelenting pressure imposed by her indiscriminate superior forced her to make the painful decision to resign from a highly promising career. Furthermore, she found herself trapped in an abusive marriage, compounded by the heartache of infertility, ultimately leading to a bitter divorce settlement. Adding to her already heavy burdens, she was one of eight siblings entrusted with the care of their elderly mother, who suffered from dementia and various health complications.

Aisha was left emotionally devastated, grappling with these immense challenges in solitude, with no visible ray of hope at the end of her dark tunnel. In the process, she not only lost hope but also her courage, confidence, and cheerfulness—three crucial attributes necessary to navigate life's trials and tribulations. She sank into deep depression and found herself hospitalized multiple times due to anxiety attacks, fuelled by her lack of interest in engaging with any activities.

It wasn't until almost five years had passed, during which she voluntarily isolated herself, that her path crossed with a noble soul—a staunch Vedantist—through a mutual acquaintance. This sage, through his wisdom, imparted to her the fundamental principles of Advaita Vedanta and, more specifically, guided her to reconfigure her SRTs, which were dominated by the 'T' factor. These teachings allowed her to grasp the profound importance of moving forward in life, aided by her own free will and the practice of Vedic meditation.

Aisha learned the powerful art of forgiveness and the ability to let go of grudges against those who had wronged her. She came to realize that those who inflict harm are, in truth, mere names and forms, lacking substance unless we ascribe reality to these illusory entities. As a result, she diligently worked to diminish the prominence of the 'T' in her life, consciously focusing on cultivating the 'R'—an endeavour that fundamentally transformed her outlook on both herself and the world around her. Although this transformation took time, it eventually bore fruit when she secured a suitable job opportunity in less than six months, due to her renewed proactive engagement with life.

Detractors of Advaita Vedanta question its practical applicability in everyday life, as its primary focus rests in cultivating awareness of the unreality of all but Brahman. It is indeed true that it does not provide instruction on extracting oil from seeds or augmenting experiential pleasure from fleeting material possessions. Instead, it imparts the wisdom of embracing Brahman, attaining eternal bliss, which is otherwise sought through action and material wealth.

As regards the negation of the world, the realized Advaitin finds nothing to negate, for there is nothing that exists other than Brahman, which is beyond negation. Brahman alone exists, permeating all actions and cognitive acts. Everything else with dependent existence is mithya—names and forms devoid of substance. Vedanta guides us to perceive Brahman everywhere, in every object, even in illusion, and to become one with it.

Therefore, we cannot contradict the truth of the physical world when perceived through the lens of the corporeal and cognitive faculties engaged in life's endeavours. However, we cannot lose sight of the greater reality of duality that begets all the quandaries of human existence. So long as we affirm the world's authenticity, we are bound to discharge all the tasks, duties, and responsibilities within the phenomenal domain, bearing in mind the tangible nature of the world.

The origin of all suffering lies in duality. The sole remedy for this predicament is the recognition that every object of experience is inherently unreal. True liberation comes with the realization that we are the pure, singular Consciousness, and boundless bliss.[25] Duality dissipates into nothing when one apprehends the veritable reality. When individuals align with their intrinsic essence, the concept of obligations and duties evaporates. For those who have shifted their perspective from the triangular paradigm to the binary construct, comprising the Conscious Spirit (Atma) and the inert world (Anatma), and have merged their corporeal and mental facets with the world, the 'I' of individuality is extinguished, and they have synchronized with the 'I' of Consciousness. Names and forms cease to exist as autonomous entities. This is not a mere hypothesis, but a tangible experience we encounter each night in slumber.

SECTION SEVEN

BONDAGE—A UNIVERSAL HUMAN DISEASE

Chapter 15

INTRODUCTION TO THE FIVE FORCES OF BONDAGE

Bondage traps individuals in the relentless cycles of suffering and ignorance. Attachment, grief, delusion, hesitation, and despondency are intricately woven together, forming the chains of captivity that hold the human spirit hostage. These forces are not isolated; they feed off and intensify one another, creating a self-reinforcing loop that clouds the mind and delays the realization of our true, inherent freedom.

Attachment arises from the innate desire to cling to people, possessions, outcomes, or ideas. Initially rooted in the need for security, it gradually deepens into an illusion of ownership and the misguided belief that external objects or circumstances can bring lasting happiness. This distortion often manifests in relationships, where attachment is mistaken for love, leading to an obsession with protecting and controlling the connection rather than fostering genuine intimacy.

Such attachment breeds dependency, anchoring the mind in a perpetual state of longing and fear—fear of losing what is cherished, and anxiety over failing to achieve what is desired. This fear inevitably gives rise to suffering, as the impermanence of the external world guarantees that change, loss, and unpredictability are unavoidable. When the object of attachment is threatened or lost, grief becomes the natural outcome, perpetuating the cycle of emotional turmoil and bondage.

Grief is the natural consequence of attachment. When anything we hold dear is taken away or changes beyond our expectations, the heart is plunged into sorrow. Grief reinforces the false notion that we are incomplete without the object of our attachment. It deepens the illusion of separation and perpetuates a sense of inadequacy. Grief anchors us in the past, hindering our ability to fully embrace the present moment and open to the transformative potential of the moment.

Delusion arises from a distorted perception of reality—an inability to see things as they truly are. It leads one to mistake the transient for the eternal, the unreal for the real, and the external for the Self. This distorted perception fuels attachment by creating false narratives around what we believe will bring lasting fulfilment. It obscures the deeper truths of existence, trapping us in a web of false identities and misplaced priorities. Without clarity, the mind remains bound, unable to discern the path to liberation.

Hesitation arises from fear, doubt, and a lack of self-assurance. It paralyses decisive action, hindering our pursuit of higher truths. Hesitation confines us to the comfort of the familiar, even when it breeds suffering. It stifles the courage and resolve necessary to break free from ingrained patterns of thought and behaviour. Without decisive action, the journey towards self-discovery remains stagnant.

Despondency emerges from prolonged struggle and the perception of insurmountable failure. It is the despair that arises when effort seems futile and goals appear unattainable. Despondency drains the energy and willpower essential for the spiritual journey. It traps individuals in a cycle of inaction, perpetuating the very bondage they seek to overcome.

These forces enumerated above are not insurmountable. They can be confronted and transcended through self-awareness, wisdom, and disciplined practice. Ancient teachings, such as those found in the Vedas and other spiritual traditions, offer tools to break free from these chains. By cultivating detachment, one learns to appreciate the world without being bound by it. By developing clarity, one pierces the veil of delusion. By fostering courage and resilience, one overcomes hesitation and despondency.

True love should not be mistaken for affection, nor does it dwell within relationships bound by the principle of give and take. It flowers only in the absence of all transactional expectations—where the idea of reciprocity dissolves, and only the selfless act of giving remains. Ultimately, liberation comes from recognizing the immortal essence within—the Self that is beyond the mind, beyond the body, and beyond the five negative forces that bind us. This realization dissolves the chains of bondage, allowing the individual to experience true freedom, unshaken by the transient nature of the external world. Only then can one fully embrace the infinite potential of the spirit, unburdened and liberated.

MAYA: THE MIRAGE

Amidst the countless lives, each donning diverse roles in the grand theatre of existence, a notable character emerges—the enigma known as Maya. Strangely, she, in her guise as the manifest, yet the invisible Delilah, wields pivotal influence over the ceaseless spectacle of the cosmos. Ignorance takes shape in her form; Maya is ignorance incarnate. Her touch conjures illusion. She is palpable, not a mere illusion. The very term 'Maya', bearing the connotation of 'non-existence', must be grasped as the absence of an effect (non-existent) brought about by ignorance, particularly concerning the world and all the entities it holds. Depending on the context, Maya unveils diverse facets—magic, illusion, and delusion.

In certain dimensions, Maya encapsulates the notion of 'mystery' within a framework where a straightforward examination of any worldly object metamorphoses it into something different, highlighting the concept that, fundamentally, everything is a fusion of diverse elements. This process gradually diminishes the very essence to nothingness, until it ultimately fades away. Each investigation reduces the world to elements, molecules, atoms, and energy until even energy dissolves into motion—an insight that reveals the illusory nature of all perceived reality. Energy in motion crafts this illusion, an unmanifest version of tangible forms. With every inquiry, the world gradually dissolves into the void, confirming the theory that the perceived world lacks separate existence from the observer, just as the vivid dream world inseparable from the dreamer, vanishes upon waking.

Similarly, no separate world exists apart from the observer, the Consciousness. Hence, the individual ensnared in lending authenticity to the waking world parallels the dreamer ensnared by their dream's reality. Like Consciousness, Maya endures eternally, in manifest or unmanifest form. Yet, unlike Consciousness, Maya is illusory, existing within the perspective of Consciousness, while Consciousness alone remains enduringly real. Her extinction arrives when man comprehends his authentic nature as Consciousness.

The feminine gender is attributed to Maya because it is the dynamic energy principle that alone evolves into the apparent world of multiplicity—a creation of sorts—at the physical level. As the projecting power of Brahman, Maya manifests the formless Absolute into the diverse appearances of the phenomenal world, though in truth, no real creation ever takes place. Consciousness alone can affirm the existence of all, as nothing pre-exists it. All that ensues may be likened to sparks within a fire. Since the sole absolute truth (Consciousness) also forms the foundation for apprehending the physical world, nothing beyond that which relies on Consciousness for existence can hold reality. Ergo, the perception of a manifold world is born of man's ignorance. From distorting the concept of creation to presenting an illusory world as authentic, Maya, like a queen bee, reigns in the hearts of men and women. Her role as the solitary architect behind the universe's creation and sustenance has earned her a feminine moniker. Her traits cluster within three spheres.

First, as personified ignorance, she conjures diversity through her power of projection. She leads jivas, the individual beings astray into a domain of illusion, projecting pure Consciousness as a world of multiplicity. Distinctions arise due to her influence.

Her second attribute is change. Concealing reality, she estranges individuals from acknowledging their true essence. They misidentify the unreal as authentic, dwelling in duality, a wellspring of suffering. Expectations, desires, and values vacillate as their minds succumb to the domain of ignorance.

Lastly, the misconception of creation's genesis rests within Maya's world. Ignorance weaves a web of enigma, challenging human intellect with myriad questions; hence, Maya is often likened to a question mark. As one delves into Maya, the cloak of ignorance and restlessness befalls the intellect. Only the one attuned to their genuine nature evades Maya's grasp, sidestepping her entanglements.

IGNORANCE (CAUSE) AND ERROR (EFFECT)

'Where ignorance dwells, error inevitably follows suit. The simultaneous presence of wisdom and ignorance lays the fertile ground for folly. Ignorance begets error; it is the cause from which the effect springs.'

Sage Gaudapada, in his *Karikas* on the *Mandukya Upanishad*, sheds profound light on this notion. To exemplify this concept, the sage employs the renowned Vedanta metaphor known as the 'Rajjusarpa Nyaya'—the tale of the rope and the snake.

In the dusky cloak of night, a man treading upon a dimly lit path spies a serpent barring his passage. Fear overtakes him. Armed with this knowledge, he flees in the opposite direction. When he retraces his steps along the same path the next morning, he discovers nothing but a coiled rope on the ground. It then dawns upon him that, in obscurity, he had mistaken the rope for a serpent. In this tale, a partial knowing of the object's presence is accompanied by a partial ignorance of its true nature. Further, the rope remains shrouded in ignorance, thus giving rise to the misjudgement of it as a serpent. Through this allegory, Vedanta imparts a cardinal lesson: both partial knowledge and partial ignorance hold peril, while absolute knowing and complete unknowing (in certain circumstances) bring serenity.

Sage Gaudapada affirms that the existence of every mortal is, in essence, a blend of ignorance and error, particularly with reference to our misconceptions concerning our intrinsic reality—the boundless Consciousness. But this truth remains concealed from our ken. Hence, a fundamental quandary of self-ignorance persists, wherein we remain unaware of our boundless Self. Ignorance begets error, and in the domain of self-ignorance, the error is the conception of a limited self.

He further expounds upon this concept by illustrating how mortals perceive themselves in their waking and dreaming states.

During the waking hours, we perceive ourselves as the finite 'Self'. The ignorance (cause) of our boundlessness gives rise to the perception of limitation (effect). Thus, we converse about our birth, aging, infirmities, and our eventual demise. In our wakefulness, we slumber, for we speak of mortality even though, in truth, humans are immortal from the vantage point of our intrinsic reality—the eternal Consciousness.

In dreams as well, the dreamer identifies as the finite self.

In deep slumber, no one experiences limitation; yet the sleeper remains oblivious to their boundless nature. This is unalloyed ignorance, untainted by error. As the mind of the slumbering soul dissolves temporarily, it does not have the capacity for folly and thus perceives itself as an infinite individual. Therefore, the error of a limited 'self' does not persist, but within slumber, ignorance of the boundless 'Self' remains.

A rope, in partial illumination, breeds partial ignorance, hence the misperception. In the shroud of utter darkness, total ignorance reigns, and nothing but accurate perception prevails, devoid of serpentine dread. In the sphere of partial ignorance or partial knowing, bondage and the cycle of existence, known as samsara, take root. A sage, possessing full knowledge, thus finds liberation from the shackles of bondage.

Chapter 16

KARMA, FATALISM, AND FREE WILL

Karma encompasses both our actions and the consequences that flow from those actions, referred to as Karma Phalam. These consequences manifest as subtle impressions, which abide as the exclusive investment of the doer. In simpler terms, karma embodies the joy (punyam) and sorrow (papam) accrued through our prior virtuous and sinful deeds, conducted through our thoughts, speech, and actions. In the earthly realm, actions triggered by desires and their absence play a pivotal role in the lives and liberation of human beings, respectively. Action, which is termed karma, is indeed at the heart of creation and existence.

In a world that places unwavering reliance upon scientific validation before embracing any theory, the karma doctrine stands akin to a man without a spine.

It is an undeniable verity that we lack concrete proof of the karma theory, much like any subject dwelling within the metaphysical world. Therefore, to assimilate the concept of karma we are left to rely upon the multitude of unforeseen events that routinely unfold in the lives of all, as a potential indicator of the workings of nature in the absence of empirical evidence. For the sake of solace, many liken Karma Phalam to Newton's law, which posits that for every action, there exists an equal and opposite reaction. This conclusion is drawn by observing the deeds that often yield no discernible outcome or results that deviate entirely from expectations.

From a rationalist's perspective, therefore, the acceptance or rejection of the theory may indeed hinge solely upon an individual's faith. However, as a society, we must not disregard the need to delve into the bedrock of the Karma doctrine, for this neglect would continue to leave countless individuals grappling with unpredictable events, uncertain of their course of action.

Science too frequently encounters situations that lie beyond its capacity to discern a cause within its field. When these challenges become insurmountable, they leave the problem unresolved, forcing the afflicted to cope with helplessness on their own, as is the case for individuals suffering from idiopathic diseases—ailments with unknown causes or mechanisms of apparent spontaneous origin. It is true that while we have a good understanding of the causes of several medical conditions, there remains a percentage of cases where the cause is not immediately clear. In some other medical conditions, the root cause has not been identified for a significant portion of cases, so these are also categorized as idiopathic. Certain medical conditions, when the cause is idiopathic, notably some forms of epilepsy and stroke, are preferentially described by the synonymous term 'cryptogenic'.

This certainly appears to be a generous gesture—bestowing upon science the benefit of doubt to fill the void in understanding, while allowing the passage of time to heal physical wounds or guide those affected towards their ultimate destination. Yet, humankind often exhibits a marked reluctance to embrace viable metaphysical solutions, particularly in the absence of scientific endorsement, to address psychological ailments that are frequently more agonizing than physical pain. The disparity is glaring: society readily invests in treating physical maladies but hesitates or falters when confronted with the complexities of mental health.

This inequity underscores a deeply imbalanced approach. The stigma surrounding psychological distress, combined with a lack of urgency to prioritize its resolution, reinforces this divide. While physical pain garners immediate empathy and action, psychological suffering is often dismissed, misunderstood, or minimized.

The choice to grasp and derive value from any theory, whether it bears the fortification of science or not, remains an intrinsic right of every human being, for belief serves as the very cornerstone of human existence. When reason falters in its quest to offer lucid explanations, or when it proves impossible to uncover the cause concealed within the effect through scientific means, our sole recourse is to find solace in inference, scriptural endorsement, and even lean upon presumptions or simple faith to alleviate the struggles that beset our primary objectives.

Our comprehension of the world and existence remains fragmentary and flawed. Not every enigma yields to reason or evidence. We subsist not merely on reason alone but also on faith, enabling us to confront life's uncertainties and ambiguities. Without faith, the motivation to pursue one's aspirations diminishes. Faith is a prerequisite for taking any action, for no endeavour can be deemed devoid of risk. Until we accomplish a task or attain a goal, it is faith that sustains us.

TYPES OF KARMA

The law of Karma unequivocally dictates that we cannot absolve ourselves of the consequences of our actions, be they positive or negative, under any circumstances, as these consequences will manifest either in our present or future lives. To gain a deeper comprehension of the doctrine of Karma, the Vedas meticulously categorize it into three distinct classifications:

Sanchita Karma (SK)

This category encompasses the amassed baggage of all unresolved karmas, carried forward by an individual from previous lifetimes, awaiting the fruition of their karmic outcomes. It represents a vast and intricate network of cause and effect, forming the core reason behind the cycle of reincarnation or the acquisition of a new embodiment. Each life serves as a stage to exhaust the karmic fruits tied to certain past actions while simultaneously providing opportunities for new actions to be performed, thereby generating fresh karmas.

This inexhaustible reservoir perpetually expands, as every life contributes to the creation and accumulation of countless karmas, many of which remain unfulfilled or unexperienced by the end of that lifetime. These unresolved karmas in each life continue to flow into the reservoir, weaving a complex tapestry of consequences that shape future existences. Beyond its role in governing reincarnation, this karmic storehouse also includes those karmas carved out as Prarabdha Karma—the portion of past karma destined to bear fruit in the present life, influencing events, relationships, and circumstances.

It underscores the cyclical nature of life and the continuous interplay between past actions, present experiences, and future outcomes. Importantly, the Sanchita Karma—the entire karmic 'warehouse'—always resides within the mind as a latent repository. However, it is the PK that dictates the trajectory of an individual's current life, steering their experiences and shaping the course of their journey within the broader framework of cosmic justice.

Prarabdha Karma (PK)

This subset of Sanchita Karma is the portion that unfurls and yields results in the current lifetime. Through a meticulously structured system, it determines the cycles of joy and sorrow experienced in a human life. This influence extends to various events and factors in the worldly realm, such as circumstances of birth, physical attributes, family background, identity, birth-related attributes and challenges, health, the quality of relationships, wealth, fame, progeny, and finally the nature of one's passing. It manifests as a consequence of one's desires, the absence of desires, or external interventions. It is not negotiable, not transferable, and not reversible. No one can evade the inexorable influence of PK and its accompanying consequences. It matters not whether one is poor or rich, famous or obscure, a politician or a religious leader, or even a spiritually enlightened individual.

To elucidate the distinctive characteristics of PK, let us delve into a real incident that brought profound humiliation to a revered and highly esteemed sage.

The arrest of Jayendra Saraswathi, the then head of the Kanchi mutt in southern India and his subsequent release after two months of incarceration in 2004, unveils a compelling narrative. The alleged involvement of the esteemed spiritual luminary (pontiff) in the murder case of Sankararaman, the manager of a temple within the same district, casts a spotlight on the inexorable principle of karma that carves its trajectory. It extends its reach to all without exception, regardless of their standing within the hierarchical order, ensuring that the repercussions of one's actions are fully experienced.

Typically, these venerated sages, renowned for their rigorous adherence to the principles of Advaita Vedanta, are said to have transcended the three fundamental energy propensities that compel us to engage in both virtuous and malevolent deeds. Through their unwavering observance of Vedic injunctions, they successfully shed the trappings of human traits, such as likes, dislikes, love, hatred, desires, delusions, anger, greed, competitiveness, and jealousy, well before their consecration. Consequently, these sagacious luminaries become highly sought after for their profound wisdom in matters of religion and philosophy, garnering the utmost reverence from high-ranking officials, celebrities, the general populace, and the ascetic brethren who ardently follow their teachings, as they bear the torch of compassion and uphold the loftiest virtues.

Therefore, one cannot help but ponder the forces that might have driven them to partake in actions that ultimately led to their downfall from the highest echelons of society. In this specific instance, there were a few who speculated that J Jayalalithaa, then the chief minister of Tamil Nadu, issued the order for the arrest of the sage, guided by the counsel of her astrologer, who had advised the detention of Jayendra Saraswathi until 23 December. This seems bizarre, but PK can draw upon a wide array of internal or external sources to bring about its fruition. Irrespective of the circumstances surrounding the episode, a man of such elevated eminence found himself compelled to endure the trials and tribulations wrought by the deeds of his past, which seemed to materialize through purportedly unlawful activities in his current lifetime.

Operation PK

Let us consider a scenario where an individual holds an outstanding balance of 100 units of karma within the Sanchita Karma basket, awaiting their future experiences. In this analogy, we shall symbolize each of these karmas as 'arrows'. Each arrow, in its essence, encapsulates several key aspects: the nature of the deed (whether it falls within the spectrum of good, bad, toxic, and so on), the duration of the karma (referring to the time spent to perform the karma), and the resulting impact it generates.

The impact of karma can only be gauged through the intensity and duration of joy or sorrow experienced by the affected entity. This is why the person undergoing the consequences of such actions is often bewildered, as they have no insight into the extent to which a good or bad deed affects the other person. For example, if an individual subjects their child to abuse for fifteen minutes, causing the child to endure anxiety and fear for the subsequent ten days, the repercussions of such karma will inevitably manifest in the abuser's life for ten days, with the same intensity of suffering as that inflicted upon the child. This principle holds for positive karma as well.

Taken collectively, these aforementioned factors play a crucial role in shaping the extent and intensity of joy or sorrow, referred to as Karma Phalam, that an individual will encounter in their journey of life. As the new body, housing the old mind, embarks on its journey, it inevitably encounters both physical and psychological pain and pleasure. Typically, Karma Phalam manifests as the fruits of past actions, bringing forth favourable or unfavourable situations in the realms of health, relationships, finances, and social status.

It's crucial to emphasize that the Sanchita Karma basket contains a diverse mix of karmas accumulated over various past lives, rendering it impossible to discern specific details through meditation, introspection, or retrogradation techniques. It is from this intricate basket that the blueprint of PK for the next life is meticulously crafted. This intricate process unfolds within the brief span of about six to nine minutes, during which the individual soul, known as the jivatma, along with the subtle mind and the physiological support provided by the ordained system for bodily functions, departs from the physical body. This departure signifies the culmination of the individual's life and marks the journey towards a new embodiment.

Therefore, the individual assumes the role of the author of the PK blueprint. According to the Vedas, those who have actively pursued virtuous deeds through thoughts, words, and actions in their present life and maintained unwavering devotion to the divine are more likely to craft a more favourable destiny for their next incarnation.

In the analogy mentioned above, when ten arrows with varying tenors are chosen from the Sanchita basket, the cumulative sum of the tenors covered by each arrow determines the duration of the individual's next life. The initial arrow's experience holds sway over the fate of the foetus, influencing the path of the developing child both in the womb and after birth. If the combined duration of karmas to be experienced falls short of the typical nine-month gestation period, it may result in a miscarriage or the birth of a stillborn child. This outcome occurs when the PK of the mother-to-be, which encompasses her Karma Phalam, aligns and intertwines with that of the developing child, creating what is classified as joint karma.

Upon the child's birth, each arrow unfolds to bring either joy or sorrow, depending on the specifics of that particular arrow's influence on the individual. The following illustration serves to explain this concept better. Kim Eun, born into a middle-class Korean family, was an endearing child. Thanks to the influence of joint Karma Phalam, her family enjoyed positive progress, witnessing a steady improvement in their economic circumstances. When an opportunity arose, they collectively decided to relocate to the USA. Displaying a keen interest in learning from the onset of her first-grade journey, Kim excelled academically, securing top grades in her class. She later clinched the championship in the Spelling Bee competition, adding another accolade to her achievements.

Pursuing her undergraduate studies in English language, she went on to ace the LSAT examination, earning the global first rank and unlocking the doors to Harvard Law School, which warmly welcomed her. Once again, Kim excelled at Harvard, graduating as a top-ranking law student, poised to embark on her corporate career. Throughout this journey, she enjoyed the positive outcomes of a past arrow symbolizing good karma, culminating in a joy-filled graduation ceremony. However, upon maturity of the positive outcomes from the previous arrow, a new arrow that came into play proved less favourable. Over the next three years, Kim grappled with the challenge of securing a suitable job, navigating through various roles until she eventually found a position as a content writer for a company specializing in web design services. She is now one among the many leading a life as a single woman in a city full of heartless beings.

Frequently, two or more arrows come to fruition simultaneously. This is why many of us experience both joy and sorrow concurrently, illustrating the intricate interplay of karma in our lives.

Agami Karma (AK)

Among the three types of karma delineated in the Vedas, Agami Karma hinges on present-moment actions and can be influenced by an individual to yield favourable outcomes in the future. Some of these karmas, not experienced in the present life, will subsequently find their way into the reservoir of Sanchita Karmas.

Typically, the quality of Agami Karma (AK) is shaped by an individual's thoughts, which are, in turn, influenced by their likes, dislikes, and tendencies (Sattva, Rajas, and Tamas—SRT) as well as the Vasnas they have cultivated over time. By understanding the implications of this intricate interplay, individuals can consciously reconfigure their SRT, replacing negative tendencies with constructive ones. They can also actively cultivate positive Vasnas through mindful interactions with the external world. Simultaneously, refining their internal thought patterns by aligning them with higher values and intentions enables them to transform the trajectory of their karmic imprint, paving the way for spiritual growth and harmony.

Forms of Agami Karma

Sattvic Karma: The foundation of all karmas lies in our thoughts. Therefore, it is crucial to cultivate virtuous thoughts before undertaking any action. When our thoughts are inherently good, our speech and actions naturally align with those virtuous intentions in general. The result of such actions is characterized by their sattvic (pure and selfless) nature. Sattvic karma is the act of directing our actions towards the betterment of a broader community, with less emphasis on personal gain.

Rajasic Karma: In this type of karma, the primary focus is on personal benefit, although it may extend to include others on a selective basis. The underlying thought process is often centred on self-gain, and actions are taken to benefit oneself, with some consideration for others if it serves the individual's self-interest.

Tamasic Karma: Tamasic karma is characterized by a singular focus on personal benefit, often at the expense of others. In such actions, the doer may not hesitate to cause harm to individuals perceived as obstacles to achieving their selfish goals. The overriding intent here is self-centred, without regard for the welfare or well-being of others.

DIVERSE EFFECTS OF KARMA

Delayed Effect: Frequently, we encounter the repercussions of karma long after the original action has concluded. For instance, the true consequence of a burn to one's finger may manifest many hours after the initial incident. Transmigration of karma consequences flowing from one life to the next life is the result of the delayed effect of karma.

Coincidence or Joint Effect: Joint karma operates on various levels, manifesting in diverse scenarios. One facet suggests that a fortuitous or calamitous encounter with a stranger can lead to significant shifts in one's destiny, sometimes resulting in a substantial windfall or a plunge into deep misery. Importantly, it is crucial to note that such coincidences may or may not recur.

Often, we find ourselves entangled in relationships within family or social circles necessitating unavoidable interactions with individuals characterized by dominant traits of a 'T' personality, radiating negative energy. In such instances, it is wise to restrict interactions to the bare minimum or even consider ending the relationship without excessive worry about potential repercussions.

This holds particular significance when evaluating relationships founded on misplaced attachment. Influenced by herd mentality, a substantial number of individuals within the triangular mode, seeking external assistance for fulfilment of desires, become entangled in one-way relationships with purported spiritual gurus or self-proclaimed godmen. These associations are often fuelled by either greed or hope, with followers forming excessive attachments and relying on the guru to catalyse changes in their PK.

However, endowed with remarkable eloquence, these gurus skilfully foster a cult following, exploiting the vulnerabilities confessed by the individuals. They show little regard for the essential duty of a guru, which is to empower followers towards independence. Instead, they render their devotees increasingly reliant on their guru to the extent that they cease to make autonomous decisions, be it the most trivial matters or significant undertakings. In the course of karma's coincidences, numerous followers may have encountered favourable results. However, there exists no assurance that such outcomes will recur or that a positive outcome will transpire at all for many, a reality seldom pondered by those of feeble disposition.

Being fully aware of this phenomenon, the gurus invest all their time in increasing their following through well-crafted strategies. After all, it is a numbers game for them, who flourish upon the theory of odds. It is crucial to remember the cause-and-effect theory, which establishes a direct correlation between our successes or failures and karma. Unaware of this truth, misguided followers perpetually imprison themselves in the relationship by attributing their triumphs to the blessings of their guru.

Blinded by the charisma emanating from these gurus, they persist in these relationships during adversities, hopeful that the guru will resolve their problems, even when the ideas presented consistently fail to yield the desired results. Victims of ignorance in such circumstances do not engage in performing new karmas necessary for resurrecting themselves. Instead, by relying on the guru to perform magic, they are prepared to endure hardships for extended periods.

The unpredictable nature of these encounters underscores the dynamic and unpredictable interplay of karma in shaping individual destinies.

Another dimension involves the interplay of Karma Phalam between individuals in a relationship, where a person, while experiencing one's Karma Phalam to a certain degree, could suffer or enjoy the partner's Karma Phalam with greater potency. It is crucial to note that only the specific Karma Phalam of one of the partners is jointly experienced by both partners without an actual transfer of karma. For example, a woman from an affluent family, married to a wealthy partner, might undergo profound financial hardships due to the changing fortunes and individual karmic experiences of her spouse, and simultaneously experience physical or mental pain due to her karmas. This intricate web of shared consequences illustrates how joint karma, through the interconnected nature of relationships, weaves a tapestry of experiences that shape the course of individual destinies.

In a different context, a poignant illustration emerges. The daughter of a highly successful medical practitioner faced challenges in securing a life partner despite her good looks and qualifications as a software engineer. After a series of unsuccessful relationships, she found her ideal match at the age of thirty-five, with wedding plans underway. However, during this auspicious period, her father's medical license was revoked by the government due to consistent negligence, leading to a patient's death. The ensuing legal battle and financial losses affected the family, causing the planned wedding to be cancelled by the groom. Despite the daughter's lack of involvement in her father's actions, the incident exemplifies the intricate alignment of individual karmas, offering a glimpse into the profound concepts of Vedanta regarding the connections we form in our lives and the circumstances into which we are born

Cross Effect:

Karma executed through actions can profoundly affect our mental state, and conversely, negative thoughts directed towards another person can have a detrimental impact on both parties.

Simultaneous Multiple Effect

This pertains to the simultaneous experience of both joy and sorrow at the same time. It also encompasses situations where we undergo sorrow due to the end of a relationship, financial loss, and illness occurring concurrently.

Karmic consequences often manifest not as isolated events but as the interplay of multiple actions unfolding simultaneously. While karma typically operates individually, experiences can overlap, and new outcomes may arise before earlier ones are fully resolved. This dynamic explains why moments of joy can unexpectedly emerge even amidst sorrow.

Transmigration

This concept encompasses the influence of past-life Karma on the acquisition of subsequent embodiments and the experiences that follow. It delves into the principle of life after death. Ignorance, the cause of reincarnation, impacts the individual soul and not the universal soul, Brahman. The array of individuals, each endowed with unique qualities, endures until the dissolution of the cosmic process. This multiplicity is intrinsic to the cosmos, inseparable from its existence. Liberated souls comprehend and wholeheartedly embrace this truth, living in harmonious alignment with it. In contrast, the unenlightened ones persist in navigating the cycle of birth and rebirth, ensnared by the effects of karma. This is the divine design, a means for the continuous refinement of the soul in each birth, ultimately leading to the attainment of immortality.

FATALISM AND FREE WILL

In stark contrast to karma, fatalism acts as a corrosive force, steadily eroding confidence and weakening faith in our innate capacity to transcend karmic repercussions. It obstructs personal growth and derails the pursuit of life's true purpose. Both karma and fatalism can entrap the unenlightened, yet their natures are fundamentally different.

Karma affirms the sovereignty of human will, offering a framework of cause and effect wherein actions bear consequences. Fatalism, on the other hand, denies agency altogether—suggesting that outcomes are fixed, rendering human effort meaningless. While fatalists remain imprisoned by the belief that destiny cannot be altered, karma offers a path to liberation through new action.

The ancient Vedas recognize this distinction clearly: fatalism is likened to an unbreakable chain, whereas karma upholds the dignity of choice. Nonetheless, those entrenched in fatalistic beliefs often misinterpret karma as equally deterministic. They argue that since every experience is predestined by PK, free will is an illusion. In their view, even the capacity to respond to adversity is preordained—leaving no space for initiative or transformation.

Vedanta challenges such assumptions as being rooted in ignorance. Unlike other beings, humans are gifted with refined intellect and fewer limitations. This enables us to exercise free will, especially in initiating new actions—Agami Karma (AK)—even while experiencing the fruits of Prarabdha Karma (PK). While PK may influence the available choices or their outcomes, free will is never entirely eclipsed. There may be uncertainty or even an absence of visible results, but the power to act remains intact.

Consider the example of someone who loses a job due to karmic necessity. They may initially attempt to find work, but if unsuccessful, could fall into despair and inaction. Yet, the doctrine of karma insists that self-conscious human beings always retain the power to act, to make choices anew. Whether those choices yield the desired result is secondary—what matters is that the potential for action itself remains undiminished.

In essence, karma and its results mirror the law of cause and effect. Free will exists within the space before action—where decisions are made. Vedantin asserts that fate does not negate free will; in fact, it demands fresh action regardless of whether outcomes align with expectations. There is always hope in action, while inaction born from fatalism breeds stagnation and despair.

Swami Nikhilananda rightly observed that the doctrine of karma is India's unique philosophical contribution to the world. However, it is often misunderstood and misrepresented as fatalism—its very opposite. Karma is about engagement and evolution; fatalism promotes resignation. Both produce consequences, but human nature is inherently inclined towards action, while inaction is often more painful and corrosive to the spirit.

Every action produces a reaction. Confusion arises particularly when we experience sorrow. We naturally seek meaning in adversity, but when we can't trace its origin to past karma, we tend to label it as fate. This leads to inner conflict and spiritual stagnation. To progress, we must interpret karma and its outcomes correctly.

Though individuals are solely responsible for their present circumstances, life remains an open field for renewal. The recognition of this truth highlights karma not as a burden, but as a catalyst for transformation. It fuels our resolve to embark on constructive paths in pursuit of a more meaningful existence.

An important point must be made here: While free will presents options, it also introduces duality—conflict and contradiction. Choices can generate hesitation. However, for those who are clear about their spiritual goal—abidance in the bliss of Brahman—there is no such inner struggle. When the destination is known and the path illumined by wisdom, decision dissolves into devotion.

The sole purpose of presenting the doctrine of Karma in detail is to remind us, as human beings, to remain ever conscious of our actions even before we perform them—indeed, even before a thought arises. It should not matter if the said karma is driven by Prarabdha Karma or a new Agami Karma.

For many, the timing may not seem ripe to fully grasp the significance of aligning with one's true Self. Yet, this knowledge can help refine one's thinking, making it sattvic. Naturally, sattvic thought gives rise to sattvic speech and action. At the very least, such awareness ensures the accumulation of good karma to be experienced in the future. Thus, the teaching is simple: think before you think.

Chapter 17

DEATH AND BIRTH

Our view of 'death and birth' as opposites lies at the core of our fear of death, often overshadowing our concerns about the challenges of life. Yet, life itself can be the greater struggle, filled with emotional turmoil, contradictions, limitations, and constant adjustments, making it a difficult journey. For those who believe in reincarnation and the cycle of karmic consequences, death is not the end but a blessing—a chance to start anew and gain from engaging in virtuous actions.

The common perception of death suggests the termination of life's trials, yet it looms even more formidable. Death merely signals the conclusion of our current life's odyssey with the vessel of our cherished bodies, and beckons the dawn of a new commencement. A fresh life awaits, clothed in an entirely new embodiment. This cycle persists until the recognition dawns upon us that we are immortal spirits, undergoing the human experience.

In the realm of uncertainty that follows death, grasping the rationales behind our diverse experiences is crucial, especially if we acknowledge the law of cause and effect as a guiding principle in the physical world. A meticulous review of one's past often lays bare a perplexing dissonance between actions taken in one's current existence and their outcomes. It's not rare to witness genuinely virtuous individuals grappling with a lifetime of hardships in areas like finance, health, and relationships. Conversely, an individual with a track record of misdeeds might revel in life's abundance. This inequality challenges the conventional notion that every action causes an equal and opposite reaction.

The brevity of a single lifetime frequently proves insufficient to fully experience the repercussions of all the karmas we perform through thoughts, speech, and action. This underscores the significance of the concept of the transmigration of jivatma, the soul, at life's conclusion. It provides the opportunity for a new embodiment, essential for navigating and resolving the consequences of past actions.

As previously elucidated, PK functions as the blueprint shaping our present life, intricately influencing our actions to align with the karmic outcomes we are destined to face. This accentuates the notion that each individual is, in essence, the architect of their destiny.

The Vedas further expound on the enduring void, lingering even after the fulfilment of all desires, as the inherent result of one's prior actions. Until the wisdom of Brahman, the essence of eternal bliss and ultimate reality, unfurls within an individual, the search for the reasons behind the gap shall persist, and individuals will find themselves tirelessly oscillating between virtuous and less-than-virtuous deeds in a continuous effort to alleviate the negative consequences of their past actions. Once this concept is grasped, the significance of engaging in virtuous deeds becomes apparent, serving as the transformative force that shapes a more favourable life through the intricate process of reincarnation.

The Vedas assert that reincarnation serves dual purposes: firstly, to address the consequences of past actions, and secondly, to steer us towards transforming our thoughts and deeds, ultimately culminating in liberation from all forms of suffering.

What really happens before death?

When death approaches, the body's vital forces begin to converge around the jivatma—the self identified with the conscious mind, or the small 'i'—residing in the heart. At this critical juncture, the jivatma reveals a subtle blueprint for the kind of body it will require in the next birth, shaped by the accumulated PK that is due for experience. This new karmic package, though essential for the journey ahead, does not belong to the true Self; rather, it is a provisional design tailored solely for the unfolding of karmic consequences in the next life. As the jivatma prepares to depart, a struggle for breath ensues, and when the upper end of the heart lights up, the departure begins. When the gross body falls away, the vital and mental sheaths remain as the vehicle of the soul. The path of exit from the physical body—whether through the eye or the head—is determined by the proportion of virtuous and malevolent actions performed in this life, as well as by the degree of devotion shown to the Divine. The jivatma, now laden with its karmic package, transitions to the body it is about to inhabit. Knowledge, work, and past experiences accompany the jivatma through this journey. 'In a way similar to how a leech on a blade of grass reaches its end, grasps another support, and draws itself towards it, the jivatma, after discarding its old body and rendering it unconscious, seizes a new anchor and draws itself towards it. In the new body, the organs, under the control of the karmic package, become active and coordinated, and an objective connection between the various forms of life remains undisturbed. Simultaneously, the physical body takes form and falls into its arrangement.'[26]

The Upanishads explain that while the body is cremated, the jivatma ascends along its predetermined path—either toward the sun or the moon. It eventually descends to Earth in the form of rain, gets absorbed by plants bearing grains, and is consumed as food by humans. This way, it enters the semen and, upon entering a woman's womb, is reborn as a human being.

However, individuals who do not follow the path of gods or the ways of their ancestors may be reborn as lesser beings, such as insects, moths, or biting creatures like gnats and mosquitoes.

Reincarnation remains a near-certainty, as the law of karma is unyielding until one finds a path to permanently liberate the soul by merging with Brahman. Despite this, the Vedas prescribe guidelines for leading a religious life and appeasing the highest deities to gain favours in the material world. The underlying message is for human beings to gain experiential insight into the futility of attachment to material possessions, and in doing so, gradually cultivate wisdom and its effects. This transformation leads to a state of profound understanding of Brahman.

SECTION EIGHT

FREEDOM—A UNIVERSAL DESIRE

Chapter 18

LIBERATION

As we conclude our exploration of the various topics of the pure Vedas, it becomes crucial to delve into the profound concept of liberation, which holds utmost significance in Vedic meditation. This necessitates revisiting the fundamental question posed at the beginning of this treatise.

If we accept the notion that our destiny hangs in obscurity on either side of the grave, what can we aspire to comprehend once life's flame dims, if, during our earthly existence we have not understood why a human soul was bestowed upon us?

The divine decree that exclusively graces human beings with the sacred privilege is 'liberation'. It signifies reaching a state of existence characterized by the complete eradication of all suffering and a permanent escape from the relentless cycle of birth and death. Liberation represents a state of ultimate perfection where there is no regression into imperfection or struggle. It's essential to grasp that achieving liberation is not about gaining something or experiencing it as a future event. Instead, it occurs instantaneously for the individuals who decide to shift their perspective and commit to abiding by it. No effort, action, or sacrifice is required.

The individual who attains the knowledge of Brahman, our true identity, is deemed to have reached the sublime state, the ultimate goal of life. On the contrary, those who fail to comprehend Brahman and recognize Consciousness as their intrinsic reality are destined to remain ensnared in the unending cycle of birth and death, enduring the suffering of bondage, and possibly even relegation to a sub-human state.

The Vedas emphasize that it is the human body, and not the divine or animal forms, which possesses the capability to engage in actions according to the various steps outlined for gaining the knowledge of Brahman, ultimately leading to liberation. Divine beings (gods belonging to the physical world) and animals merely experience the consequences of their past deeds and are incapable of performing actions that yield new results.

It is vital to clarify that liberation is not an outcome of acquiring the knowledge of Brahman; instead, the knowledge itself is liberation. It is the profound realization that exists eternally within every creation as the intrinsic self, and this understanding is uniquely attainable by human beings.

One who understands the Self discovers liberation; not even the gods can hinder this realization, for they recognize that the Self is the very essence of Brahman and the soul of the gods themselves. This understanding leads to a state of immortality, signifying indestructibility rather than eternal existence in heaven, as expressed by Swami Nikhilananda.

Given that every human being is born with the greatest privilege of freedom, actively seeking liberation seems both pitiable and futile. Those who perceive themselves as the eternally free Consciousness remain unburdened and ever free. The individual small 'i' is reduced to merely playing a role in a grand drama or an ephemeral dream with this new-found perspective. This doesn't imply that those who have discovered their real nature and aligned with it shirk their duties and responsibilities.

In stark contrast, individuals who primarily identify with their body and mind find it challenging to break free from their shackles. They are deeply entwined in the roles they play in the world as father, mother, brother, sister, and more within the family and society. Consequently, they must fulfil various duties and rituals dictated by these roles, encountering both favourable and unfavourable experiences. Ignorant individuals cannot escape the afflictions brought about by the ever-changing world or the karmic consequences of their past actions. This occurs because they fail to recognize that the world and its various objects are mere benign names and forms that cannot bind an individual unless they choose to be bound.

Yet, as long as one remains trapped in the triangular format (tripurti), they will depend on the transient world for security, peace, and happiness. Their life becomes one of suffering, occasionally punctuated by fleeting moments of pleasure, while the true understanding of liberation eludes them. To realize peace, individuals must relinquish the delusions rooted in the empirical perspective and elevate themselves from their limited individual self to their higher nature, which is their true essence. This transformative shift in thought patterns is what is meant by liberation.

TWO TYPES OF LIBERATION (MUKTI)

Vedanta presents two paths to liberation: one anchored in the Self and the other in the domain of the mind. The primary liberation, Mukhya Mukti, revolves around the realization that 'I am eternally free.' This insight arises from the diligent study of Vedanta and deep contemplation. For this form of liberation, a profound comprehension of Vedantic principles—which emphasizes that freedom is an intrinsic state, unaffected by one's mental condition—is all that is required. This understanding alone paves the way to liberation, as it resonates with one's fundamental nature.

The secondary liberation, known as Gauna Mukti, is tailored for those embarking on their spiritual journey. It entails freedom viewed through the lens of the mind and unfolds in two progressive stages with a focus on refining and transforming the mind. The ultimate goal is to elevate the quality of life, which is intrinsically linked to the quality of one's mind. Striving for an improved quality of life is a fundamental aspiration for individuals in the practical world, regardless of their attainment of Self-knowledge. The path to mental refinement culminates in the initial stage of secondary liberation known as Jivan Mukti. At this stage, individuals persist in the practice of introspection with the overarching objective of reaching the second stage of secondary liberation upon death, known as Videha Mukti. This stage entails the subtle mind merging with Brahman, effectively ending the cycle of birth and death.

While primary liberation emphasizes listening and contemplation (Shravanam and Mananam), achieving secondary liberation relies on internalization (Nidhidhyasanam). This process entails continuous assimilation, as the complete refinement of the mind—essential for secondary mukti—is inherently challenging. Yet, many individuals immersed in the practical world gravitate towards secondary mukti, finding it difficult to pursue primary liberation due to their focus on materialistic objectives. Sage Gaudapada, in his *Mandukya Karika*, highlights the importance of refining the mind as a crucial prerequisite for delving into Vedantic teachings.

The focus of those pursuing secondary mukti shifts to tempering the mind by reducing attachments (Raaga) and aversions (Dvesha) upon individuals attaining Self-knowledge. This becomes the primary practice for achieving Jivan Mukti or elevating the quality of the mind, ultimately leading to an improved quality of life. Vedanta encourages individuals to aspire to primary liberation even if they initially lean towards secondary liberation. The essence of Vedantic teachings lies in emphasizing the relative insignificance of the mind, and advocating an understanding of humanity's true nature as Consciousness—eternally free and impervious to mental conditions.

Vedanta also cautions individuals who are satisfied with secondary liberation about the potential danger of becoming enslaved by attachments (Raaga), which can detrimentally affect the quality of the mind. Vedanta recognizes that fully eliminating attachments and aversions is a challenging endeavour, and it thus encourages individuals to transition from a concentration on mind-centred secondary liberation to a focus on Self-centered primary liberation.

Certainly, acquiring any kind of knowledge in the physical domain demands arduous labour and unwavering dedication over an extended duration. Similarly, the pursuit of supra-rational wisdom is no exception, as it extends beyond the realm of mere logic and the grasp of sensory tools, necessitating a more formidable exertion. This proves to be a tough challenge for the human mind, which is already shaped by the lexicon of words, the realm of thought, the notions accumulated from personal experiences, and the influences of the external world.

The challenge is further intensified by two additional factors. First, the knowledge and experiences accumulated over one's lifetime are often mistakenly regarded by the individual ego as the ultimate essence of wisdom. This misconception reinforces egotism, which becomes the primary obstacle on the path to realizing Brahman. Second, the pursuit of Brahman is often dismissed as utopian, offering no immediate gratification. As a result, the intensity of one's dedication and commitment to this higher pursuit becomes essential to overcome these hurdles and attain its profound rewards.

Regrettably, the mind, still entangled in its deeply rooted preconceptions, remains bereft of the capacity to apprehend the secret knowledge. Only after engaging in the various prescribed practices for remoulding the mind, and rigorously purging any prior knowledge gleaned from sources other than the Vedas can one hope to overcome this obstacle. Without this transformative process, the journey may indeed prove to be a challenging and painful struggle.

Unlike the pursuit of knowledge in the physical sciences—where progress is often hindered not by a lack of capability but by a lack of willingness, since skills can be cultivated through academic resources and practical training—the quest for knowledge of Brahman follows an entirely different path. While scriptural texts may offer guidance, true realization does not depend on intellectual ability or even mere intention. It is awakened and sustained only by an intense, inner yearning to grasp the deepest truths of existence. Subsequently, it hinges upon one's unwavering commitment and dedication to embark on a formidable journey of self-realization, deeply rooted in personal experiences. It mirrors the endeavours of intrepid individuals driven by an insatiable quest for new knowledge, who venture into the uncharted domains of the physical world, where established methodologies have not yet found their footing, and, in time, stumble upon the treasures of unexplored wisdom.

It is a spark, an exceedingly rare spark, an indispensable catalyst that ignites one's spiritual odyssey. It does not emerge from the crucible of life's trials, the tumultuous tribulations of love, or the ever-shifting tapestry of joy and sorrow. Inspirational sermons delivered by influential orators and even extraordinary encounters fail to kindle this enduring flame. It is a gift bestowed upon the preordained few, their destinies woven from a transcendental loom.

By delving into this wisdom through ancient treatises, the revered *Prakarana Granthas*, or by simply attuning one's ears to the sagacious whispers of the wise who dwell in the silent ocean of Brahman, having acquired knowledge through the processes outlined in the Vedas may plant a seed destined to sprout whether in the present life or in lives yet to come.

The refusal to acknowledge a reality beyond the ever-changing world of self-deception, selfishness, hatred for life, and obsession with material prosperity is a universally misguided notion, regardless of the terms in which it is expressed. According to the *Varaha Upanishad*, every action, from simple acts like breathing to satisfying hunger, should bear witness to the presence of such an entity, seen as a worship of Atman, the inner essence.

This recognition arises from the need to shift from being a victim of one's ignorance to its dissolution through the realization of Brahman—the true Self underlying all existence. This realization culminates in the liberation of the Supreme Self from the entanglement of the mistaken notion that it is integral to the body–mind duo.

Chapter 19

PATH TO DISCOVER FREEDOM THROUGH KNOWLEDGE

PREPARING THE MIND

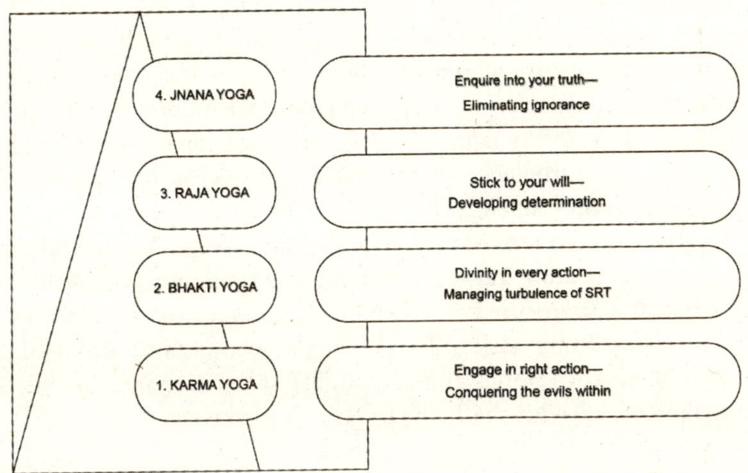

The path to this liberation is divided into four steps: Karma Yoga, Bhakti Yoga, Raja Yoga, and Jnana Yoga. Yoga serves as the means to unite the small 'i' with the grand 'I'. Although Karma Yoga occupies the lowest rung, seemingly distant from the realization of truth, it is an indispensable prerequisite. Without engaging in Karma Yoga, one cannot rightfully gain knowledge of Brahman. It functions as a foundation, akin to high school education, before entering the corridors of the university. Therefore, there is no genuine choice between Karma Yoga and Jnana Yoga; both are indispensable components of the transformative journey.

Despite the categorization of yoga into four rungs, they are inherently interconnected. By introducing bhakti as the weft into the warp of karma, the fabric transforms into Sattvic Karma, crucial for the reconfiguration of SRT.

The act of engaging in any action tends to foster a sense of duality, creating a division between the doer and the deed. This division has resulted in contradictions, complexities, unhealthy competition, and malicious motives, all contributing to stress and sorrow. The Vedas proclaim, 'Those who believe in duality are not masters of their own selves and go to perishable regions, while those who realize the reverse become their own kings.'

As long as an individual demonstrates devotion to the Lord as a perceived entity with a name and form, duality persists in Bhakti Yoga, too. Nevertheless, when practitioners of Bhakti Yoga perceive Brahman throughout the entire universe, they can maintain determination, particularly in Raja Yoga, directed at liberation through knowledge. This ability makes Bhakti Yoga superior to Karma Yoga, as it calms the turbulence of the mind and dispels the illusion of manifold existence. Similarly, Raja Yoga is deemed superior, serving as the most critical requirement for acquiring knowledge. Verily, without bhakti complementing karma, sustaining determination, especially in Raja Yoga practice focused on attaining liberation through knowledge, becomes a daunting task. The individual who attains knowledge through Jnana Yoga stands as an admirable human, engaged in selfless action dovetailed with the highest form of bhakti.

KARMA YOGA: CONQUERING THE EVILS WITHIN

Renouncing duty, as per the teachings of the Gita, is deemed incorrect. Since humans can never be entirely free from action, the optimal path is to discover freedom within action through the practice of Karma Yoga. When yoga is seamlessly integrated into karma, the executed action transcends into a form of worship of the Lord. A Karma Yogi, therefore, commits to action for the sake of the action itself, not merely for personal gains. As a result, the quintessence of the five virtues—tolerance, alignment of thought, speech, and action, empathy, contentment, and truthfulness automatically flow through the veins of a Karma Yogi, while getting rid of the evils from within.

The practice of Karma Yoga is not to be misconstrued as a mere mechanical activity. Its purpose is to discipline the mind, fostering the ability to stay determined in union with the absolute truth—Consciousness. This practice encompasses several virtues:

- **Kshama (forbearance):** Embracing the truth that everything within the field of time and space (the world) is in perpetual flux. Responding with violence holds no merit; instead, tolerance becomes the key virtue to maintain inner calm.
- **Arjavam (alignment):** Signifying the alignment of thought, speech, and action. Achieving this alignment involves employing the 'S' factor before contemplating any action.
- **Daya (empathy):** Advocating for constant compassion towards every person and appreciating the situation from the perspective of others.
- **Toshaha (contentment):** Cultivating contentment with one's current circumstances. This can be achieved by regarding the outcome, be it favourable or unfavourable, as a gift from the omnipotent. It does not denote suppression of legitimate desires.
- **Satyam (truthfulness):** Upholding truthfulness as a steadfast principle. It is acceptable to withhold the truth only when its revelation could gravely impact another.

Key features of Karma Yoga

- Non-attachment or indifference to the fruits of action.
- Dedication of every action to the divine.

Karma Yoga fundamentally involves the preservation of mental equanimity, irrespective of the consequences stemming from adherence to the preceding two principles of Karma Yoga. In this path, no effort is squandered, and no impediment prevails. There can be no harm wrought by it. Even a modest measure of the virtue arising from such actions shall empower one to vanquish fear.[27]

Central components of Karma Yoga

- **Action:** Each action must embody the sattvic quality performed as an act of worship to the Lord.
- **Attitude:** The approach towards the outcome must also be pure, acknowledging it as a gift from the divine.

Though Karma Yoga, in its essence, cannot bestow the sought-after liberation, it remains indispensable. Action, an inherent aspect of our nature, assumes an imperative role, and when executed diligently, paves the way towards acquiring the knowledge that leads to liberation.

The Bhagavad Gita, in its wisdom, extols karma to the status of yoga, rendering it the reverence it rightly deserves.

BHAKTI YOGA: MANAGING THE TURBULENCE OF SRT

Devotion and respect towards the divine or any individual cannot be driven by fear. True reverence arises from a genuine and heartfelt connection rather than being a product of intimidation.

In the nascent phases of one's spiritual odyssey, bhakti plays a pivotal role not only in calming the restless mind but also in redirecting its focus away from the fleeting allure of sensory pleasures, facilitating concentration on the realization of Brahman. It induces a metamorphosis in human nature, a transformation echoed in the sacred verses of the Bhagavad Gita.

The timeless wisdom expounded in the Bhagavad Gita categorizes bhakti into four discernible classes, concurrently deeming any form of devotion grounded in sincerity as virtuous. Those in distress, seeking relief; those desiring wealth to enhance material possessions; those devoutly seeking the truth; and those who have realized the truth—their real Self. Devotees in the first three categories desire rewards and seek favours. In contrast, the worshippers in the fourth category exhibit an unparalleled singularity of purpose. Their devotion is undiluted and selfless, characterized by a profound surrender to the divine. They seek nothing, reject nothing, embodying an attitude of non-utilitarian worship—a pure and unadulterated communion with the sacred, transcending the mundane realms of desire and expectation.

The immanent God, in His omniscient wisdom, discerns that the yearning for divine favour, when rooted in legitimate aspirations, gradually transforms into sublime love. In the final stage of bhakti, true devotion blossoms, ushering the seeker into sacred communion with the very source of everything perceived by the senses. By then, those imbued with the 'S' factor at their core elevate themselves to the echelons of immanent divinity. For them, the ardour of divine love mirrors the fervour that ignorant souls harbour for the transient comforts of the material world. They perceive the transcendental God alone in all the diverse phenomena of the universe.

In the wealth of God's infinite manifestations, they peel away the layers of illusion that shroud the universe to unveil the absolute truth that permeates all creation. When wisdom graces our being, duality dissolves, revealing a profound essence of unity. Nevertheless, the venerable Vedas declare that the benevolence of the divine is not exclusive; it extends its gracious hand to every category of devotee. However, this divine munificence is granted only when the aspirant seeks legitimate favours, those meant to fulfil basic needs through rightful means.

It is not as though this grace descends into one's war chest through the roof of personal abode. The practice of devotion contributes to the cultivation of the 'S' factor, a factor integral in elevating positivity and enhancing cognitive faculties. This becomes particularly pivotal when exercising free will to discern and choose judiciously among available alternatives, thereby steering one towards the realization of success in one's endeavours.

The ultimate goal of all forms of devotion should serve two key purposes: first, expressing devotion through prayer should encourage a mindful pause before every action, ensuring that it causes no harm to oneself or others. Second, devotion should be practised to cultivate independence from the external world, including reliance on deities worshipped within the domain of the universe.

It is imperative to note that no form of devotion to gods within the universal framework should act as a catalyst for cultivating material desires or their fulfilment. Such an approach can lead to disappointment and foster complacency, ultimately hindering the pursuit of well-directed efforts.

Devotion undoubtedly fosters respect towards other living beings and facilitates the practice of righteous deeds. It serves as a crucial tool for managing desires, especially when the outcomes of past actions (Karma Phalam) are unfavourable, leading one to struggle in fulfilling even legitimate desires. Consequently, individuals may resort to selfish and immoral acts. During such times, devotion becomes vital for detaching from the consequences of one's actions and preparing to face potentially more adverse outcomes.

True bhakti confers upon the individual an ineffable boon of love that transcends the confines of all experienced emotions. The act of worshipping God, adorned with a specified name and form, as opposed to directing one's devotion towards the absolute unmanifest Brahman, is not deemed the loftiest form of reverence. Instead, it assumes a position of lower order, as it is perceived as a mere mental projection originating from the human mind. Such a practice inevitably circumscribes the formless God within the finite boundaries of human comprehension, diminishing the vastness and transcendence inherent in the divine.

Nevertheless, the profound wisdom encapsulated in the Vedas acknowledges the validity of this lower form of worship—adoration directed towards a personal God. This form, which is relatable and accessible, serves as an essential preliminary step on the path to attaining supreme bhakti. Thus, the worship of a personal God, though perceived as a lower order, is recognized as a crucial phase in the spiritual journey, paving the way for the eventual realization of the ineffable, formless divinity beyond the grasp of conventional senses.

The crucial caveat lies in always remembering that the personal God, in whatever form of worship, must be perceived not as separate but as a reflection of Brahman. The grace bestowed upon the worshipper ultimately emanates from the supreme Brahman, in recognition of their sincere devotion, whether directed towards a personal deity with or without name and form. After all, such worship ultimately honours the Brahman that pervades all existence. Without this understanding, the seeker risks remaining confined to form-based worship, unable to progress towards the realization of the ultimate truth.

RAJA YOGA: DEVELOPING DETERMINATION

This deliberate practice is crafted with a purpose—to cultivate the fortitude of unwavering determination, not through suppression, but through the conviction that nothing in the world inherently possesses the essence of bliss. The allure of gold, which captivates the senses, is but a superficial fascination, a crucial insight paving the way for an enriching journey towards knowledge. In the realm of Raja Yoga practice, the principle of Vairagyam, or resolute determination, takes centre stage. It hinges on the profound understanding that no thing perceived as a sense object can bestow upon us the ultimate desire—eternal bliss. This realization becomes pivotal for the adept Karma Yogi to triumph in their endeavours.

The revered sage Shankaracharya, in his insightful teachings, emphatically stated that reaping genuine benefits from knowledge, including the profound wisdom of Brahman, is impossible without an unwavering determination. In other words, once knowledge is free from doubts, we must stand resolute and impervious to opposing views and opinions. It is asserted here that any knowledge lacking such determination, known as Vairagyam, is rendered devoid of genuine value. In the pursuit of spiritual ascent, the harmonious fusion of knowledge and resolute determination becomes an indispensable union, propelling the seeker towards the sublime goal of realizing the eternal bliss that transcends the ephemeral allurements of the sensory world.

JNANA YOGA: ELIMINATING IGNORANCE

The mystery enveloping the human experience, we have discerned, is the offspring of our profound ignorance and can only be remedied through the illumination bestowed by the knowledge of the 'One that unfolded into many'. Reflecting upon this, we may ponder: when the sense of 'I' takes possession of any, the world unfurls in marvellous diversity, and who could articulate the boundless ocean of mystery that emanates from this? Indeed, counting the sands on the seashore appears a more feasible task than elucidating the legion of adversities springing forth from the singular cause of the misguided sense of separateness. Nothing but the knowledge of Atman can bestow salvation, as imparted the venerable sage Thayumanavar.

Jnana or wisdom emerges as panacea for the tribulations of life. 'He who attains wisdom in this life attains immortality,' illuminates the *Kena Upanishad*.[28] It entails the profound realization that 'nothing within the phenomenal world exists independently of Chaitanya or the Brahman, who is both the observer and the observed, pervading all aspects of existence with impartiality. This profound understanding acknowledges the unity within diversity and recognizes the true essence that transcends apparent distinctions. It involves the realization of the self through the restraint of the senses, dedicated service to the guru, and the contemplation and meditation upon Atman, guided by the practices elucidated by the guru for attaining realization, as expounded in the *Niralamba Upanishad*.

Chapter 20

WHO IS A FREE INDIVIDUAL?

Fostering and upholding mental discipline stands as a pivotal requisite before and after attaining the wisdom of the Self. In this context, the fourfold discipline, undertaken both in preparation for seeking knowledge and post its acquisition, engages in targeted practices to diminish karma linked to attraction and aversion. This realignment of various layers within the individual's personality triggers a profoundly sought-after inner transformation. A radical shift in perspective ensues. Nevertheless, the individual self, the small 'i', does not perish or vanish from existence due to this realization. Standing apart, the Jnanis look upon the entirety of existence, including his corporeal form, as a lower order of reality, intended merely for amusement.

The enlightened individual constantly recognizes, in every moment and circumstance, that everything existing in the universe is merely an extension of their Self, upon which the awareness of body, mind, and the external world has been overlaid. The person with Self-knowledge resides, moves, and exists within the richness of this self-consciousness. They consistently remain unattached to the actions carried out by their body, mind, and senses, experiencing complete liberation from the grip of egoism. All their actions are superficial and do not diminish the exalted state of Consciousness. The distinction between an uninformed individual and a wise person does not lie in their actions, but rather in the awareness accompanying their deeds. Consequently, despite external similarities, these two individuals stand worlds apart.

A sage established in Consciousness remains untroubled by his impending demise or that of his kin. Unlike a conventional ascetic who forswears the untenable responsibilities of a householder, he diligently fulfils his necessary duties. Yet, he remains untouched by the outcomes of his actions, which might not align with his anticipations, given his lack of expectations; he is consistently content, having relinquished attachment to the body executing the deeds. The notion of renouncing duties (karma sanyasa) holds no relevance for him. Not due to a shift in external conditions, but rather a transformation within, liberating him from rigid anticipations.

Being the very Consciousness, he doesn't enact any deeds across the three temporal dimensions. He is ever beyond time and action. The domain of performance and renunciation pertains to the ignorant people, who identify exclusively with their bodies. Hence, he entertains no notion of a doer. Consequently, he refrains from classifying the world into favourable and unfavourable, welcoming future shifts with equanimity, impervious to the delusions of the world. His mind remains unburdened, without fixed expectations, though some non-binding preferences might persist when options present themselves. He is not swayed by strong likes (attachments) or dislikes (aversions) towards worldly things. Neither does he harbour a yearning for liberation nor a craving for desirelessness. Detached from obsessions, his mind resides in perpetual tranquillity, permitting the body and mind to engage in their intended roles, recognizing it as a mere theatrical enactment.

His desire for longevity doesn't stem from attachment to life; he rather permits life to unfold as dictated by his Prarabdha Karma. While amidst relationships and possessions, he doesn't rely on any of them for security, serenity, or happiness. He envisions a life divested of these elements, prepared to relinquish anything at any juncture. Emotionally unentangled, fear of loss, including that of his own body, eludes him.

When fulfilling societal obligations, he engages with the triangular perspective, deeming them requisites of the grand drama's role he assumes, excelling effortlessly. Yet, when attending to personal life, he adopts a binary outlook, regarding himself as eternally free. He acknowledges that the tendencies of the mind still bear the imprints of past conditioning but ensures they don't sway his conduct, for he remains vigilant as the witness Consciousness. Amidst the fluctuations of the mind due to karma, he doesn't identify with its turbulence. Self-judgement doesn't engage his mind. He cultivates an attitude of composure as his body navigates health oscillations, remaining undisturbed, analogous to how space remains unsoiled by smoke. His mastery over the senses keeps his thoughts, speech, and actions harmonized.

In summary, he operates within the functional world akin to others, yet he remains unbound by it.

As for whether the lower 'i' of an enlightened individual might indulge in wrongful deeds in the guise of Prarabdha Karma, this stands as a debatable query. Such a scenario becomes implausible, for he has ingrained dharma (strong moral values) and nurtured virtuous tendencies (vasna) through prolonged practice of diverse disciplines, endowing his mind with unwavering adherence to teachings.

The composed individual understands that objects perceived are inherently devoid of true substance, hence they do not differentiate between what is deemed acceptable or unacceptable. Furthermore, having relinquished worldly attachments from the mind, they transcend the dualities of existence. Freed from desires, the experiences that arise naturally evoke neither pain nor pleasure for them.[29] By neutralizing Raaga and Dvesha, the binding agents, he abstains from participating in immoral actions. Bondage doesn't stem from worldly occurrences but rather from our judgements, our 'R' and 'D'. Hence, it is imperative to transform desires into preferences, not compelling needs; otherwise, they result in bondage and distress. The one who declares, 'Ahankaara, the small "i", is a drama or a dream,' finds Raaga and Dvesha transmute into non-binding preferences.

SECTION NINE

APPLIED VEDANTA

Chapter 21

BHAGAVAD GITA—ETERNAL WISDOM FOR THE CORPORATE WORLD

The Vedic scriptures convey the profound concept that human life is granted to us not for its culmination in death but for attaining immortality through spiritual liberation.

The world is a battleground of opposing forces—good versus evil, deeds versus duty, morality versus immorality, righteousness versus wickedness. In the construction of the world order, hate coexists with love and anger with compassion, jealousy with empathy, darkness with light, and bad karma accompanies every good deed. 'If the world were devoid of evil and ugliness, there would be no incentive to seek the truth, and the pursuit of knowledge through the Vedas would be unnecessary,' articulated Dr Radhakrishnan.

A fundamental prerequisite for attaining liberation lies in performing karma according to dharma—the cosmic law that delineates behaviours, duties, rights, rules, virtues, and the righteous way of living, manifested through morally upright human conduct. It underscores the notion that, while it may not be possible to completely eradicate evil and imperfections from the world, enforcing dharma is imperative for mitigating these challenges.

INSIDE BIT WEISER ENTERPRISE: CAPTURING THE ESSENCE OF THE BHAGAVAD GITA

The impending fate of a chain of stores in Dresden, Germany, celebrated as the most esteemed milk outlet, hung in the balance, awaiting a decisive verdict early the following morning.

Druid Fischer, who had tragically lost his eyes in a harrowing car accident on a harsh winter day in the year 2000, was compelled to pass on the mantle of Bit Weiser Enterprise, a company forged by two brothers in 1963. Following the demise of his younger brother, Druid, alongside his uncle Mueller, had meticulously cultivated the business on the bedrock of honesty and righteousness.

Despite Druid's earnest desire to entrust the reins to his nephew Yohan, the oldest of the three siblings—an embodiment of virtue—instead of his elder son Dyrk, who embodied treachery and deceit, fate took an unforeseen turn. Dyrk managed to usurp the throne through cunning machinations, initiating a perilous course of action. In the absence of Yohan's valiant brother Arnold, pursuing a Ph.D. in the USA, Dyrk schemed to undermine Yohan, laying the groundwork for a potentially destructive turn of events.

THE HUMAN DEVIL

As anticipated, within a mere three years at the helm, Dyrk managed to tarnish the once-pristine reputation of the enterprise, affectionately known as the world's premier milk supplier, celebrated for its offerings of the nation's finest cheese selections and other delectable delicacies. The saga of downfall unfurled through a nefarious web of malpractices, orchestrated with the dual goals of amassing personal wealth and indulging in sensual pleasures, callously disregarding the trust bestowed by loyal customers, and disrespecting basic morality. From deceitful acts targeting esteemed customers to the exploitation of female workers through immoral practices, Dyrk exhibited the traits of an intelligent tyrant, revealing a propensity for viciousness and exemplifying a regime marked by brutality and ferocity.

Fortunately, the Bit Weiser board, which intervened early, successfully halted the progression of atrocities by making an informal decision to terminate him. This timely action was a saving grace that prevented him from acquiring the infamous label of a reincarnation of Pol Pot, the former prime minister of Cambodia, who caused the deaths of more than one million people within three years through forced labour, starvation, disease, torture, or execution.

It all began with the egregious act in which 126 children suffered severe consequences due to the consumption of milk tainted by the unethical practice of dilution with unpurified water. This incident marked the initial fracture in the foundation of the enterprise, which had been built on the pillar of honesty.

Upon being confronted, Dyrk, who wielded considerable sway over a board primarily constituted of family members, adeptly managed to quell concerns temporarily with deceptive promises.

However, in a relatively brief span, the tipping point emerged when a courageous intern brought to light covert plans to divert funds for promoting drug trafficking, revealing a sinister collaboration between Dyrk and the organization's accountant. Such revelations stand as a stark manifestation of the callous actions of a power-driven individual, characterized by a blatant disregard for ethical boundaries—a disquieting emblem of a 'T'-dominated personality.

The need for a change in leadership became apparent and imperative as the enterprise grappled with the repercussions of such flagrant conduct.

WHEN DARKNESS ASCENDS, A SAGE EMERGES

Krisn, a cherished childhood friend of the family holding 11 per cent of the company's equity, decided to call Arnold to return in the best interest of the broader community. Possessing not only a formidable academic background in physical science but also the highest echelons of human wisdom, Krisn had delved into metaphysical truths, shaped by the profound insights of luminaries like Max Mueller and more notably inspired by Schopenhauer's seminal work *The World as Will and Representation*, which drew profound influence from the *Chandogya Upanishad*—one of the ten principal Upanishads of the Vedas. 'The study of the Upanishads has been a source of great inspiration and means of comfort to my soul. From every sentence of the Upanishad, deep, original, and sublime thoughts arise, and the whole is pervaded by a high, holy, and earnest spirit,' wrote Schopenhauer.

A paragon of 'S' at his core, Krisn commanded admiration from all who knew him, and his words carried unparalleled weight, inspiring those around him to action. Arnold, possessing a harmonious blend of 'S' and 'R' factors, made a profound decision to forgo his academic pursuits in deference to fulfilling his duty according to dharma—a principle that Arnold recognized and chose to embody in his actions.

The time to decide between right and wrong had arrived: a pivotal motion to oust the head of Bit Weiser was about to be proposed. The two opposing factions, united by common ancestry, had gathered. The boardroom had transformed into a battleground, where silence echoed within its walls, creating an ominous atmosphere. As the forces of the divine and the demoniac prepared for the impending conflict, the air was charged with the palpable intensity of a moral struggle served as tangible evidence of the profound clash of principles personified by the two diametrically opposite individuals.

DIVINITY, HUMANITY'S SUPREME ASSET

Dyrk gazed around the table, making one final assessment of his success by meticulously evaluating the strengths of his allies. Among them were his highly principled grand uncle and his blind father, both supporting him under duress, along with other influential family members backing him out of fear of his ferocity. Despite being backed by a united team capable of quashing any motion against him, the incumbent leader couldn't help but feel restlessness within.

As he grappled with this internal turmoil, he realized that the sheer absence of the divine within him was the root cause of his internal fear. 'If you hold me in your heart, you'll find a sense of security, even if your material possessions are minimal,' declares the Lord. The essence is clear: without devotion (bhakti), mere possessions cannot provide true security.[30] On the contrary, Arnold harboured confidence in a triumphant outcome as he gauged his strength through two pillars: the steadfast backing of his learned confidant Krisn and his devout dedication to God.

He reasoned that Krisn, a person of extraordinary wisdom, would not have summoned him without crafting a meticulous plan designed to succeed, even in the face of the substantial support his cunning cousin might have amassed through the means of fear and mandates.

Amid the sombre atmosphere, the authoritative grand-uncle took the lead in enumerating the agenda for the meeting, which was to decide on the singular topic of new leadership. The hushed whispers from all corners and the palpable anticipation of the long-awaited conflict shattered the silence as Arnold prepared to initiate the key motion. In a moment of introspection, Arnold realized that this struggle would necessitate abandoning the cherished ideals of life, race, and family—values of reverence for elders, and affection for his cousins that he had faithfully upheld until that point.

ATTACHMENT, GRIEF, DELUSION, HESITATION, AND DESPONDENCY

Despite being endowed with an abundance of 'S' and an appropriate level of 'R', Arnold failed to realize that his strengths were meant to serve a higher purpose. Instead, his thoughts were consumed by the fact that those he was about to confront—his cousins—were bound to lose, irrespective of their conduct or character. Caught in this emotional conflict, he believed that upholding justice and protecting righteousness would mean turning against his entire family—a burden he was not prepared to bear. His thoughts were clouded by extreme negativity, envisioning a potential victory in the leadership battle, resulting possibly in a tragic end for his cousin and family, their dreams and aspirations obliterated by shame. This realization weighed heavily on Arnold's mind. Typically, in situations like these, we tend to forget that the enemies we are fighting are human beings with feelings, a shared characteristic of relationships in the contemporary era.

The pivotal question echoing in his thoughts was: how much was the victory worth if it entailed the disintegration of a family that once lived to accomplish shared aspirations to benefit a community? His compassion for Dyrk lacked the transcendent quality of divine empathy, manifesting instead as a form of self-pity. This self-indulgent sentiment seemingly provided a rationale for his choice to avoid an action that would entail causing harm to his people.

Drawing nearer to Krisn, Arnold confided his overwhelming sense of sadness, expressing his decision to abandon the path he had initially chosen when he saw his adversaries with a sense of belonging. His choice was driven more by social obligation than a commitment to the prevailing truth. Despite recognizing the malice of his enemy, Arnold hesitated to counter one sin with another. Guided by the principle of 'conquer the anger of others by non-anger; see no wrong in those whose minds are overpowered by greed, who see no crime in the destruction of family and friends,' Arnold wrestled with the moral dilemma.

While his adversaries may have been blind to wrongdoing, he was concerned about the potential for a greater sin— destroying members of his own family merely to satisfy his greed for control of the enterprise. Inaction gained momentum where action was imperative. He was torn between the worldly pull of love and attachment, which urged him to reconsider a decision made with great deliberation and the moral need to confront tyranny in the pursuit of justice and higher ideals. The dilemma Arnold faced is a recurring theme in human life, manifesting in various forms. At its core is the profound attachment we cultivate for the fleeting fantasies of the objective world, encompassing people, objects, and events. This attachment often misconstrued as love or compassion clouds our judgement, compelling us to engage in inappropriate actions, even when disillusionment lurks within the allure of the glamorous world.

Rather than addressing the root cause of delusion and grief, which are the offspring of attachment—an undeniable reality we all experience—we tend to fixate on imagined outcomes of actions, also fuelled by the delusion that obscures our intellect. This state persists until divinity is restored and wisdom illuminates our path. It is a transformative process that reflects the evolution of an individual soul, momentarily estranged from spiritual reality.

Arnold undergoes inner conflict and struggles with the temptation to deviate from his duty, which the divine in him reveals. Yet, during the initial phase of introspection and self-reflection, much like any intelligent person, Arnold chooses to rely on personal experiences to evaluate the ordained path. Confronted by the dilemma of whether to advance or retreat, he navigates the precarious balance.

However, as the persisting agony begins to tighten its grip on Arnold, his need for external guidance intensifies. Faced with the anxiety and insecurity he had unwittingly cultivated, Arnold turns to Krisn for solace and direction.

He was among the fortunate few, for not everyone is ordained to receive Vedic teachings, which Krisn graciously provides to him as a mentor. Guiding Arnold through the intricate labyrinth of his inner turmoil, Krisn imparts profound knowledge, unravelling the answer to the universal question: the purpose of human existence. The transition from inner conflicts to spiritual evolution, culminating in the revelation of existential truths, serves as the pivotal highlight of Arnold's spiritual journey.

BONDAGE: A DISEASE EXPERIENCED BY ALL

Krisn swiftly discerns the predicament Arnold was confronting. As a victim of ignorance, he was ensnared by 'attachment', a profoundly toxic phenomenon from which no one can escape, even though we recognize it as the fundamental cause of all the problems it brings and, more importantly, the human affliction known as bondage that traps every human being in an inextricable cycle of birth and death. Despite his intelligence, Arnold was confounded by a lack of wisdom, a quality found in those who have discovered their true inner Self.

Such individuals embody compassion yet remain unbound in relationships. While emotions hold value and are considered a necessary virtue, the wise do not allow them to sway their intellect. Instead, they engage with emotions without letting them dictate their actions. For the wise, emotions become tools for deliberate actions rather than triggers for reactive responses.

Caught in the web of delusion, Arnold seeks a way out. Instead of retreating from the contemplated plan, he earnestly requests deferring the proceedings by a day, following the counsel of Krisn. This unexpected move surprised everyone, diffusing the much-anticipated action from someone known for actions that consistently yielded positive outcomes.

THE FUTILITY OF ADVICE

Unacquainted with the formal teachings of the Vedas, Arnold would face the challenge of comprehending the intricate complexities of life born out of ignorance and the ensuing internal turmoil. Like the common populace, Arnold would continue to seek solace in the external world while wrestling with his predicament, persevering until a precise diagnosis is attained. In such circumstances, individuals possessing a blend of worldly wisdom and resistance to change demonstrate remarkable tenacity. They persist, reluctant to easily surrender their intellectual prowess, even at the potential risk of detriment. It is not uncommon to witness individuals brimming with egoism ruin their lives simply because they remain adamant and do not seek help when needed. Arnold was no exception to this rule.

Krisn offered no resolution to Arnold's ongoing dilemma as he was aware of his personality that refrained from seeking help until rendered utterly helpless. Instead, he enumerated various actions of the past that had garnered him unmatched acclaim within the family, emphasizing the inevitable descent into disgrace should he decide against a carefully considered course of action. 'Until individuals are willing to acknowledge their helplessness and relinquish their egoism entirely, any advice offered remains as futile as attempting to nurture arid land.'

According to the wisdom delineated in the Vedas, counselling exerts its most profound impact when individuals question their intellect, signalling a state of helplessness. Essentially, this profound perspective embodies a crucial lesson: the necessary course of action to be followed when confronted by failures. It entails the imperative shift from erroneous thinking rooted in Tamas, to cultivating doubt, a characteristic of Rajas, and questioning decisions before acquiring the correct knowledge that embodies Sattva.

In their preliminary talks, Krisn seizes the occasion to jog Arnold's memory about past occasions wherein he championed the cause of justice, often embarking on audacious exploits with the prospect of inconveniencing a few to safeguard the welfare of many. He draws parallels between his valour and the illustrious warriors of yore who waged fierce conflicts in the name of upholding virtue and societal harmony. Furthermore, he playfully taunts Arnold, suggesting that retracting from the commitment to combat the nefarious would besmirch his manly honour and integrity.

Arnold did not pay attention as he was caught in a loop, reiterating his thoughts and even justifying his stance from a spiritual angle, asserting that he would incur a heavy karmic debt, one which he'd have to settle sometime in the future. A bewildered Arnold begins to question the purpose and legitimacy of their resolve to remove Dyrk. For the first time, he voices scepticism about the likelihood of winning the vote of confidence and expresses a desire to return to the USA. It wasn't just about securing the mandate to take control of the company by ousting his cousin; it was a deep-seated issue of grief that would persist and disrupt his entire life.

His mind grappled with a tumultuous blend of anxiety and doubt, accompanied by an overwhelming yearning for assured victory. The divine's mysterious method appears to involve shrouding the path of virtuous individuals in additional darkness and sorrow, only to graciously unveil the radiant light of joy in due course. This unique process should be construed as a symbolic manifestation of the Supreme Consciousness, a distinctive means to suggest to His devotees the necessity of recognizing and gradually eliminating the presence of inherent imperfections of the individual soul and transcending the limitations of their ultra-powerful minds.

It serves as guidance towards an elevated state through the intricate weave of trials and tribulations, distinct from the dependence on a personal deity that the helpless individual resorts to while struggling in the triangular mode comprising God, the world, and individuals. Nevertheless, amid an individual's world falling apart, where relief seems elusive, one cannot be left to mercy. One must turn to the divine within, even if devotion to the infinite Lord is expressed through an external energy or deity.

Arnold yearned for respite from the anguish, which he realized couldn't be achieved through pre-meditated action or philosophical enlightenment alone. His desire was for solutions to the prevailing dilemma, seeking clarity through a profound understanding of the law of dharma. In that moment of despair, Arnold's sinking heart yearned for solace in the words of wisdom, leading him to the decision to confide in his friend and declare, 'My thoughts are in disarray, and I find myself unable to assess the situation with clarity. I want to withdraw and go back. I believe I need your guidance, please decide for me, please give the instructions as to what I should do.'

AWAKENING TO THE TRUTH

Arnold, with his closed mind, posed a formidable obstacle to the task at hand. Krisn understood that breaking through the barriers of Arnold's mindset wouldn't be easy, but he was determined to navigate through the complexities.

In confronting the overarching problem of Arnold's suffering caused by bondage, Krisn recognized the urgency of addressing the immediate issue of attachment that obstructed his ability to move forward with the decisive plan to oust Dyrk—attachment to the transient body and attachment to various entities associated with his body. Arnold's hesitancy, rooted in ignorance, prompted Krisn to acknowledge the importance of enlightening him to dispel this lack of understanding.

Additionally, Krisn took into account Arnold's upbringing, which instilled profound teachings about the importance of performing virtuous deeds and refraining from engaging in detrimental actions, echoing the principles found in the Vedas. Recognizing these aspects, Krisn aimed not only to alleviate Arnold's immediate predicament but also to impart wisdom that could guide him on a path aligned with virtuous conduct and enlightenment.

Accordingly, Krisn considered different strategies to open up a channel of communication and understanding. He knew that patience, empathy, and a careful choice of words would be essential in reaching Arnold. The journey ahead was uncertain, but Krisn was perfectly qualified to approach it with resilience and a willingness to reach the intended goal. To accomplish his goal, he approached the problem of attachment from philosophical, ethical and worldly angles.

JNANA YOGA: KNOWLEDGE OF THE SUPREME SELF

In the initial stride to free Arnold from his delusions, Krisn, his trusted and compassionate companion, leads him on a philosophical journey. He accentuates the disparity between the essential (the higher Self) and circumstantial (lower self) aspects of human existence, and highlights how sages attain knowledge of their higher Self through renunciation of duties and remain undisturbed by worldly events. Simultaneously, Krisn delves deeper, expounding on the Supreme Self. He emphasizes that fulfilling one's duty in alignment with a divine purpose—prioritizing the greater good and upholding social order—does not amount to committing a sinful act.

Krisn guides him on the proper execution of karma in the world, shedding light on the principles of dharma (the universal law that keeps life and the cosmos in harmony) that govern righteous action. In situations demanding the safeguarding of good, one might even be compelled to act against one's conscience, if it requires confronting and eliminating evil to establish righteousness.

'There is no need to mourn those for whom mourning is unwarranted. If Dyrk contemplates drastic measures to terminate his life due to humiliation, it is the decree of his Prarabdha Karma that will orchestrate circumstances culminating in a dramatic conclusion through self-infliction, regardless. The inevitability of death awaits the one who is born in some form or the other, just as assuredly as birth awaits the one who has died. Therefore, there is no cause for sorrow over what is inherently unavoidable. Furthermore, rebirth is an immutable law of nature. Our existence is transient, and the certainty of death looms over us all the time. The privilege of being born as a blessed human comes with the responsibility to embrace pain and suffering in pursuit of righteousness. This is wisdom,' declares Krisn in his first sermon.

Grief, sorrow, disturbance from material events, and deviation from the path of duty all signal susceptibility to the influence of ignorance. In addressing these issues, Krisn advises Arnold to confront the current situation without hesitation, regardless of the potential consequences for Dyrk. He reassures him that the eternal essence, embodying Brahman, remains indestructible.

'Human beings are unmanifest in their beginnings, manifest in their middles, and unmanifest again in their ends. Where is there room for lamentation in this inevitable cycle, my dear Arnold?' Even in the face of Dyrk's contemplation of ending his life following a humiliating experience, it is crucial to understand that Arnold's grief was misplaced. The inner essence of every object in creation is invulnerable and impervious to any legitimate or illegitimate treatment directed towards the individual soul.

'The dweller in the body of every one is eternal.' This fundamental concept underscores the enduring nature of the eternal essence, offering solace and perspective amid life's challenges. Despite life culminating in death, progress coming to a halt, and everything being transient, the presence of the eternal is discernible in every facet of existence. The passage of time brings about this realization, whether through unforeseen accidents or deliberate actualization.

Krisn emphasizes the immortality of the supreme soul, stating that the universal spirit empowering Dyrk's existence will persist indefinitely. The inevitability of death, however, does not serve as a justification for actions like murder, suicide, or war. Intentionally wishing harm upon others or on ourselves is unjustifiable, considering that all individuals are destined to confront mortality eventually.

At the end of the initial teachings, Arnold grasps the synthesis of the immortal Self and the perishable body within human existence. He also recognizes the importance of preserving the body as the sole instrument for advancing individual interests in the phenomenal world. However, while comprehending profound truths about human existence, the idea of following the path of a sage, who renounces worldly duties to acquire knowledge, appears highly appealing to him, a proposition seemingly aligned with his immediate interests amid his current predicament.

When Arnold starts expressing his desire to consider the possibility of becoming a sage, Krisn redirects his focus emphasizing the significance of embracing the right duty—an aspect Arnold was contemplating to avoid amid prevailing agony, despite 'action' being a deeply rooted trait in his personality.

Intriguingly, while writing this segment of the treatise, I reminisced about how the teachings of the Bhagavad Gita bestowed profound clarity in the days preceding my commitment to leading the life of a monk. Notably, this choice empowered me to direct my energies towards selfless humanitarian endeavours, as a reverent devotion to the divine fount of all, shunning the pursuit of bliss in the comfort of a secluded existence.

KARMA YOGA: ADJURATION TO A SENSE OF DUTY

'There is no nobler duty than engaging in a fair battle for a warrior', says the Gita. The law of action dictates that anyone with noble thoughts must actively contribute to maintaining social order and refrain from renouncing duty in favour of embracing an ascetic life. Opportunities to serve humanity become a pathway to heaven for those aligned with such principles. Ascending to greater heights is possible through the conscientious performance of one's duty, whether viewed from a metaphysical or worldly perspective.

'If you shy away from this lawful battle due to false sentiments, weakness, or cowardice, you will fail in your duty and incur sin. Besides, you risk being remembered and ridiculed in family and social circles as the one who evaded duty out of fear, long after you are gone. Vulgar words will be uttered, tarnishing your greatness, and there can be nothing sadder than that,' says Krisn to bring Arnold back to the present reality. It is crucial to emphasize that the central teachings of the Gita underscore the principle that one should not undertake actions with the anticipation of receiving praise or withdraw from them in fear of blame. According to its guidance, we do not incur sin if we approach our activities with an attitude of equanimity, treating pleasure and pain, gain and loss, victory and defeat as equals rather than opposites.[31] As the human mind naturally gravitates towards the pursuit of desires and the attainment of worldly pleasures, our actions often become centred around these ephemeral goals rather than us engaging in actions that lead to the pursuit of eternal bliss. It is vital, therefore to distinguish between true karma and ritualistic karma, for even those who comprehend that the eternal essence remains untouched by transient worldly events may face challenges in undertaking righteous actions without cultivating 'Buddhi Yoga'—yoga of the intellect, different from Jnana Yoga. Krisn succinctly elucidates this practice, emphasizing the necessity of training the mind to gain insight and achieve a state of equanimity (samata) while engaging with the entities of the world.

Buddhi Yoga involves directing deliberate intellectual effort to guide the mind that is perpetually tied to the senses. When the mind is purged of impurities through Karma Yoga practices and external inclinations are restrained through bhakti or Upasana Yoga, the intellect becomes fully illuminated by Consciousness. In this state, the mind aligns itself with the cosmic purpose, allowing the radiance of Consciousness to remain undistorted.

Harmony with the supreme spirit is achieved, even as one fulfils societal obligations while being present in the world but not entirely consumed by it. This state requires a single-minded focus, intentionally cultivated by discerning individuals. Liberation from distractions is paramount, not through theological or religious pursuits, but through first hand spiritual experience of the truth. Unfortunately, this profound wisdom eludes those trapped by their desires, ensuring their rebirth as a consequence of actions and rites performed solely for the fulfilment of worldly pleasures.

The first portion of Vedic teachings guides us to engage in actions with a desire for recompense, whether in a temporary heaven or a new embodied life. In contrast, Buddhi Yoga serves as a transformative path that directs us towards liberation. Rather than perpetuating a cycle driven by desires and their anticipated outcomes, Buddhi Yoga encourages a profound release. It beckons practitioners to transcend the immediate pursuit of rewards and embrace a higher state of consciousness, liberating themselves from the perpetual cycle of desires, actions, and subsequent rebirths.

In essence, the initial segment of Vedic teachings underscores the necessity of working with desires, crucial for sustaining functional life driven by SRT—the energy propensities of the mind. Conversely, Buddhi Yoga, as expounded in the subsequent section, illuminates the path to transcendent freedom beyond the confines of such cyclic existence.

INDIFFERENCE TO THE RESULTS OF ACTION

Arnold's scepticism about achieving a decisive victory aligned with his discomfort in pursuing a selfish interest to attain a leadership position in the enterprise. This inner conflict weighed heavily on his mind, creating hesitation against a well-thought-out and necessary plan of action.

Krisn introduces Arnold to another significant concept from the Gita with the sole objective of influencing him to take action recognizing it as the imperative need of the hour. 'You have the right to action alone, and never to its fruits; let not the fruits of action be your motive. Nor should there be any attachment to inaction within you.'[32]

Success or failure is not solely determined by the individual but is influenced by various factors beyond our control. What truly matters during the execution of an action is goodwill—the fulfilment of the divine purpose. The Gita encourages a perspective that transcends the fixation on results, such as acquiring fame or wealth. Instead, the focus should be on cultivating indifference to the outcomes of an action—without compromising the need for planning—thereby maintaining the equipoise of the mind even when the result deviates from one's initial aspirations. It takes practice to master one's sensitive nature, anger, and despondency. This shift in perspective is crucial for navigating the uncertainties and challenges inherent in pursuing goals.

THE RELEVANCE OF THIS PHILOSOPHY IN THE MODERN ERA

This important concept, deeply rooted in Vedic philosophy and spiritual traditions, finds expression in the idea of 'Nishkama Karma'. It encourages individuals to fulfil their duties with dedication and sincerity, underscoring the significance of not becoming excessively attached to the results, yet remaining focused on minute details when performing the task.

In a modern era that places a premium on achievement, success, and external validation, embracing this philosophy may be challenging but is fundamentally crucial. Understanding the relevance of this principle becomes paramount as societal pressure to meet expectations, achieve goals, and excel in various domains frequently gives rise to heightened stress and anxiety. The pervasive emphasis on success metrics, such as grades, wealth, and fame, often obscures the intrinsic value of the journey itself and the importance of actions undertaken.

Imparting the wisdom of maintaining mental equilibrium in the face of success or failure is especially vital for the younger generation. Life's inherent uncertainty and the lack of control over outcomes necessitate the ability to detach from results. This detachment doesn't imply abandoning goals or aspirations but approaching them with a sense of purpose and commitment, recognizing that external outcomes do not singularly define one's worth or the value of one's efforts.

Developing resilience, adaptability, and a well-balanced outlook on success and failure is essential for maintaining mental well-being. This development requires fostering a mindset that places value on the journey, appreciates personal growth, and recognizes setbacks as chances for learning and advancement. Ultimately, it involves discovering joy and satisfaction in the process, irrespective of external judgements deeming it a success or failure.

THE INSIGHT OF BUDDHI YOGA

Krisn emphasizes that merely performing duty for the sake of results is inferior compared to Buddhi Yoga, despite the urgency to put Arnold into action. Those who operate from this intellectual standpoint effortlessly distance themselves from both good and evil, rising above ethical principles. Such individuals transcend selfishness, rendering them incapable of engaging in harmful actions.

Moreover, those who are wise and spiritually connected, having renounced attachment to the outcomes of their actions, liberate themselves from the predetermined outcome of an action and its attendant sorrows. Such enlightened individuals don't find it necessary to perpetually rely on the sacred scriptures of the Vedas, for the adoption of Buddhi Yoga decisively empowers these individuals to transcend rituals and fulfil their duties without becoming attached to the results. The Gita emphasizes that the crucial question lies not in what we do, but in how we do it, and the spirit with which we act.

After absorbing Krisn's profound insights, Arnold becomes intrigued to learn about the characteristics of an enlightened individual firmly grounded in the spirit. His motive was to understand what it would take to embody such qualities, considering a potential shift from a familial life to the path of a renounced monk. To help Arnold understand that embracing the life of a true monk is more demanding than pursuing a familial existence, Krisn adeptly weaves his narrative with several key attributes characteristic to such individuals:

'Elevated souls, unencumbered by personal interests, emerge as catalysts for positive transformations in societies to which they are not inherently connected. These sagacious individuals naturally assume the role of influencers, shaping and upholding the collective conscience of society through their exemplary actions. By transcending religious constraints, they present a formidable challenge to the realms of corruption and deceit. What sets them apart is their detachment from the pursuit of fulfilment through passion-driven actions, seeking contentment in the realm of the spirit.'

Monks dedicated to serving society undertake a noble endeavour that demands adherence to a series of rigorous disciplines and routines. These practices form a stringent code of conduct, extending beyond the physical realm to encompass ethical and spiritual guidelines. Genuine sanyasis renounce all desires, finding contentment within their spirit. Their minds remain undisturbed amidst sorrow, and free from desire amid pleasure. Having triumphed over desire and passion, they neither rejoice nor lament when faced with good or evil.

The enlightened beings abstain from indulging in sensory objects, much like a tortoise withdrawing its limbs into its shell. This withdrawal is an expression of their wisdom. While common beings are captivated by the allure of sensory objects, disciplined souls remain focused on understanding reality. Consequently, the sources of pleasure and even the taste itself turn away from the embodied soul. Disciplined individuals are vigilant and awake to the true nature of reality, a realm to which the unwise remain oblivious.

Recognizing the imperative to elucidate the perilous consequences of attachment, Krisn underscores that fixating on sensory experiences begets a profound sense of attachment. This attachment, in turn, gives rise to both legitimate and unwarranted desires. While desire and passion are generally deemed essential for societal growth, on an individual level, unfulfilled desire provokes anger. From anger emerges confusion, and this state of confusion leads to a loss of memory. The decline in memory sets the stage for the erosion of intelligence, ultimately culminating in the inevitable demise of the individual.

Worldly objects enhance or diminish the value of the false image (ego) one creates for oneself, compelling the individual to protect their identity through love and hate. Harbouring both hatred and excessive love for the senses are misguided approaches. What is required is to counter not a forced detachment from the world or the annihilation of sensory experiences, rather an internal withdrawal. This profound transformation occurs when the enlightened individual perceives the supreme reality in every object, marking a significant shift in their perspective through inner renunciation and self-discipline.

As the clock neared five in the morning, Krisn knew it was time to conclude his teachings, leaving room for introspection before the crucial moment approached. In the final phase of his lecture, he echoed verses from the Gita, which emphasize that wise individuals, even after attaining liberation, can and should fulfil their duties. This stance opposes the notion that all action, originating from ignorance, ceases with the dawn of wisdom. However, the Gita does not advocate the total renunciation of work; actions are not to be set aside. It encourages the transformation of all actions into selfless endeavours, giving up attachment and desire for fruits. Sage Shankaracharya clarifies that the principle applies to Karma Yogis and not to jnanis, who have attained Self-knowledge and aligned with Brahman. Jnanis, in his view, engage in actions merely for others, as he believes that knowledge is incompatible with work.

The Gita emphasizes the importance of cultivating restraint and achieving freedom from desires, as well as overcoming the attachment to material possessions, both of which are integral to attaining spiritual perfection. The scripture advocates for inner renunciation, which involves conquering the lower nature of an individual marked by ignorance, negativity, and inertia. Notably, this concept of renunciation doesn't imply withdrawal from work but denotes a transcendence of the egoistic and materialistic aspects, encouraging active engagement with a sense of detachment.

BHAKTI YOGA: SURRENDERING ALL ACTIONS TO THE DIVINE

The principle of acting without attachment or the desire for outcomes of one's actions is indeed one of the most formidable challenges for humans, requiring divine blessings. Observing Arnold's confused state, Krisn emphasizes that divinity plays a crucial role in empowering individuals who may desire to fulfil their duties for the betterment of humanity but lack the willingness to do so. He suggests that inner peace can be attained through prayers, chanting, and various forms of expressing devotion to the divine.

Quoting the sagacious words of sage Shankaracharya, Krisn shares his conviction with Arnold by stating, 'Attaining unity with Brahman and maintaining tranquillity in the silent spirit embody the highest form of devotion. In this pursuit, both jnana, the pinnacle of wisdom, and bhakti, utmost devotion, converge towards the same ultimate goal. The synthesis of knowledge and devotion creates a harmonious pathway to spiritual enlightenment and realization, even amidst active engagement in worldly responsibilities and the fulfilment of one's obligations. With an unwavering focus on Brahman and under the benevolent grace of the divine, all endeavours shall find enduring residence within the royal abode.'

Devotion to the Lord serves yet another distinct purpose—allowing the divine to enter the individual soul (jivatma), purifying and reshaping the SRT, our inner personality, and making us universally endearing. The ever-present Lord awaits only our sincere appeal, the Gita affirms.

This integrated approach allows individuals to navigate the complexities of life with a sense of purpose and inner tranquillity, transcending the dichotomy between spiritual pursuits and worldly duties.

'Every individual is endowed with the right to choose between freedom and bondage. Believing that we can resist the will of God shall inevitably lead to sorrow. The defiance of the Lord is an egoistic pursuit devoid of inherent power. Therefore, if you decide to relinquish your resolve due to delusion, you can be assured that your nature will compel you to act, even against your own will. Such is my conviction,' says Krisn, gently guiding Arnold towards action without undue coercion.

The interplay between our inherent nature (SRT factors) and its consequential compulsions is orchestrated by the divine through karmic repercussions, denoted by various terms like 'luck', 'fate', and 'destiny'. Embracing the truth that the Lord resides within the heart of all beings as the innermost essence of our existence enables us to surrender all actions to God and transcend our egoism. Krisn calls upon Arnold to collaborate with God and fulfil his duty. He must yield himself in service to the Lord. This surrender will dispel his illusion, sever the bond of cause and effect, and guide him to attain the luminous light devoid of distortions.

Arnold gazes at his erudite friend, who assumed the role of a Guru from the moment he declared his state of helplessness and sought his friend's advice, as Krisn continues with his preachings.

'What needs to be done is in harmony with the cosmic purpose. Do not relinquish work that resonates with your character.' He paints a picture of the wise individual liberated from ego and doubt, who harbours no aversion to disagreeable actions and no attachment to agreeable ones. The freed soul, Krisn emphasizes, operates as an instrument of the Lord, upholding the cosmic order through selfless duty. The crux lies in recognizing ordained duty devoid of selfish interests.

After imparting this profound wisdom, the greatest of all secrets, Krisn relinquishes the decision-making to Arnold. There is no coercion; instead, he allows events to unfold naturally. Unlike common tendencies rooted in control or force, his approach is one of gentle persuasion. The Lord stands ever ready to guide and support, but never commands or coerces.

In a classic demonstration of inclusive leadership, Krisn acknowledges and respects his friend's capabilities. He assures Arnold of his readiness to offer guidance should challenges arise, eschewing the imposition of solutions and recognizing the growth potential in mistakes. He encourages Arnold to think independently, embark on a journey of Self-discovery, and act based on personal beliefs rather than unquestioningly adhering to authority. The ultimate goal is for Arnold to cultivate a profound sense of ownership over his ideas, free from the constraints of his teacher's imposition.

FINAL APPEAL

'By dedicating your life, actions, feelings, and thoughts, and surrendering yourself to God, divine guidance becomes a steadfast companion in life's struggles, dispelling any fear. Fix your mind on the Lord, and be devoted, allowing yourself to draw near to Him. I am confident that you are dear to Him; that's the message I wish to convey,' says Krisn.

CONCLUSION

At half-past eight, as the board members assemble, Arnold enters with a new-found radiance, a glow hitherto unfelt by his family members. Initially leaning on his friend—a compassionate teacher and erudite scholar exuding kindness—he whispers, 'Through your grace, my dear friend and teacher, I now stand resolute with my doubts dispelled. I shall act per your guidance. My gratitude to you is boundless for imparting the essence of the Bhagavad Gita, encapsulating the core of all Vedic scriptures, and offering practical insights for navigating life's challenges. In just four simple steps—right action, devotion, determination, and knowledge—you've illuminated why, as humans, we need not worry nor grieve. I've acquired the formula to attain a state free from suffering, liberated from bondage. Each time I revisit these wondrous teachings, I shall cherish them with renewed thrill and astonishment.'

The chairman of the board formally announced the results upon completion of the voting process. 'The unanimous decision to remove Dyrk as the head of the enterprise reflects a collective agreement recognizing the imperative for change. With Yohan—Arnold's older brother—assuming the leadership role, there's a renewed commitment not just to oversee daily operations, but also to reconstruct the company's image. This shift is viewed strategically, introducing fresh perspectives and innovative approaches.

In acknowledging the potential impact on Dyrk's family, an additional resolution is passed to provide them with annual compensation. This step is aimed at mitigating likely financial challenges, ensuring the family can maintain its accustomed standard of living. The emphasis extends beyond business restructuring; it underscores a commitment to compassion and fairness in addressing the consequences of the leadership change. The ultimate goal is a seamless transition that cultivates positive growth for both the enterprise and the individuals directly affected by the decision.'

The teachings of the Gita embody a profound system of spiritual discipline and guidance, constituting a comprehensive form of yoga. This holistic approach integrates philosophy, ethics, pure religion, and practical principles to facilitate Self-realization, inner harmony, and a profound connection with the divine. 'In its practical application to our lives, the Gita emphasizes the importance of uniting vision (yoga) and energy (dhanuh), and not allow the former to disintegrate into madness and the latter into savagery,' as aptly described by Dr Radhakrishnan. Indeed, the teachings of the Gita call for a harmonious balance between spiritual insight and practical action to effectively navigate life's complexities.

SECTION TEN

INTERNALIZE KNOWLEDGE THROUGH VEDIC MEDITATION

Chapter 22

THE NEW WORLD ORDER

The paradoxical nature of our progress becomes vividly apparent in today's landscape, where the remarkable achievements of science coexist with glaring disparities among individuals. This striking dichotomy serves as a profound reflection on the current state of our society. Undoubtedly, the technological revolution has brought unprecedented opportunities and innovations, promising an enhanced life for humanity as a whole. However, the plight of the average person is disheartening. In this dynamic environment, everyone aspires to share in the abundant benefits stemming from explosive growth, irrespective of whether one possesses the requisite means. Nevertheless, only a privileged few enjoy the rewards, leaving the majority to merely contribute without reaping their rightful benefits. Stranded at the periphery, many are forced to feign contentment with whatever morsels they manage to attain, concealing a deeper sense of discontent arising from the absence of legitimate gains.

Does the surge in the digital domain genuinely represent a metamorphosis of our existence, as fervently asserted? A candid response would lean towards negation, as what has truly transformed is merely the avenue through which we pursue happiness, now facilitated by technology. Experiential pleasure, often mistaken for true happiness, is merely a counterfeit—an illusion mediated by technology and external stimuli, offering fleeting gratification but lacking lasting fulfillment. The once heartwarming moments that elder parents savoured while anticipating the arrival of funds through a money order, followed by the exchange with the weathered hands of the aged postman, have receded into obscurity. The delight derived from those fleeting human interactions has now yielded to the impersonal efficiency of a banking notification or a terse text message affirming a deposit. The thrill experienced by a young adolescent anticipating a rendezvous with a neighbour under the twilight sky has now mutated into exasperation and distress, fostered by the prolonged wait for digital communiqués from a young acquaintance, whose delays often defy comprehension.

It's a conundrum of abundance. With an array of fifty distinct bread varieties, a palette of a hundred or more car models, a plethora of diet charts numbering in the thousands, and an expansive web of dating sites housing millions of profiles, the process of evaluation has transmuted into an arduous ordeal bereft of the once fervent excitement. The initial thrill dwindles precipitously, eclipsed by an inevitable state of confusion. An inordinate amount of time is now expended on exhaustive research before acquiring an object or service, or engaging with individuals digitally, yielding experiences that are scarcely distinguishable from the ordinary. The satisfaction derived from a complex and intricate process remains limited, reminiscent of times past, emphasizing that the monumental digital revolution has left a minimal imprint on the human psyche. Quickly, the mind redirects its focus towards the pursuit of unnatural or superfluous desires.

From a ten-year-old child to a septuagenarian, the contemporary landscape imposes a greater burden of stress due to a multitude of factors, unlike in the past, when the sources of unhappiness or stress were limited in number. It is true that technology undeniably yields a plethora of goods. Yet the intricate tapestry of a capitalistic society renders these riches inaccessible to the common man. Even amidst an abundance of creature comforts, humanity remains perennially entangled in sorrow with occasional bouts of contentment. No one is immune to the pangs of agony, stress, or despondency. Could this not be the opportune moment to reflect on the wisdom imparted by one of the foremost technology visionaries of our era?

The message resounds loud and lucid. Let us lend a ear to the words believed to be uttered by Steve Jobs during the twilight of his life.

'At this moment, lying on the sick bed and recalling my whole life, I realize that all the recognition and wealth that I took so much pride in, have paled and become meaningless in the face of impending death.

Non-stop pursuit of wealth will only turn a person into a twisted being, just like me.

God gave us the senses to let us feel the love in everyone's heart, not the illusions brought about by wealth. Material things lost can be found. But there is one thing that can never be found when it is lost—life. Whichever stage in life we are at right now, with time, we will face the day when the curtain comes down.'

Deceived by the myriad offerings that have burgeoned due to remarkable strides in science and technology, the common man finds himself ensnared in a state of vexation, trapped between his yearnings and the unyielding grasp of denial. Meanwhile, the unfeeling world persists in its pursuits to propel organic expansion even further. While it is conceded that science has indeed provided mankind with tools to navigate life more effectively, it has also given rise to the unwarranted assertion that every augmentation in our dominion over nature is unequivocally beneficial.

However, as articulated by Dr P. Nagaraja Rao, 'The gifts of science and technology are not qualifiedly good in themselves. We have so many undesirable elements wrapped up in the gifts of science.' This emerges from the reality that the mind, which comprehends a multitude of external objects and experiences a gamut of emotions attached to them, remains estranged from self-understanding; it remains oblivious to its desires.

From the break of dawn to the wane of dusk, individuals from all strata of society find themselves endlessly entangled in a ceaseless whirl of actions, driven by unchecked desires spurred by their sensory faculties and steered by an ambivalent mind. In this ceaseless striving, a select few manage to actualize their aspirations, while many grapple incessantly, only to eventually succumb in their pursuit. For the majority, life resembles a pendulum that incessantly swings amidst opposing poles, frequently pausing for prolonged intervals at the end characterized by anguish. For them, life embodies a panorama of disillusionment, grief, and misery.

Endeavours to rebel against this prevailing reality generally yield scant fruitful outcomes, for their aspirations remain but speculative conjectures and their actions transpire under the aegis of ignorance of their authentic selves. Until this veil of ignorance is lifted to reveal the truth, humankind shall persistently retrace the very errors they have committed in the past. In their quest to transcend sorrow, individuals channel their focus into amassing material comforts, often oblivious to the fact that it is the very longing for material possessions that engenders their suffering. People tend to desire more when they feel a sense of lack or emptiness, whether it is in terms of material possessions, emotional fulfilment, or other aspects of life. As long as ignorance persists, a perpetual sense of emptiness shall linger.

It would be an even more regrettable fallacy to entertain the belief that the affluent and renowned are immune to participating in this sombre narrative. Anxiety, depression, and various other psychological afflictions—ailments that confound medical science's attempts at resolution—grasp individuals indiscriminately.

However, the majority remains disinclined to heed the pleas of the minor faction advocating fervently for an equilibrium of growth—harmony between heart and intellect, the synergy of physics and metaphysics. While every individual within the realm possesses the faculty of intellect, it remains befuddled and tainted. Consequently, unless this intellect finds unity with divinity, the trajectory of scientific advancement stands to jeopardize society's well-being.

THE DEHUMANIZATION DILEMMA: THE RISE OF AI AND THE LOSS OF SELF

The relentless yearning of humanity to assert dominance over nature, subjecting it to its will, is a venture of daunting proportions. Within the span of the forthcoming fifteen years, or even less, artificial intelligence might ascend to such a zenith of supremacy that it shall not only govern the journey to a destination but dictate the very destination itself. Conceivably, it could exert dominion over the human psyche, shaping not only actions but also intuition and anticipations. It might decree the spectrum of desires, the amplitude of emotions, and even orchestrate the rhythm of elation and melancholy.

The complete relinquishment of biological intelligence by man, juxtaposed with the eventual ascendance of artificial intelligence over nature, might seem implausible. Yet, we mustn't dismiss the readiness with which humanity is poised to forfeit its intrinsic nature, its propensity for contemplation and introspection, thereby sacrificing its liberty as well. As elucidated by Dr P. Nagaraja Rao, a sagacious philosopher, 'Human beings when exposed to such technology would become uninterested in freedom and the right to dissent. Men would become like those birds which have learned to gulp up a good living without using wings and consequently renounce the privilege of flight and remain grounded forever.' The seer offers a subtle glimpse into the path humanity is likely to tread in the times to come. The rapid process of dehumanization at the hands of man himself is evident through his evolving role, behaviour, and paradigm towards existence.

A multitude of individuals perceive the aforementioned phenomenon tentatively. A considerable batch of humanity displays a willingness to capitulate to technology, while generally evading exploration of alternatives that hold the potential to alleviate the afflictions stemming from a perturbed mind, a phenomenon attributed largely to ceaseless and vehement desires. Indeed, few individuals lead lives suffused with unconditional bliss, steering clear of the ephemeral enticements proffered by a capitalistic society. Not out of deprivation, but a conscious choice inspired by conviction and free will. Regrettably, the pursuit of the underlying secrets to lead a life of contentment seems to elude widespread interest. Even practitioners of modern complementary alternative medicines, determined to profit from the milieu, find themselves engaged in endeavours primarily focused on furnishing immediate alleviation. Their designs appear fixated on offering symptomatic solace for afflictions stemming from a perturbed mind, rather than addressing the quandary at its root.

Meditation, among a multitude of other practices, an age-old method designed to confer substantial and enduring benefits, has, in the current epoch, undergone a dilution of its intrinsic meaning and worth, owing to its integration with commercial inclinations. In the modern paradigm where time investment is appraised solely against measurable gains, the practice of meditation finds itself in competition with a gamut of diversions that promise fleeting solace through transient distractions. Predictably, the current circumstances provide fertile ground for individuals overwhelmed by the pressures of contemporary existence to succumb to counterfeit meditation methodologies. Yet, the modern viewpoint, though in vogue, cannot negate the fact that authentic meditation produces lasting outcomes today, just as it did in the past when individuals embraced a tranquil way of life.

The primary source of human woes is ignorance, closely followed by the misconception of the world's dual nature. Ignorance here does not refer to a lack of scholarly wisdom; rather, it pertains to the lack of awareness of one's true Self, as expounded upon throughout this text. While man's authentic Self, the 'supremely blissful Consciousness', stands independent and absolute in reality, his illusory self, the individual, lacks such independence.

This unawareness of the truth renders him ignorant. Destruction of ignorance is not possible through any action for it is not in conflict with ignorance, declared Shankara in his *Atma Bodha*. Dwelling within the realm of duality, an individual incessantly engages in various endeavours to satisfy his desires, a consequence of his ignorance. Additionally, since all notions of duality stem from ignorance, actions stemming from this misconception, such as considering oneself the sole doer, only serve to reinforce ignorance rather than eradicate it.

Knowledge alone dismantles ignorance. Advocates who emphasize the necessity of performing actions based on knowledge for their fruition contend that knowledge by itself remains unproductive, be it regarding material or transcendental understanding. Yet, a person rooted in non-dual Consciousness seeks nothing, for he recognizes that liberation is his inherent essence. What action should he undertake when he has no objective to fulfil? Such an individual, while carrying out worldly duties and responsibilities, perceives everything as part of his role in the grand cosmic play. He lacks any yearning for liberation, as he is eternally free upon realizing his true nature. He even lacks the desire to be desireless.

Chapter 23

THE MYTH OF MEDITATION

The meditation practice currently in vogue is a distortion of the original form, reminiscent of classic misrepresentation. It does not align with either the true essence of the term 'meditation' or the purpose for which the practice was originally conceived. Furthermore, the myriad variations in this practice, stemming from differing interpretations and teachings of diverse traditions, often perplex and undermine the very purpose it seeks to fulfil.

The central aim of the prevailing practice is to ease the mind, with the hope of alleviating stress and anxiety. However, this modern approach lacks the defining characteristics that would properly exemplify the genuine meaning of meditation. Nevertheless, for reasons not easily comprehended, scholars have associated it with meditation. Not astonishingly, engaging in an endeavour to tranquillize or pacify the mind, an action that is now universally deemed as meditation, only yields a small fraction of what true meditation is intended to achieve.

Presently, the common understanding of meditation is derived from an extended definition of the term rather than its original import. Given the swift pace at which contemporary individuals pursue their tasks, they are swiftly enchanted by any offer, provided there is a reward upon the completion of an activity, however fleeting or illusory it may be. For those ensnared in lives filled with stress, the solace of a serene mind surpasses even a hearty meal in significance.

Moreover, when the all-powerful realm of medical science endorses the practice's benefits in such a substantial manner, modern man finds neither the time nor the inclination to undertake further investigations. Hence, he readily embraces any practice labelled as meditation, without much scrutiny. Such is the potency of linguistic distortion.

Despite the aforementioned points, this tome does not endeavour to undermine the positive strides that millions have found, nor to assert the dominance of one concept over the lauded existing practice—favoured universally as a 'one size fits all' solution. Neither is its purpose to partake in a war of words. Yet, to avert our gaze from the weighty toll exacted by the disregard for semantic precision regarding the term 'meditation' is to teeter on the brink of absurdity.

A thorough examination of the popular practice is not deemed necessary except for addressing two notable shortcomings, as the realms of practice and proposition emphasized in this text belong to different domains, each pursuing distinct objectives. Moreover, there exists no intent to diminish the present practice, which centres on pacifying the mind. In truth, a tranquil mind provides solid footing for the meditation practice advocated in this treatise. This practice emphasizes the importance of accepting the world's diversity as it is, while also rising above the dual nature of cosmic law, which is apparently shaped by opposites. Therefore, the primary aim of this work is to present a practice rooted in the primal definition of the term 'meditation'. This practice is genuine, all-encompassing, and capable of yielding monumental outcomes. Above all, it strives to uncover the indubitable truth regarding Consciousness and the means to attune with it, to alleviate the suffering of man.

Consciousness is the prevailing force in all the thinking that accompanies every human encounter. It is only through Consciousness that the world of objects, the body, and various mental states become known. The mind and body attain sentience, functioning as the knower and the doer, solely due to the reflection of Consciousness with its independent existence. It is the absolute truth, transcending all religions, rituals, and practices. Thus, no prerequisites based on religious tenets are imposed. It stands in perpetual harmony with all we know and yearn to know.

To meditate is to engage in thoughts, mull over notions, and contemplate deeply. Introspection, rumination, self-examination, concentration, and pondering are meditation's kindred expressions. Yet, what the world has embraced as meditation has nothing to do with deep thinking. In essence, it manifests as a regimen, demanding modest mental exertion. It directs the mind's focus, under tutelage, to linger upon a chosen object or endeavour—a breath's rhythm, or even a humble raisin chewed deliberately to remain attuned to the present moment. Another variation explores the dynamic relationship between the body and mind. This too requires active engagement of the mind to gain any insight.

The core idea behind the current practice is to shift attention away from dwelling on the past or worrying about the future, thereby calming the mind and helping one remain anchored in the present moment. While these methods are undoubtedly rooted in noble intentions, they often produce only limited and short-lived results due to two inherent shortcomings. An article featured in *SciTech Daily* (9 October 2023) echoes the sentiment expressed above, as it asserts, 'Mindfulness therapy has gained widespread popularity as a means to help individuals cope with stress, and many people have reported significant benefits from practising it. However, Odysseus Stone, PhD from the University of Copenhagen, believes that many of the philosophical assumptions about human beings and their relationship to the world on which mindfulness is based are quite dubious and should be examined carefully.'

Essentially, the article underscores a fundamental concern regarding the authenticity of the purported benefits associated with the widespread adoption of mindfulness, which has found diverse applications in educational, healthcare, and occupational settings through the proliferation of mindfulness-based therapies and meditation practices.

Mindfulness encourages viewing passing thoughts and emotions as fleeting clouds in the mind, avoiding excessive attachment. However, this approach becomes problematic when applied universally, especially to deeply held beliefs and societal issues. It also intersects with the attention economy, where tech companies compete for our focus. While mindfulness offers tools to control attention, critics argue it shifts responsibility for structural problems to individuals. Additionally, the concept of living solely in the present moment, a central tenet of mindfulness, raises questions about the importance of past and future narratives in our lives and the nature of the 'pure now'. These ideas challenge us to consider the nuanced implications of mindfulness in our complex world.

The initial shortcoming arises from the challenge of sustaining focus on any task beyond a brief span, especially for individuals whose thoughts are dominated by persistent, pessimistic reflections or by matters necessitating immediate action. The second and greater restraint lies in its dependence on redirecting negative thoughts by concentrating on an undertaking, rather than obliterating the root cause from whence negative thoughts spring. While we concede the accrual of favourable advantages from participation in such techniques, we cannot disagree that it amounts to a renewed endeavour to furnish only symptomatic relief to an ongoing quandary.

Hence, a person must repeatedly embrace this practice to mollify the same age-old inner struggle, which keeps returning in cycles—even though each meditation session should ultimately reach its natural conclusion. Assuredly, none of these methodologies is contrived to fathom the genuine origin of human afflictions, whether tied to strain or the inability to grapple with life's capriciousness, for none of these qualify as true meditation. It is worth noting that the architects of modern meditative techniques could not have contrived a practice now ubiquitously acclaimed, without delving into profound meditation grounded in the original meaning of the term, whether or not they were aware of the principles thereof.

In recapitulation, everyone should continue the valuable practice of calming the mind—but avoid calling it true meditation. Begin your genuine meditation practice to understand and eliminate the root causes of the challenges confronting humanity. Think, reflect, and contemplate in earnest. The key lies in comprehending the nature of the mind, its inherent relationship with Consciousness, as well as its pivotal role in the interplay between Consciousness and the body. First, it's crucial to cultivate and maintain the appropriate thought patterns that are essential for preserving a state of inner tranquillity when confronting opposing pairs of experiences. Subsequently, delving into the core of human challenges and addressing them through the practice of Vedic meditation becomes the crux.

This meditation practice's outcome remains consistent across the cosmos, given that its central focus is on Consciousness—the sole absolute and undeniable truth spanning the universe and beyond. As one progresses towards the realization of their elevated essence, a spontaneous purification of the mind becomes perceptible. Those who engage in this practice will witness two key outcomes: a remarkable improvement in overall quality of life for everyone, and, for some, complete freedom from the bondage of desires.

VEDIC MEDITATION—SUPREMELY DIFFERENT

Verily, Vedic meditation proposes a vigorous, yet effortless engagement of the mind, to perceive the world and its sundry objects with a transformation in the pattern of thought. It is but a change in perspective, a shift in vision, lacking any attempt to alter the external world or bring about any metamorphosis in the corporeal state of the body. To put it plainly, it is a step-by-step systematic progression of the mind, to apprehend and dispel ignorance, which is the very root of man's tribulations.

It is an endeavour undertaken to dispel ignorance about our true essence, our authentic Self, and to establish a connection between theoretical knowledge and its practical realization. This is achieved through focused introspection and contemplation. During this process, unnecessary thoughts are filtered out, allowing the individual to concentrate—through heightened awareness—on those that hold significance.

This meditation is not a revolutionary novelty, but a hoary and well-established practice, a procedure embraced by all illustrious personages to excel in their respective domains, be it sports, acting, or academia. Great scientists such as Sir Isaac Newton and Einstein, knowingly or unknowingly, may have delved into the depths of meditation to unearth significant truths of the physical cosmos.

Thus, meditation's practice must engage the mind fervently to achieve an objective by engendering and concentrating on rightful thoughts that culminate in resolving psychological battles experienced by men, women, boys, and girls of all ages, or to spark the revelation of fresh insights and ideas relevant to the material world. Or for the comprehension of supra-rational wisdom that pertains to the realm of our inner world.

Surely, the rationale and purpose must be lucid prior to the commencement of any meditation, and the practice ought to cease upon accomplishment of the objective. Cultivating the appropriate disposition and predisposition through prescribed preliminary disciplines are prerequisites to persisting resolutely with wisdom. A seeker aiming to uncover the truth is counselled not to unreservedly accept the wisdom expounded in Vedic scriptures before subjecting the same to logical scrutiny (yukti) even though there exists a complete dearth of conjecture or speculation. The reliance upon scriptures is emphasized because the wisdom sought lies beyond the scope of the six methods available for acquiring knowledge in the phenomenal world.[33]

In a world divided between fervent religious extremism and the complete abandonment of faith in favor of science and technology, the only true path to healing humanity's suffering lies in returning to the ancient practice of meditation, prescribed long before the seventh century BCE. This timeless discipline offers a balanced alternative, transcending both blind belief and cold rationalism.

Assured outcomes await the individual who is prepared to adhere to a regimen of discipline and maintain unwavering resolve, relinquish ego, cast off the veil of self-delusion, and simply embody goodness while resolutely upholding the transformed perspective.

The conditions mentioned are not as arduous as they might seem. After all, the true catalyst for the pivotal moments in the lives of all renowned individuals is their momentary adherence to three fundamental prerequisites, which emerge opportunistically (finding themselves in the right place at the right time). When comprehended accurately, relinquishing ego becomes the simplest task, for it entails letting go of something that was never truly yours to begin with. Self-deception arises whenever one deceives oneself; it constitutes a purposeful transgression against one's moral compass. Equipped with a superior set of faculties, you can easily evade pretentiousness by harmonizing thoughts, speech, and actions to dispel self-deception. Every human embodies a mixture of virtues, vices, and imperfections. To embrace goodness and become a virtuous human, you must consciously infuse every action with a measure of kindness.

Chapter 24

CONTEMPORARY MEDITATION—A FRESH PERSPECTIVE

The prevailing misconception that surrounds the term 'meditation' is egregiously misleading, as it deviates drastically from the word's original essence. Thus arises the imperative to pose a single question before embarking upon the venture of meditation: do I genuinely comprehend what I seek from this practice?

The burgeoning popularity of modern meditation methodologies, despite their lax interpretation of the term, is heartening. However, it also serves as the cause of disillusionment for many. It is observed that a considerable number who presently find themselves disenchanted with this practice were surreptitiously influenced by individuals with a limited or shallow grasp of spirituality. Likely, their entry into the realm of spirituality was inspired by a sense of enigmatic allure.

Regrettably, since these self-proclaimed gurus fail to divulge the authentic purpose for which meditation was conceived, a sizable fraction of practitioners prematurely abandon the endeavour due to disillusionment or because the outcomes fall drastically short of their inflated expectations. Adding to this dilemma is the venal agenda of commercial-minded opportunists who emphasize meditation's auxiliary benefits—conditioning the mind with fleeting excitements—while failing to acknowledge its true intrinsic value, both in the immediate and extended trajectories.

Indeed, it's true that those who engage in meditation often exhibit heightened emotional control and a sense of tranquillity, a reality substantiated by empirical data within the sphere of medical science. This outcome is an incidental benefit, manifesting during those precious moments when the practitioner enters a state of silence, hopefully withdrawing their senses from the tumultuous external world. However, it must be underscored that the original purpose of meditation wasn't to seek transient respite from stress or psychological distress caused by myriad factors emerging from the so called 'economic progress', as these afflictions were not as prevalent then as they are in contemporary times.

Meditation is bestowed with a dual nature, each facet addressing distinct exigencies. The first purpose is to shape and refine the mind, preparing it for the journey of spiritual ascent. In this process, three objectives are accomplished: firstly, an enhancement in the quality of life devoid of undue reliance on technology while addressing real life miseries and conflicts; secondly, the attainment of Jeevan Mukti—emancipation from the entanglements of the material world; thirdly, Videha Mukti—a liberation from the cycle of birth and death.

The second purpose of meditation is even loftier, centred around transcending the material world to realize the higher truths. Meditation wields the power to dismantle all obstructions on the path to eternal liberation, Nitya Mukti.

The transition that humanity has undergone over the past century, propelled by economic progress, stands as a testament to remarkable human achievement. From the advent of steam engines to the marvel of maglev high-speed trains, from the harrowing beginnings of human surgery to the marvels of robotic surgical procedures, the transformation is indeed remarkable. Yet, the refusal to acknowledge the lopsided nature of economic growth is an equally striking testament to human hubris. The widening chasm of inequality, a direct consequence of growth driven by capitalism, has plunged billions into distress, grappling with their inability to satiate the insatiable demands of their senses.

As Ronald Purser in his treatise titled *McMindfulness* notes, 'People are expected to adapt to what this model demands of them. Stress has been anthologized and privatized, and the burden of managing it outsourced to individuals.' We now find ourselves at a juncture where the possibility of rectifying the situation seems nearly inconceivable—a reality wherein the common individual is fated to suffer or perish amidst suffering. Amid a climate of exaggerated claims, the profound truth that even the wealthy are not immune to discontent only heightens the gravity of our predicament.

The pursuit of creating an abundance of creature comforts in the endeavour to amplify pleasurable encounters, all while harbouring the hope of assuaging pain by default, constitutes yet another fallacy within the grand scheme of growth. 'Pain' and 'pleasure' stand not as mere antithetical sentiments; rather, they maintain their distinctive essence. The advent of one does not necessarily signal the departure of the other, contrary to the presumptions of those steering the economic machinery. These twin forces coexist, flourishing independently.

How could humanity permit both knowledge and suffering to flourish in tandem? How could humans adopt such a cavalier attitude towards suffering and accept its repercussions as an irreversible decree?

Amidst the sombre overcast enveloping humanity, the knowledge at our disposal to rein in the unruly mind and govern thoughts, thereby quelling all forms of mental anguish, emerges as more than a mere silver lining. The ancient Indo-Aryan sages turned their minds towards the practice of meditation—contemplation—to attain Para, the higher knowledge that unveils the transcendental verity of the imperishable. Acquiring this subjective wisdom, which transcends the domain of physical sciences, demanded the mastery of the mind, an evolution towards a heightened faculty of understanding known as 'bodhi'.

The aspirant of this wisdom awakened the latent potency of the mind and senses through concentration and self-restraint. 'By withdrawing the senses from outer objects, he made the scattered mind to focus on one point. And as the power of concentration increased, the seeker became aware of deeper phases of existence,' as eloquently penned by Swami Nikhilananda.

We find all these teachings encapsulated within the annals of Vedanta texts. The choice to learn, comprehend, and apply this profound knowledge (sphota) rests upon the individual's volition or karma. Should one engage in meditative contemplation upon this knowledge with due diligence, palpable and enduring outcomes shall undoubtedly emerge, manifesting as substantial enhancements in the tapestry of life's quality.

A prerequisite step, preceding the meditation on this concept, involves delving into the 'absolute truth'—the bedrock underlying every facet of this phenomenal world (which constitutes a lower dimension of reality). Thus, the central purpose of Vedic meditation lies in contemplating the multifaceted dimensions of the singular truth, the truth intrinsic to oneself. It forms an integral part of a holistic process (Shravanam—hearing, Mananam—introspection, and Nidhidhyasanam—meditation), a journey culminating in self-realization of the knowledge about the 'absolute truth', acquired through the perusal of texts and the guidance of a qualified guru. In essence, meditation becomes a practice to reconfigure thought patterns, ensuring the mind becomes a repository of thoughts essential for leading a tranquil existence.

A FALLACY OF INTERPRETATION: A BEACON OF IGNORANCE

At its core lies the erroneous identification of the individual with the composite of body and mind—a field of lower reality. This fallacy originates from the mistaken belief that matter (the body and mind) and spirit form an inseparable unity. Predicaments arise when the individual bestows reality upon the body and mind, entities that lack independent existence. Upon aligning with the body, the immediate ramifications are the emergence of Ahankara (the Ego) and Mamakara (the sense of possession), unfailingly leading to anxiety, and the pilfering of inner peace.

A plethora of sensations—arrogance, conceit, false dignity, preferences, aversions, love, hatred, attachments, and distress—all cascade forth as an integrated package. The ego, germinating from this erroneous amalgamation with the body and ignorance concerning one's genuine identity, emerges as the primary fount of human sorrow and suffering. Desires and attachments, progeny of nescience, play a mediating role.

Divergence in name and form (referring to the body–mind complex) is crucial for practical transactions and the corresponding experiences. However, identifying solely with the body and mind, both representing pure matter, makes one vulnerable. This leads to inner turmoil, hindering even the fleeting tranquillity that the mind can offer.

Chapter 25

GETTING READY

The purpose of Vedic meditation is to attain the wisdom known as Brahmavidya—the knowledge that reveals the higher aspect of the Self. Its ultimate aim is the complete eradication of suffering and the realization of supreme bliss. Brahmavidya forms the very foundation upon which all true knowledge rests. 'The fire of knowledge, kindled by discrimination between the Self and the non-self-consumes ignorance with its effects,' proclaimed Shankara. It transcends all we have known or will know through our sensory faculties. It predates all experiences and actions, rendering it beyond the grasp of ordinary human senses. Grasping the infinite with our finite faculties makes this journey challenging, leading many spiritual seekers to prematurely halt their progress.

Thus, the compassionate guidance of a capable guru is paramount in dispelling fear and reaffirming the invaluable rewards of embarking on the spiritual journey. The true essence of this expedition lies in discerning the disparity between the Consciousness tainted by ego, the 'i' consciousness, or the empirical self, and the 'I', the pure Consciousness, or the transcendent Self.

To tangibly realize the absolute truth, intellectual comprehension must be coupled with unwavering moral disciplines and a resolute spirit to acquire and apply this knowledge. Mental discipline is an initial prerequisite, both to qualify for attaining knowledge and to sustain determination and reap its benefits. Thus, the practice of ethical virtues and the mastery of the senses, which possess inherent outward tendencies, remain foundational in this blessed odyssey.

The teachings of Vedanta are never a burden upon a conventional existence, for they do not wield control but rather contribute to a more serene life. The spiritual expedition proposed does not encroach but assists an individual in fulfilling his roles, responsibilities, and duties more effectively within the material world. It firmly proclaims that any person can achieve absolute freedom from all bondage, provided two prerequisites are met. Firstly, the individual must be eligible to pursue this wisdom; otherwise, although knowledge might be acquired through the processes of Shravanam (listening), Mananam (contemplation), and Nidhidhyasanam (meditation), it may not be steadfastly retained. Secondly, the individual must gain the insight that they are not the body–mind complex, but indeed the unadulterated Consciousness.

To glean the benefits from this acquired knowledge, the individual's mind must be refined. The seeker of this wisdom thus advocates shaping the mind to cultivate self-discipline. Yet, self-discipline does not equate to stifling innate emotions or demeaning oneself; rather, it entails altering the thought paradigm. Ample preparation, fostering the right disposition, and cultivating readiness to detach from excessive material pursuits are indispensable prerequisites.

As B. R. Rajam Iyer elucidated in his preface to another prominent Vedanta text, 'till one makes sure that one's mind has been completely purged of all preconceptions or prejudices which are the offspring of attachment, one cannot hope to command the concentration of mind needed for climbing the topmost steps leading to truth.'

Vedic meditation necessitates qualification, adhering to the fourfold regimen known as Sadhana Chatushtaya. Its goal is to purify the mind and establish conditions that facilitate the process of learning.

Alongside the four prescribed disciplines outlined below, three forms of ascetic practices—namely, asceticism of the body, speech, and mind—are advocated. All these endeavours are aimed at training the mind to discern its relationship with Consciousness, the ultimate reality. Focused concentration is imperative when embarking on the journey to comprehend metaphysical truth. It entails nurturing inner tranquillity and reigning in the senses. This is achieved through virtuous conduct, dispelling malevolent thoughts, venerating personal deities, adhering to religious rituals, and performing offerings—all directed at cleansing the mind and aligning one's persona.

The aspirant must ascend the three-tiered staircase, progressing from being a karmi (executor of actions), intensely desiring to acquire the knowledge, to metamorphosing into a jnani (one who has acquired wisdom). Throughout this transformative process, the aspirant must engage in Vedic meditation, initially to acquire the sought-after knowledge and subsequently to preserve it. Concurrently, to quote Nikhilananda, 'intellectual understanding of Vedanta must be followed by transformation of life; otherwise, it is of no practical benefit to the aspirant'. It is crucial to remember the immutable verity that even as unenlightened individuals engage in specific meditation to explore higher knowledge of Brahman, they perpetually remain Brahman and experience no alteration.

SADHANA CHATUSHTAYA—THE FOUR DISCIPLINES

1. Discrimination: Nitya Anitya Viveka

This primary directive involves clear comprehension and the essential discrimination between Absolute (unchanging) reality and relative (changing) reality. The essence of Vedic meditation lies in the direct realization of the ultimate truth, which emerges after grasping that the spirit or Supreme Consciousness is the unchanging reality, while everything else—all objects of experience—remains ephemeral; and the realm of multiplicity is transient. This understanding of eternal truth is not to be misconstrued as a theological doctrine but rather a demonstrable truth forged through a threefold criterion—authoritative scriptures capturing the insights of ancient sages, intellectual inquiry, and self-realization through individual experiences.

An object or a substance like the spirit must stand free from contradiction, possess self-sufficiency, and remain immutable across the past, present, and future to be deemed genuine. Every entity in the cosmos, including the human body and mind, relies on the spirit for one or more reasons and, hence lacks self-sufficiency. Moreover, all objects entwined in the gamut of time and space shall inevitably undergo alteration and dissolution, thus lacking the attribute of unchanging reality and, consequently, not being classifiable as real.

In contrast, the spirit stands self-sufficient, undisturbed by the metamorphoses undergone by diverse objects. It is the bedrock of time, space, and objects, and hence remains unaffected by their phenomena in the objective realm. Consciousness transcends temporal constraints; it is not the product of any specific cause. Therefore, it is untenable to consider the knowledge of Consciousness as subject to time. Consciousness neither grows nor diminishes. It is static and the sole unchanging reality. It is peerless. It is ever present.

The dependence of the individual's body–mind complex, a composite matter for all the functions on Supreme Consciousness, is substantiated by the threefold states of human experiences—waking, dreaming, and deep sleep. It is essential to understand that everything—from our own body and mind to the cosmos—belongs to a lower order of reality. It lacks independent existence, arises and dissolves, and is therefore impermanent.

Waking: In this state, man engages with the external world through the interplay of jnanendriyas (organs of perception) and sense objects (sound, touch, form, taste, and smell). The sequence of pleasurable and distressing interactions fosters the emergence of reactions such as Kama (desire), Krodha (anger), Lobha (greed), Moha (delusion), Madam (arrogance, vanity), and Matsaryam (jealousy). The absence of interaction entails an absence of reaction or concerns.

The instruments of perception or the sense organs guided by the mind give the knowledge about the existence of various objects and oneself. Awareness of past, present, and future experiences is enabled through sentiency lent by the Consciousness, which the mind acquires as a reflection of the radiant spirit, encapsulated within the body. Stated differently, Atman, the Supreme Consciousness residing in every being, identifies with the human experience during the waking state, all the gross objects of the world, and the physical body (sense organs) of the individual. The mind not only perceives the external world but also records experiences from interactions, emotions, and impressions called Vasna or samskaras. During the waking state, the active mind and senses function only due to the identification of Consciousness, facilitating experiential engagement with the world.

Dreaming: This phase involves a reiteration of experiences from the waking state, albeit with dormant or withdrawn sense organs. It renders the physical body unconscious while generating a dream body, within which the individual experiences the dream. Knowledge arises from registered impressions (vasnas) collected during the waking state of the long past, coupled with the imaginative projections of the mind, manifesting as dreams. Pleasures and pains are not genuinely experienced in dreams; instead, the mind assumes the role of forming impressions, associations, and corresponding emotional experiences. In this state, the Supreme Self does not identify with the physical body, rendering the external world non-existent. Nevertheless, the Consciousness associates with the dream state and the Vasnas contained within the subtle mind, the dream world, and the dream objects. No new experiences are amassed during this phase. However, objects in the dream are visible only with the light of Atman.

Deep Sleep: During this stage, neither the external nor internal world is perceptible. There is no experience through an active mind or organs, which facilitate various experiences in the other two states. In the state of deep sleep, the sense organs, mind, and the sense objects of the world converge and dissolve into the Self, assuming a seed-like or potential form. Consequently, the individual remains oblivious to any occurrences, even his existence.

Since the mind is latent during deep sleep, there isn't even the experience of 'I am sleeping.' What persists is profound relaxation, etched into the passive mind, known as the causal body or seed form. Emotions, worries, anxieties, and bodily pain dissolve temporarily. Since the sense organs are resolved or withdrawn, there is no experience. Yet, upon waking, one retains the memory of sleeping, recognizing the brief absence of life. Simultaneously, connections with previous thoughts swiftly resurface. Even within this experience-less deep sleep, a form of experience exists, reinforcing the absence of ignorance. 'The effulgent infinite spirit makes the body insensible in sleep but It remains awake taking with It the particles of the organs.'[34] During this phase, Atman aligns with deep sleep and the causal body, where all exist in latent form.

This exposition affirms Atman's eternal presence as a witness to the three states of human experience.

The day the mind—acting as the intermediary between Consciousness and the physical body within the subtle body—departs, the connection with the spirit severs, marking the culmination of one's life. Subsequently, the human body resembles a lifeless piece of wood devoid of the spirit's link.

Thus, the spirit, the eternal Consciousness, rightfully earns the epithet of life force energy. It transcends mere existence; it is the very foundation of existence, as everything comes to being only in its presence. The ability to discern the illusory nature of the phenomenal world, as opposed to the unchanging reality of the Absolute—which lies beyond sensory experience—is a vital catalyst in the journey of Vedic contemplation. This marks the foundational discipline one must cultivate: the art of distinguishing the real from the unreal, the authentic from the counterfeit.

2. Determination: Ihamutra Phala Bhoga

After the seeker has imbibed a lucid comprehension of verity and illusion, Vairagya, or detachment, emerges as a newfound disposition towards the material trappings of the world, incapable of bestowing boundless felicity. This discipline dispels the obscurity enshrouding one's genuine Self, permitting a sojourn within the perpetually joyful Consciousness. Vairagya, furthermore, stands as an indispensable trait for the spiritual aspirant, empowering steadfast adherence to truth when the material realm tantalizes with irresistible allurements.

3. Six Treasures of Discipline: Shadga Samadhi Sampatthi

i. Sama (Inner Harmony; the control of mind)

The outward-reaching senses, as acknowledged in the *Katha Upanishad*, possess a deliberate flaw within their design. This flaw impels humankind to chase pleasure through external objects, despite the inherent limitations that result in finite gratification from such pursuits. As long as one remains fixated on this outward journey, one remains ensconced in obscurity. Recognizing the 'Knower of All' demands a firm conviction that the pursuit of external objects, regardless of their pleasure, cannot provide the security and tranquillity one seeks. Sama embodies the capacity cultivated to divert the mind from sensory enticements, to harness each sense faculty for the acquisition of absolute truth. It's not a product of aversion towards worldly objects, but a consequence of the conviction that all within time and space are subject to change, and lack the attributes necessary for fulfilling one's desires.

ii. Dama (Self-Mastery; control of the senses)

Complementary to Sama, Dama is the art of reigning in the senses, preventing them from succumbing to the fleeting allure of material pleasures. This mastery is the gateway for a seeker to delve into meditation upon the truth. As the mind dances to the tunes of the sense organs, merely controlling the mind is insufficient.

iii. Uparati (Selfless Action)

Uparati signifies engaging in actions within the functional world with the intent of benefiting others. Termed as Sattva Karma, the individual here is primed to undertake entirely altruistic actions. Every action yields him greater joy compared to those who engage in deeds with the expectation of favourable outcomes. However, he does perform actions essential for the sustenance of life. While some Vedantists may advocate embracing monastic life and forsaking worldly obligations, the true practice of this discipline entails residing within the world while not being bound by it.

iv. Titiksha (Resilience)

Titiksha is the attribute enabling a person to endure life's harshest trials without complaint. Once cultivated, this quality frees a person from the desire to counter the pain that arises from their karmic actions. They serenely accept whatever comes their way. They keep in mind the transient nature of the world, thus remaining unperturbed by the dualities of life's experiences, which are creations of the mind. Such a practitioner remains impervious to physical injuries to a certain degree, and free from mental distress.

v. Shraddha (Devotion to Guru)

Shraddha is the unwavering faith disciples nurture towards their guru—one who is adept, wise, and knowledgeable about the path leading to the ultimate goal of all spiritual seekers. The disciple's relationship with the master is built upon absolute reverence and devotion, forming the bedrock for attaining invaluable wisdom. It is not blind faith but truth before faith. This reverence transcends conventional scepticism. It differs from the teacher-student dynamic in worldly academic settings.

vi. Samadhanam (Dwelling in Consciousness)

After dedicatedly practising the aforementioned disciplines, the spiritual seekers ready themselves to gather their thoughts, enabling unwavering focus on the Supreme Consciousness, and basking in eternal bliss.

4. Desire for Liberation: Mumukshutvam

The ultimate aspiration of every spiritual seeker lies in liberation—release from the chains of worldly entanglements. A fervent desire forms the base for the fulfilment of any aspiration. However, when individuals comprehend their intrinsic essence, identical to the eternally free Supreme Consciousness, the yearning for liberation becomes superfluous. In this knowledge of Brahman, ignorance dissipates, and liberation prevails.

The assimilation and application of the aforementioned four disciplines thus stand as vital prerequisites for shaping the mind before embarking upon Vedic meditation. The imperative to harbour resolute determination outweighs the very acquisition of knowledge, a refrain underscored repeatedly in Vedanta's teachings. This alone shall ensconce the mind in tranquillity, unwavering amidst every circumstance.

MASTERING DETACHMENT (NON-ATTACHMENT)

Two facets of non-attachment warrant a deeper comprehension. One pertains to detachment from all objects of experience that do not belong to the domain of the Supreme Self. This competence can be cultivated by discerning the truth from the illusory, recognizing that experiential joys, though momentarily enticing, cannot yield enduring happiness. Eight malevolent forces enter during the early phase after birth, allying with the senses that project outwardly.[35] In unison, they generate deposits of impurities within the mind, manifesting as repugnant thoughts. These thoughts then form the basis for actions, conduct, and disposition. Hence, humanity remains perennially discontent with amassed possessions.

Nurturing mastery over the mind while failing to cultivate detachment towards worldly treasures may prove detrimental, especially for those not yet primed for the inner journey, as it can deepen attachment, inflate ego, and divert the seeker from true self-realization.

Secondly, the act of turning away from material possessions ought to arise organically from within, rooted in conviction. The suppression of desires, aimed at asserting dominion over the mind, might yield contrary outcomes. Ergo, the governance of the senses through the myriad disciplines delineated above must be harmonized with nurturing non-attachment. This equilibrium stands pivotal in steadying the mind during the nascent phase of the spiritual expedition. Thus, the guidance of a guru becomes imperative. To follow the precept of non-attachment doesn't render an individual devoid of societal connection or empathy. Detachment truly conveys relinquishing the possessive inclination.

EMBODYING STILLNESS AND DETACHMENT IN THE FAST-PACED MODERN WORLD

Both are achievable through a steadfast understanding that Consciousness is our intrinsic reality, while the body–mind complex is merely an incidental phenomenon. As witness Consciousness, it remains detached, serene even amidst the chaos of daily life. Consciousness, by its very essence, is unattached to anything, yet nothing escapes its observation.

A fitting metaphor for this is light: it illuminates objects without being affected by their changes. Similarly, Consciousness observes all experiences without becoming entangled in them.

To live with this awareness, even while fully engaging in the world, requires constant acknowledgement of our true nature as Consciousness itself. The body and mind are simply tools—functional instruments enabling us to navigate and transact with the world without losing sight of our inner stillness and detachment.

Chapter 26

INTRODUCTION TO VEDIC MEDITATION

The Vedic meditation practice, as previously outlined, comprises three integral facets: Shravanam (hearing), Mananam (contemplation), and Nidhidhaysanam (reflection). This structured approach is designed to facilitate the understanding and realization of Self-knowledge inherent in teachings of vedanta.

Shravanam marks the initiation of the learning journey, involving a systematic examination of the philosophy over a period. The goal is to distil the essence of Vedanta, accomplished through dedicated engagement with the scriptures under the guidance of a competent guru. This endeavour dispels the illusion that the disciple is an imperfect entity, unveiling the truth that, in reality, they are the defect-free Brahman.

During the **Mananam** phase, the individual undergoes a process of liberating the mind from doubts and intellectual obstructions. This process is crucial for solidifying the idea rooted in the concept of non-duality (Advaita Vedanta) that the authentic Self (Atman) of the individual is inherently and eternally Brahman, which is the ultimate reality or cosmic spirit in Vedanta philosophy.

The removal of doubts and intellectual obstacles is seen as a means to realize this inherent oneness and experience a state of Self-realization through the next stage of Vedic meditation.

Nidhidhyasanam is the final phase in Vedic meditation, emphasizing the importance of internalizing teachings, freeing the mind from erroneous beliefs, and cultivating doubt-free knowledge. The notion of deconditioning the mind from false beliefs and limitations is central to the transformative journey.

Abiding in the truth becomes paramount in reshaping a mind ensnared by misconceptions—a mind tethered to perceived limitations and reliant on the external world for solace, security, and joy. Those who depend on the external realm face a decisive dilemma: either yield to its unpredictable whims or bear the consequential costs, as the world stands capricious and beyond control. Consequently, endeavours to construct a meaningful life on the ever-shifting sands of this dynamic sphere prove unattainable.

Having elucidated the nature of the immeasurable Brahman in the preceding sections and with the expectation that the reader, through self-introspection with a purified mind, has attained a logical understanding of one's true Self, this section will concentrate on the internalization of that Self knowledge.

Meditation, in its essence, can be comprehended as the act of substituting one set of thoughts with another, or as an endeavour to redirect the flow of thought towards a specific objective. The triumph of even the most rudimentary meditation practice hinges upon securing the cooperation of the mind, a task that is oftentimes the most arduous, and frequently the chief cause for many abandoning the practice prematurely, disheartened by outcomes that fall short of their expectations.

Any form of meditation possesses the capacity to instil a fundamental serenity within the mind. However, delving into the intricacies of the mind, understanding the roots of its agitation, and acquiring the means to surmount it hold greater significance in achieving optimal results. This marks the initial step. In the pursuit of calming the mind, the methodology involves engaging the mind itself, a task fraught with challenges. The mind, inherently, is predisposed towards negativity, beset by the presence of eight detrimental influences that take root in early life. The purification of these impurities necessitates the practice of Karma Yoga.

The mind, being extroverted by nature, and the emotional constitution of the meditator, dominated by either of the two energy propensities (Rajas and Tamas), engaged in perpetual conflict, further contributes to its restlessness. The resolution to this discord lies in cultivating Sattva, the third energy propensity to reconcile the warring factions. The most accessible avenue available to us is the performance of Sattvic Karma—noble activity—wherein the focus is directed towards benefiting a greater number of individuals. This alone catalyses resetting our thoughts towards the noble disposition. Consequently, our words and deeds align naturally, ushering forth a profusion of positivity.

At this point, it is important to clarify that our analysis is not centred on a traditional meditation practice, commonly referred to as

Upasana Yoga, which focuses primarily on calming the mind. Instead, we explore Vedic meditation, intricately crafted to attain the highest aspirations of humanity. This distinctive pursuit requires a thorough understanding and an alternative approach.

THE PURPOSE OF MEDITATION

The role and purpose of Vedic meditation, as elucidated in the Upanishads, bear distinct characteristics (what Vedic meditation is, and what it is not):

1. Vedic meditation is not a pursuit aimed at achieving liberation, for liberation is not an external objective to be sought within the human existence. Rather, it is an inherent aspect of our being, inseparable from our essence. Liberation is an innate reality, a siddha vastu, not an outcome of external efforts. It resides in realizing and embracing this truth. Knowledge alone serves as the pathway to uncover the liberation that already resides within us.
2. It does not serve as a means to attain knowledge of the absolute reality.
3. Vedic meditation is not geared towards obtaining extraordinary or mystical experiences, as is often the aim in other meditative practices. The Vedas acknowledge the possibility of such experiences for yogis but assert that these encounters are linked to objective knowledge, residing within the realm of the external universe and therefore transient.
4. The primary objective of Vedic meditation lies in acquiring knowledge of one's true Self, residing within the spiritual realm and transcending objective knowledge. Given that the seekers are endeavouring to comprehend their nature, meditation cannot serve as the means to ascertain the truth about oneself, as the meditator cannot simultaneously assume the dual role of the subject and the object. Consequently, meditation cannot bestow liberation, which entails rediscovering our authentic Self.

   It is crucial to note that the seeker of liberation must abstain from chasing extraordinary or mystic experiences, for they remain unrelated to Self-knowledge. Such pursuits would confine the seeker within the finite world of Anatma (non-self) and perpetuate the cycle of samsara (the cycle of birth and death).

The primary purpose of meditation is twofold, as expounded upon in the ancient scriptures: firstly, it serves as a preparatory ground for the receptive mind, like the tilling of soil before sowing the seed. This initial form of meditation, referred to as 'Upasana Dhaynam', holds significance in the tuning of one's mental faculties, a necessary exercise to prepare the mind before acquiring knowledge. Subsequently, the seeker must glean knowledge concerning their true identity by employing the prescribed means found within sacred texts. The underlying principle is the same as our inability to gaze upon our own eyes which see the whole world; we require a mirror to perceive them.

Similarly, when endeavouring to fathom our authentic selves—where the knower must become known—self-reliant efforts cannot yield this understanding. What is essential is the guidance provided by scriptural teachings, known as 'shabda pramanam'. This knowledge is acquired through the two-fold process of Shravanam (listening) and Mananam (contemplation) inherent in Vedic meditation. It surpasses any lower form of meditation meant for calming the turbulence of the mind momentarily; that which cannot facilitate the discovery of Self-knowledge—the consciousness that underpins all our experiences.

This knowledge instigates a profound transformation in the individual's character, leading to the attainment of mental equanimity, as proclaimed in the scriptures. Unfortunately, many struggle to achieve this equanimity due to various obstacles, with deep-seated notions (vasnas) and erroneous beliefs about our true identity, acquired during childhood, being chief among them. The elimination of these obstacles requires time and diligent effort.

The second purpose of meditation is Nidhidhyasana Dhyanam—a contemplative process meant to assimilate knowledge of the Self until it becomes lived reality, culminating in inner peace: the first fruit of Self-awareness. In daily life, however, it is often not the conscious mind but the subconscious, conditioned by past impressions (samskaras), that drives our behavior, especially our reactions. This is why we may react impulsively—when confronted with another's harsh words or unacceptable actions—and only later regret our response. Such lapses occur when Self-knowledge remains at the intellectual level without penetrating deeper layers of the mind. Through steady Nidhidhyasanam, knowledge is impressed upon the subconscious, gradually reshaping one's inner personality. As this transformation takes root, instinctive reactions give way to natural equanimity, compassion, and clarity—signs that wisdom has moved from mere thought to enduring realization.

The process of Nidhidhyasanam necessitates:

1. An attentive lifestyle: engaging with the world in accordance with Vedantic teachings.
2. Meditation: the internalization of teachings to facilitate the requisite transformation of one's personality. It entails maintaining inner serenity in the face of external disturbances through continual affirmation of one's true Self, the ever-unperturbed Consciousness.

Chapter 27

COUNTERMANDING OBJECTIONS

Comprehending the potency of Vedic meditation, against primary objections, is deemed requisite for fostering a foundational degree of faith and conviction in the notion, paving the way for its acceptance and embrace.

First objection: the proposed practice, which suggests subjecting the mind to intense contemplation, presents a novel threat to the already taxed mind, burdened by countless unresolved concerns. In the present age, man requires his mind to find peace, allowing him to channel his energies on many endeavours other than solely attending to daily sustenance. What utility lies in any disruptive practice if it fails to fortify his aspirations for legitimate worldly comforts? Ailing individuals demand prompt medical attention; the famished seek nourishment, and Cleopatra yearns for Mark Anthony. To address these needs, the mind must be spared, its faculties unencumbered by prolonged reflection on some ethereal entity labelled as Consciousness and striving to harmonize with it.

Second objection: indubitably, man must consistently engage with the world for his manifold transactions, not with Consciousness. Consequently, man has found no reason to rediscover his inherent essence while making strides over the past century, progressing from walking on the earth to reaching the moon and beyond. He is well aware of his birthright as a conscious being and harbours no doubts concerning its continuity from his entry into existence until his exit. Thus, labouring to comprehend some cosmic principle seems futile. Why shift from driving on the left to the right when equilibrium reigns? The adoption of a practice to alter one's perspective shall remain a distant prospect for a man deeply entwined in the blueprint he charted for his future within the phenomenal realm, long ago.

Third objection: conforming to Consciousness is prone to clash with the mind, corroding dynamism and the spirit of competition within man, perhaps even segregating individuals into the camps of saints or atheists.

Fourth objection: the notion of Vedic meditation seems akin to intellectual provocation. Its pragmatic application in the crucible of real-life situations is open to debate. Can the rhetoric of optimism materialize into action?

A Vedantin would hold that such derision, verily, arises from cogitative inference born of limited cognizance. The fruit of such ratiocination—being rooted in the finite faculties of reason—is oftentimes tinged with scepticism. For reason, when wielded as the sole instrument of understanding, becomes a tool of doubt, withholding assent until all is proven to the satisfaction of empirical logic.

To aid the discerning reader in appreciating the deeper import and enduring value of Vedic meditation in the face of such arguments, I present the following rebuttals.

Admittedly, mankind is in ceaseless engagement, striving to fulfil desires and thereby enhancing the quality of life to attain security, tranquillity, and felicity. In their fervent pursuit of creature comforts, fame, relationships, and wealth, individuals strain every fibre of their being to satisfy the restless urges of the senses. Yet, personal experience repeatedly reveals a sobering truth: external acquisitions—tainted by inherent limitations—seldom yield lasting fulfillment. Still, like benighted souls posing as sages, they continue circling the same path, unable to recognize that no finite accumulation can complete the finite self. Worldly possessions, after all, are merely instruments—not ends in themselves. Interestingly, individuals with modest means often seem to grasp the above truth early, choosing a more serene existence through compromise. Though not necessarily enlightened, these individuals have certainly understood that life's quality doesn't revolve around the quantity of material wealth accumulated. Instead, it's contingent on the state of mind, which remains susceptible to various influences even after desires have been met. Underestimating the profound impact of unfulfilled aspirations on the mind, therefore, is a crucial oversight we must avoid.

The oft-touted doctrine of forsaking desires to alleviate suffering is met with rejection due to its impracticality in the realm of real-life situations. Thus, the sole recourse that remains is the management of the repercussions when buffeted by karmic consequences. In readiness, comprehending the causes for non-fulfilment of desires is foremost. The inception of action to attain fulfilment of a desire heralds the commencement of man's struggle. And within this struggle lies the bridge connecting desire with its consummation or lack thereof—a linkage reliant not solely upon the individual's exertions, but also upon the intervention of an extrinsic force—Karma Phalam, a peculiar formula of nature perchance ordained to subdue chaos through inequity. Arguably, it is an unwavering and just bestowal of outcomes peculiar to humankind alone.

Imagine a world where every aspiration to opulence was fulfilled—anarchy would ensue. Providentially, such a state shall never come to pass, for the doctrine 'to each according to his karma,' a metaphysical verity, shall endure, even if spurned by the masses. This timeless principle finds validation not only in sacred texts but also in countless real-life events that defy logic, privilege, or planning. Despite living in a world governed by causality and effort, outcomes often unfold in unexpected ways—pointing to an unseen law of karmic return that transcends human control.

Consider the son of a legendary Bollywood actor—despite his father's towering fame, powerful connections, and repeated opportunities, he failed to make a mark in the film industry. Neither lineage nor influence could override the son's karma. His journey, like everyone else's, unfolded according to the unique trajectory shaped by his past actions, not the merit or momentum of his father's legacy. Contrast this with newcomers from humble beginnings who, without backing or glamour, rose purely on merit and perhaps the unfolding of favorable karmas.

Indeed, it is disconcerting to reckon with reality when the fruits of labour bear no nexus to the endeavour, sagacity, or intent. Perhaps, this trait of karma fosters belief in the migration of the principle of cause and effect, in the potentiality of life beyond mortality.

Having thus established that unrest of the mind springs not solely from unfulfilled desires, it is incumbent to unveil the strata obscuring other causal agents by retracing our steps to the root.

The mind, a progeny of nature, also serves as its emissary, pivotal in kindling sentience within the corporeal and cerebral complex. It achieves this via its unidirectional communion with Consciousness throughout a mortal sojourn. As the preeminent commander, it is privy to all transpiring within the corporeal confines, yet it remains oblivious to itself. It is not aware that, as pure matter it thrives on borrowed existence. Oft plagued by an identity crisis engendered by antithetical proclivities—referred to as SRT factors—it is the secondary, yet weighty component after the ingrained ignorance, shaping its constitution. These factors, verily, orchestrate the thoughts, deeds, comportment, and character of the individual. The mind, then, is both master and thrall to the cogitations it begets.

THE AWAKENING WITHIN: VEDIC MEDITATION FOR INNER EQUILIBRIUM

Vedic meditation stands not as a disruptor or a rival to contemporary practices, for it resides on a distinct plane, catering to a grander purpose. Its stance is one of cooperation, devoid of intentions to undermine existing methods, thus avoiding any unwanted quarrels. The central objective of this discipline is to attain the most essential knowledge required to break free from constraints and refine the mind, a necessity for enhancing an individual's existence. While a modicum of intelligence suffices for acquiring such profound wisdom, the mental obstacles in acknowledging, integrating, and applying this wisdom in practical life find resolution through the intricate procedures embedded within Vedic meditation.

According to a recent survey conducted by the Springtide Research Institute, it was revealed that one in every three adults in the Gen Z demographic, aged eighteen to twenty-five, 'acknowledges the existence of a higher power'. Additionally, the survey pointed to a growing interest among young people in matters of spirituality, along with a discernible shift away from dogmatic and traditional religious affiliations and beliefs. On a positive note, there seems to be a contemporary resurgence characterized by the youth's enthusiastic embrace of authentic Yogic and Vedic meditation practices. They display strong curiosity in understanding both the scientific and metaphysical underpinnings of these practices.

As Dr Bob Moorhead writes eloquently in his poem, *The Paradox of our Time*—the paradox of our time in history is that we have taller buildings but shorter tempers, wider freeways, but narrower viewpoints. We spend more, but have less; we buy more, but enjoy less. We have bigger houses and smaller families, more conveniences, but less time. We have more degrees, but less sense; more knowledge, but less judgement; more experts, yet more problems; more medicine, but less wellness.

We've learned how to make a living, but not a life. We've added years to life, not life to years. We've been to the moon and back, but have trouble crossing the street to meet a new neighbour. We've conquered outer space but not the inner space. We've done larger things, but not better things.'

An enlightened being, it is said, possesses a mind unburdened. The notion that self-awareness reigns supreme among all understanding is captivating. The drive to delve deeper, especially during the early stages, might impose a favourable strain on certain minds. Yet, with progression and the honing of the skill to sift through superfluous thoughts, wondrous truths unfurl gradually. Concurrently, the techniques tailored to disentangle diverse and intermediary thoughts intertwined within the mind aid in augmenting the capacity to focus, thus enabling the achievement of novel feats in the practical realm.

The soaring march of economic progress on one flank and the lengthening of human life span on the other have, amidst various trials, significantly augmented the likelihood of prolonged mental distress for individuals. This affliction, which is now understood, often takes root in his psyche at a remarkably tender age in the present day. Man, despite traversing the sands of a century, has not gained a surfeit of sagacity. He scarcely entertains the notion of his profound ignorance while he accords himself rewards and unmerited accolades, attributing his intellectual prowess to the material-fed recesses of his mind. Yet, in all verity, the origin and impetus behind his achievements eternally reside in Consciousness.

The more he esteems his borrowed wit as the fount of his advancement, the farther he veers from the wellspring. The manifold quandaries that besiege man's existence emanate from, and are exacerbated by his attachment to the corporeal vessel and the ruminations it houses—the entities rooted in a lesser stratum of reality. As a progeny of nature, the intellect remains impotent to operate independently in its pursuits of acquisition, retention, or utilization of knowledge sans the indwelling presence of Consciousness, which presides over each act of cognition.

Vedic meditation unfurls before him his genuine essence, the ultimate verity that traverses a loftier echelon of existence. Thereafter, he ceases to take Consciousness for granted, striving to forge a closer communion with the wellspring. And once he finds alignment with Consciousness, the pure intelligence, he ascends to a state congruent with his true nature, a state impervious to the most vehement corporeal perturbations. Possessing a calm mind, he stands primed to usher forth greater material comforts, all the while retaining equanimity towards the capricious mutability of the world.

He will accept the iniquities of life without chagrin, for Consciousness, the perennial revealer of truths, stands as a bulwark of dependability, sustainability, and predictability. His faith in Consciousness, as the compass guiding his path, burgeons. This metamorphosis renders him a consummate theist, disrobing him of artifice; a persona more amicable to his surroundings. He views the world with heightened objectivity, liberated from erstwhile dependence on religiosity and rituals to mould his attitudes, nurture his moral bearings, and concretize his convictions, transcending into an unalloyed theist.

'The contention that the widespread advance of wealth shall invariably uplift the stature of every soul in the economic fabric is a presumption as ill-considered as the age-old indictment that Vedantic notions would dismantle all societal progress and material prosperity, rendering existence bereft of value for it is incapable of such crime,' argued Rajam with conviction. He discerned the astuteness of the fact that man, in his journey through the tapestry of the relative realm, must rely upon both his corporeal vessel and his conscious faculties. Yet, the tenets of Vedanta stand resolute as the sole instrument at his disposal to refurbish his mental equilibrium, particularly when the ego traverses the unavoidable trials of an earthly sojourn.

This wisdom extends its embrace to all but finds a distinct affinity with those vigorous and astute souls who regard the onslaught of adverse circumstances as arbitrary and unjust retribution for having embarked on the human voyage. It is tailored for those who grapple with reluctance in acknowledging the edicts of the intertwined forces of nature and karma—edicts immutable by nature. In truth, the doctrine of Vedanta extends its embrace to any aspirant harbouring the hope to confer meaning upon existence, regardless of the circumstances that may invade.

Even after realizing their true nature, no one is free from the ups and downs of life—pain and pleasure still arise, shaped by their own accumulated karma, which must run its course. However, those who stay anchored in the knowledge of their true Self remain mentally calm amidst life's storms. Through dedicated discipline and the practices laid out in the Vedas, they learn to accept life as it is, without resistance. These teachings aren't just methods—they prepare the seeker to gain deep Self-knowledge. As a result, negative thoughts don't trap them, nor are they shaken by the ever-changing world around them. During meditation, at their volition, they can stave off all perturbing influences from their contemplative sphere. Their resolve continues to be unwavering in remaining harmonized with their perennially unchained and abundantly complete essence. Simultaneously, they remain engaged with the world at large, just like any other person, but they are unmoved by the fruits of their undertakings—some of which yield optimism, while others end in desolation. Serenity ever envelops their mind. Neither the trials of existence nor the spectre of impending mortality perturbs them. Mundane events, which punctuate human life, hold no allure for them, nor do they stir trepidation. Birth and death, growth and decay, are but inconsequential to one who abides in unison with one's authentic Self.

The potent shroud of Maya, an all-encompassing veil of ignorance, firmly keeps the common man distanced from the precincts of his genuine essence. The path to emancipation through enlightenment is, in equal measure, a rigorous journey for him. The attainment of saintliness, contrary to casual parlance, is no facile pursuit. It materializes only upon the relinquishment of personal possessions and the abandonment of one's identity. Be it known that the nexus between sainthood and self-awareness is non-existent, as proclaimed by the Vedic scriptures.

The acquaintance with one's own true nature is independent of such considerations. It is enlightenment, accessible to all, irrespective of life's stage.[36] Neither a metamorphosis of form nor a shift in faith is ever requisite. Given that Vedic meditation's objective is the realization of the immutable verity, the steadfast reality, it inherently lacks the potential to impede any soul's progress.

DISSOLUTION OF ATTRACTION (RAAGA) AND AVERSION (DVESHA)

The deliverance of the tumultuous mind finds its sole sanctuary within the realm of Vedic meditation. This method is meticulously fashioned to fulfil three paramount objectives: a) relinquishing the clutches of allure (Raaga) and repulsion (Dvesha) towards the world, which in turn influences our ability to stay focused or be distracted; b) encompassing both external manifestations and one's internal faculties; c) orchestrating the flow of thoughts, and remoulding the constituents of the SRT framework. The path of Vedic meditation becomes a vehicle for skilfully navigating allure and repulsion, for it is this dyad that fundamentally foments the inner turbulence. 'Attraction' denotes the clinging, the yearning, the grasping onto material objects, and the expectations entwined therein. 'Aversion', conversely, signifies the recoil, the mental dismissal, the resistance towards circumstances bereft of alternatives.

A mind caught in the web of attraction and repulsion is constantly judging—every experience, every situation, every person. This nonstop evaluation often leads to disapproval, which then gives rise to a wide range of negative emotions. Nearly all forms of emotional pain can be traced back to the disapproval of someone, something, or some event.

It is only when one realizes that the world operates on an underlying duality—where everything is perceived to exist alongside its opposite—that true understanding begins to dawn. Upon deeper reflection, one comes to see that these so-called opposites are not in conflict, but are complementary, designed to offer varied experiences of the same underlying substratum.

Upon each engagement in Vedic meditation, a fresh layer of truth is steadily unveiled, gradually reducing the dominance of attraction and repulsion. Consequently, a diminution in the prevalence of adverse reactions transpires, resulting in an elevation of the mind's quality. More specifically, this form of meditation aims to concentrate its efforts on curbing the frequency, intensity, and recovery duration of emotional perturbations.[37] A mind of superior quality is endowed with resilience, permitting it to swiftly rebound to its equilibrium, even when buffeted by the tides of emotional turmoil.

Central to the process of refining the mind is the focal point of neutralizing Raaga (attraction) and Dvesha (aversion). This quest takes us deep into the essence of existence, the understanding that the world is an amalgamation of opposing pairs, pervasive across all domains, including matters of faith and philosophy. Thus, should one find favour in a particular aspect, its counterpart shall invariably evoke disdain. The key to eluding the sway of attraction and aversion is to embrace the pairs, an acknowledgement that duality is the very fabric of our world; they stand as two points on a continuum, marking the journey's commencement and culmination. As the ebb and flow of opposing forces are inherent to the relative realm, they cannot be extricated. Our endeavour, then, should centre on embracing them devoid of judgement, releasing rigid expectations, and transforming our stance to greet both with poised equanimity.

This phenomenon arises through the profound practice of meditation while dwelling in the serene depths of Atman. In a remarkable revelation from Consciousness, it becomes evident that conflicts between opposites fade as thoughts about the two facets—this and that—of a coin gradually dissipate. For those who embrace this practice, the traditional demarcation between day and night no longer exists as opposing forces; instead, they meld into the fundamental unity of the twenty-four-hour cycle, encompassing both day and night. It's akin to a child, untouched by judgement, playing joyfully with its excrement, entirely unfazed by distinctions between pleasant and foul, and without concern for categorizing it as good or bad.

Not only does the world exhibit the feature of inherent duality in its nature, but our actions also inherently embody this principle in the form of commissions and omissions. This can be readily observed when reflecting on our life experiences. As finite beings with limited knowledge and understanding, we are prone to both omissions and commissions. At times, we may unintentionally omit certain actions, while on other occasions, we consciously commission actions, choices, or responsibilities. This interplay of commissions and omissions shapes the tapestry of our lives, revealing the dynamic nature of human existence.

Recognizing this, an adherent of Advaita Vedanta does not nurse remorse for the errors of yore. He remains unmoved by contrary viewpoints held by proponents of disparate systems, recognizing that these systems, entrenched within the realm of functionality and phenomena, fall short of encapsulating the absolute truth. To him, the illusory dyad of subject and object dissolves.

The sole formula for mitigating the reverberations that the ever-shifting world imposes on the mind lies in traversing the threshold into the non-dual realm, where the constraints of relativity, and thereby the dominion of attraction and aversion, cease to subsist. This journey is one of convincing the mind and ascending beyond the realm of duality.

It is proclaimed that an aspirant who, under the guidance of a guru, learns to practice 'nirveda' (transcendence of attraction and aversion), which culminates in 'samata' (equanimity amid provocative circumstances), eventually flowering into 'yukti' (Vedantic inquiry that unfurls the knowledge of the absolute truth), transcends the shackles of bondage.

OVERCOMING ATTACHMENT

Comprehend the limitations that encircle the world, for any entity within the objective realm, regarded as a source of delight, shall in no time transmute into a source of sorrow.

Acknowledge the verity that the tangible façade of the world is nought but an interplay of nomenclature and semblance, a fusion of the quintessential elements of nature, crafted into diverse contours. This epiphany alone shall serve as the conduit for man to abide within his authentic essence.

The fetters of habitual attraction and aversion, ingrained as vasnas present a formidable challenge to surmount. Erasing the impressions of attraction and aversion that amass through the hours of the day must find resolution through the act of meditation.

The elements intersecting a person's life converge as a result of the intricate threads of karma, and in the same manner, those very threads will disperse with the ebb and flow of karmic currents. Embracing this awareness will lead to a gradual reduction in attachment.

Chapter 28

PREPARATION, DISCIPLINE, AND PROCESS

THE TWO IDENTITIES OF INDIVIDUALS

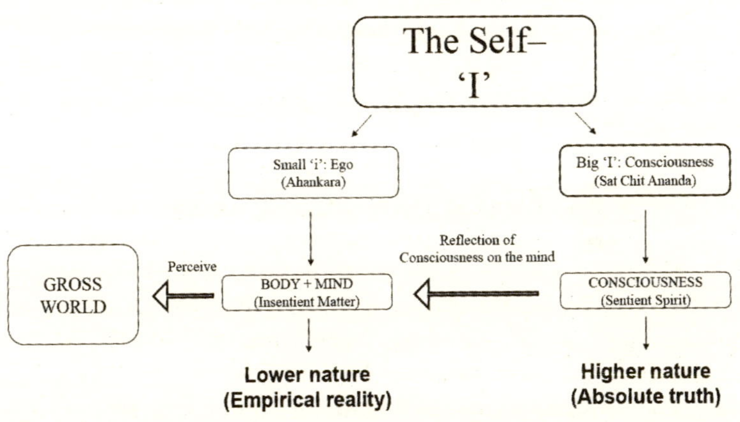

Before embarking upon and culminating the practice of meditation, the correct understanding and discrimination of the two 'I's are indispensable. The ever-changing 'i' pertains to a lower echelon of reality—the individual self, encompassing the composite of body and mind, known as Kshetra, in conjunction with the reflected consciousness. This term, 'reflected consciousness', is employed to accommodate two distinct aspects. Consciousness reigns as the sole, enduring truth, transcending the dissolution of time. As elucidated by the Jagat Guru, 'The Self within is one only; two inward Selves are not possible. But owing to the limiting adjunct, the one Self is practically treated as if it were two, just as we make a distinction between the ether of the jar and the universal ether.'

From the vantage point of this ultimate truth, nothing belongs to Consciousness, for nothing exists beside it; it stands alone in existence. Yet, from another perspective, the entirety of the world belongs to it, as each entity within the phenomenal realm relies upon its substratum—'consciousness'—for its sustenance. While this assertion holds, the converse is equally valid, for Consciousness neither hinges on external elements for existence nor necessitates the world's presence to validate its being. Its validation emanates from within itself. It endures eternally, with or without the presence of the world.

Thus, Consciousness establishes its independent, relationless state, akin to the analogy of the desert and the mirage. The material body and the universe remain concealed without the illuminating light of the Self, the Supreme Consciousness. The Self is inherently radiant and serves as the foundational substratum. Hence, the Ashtavakra Gita asserts: 'All this universe is truly mine, or indeed, nothing is mine at all.'[38]

ALIGNING WITH THE REAL SELF: CONSCIOUSNESS

'There is a self-existent Reality, which is the base of our awareness of our ego—I. That Reality is the primordial witness. It is the luminous Spirit Itself', affirmed Jagat Guru Adi Shankara. That eternal reality is widely recognized as the life force, the awareness principle, and Consciousness within the realm of spirituality. It serves as the foundational essence and the true identity of all entities within the phenomenal world. The process of perception and experience commences and concludes solely due to our awareness of events in the presence of Consciousness.

The human body–mind complex remains conscious as long as it remains connected to the Supreme Consciousness with eternal existence. Man, in the absence of Consciousness, is unable to undertake any task, including the recognition of his name and form. His genuine identity and true Self lie in Consciousness. Due to ignorance, man commits two fallacies. Not only does he falsely associate himself with his name and form, but he also attributes all his capabilities to his body and mind, giving rise to his ego, the individual self. This erroneous identification, stemming from ignorance, obstructs his understanding of his role and life's purpose.

Thus, the solitary goal of Vedic meditation is to assist man in discovering the hidden truth about his real Self; the truth about his higher nature, and identifying with it. In the Vedic scriptures, Consciousness, the unchanging Reality in the individual, is called Atman and Brahman in the Universe. However, the two are the same; one uniform, homogenous, immutable and all-pervading spirit. Again, these two or more names describe the indescribable principle and are often interchanged at various reference points.

Therefore, a spiritual seeker should not equate the absolute truth with body and mind, which is the relative truth. Nonetheless, the ignorant man thinks of his body–mind complex as a conscious entity by itself, and ignores the significance of its dependence on the self-independent Consciousness for survival. Thus, contesting the independent, relation-less status of the Supreme Consciousness is the mother of all ignorance. 'Into blinding darkness enter those who worship ignorance'.[39]

The law of cause and effect stands as the very rationale for man to encounter an array of consequences, inevitable as long as he continues to traverse the path of both virtuous and evil actions. Indeed, it is the profound grasp and immersion in the omniscient principle that empowers one to embrace life's favourable and unfavourable episodes with a steady heart. This understanding definitively extinguishes the penchant for regretting the past and fretting over the future. 'Knowledge or wisdom then is the panacea for ills of life,' as proclaimed in the *Adhyatma Upanishad*. Restructuring thoughts concerning subject and object, coupled with a gradual shift of focus from the ever-fluctuating 'i' (the complex of body and mind) to the immutable 'I' (the Supreme Consciousness), forms the cornerstone of this Vedic meditation.

The transformation from relying on the external world to relying on God (cosmic energy) within time and space, to eventually relying on oneself stands as the path to be embraced. Notably, no observable alteration transpires at the material level during this transformation, nor when man rediscovers the veracity of his elevated essence. When he finds intellectual alignment with the adorable absolute truth, also known as Tadvana, he identifies himself as the Self, yet he does not manifest behaviour discordant from the rest of humanity. On the contrary, he becomes an object of admiration. His altered perspective permits him to perceive the world more objectively than before. Embracing Consciousness as the sole truth, he garners the audacity to dismiss the realm of multiplicity—a realm encompassing names and forms—as mere illusion.

Subsequently, he recognizes the ultimate truth within every entity. In this recognition, he readily dissociates from his body and mind, perceiving them as inert elements belonging to the inert world. Even as the body and mind continue to generate an array of experiences through their interactions with the world, he stands aloof intellectually from the multitude of events transpiring within and around him. All the while, he resides in the realm of pure consciousness. He perceives the world and every entity therein as a reflection of the Self. Consequently, he transcends the realm of likes and dislikes. He embraces the world as a lower order of reality without any kind of discrimination.

The diverse entities, with their distinct names and forms, each characterized by unique needs and priorities, emerge as the offspring of misperception harboured by the ignorant. Thus, an individual who attains knowledge of his genuine Self, known as sthita pragya, remains emotionally detached and harbours no expectations from anyone or anything. He exemplifies self-control, composure, and withdrawal.

Neither attraction nor aversion for the world touches him. Yet he retains compassion and empathy for those who suffer. He laughs and he cries. 'It is not the love for the wife that the wife is dear, but for the love of the Self that the wife dear,' as declared in the *Brihadaranyaka Upanishad*. Therefore, he is never inconsistent when extending love and affection even to those who consistently demonstrate unacceptable behaviour. He remains untroubled by evil; instead, he overcomes all evils. He emerges untainted, free from doubts. Vedic meditation elevates him to a realm where he beholds the unknowable, the omniscient; he transcends the confines of cause and effect. Empowered thus, he remains unaffected by the inevitable pairs of experiences, for these merely constitute disturbances occurring within the benign realm of names and forms.

GENERAL AND SPECIFIC PREPARATIONS

Both general and specific preparations are vital to optimize the outcomes of meditation.

In the pursuit of discipline, our primary focus should be on cultivating the willing cooperation of the mind, as it lies at the core of the meditative experience. Without the voluntary engagement of the mind, meditation cannot manifest its intended benefits. The very mind that undergoes a spectrum of emotions throughout the day is the instrument we employ in our meditative practices. Consequently, our foundational preparation is centred on acquiring the skill of preserving equilibrium within the constantly fluctuating realm of the mind. This skill becomes crucial as the mind must harmonize with the ever-changing external world during waking hours and assume a pivotal role in the focused contemplation of meditation.

A simple analysis reveals why, within moments of beginning meditation, the mind tends to restlessly wander. Each encounter we have with the tumultuous onslaught of words, actions, and situations in the external world leaves deep scars in the recesses of the subconscious. The injured psyche may not immediately grasp the gravity of these wounds, as the conscious mind is typically occupied during such moments. However, during meditation, when the conscious mind remains unengaged, a deluge of thoughts erupts from these simmering subconscious scars, swiftly disrupting and hindering the serenity we aim to attain.

Hence, it becomes imperative for us to cultivate the capacity to prevent turbulent disturbances from etching negative impressions in our psyche during our interactions with the external world. Engaging in Karma Yoga emerges as our primary avenue for cultivating a balanced mind, as emphasized in the Bhagavad Gita.

How do we stop unwanted thoughts from bothering us during meditation?

The confusion around meditation often stems from the varied perspectives of different teachers. To clarify, an effective approach begins with setting a clear intention for each session by asking yourself, 'What do I seek from today's meditation?' This involves channelling scattered focus into a singular point. In Vedic meditation, this means systematically discarding random, extraneous thoughts, and concentrating on a chosen focal point. The key lies in recognizing when your focus strays and gently redirecting it to thoughts aligned with discovering your true Self or with the intended goal of meditation. With consistent practice, this method naturally cultivates the ability to sustain a single, purposeful thought throughout each meditation session.

Furthermore, anyone seeking peace through meditation must grasp the purpose of karma in life. As outlined in scriptural teachings, individuals often pursue two primary objectives: Artha (economic well-being) and Kama (sensory pleasures), in their quest for happiness. However, practitioners of Karma Yoga adopt a different approach, treating their actions as Pancha Maha Yagna (the five great sacrifices), and embracing Nishkama Karma—selfless actions performed without attachment to personal desires, focusing instead on fostering inner spiritual growth.

In doing so, they willingly let go of or minimize their focus on actions solely aimed at material prosperity. By relinquishing concerns about material gains, Karma Yogis maintain a sense of equanimity and remain unperturbed by the outcomes of their actions, whether they unfold favourably or unfavourably.

Such a Karma Yogi epitomizes a true sanyasi, distinct from those who have forsaken external possessions alone. True renunciation is not confined to external possessions. Hence, one must renounce all factors capable of agitating the mind, with freedom from worry about the future ranking as paramount. Such an individual earns the title of a Sankalpa Sanyasi, a resolute monk. The Karma Yogi is not akin to someone sitting in a serene meditative pose with a wandering mind. Their meditation remains undisturbed, for their mind is wholly present in the moment.

It is essential to emphasize that the practice of Karma Yoga, in isolation, does not confer Self-knowledge; rather, it serves as an intermediary or saadhana, preparing the mind for the acquisition of knowledge. As one progresses, a natural transition to the next level, namely Jnana Yoga (discussed elaborately in preceding sections), becomes imperative. Hence, it becomes fitting to moderate one's engagement in Karma Yoga when the mind achieves sufficient purification. This occurs when the practitioner no longer harbours cravings or aversions towards sensory pleasures or the actions required to attain them. Such an individual is termed a Sarva Sankalpa Sanyasi, one who has cultivated a wholesome, resolute mind unburdened by concerns about the future, and firmly grounded in the present.

On the contrary, individuals facing adverse consequences resulting from their past actions may find it challenging to enlist the cooperation of their minds. Such individuals must note that attributing all life events solely to Prarabdha Karma borders on fatalism; instead, it is crucial to acknowledge and exercise our inherent free will—an intrinsic capacity available to everyone—while gradually seeking the cooperation of the mind.

The Supreme Self, the consciousness underlying the limited 'i' (comprising body, mind, and reflected consciousness), resides within each of us. Embracing this profound truth nurtures a harmonious relationship between the mind and the Supreme Self. However, when disproportionate importance is placed on the transient aspects of the body and mind, we inadvertently position the Supreme Self as an adversary through contrasting implications. This misalignment fosters conceit, hindering the mind's ability to maintain calmness during meditation. Recognizing this reality and tempering unnatural desires and unwarranted cravings, the small 'i' can serve as a valuable conduit to our greater advantage, connecting us to the expansive realm of the greater 'I', which represents the ultimate goal of Vedic meditation.

This recognition unfolds in two distinct stages. Initially, it involves a transition from the realm of 'changing thoughts' to the realm of 'changeless Consciousness'. However, upon reaching this stage, there may arise a misleading inclination within the meditator. One might erroneously believe, 'I (the complex of body and mind) have successfully identified the unchanging Consciousness within.' While this is certainly a form of knowledge, termed as Jnanam (knowledge), it does not represent the correct 'truth' sought in Vedic meditation. The next step is crucial, moving towards the final stage where one declares, 'I am that consciousness, which gives me the awareness that I possess this body and mind—an incidental tool employed for life's transactions.' This is the 'truth' known as Vijnanam.

This shift in thinking constitutes the core of Vedic meditation, a quest to discover the authentic 'I' and embrace it fully. As a result, the perceived limitations of the body and mind fade away, for the individual no longer identifies with the 'limited self'. Consequently, all fears of death, illness, anxiety, and dependence on the external world for peace and happiness dissolve. Individuals who reach this state become the masters of their being. This is the correct understanding of the often-misrepresented term 'enlightenment'. Yet, the notion of a superhuman entity endowed with supernatural powers finds no place here—a trait more commonly associated with individuals experiencing bipolar disorder.

Wisdom shields such individuals from the oscillations of life's dualities—be it the extremes of heat and cold, or the nuances of favourable and unfavourable circumstances. Such individuals harbour no aversion towards objects of lesser value nor undue attachment to those of greater worth. Their judgement isn't swayed by human-assigned measurable values; instead, their perspective transcends the superficial, allowing them to perceive the true essence of all living beings—the Atma. To them, all distinctions fall within the realm of Anatma. Consequently, they recognize inherent virtue in everyone, fostering a profound and inclusive worldview. Crimes, in the eyes of a Jnani, are but temporary impurities upon saintly souls, like the moss that momentarily mars the divine fragrance of sandalwood.

The wise understand that every soul merits love, and they direct their efforts towards purifying others without harbouring any hatred. On a physical level, they neither experience attraction nor aversion towards anyone, having transcended the sway of likes and dislikes. They are unattached because they do not rely on anything in this world. Hatred, they comprehend, is merely another form of dependency, stemming from the absence of desired objects. As a result, a Jnani remains impervious to the presence or absence of anything in the world. The minds of wise individuals, adorned with virtuous thoughts, are inherently calm. This tranquillity enables them to concentrate on the objective of meditation, guiding them steadily towards the ultimate goal.

The specific disciplines to be observed just before embarking on the path of meditation are as follows:

Firstly, one must comprehend that meditation's effectiveness hinges on meticulous adherence to these preparatory steps. The primary aim is to elevate one's consciousness from its ordinary waking state to a loftier realm, eventually achieving union with the Supreme Consciousness. Succumbing to the allure of the mundane and material aspects of life leads to an imbalance in one's reflected consciousness. Consequently, the meditator must divest the mind of all external stimuli that trigger sensual desires and immerse themselves wholly in the chosen object of meditation. This process necessitates the cultivation of unwavering focus, a single-minded concentration through discrimination of the real and the unreal.[40] Furthermore, the Bhagavad Gita prescribes eight specific disciplines to be observed to optimize the results of meditation:

1. **Solitude (Ekaki):** Until one attains mastery over sama (control of the mind) and dama (control of the sense organs), achieving a state of being unaffected by both tangible and intangible sensations from the external world, the spiritual aspirant is advised to seek seclusion. This retreat should take place away from the presence of others, preferably in a tranquil environment that can invoke inner purity and silence, a silence that is profound enough to be heard.
2. **Timing (Kala):** Preferably, meditation should be conducted during the Sattvic Kala, the early hours of the day, even before the birds herald the dawn. At this juncture, the propensities of Rajas and Tamas within the meditator are at their nadir, allowing Sattva to dominate the mind and facilitate focused meditation.
3. **Duration:** The duration of meditation may vary, with quality superseding quantity. The key is to meditate for as long as the mind remains fully engaged and available.
4. **Seat (Asanam):** The seat of meditation should be personal and exclusive, not shared. It should possess a balance between firmness and softness, ensuring that it remains stable and unobtrusive, eliminating potential distractions that might hinder the meditative experience.
5. **Body Posture (Sharira Sthithi):** When seated with legs crossed, it is recommended to ensure stability. Additionally, the neck and body should be kept erect at right angles to the floor, promoting a posture that supports comfort and mindfulness during meditation.
6. **Controlled Breathing (Prana Saamyam):**[41] Breathing during meditation should be deliberate, slow, and rhythmic. Prana Veekshanam, the mindful observation of the breath, is preferable to conventional Pranayama. This practice recognizes the intimate connection between thoughts and breath. Thoughts are associated with the knowledge sheath of the subtle body, which powers knowledge—Jnana Shakti of Vijnanamaya Kosha; breathing (prana) through its association with the vital sheath, the Pranamaya Kosha powers the organs of action—Kriya Shakti of karmendriyas,

and both are connected to the energy of Consciousness—the Maya Shakti.

7. **Restraint of the Five Senses (Indriya Nigraha):** Disturbances in meditation arise when external stimuli enter the mind through the five senses. Hence, it is imperative to withdraw the senses through deliberate awareness by averting the mind's attention. A helpful technique is to keep the eyes half-closed, as though focused on the tip of the nose.
8. **Withdrawal of the Mind (Mano Nigraha):** This involves setting aside thoughts associated with worldly roles and responsibilities, allowing the mind to become still and focused. Often, the mind is plagued by regrets from the past or anxiety about the future. Overcoming these distractions requires deliberate effort, grounded in a conviction of their futility. This negative process enables the mind to concentrate on the Self. Connecting with a higher power, such as God or one's guru, is recommended to facilitate this. By invoking the guru within oneself (gurum pranamayam), one aligns with the guru's teachings, which predominantly centre on Self-knowledge (Brahma vidya) and the realization of Brahman.[42]

Additionally, the condition of both the body and the mind holds significance, as articulated by Sir Radhakrishnan: 'Through thoughts, we appeal to the intellect; through silence, we touch the deeper layers of our being. The heart must become clean if it is to reflect the Atman. The living presence of Atman is revealed in silence to each one according to his capacity and need. What is needed is the will and perseverance to follow it up.'

Meditation and moderation are likened to the two legs of a spiritual journey towards Self-discovery. Practising moderation in various facets of life, including eating, resting, activity, and sleep, is essential. Meditation becomes a source of inner peace for those who maintain moderation in all aspects of life. This equilibrium is attained when the ego, the individual self, is harmonized with the higher Self, the Atma.

The attainment of the meditation's objective necessitates the vigilant regulation of both mind and body. Patanjali Risi, the venerable master of yoga, prescribed the practice of meditation only after traversing the rigorous path encompassing the eight disciplines elucidated in Ashtanga Yoga, as outlined in the Patanjali's *Yoga Sutras*.[43]

Moreover, intellectual conviction, known as Buddhi Nischayaha, plays a pivotal role in the success of meditation—one must firmly believe in the significance and benefits of Vedic meditation in the pursuit of spiritual growth. This meditation should be diligently practised over an extended duration.

It is essential to recognize that regular, unwavering practice is imperative; sporadic attempts yield little fruit. During meditation, one should direct the mind without attachment to desires and remain indifferent to material possessions. If the mind remains entangled in the web of ego, the petty 'i', it becomes impossible to contemplate the concealed inner essence of our being. As Jesus proclaimed, 'It is easier for a camel to pass through the eye of a needle than for a rich man to enter the Kingdom of God* upon observing the deep sorrow of a wealthy individual' (St. Luke).

*The Kingdom of God, in this context, refers to Brahmapura—the sacred abode and royal palace of the Atman, the Supreme Self—dwelling within the heart of every individual.

The spiritual seeker must also grasp that the prescription of meditation is not intended for Self-realization but primarily serves as a means of purging the mind of—malam *and* vikshepa— impurities and the tumult arising from an outward-focused disposition. When meditation is practised prior to the acquisition of Self-knowledge, it is termed Upasana. In contrast, meditation undertaken subsequent to scriptural studies and attaining the knowledge of Self, referred to as Nidhidhaysanam, serves the purpose of internalizing acquired knowledge.

It is crucial to note that no amount of knowledge can facilitate transformation unless there is a profound shift in emotional disposition. The pursuit of Self-knowledge is not exempt from this fundamental principle. Hence, it remains imperative to engage in Vedic meditation even after acquiring knowledge until one has fully purged the habitual Vasna—the inclination to identify with the physical body (deha abhimaana vasna). Dr Radhakrishnan aptly emphasizes that disciplined disinterestedness is the primary requisite for this endeavour, and to achieve this, we must remove ourselves from the equation.

In summary, the key to reaching the goal of meditation lies in maintaining control over both the mind and body. Patanjali Risi's teachings in the *Yoga Sutras* emphasize the critical importance of these disciplines. Furthermore, unwavering intellectual conviction in the value of Vedic meditation is crucial, and persistent, regular practice is essential. This is because meditation serves not only to purify the mind but also facilitates the transformation of one's emotional disposition, ultimately culminating in the realization of the Self.

ASHTANGA YOGA: A GLIMPSE

The practice of Ashtanga Yoga, introduced by Patanjali, serves as the framework for the integration of personality in Vedic meditation. This eight-fold path is explained below:

1. **Yama**—the five don'ts:
   a. **Ahimsa (Non-violence):** This foundational principle entails an unwavering commitment to refrain from causing harm, whether through thought, speech, or action, to self and any living being. Its end purpose is to regulate our tendency to harbor hatred.
   b. **Satyam (Truthfulness):** Truthfulness is more than mere honesty; it involves aligning one's inner thoughts with spoken words and corresponding actions, forging harmony within the personality.
   c. **Astheyam (Non-stealing):** This tenet extends beyond the act of theft and urges us to seek happiness within rather than taking away the happiness of others. It underscores the importance of contentment.
   d. **Bramhacharya (Chastity):** Practising chastity in words, thoughts, and deeds towards individuals of all genders is the cornerstone of spiritual life. It forms the bedrock that fortifies one's connection to higher consciousness, fostering a sense of purity and integrity in interpersonal interactions.
   e. **Aprigriha (Non-avarice):** This principle advocates transcending greed and emphasizes concentrating on genuine needs by curtailing the desire for material possessions to the essentials required. Specifically, it involves restraining the impulse to acquire the belongings of others, fostering a mindset of contentment and simplicity.
2. **Niyama**—the five dos:
   a. **Saucha (Purity):** Saucha encapsulates the practice of

maintaining purity in the body, mind, and surroundings. It involves fostering clarity and cleanliness in both thoughts and actions, creating a harmonious alignment between the internal and external aspects of one's being.

b. **Santosha (Contentment):** Contentment emanates from refraining from the relentless pursuit of material possessions, which often serves to project a false image. It entails discovering satisfaction in simplicity and finding joy in the present moment. Additionally, contentment involves being at peace with the outcomes of one's actions and being prepared to embark on the next course of action, embracing both success and challenges with equanimity.

c. **Tapas (Austerity):** Austerity practised in body, speech, and mind instils the discipline required to persevere in meditation, fostering inner strength and resilience.

d. **Swadhyaya (Study of Scriptures):** Engaging in the study of scriptures is a pathway to Self-discovery, offering profound insights into the nature of the self.

e **Ishwara Pradhana (Devotion to God):** This aspect emphasizes devotion to God and alignment with the consciousness of the divine, serving as a guiding force in one's spiritual journey.

3. **Asana (Posture)**—this discipline pertains to the correct positioning of the arms, legs, and upper body, optimizing the results of meditation by disciplining the gross body (Annamaya Kosha).
4. **Pranayama (Breathing)**—this consists of exhalation and inhalation, and retention of breath. The conscious control of breath impacts our emotional disposition and must be undertaken under the guidance of a qualified teacher to regulate the subtle bodies (Pranamaya Kosha).
5. **Pratyahara (Withdrawl)**—similar to Dama, as prescribed in the sadhana chatushtaya of Vedanta, pratyahara involves withdrawing the sense organs from their respective sense objects. This practice is grounded in the conviction that these external stimuli cannot provide lasting happiness.
6. **Dharana (Concentration)**—this step entails redirecting the mind away from worldly distractions, enabling the seeker to focus on the chosen object of meditation or the thoughts of Brahman.
7. **Dhyanam (Meditation)**—this stage involves the intermittent resting

of the mind on Brahman. The meditator maintains focus on the chosen object during this phase. It is not uncommon for the mind to experience distractions, especially in the initial stages of meditation.

8. **Samadhi (Absorption)**—in the state of samadhi, the mind naturally becomes absorbed in the object of meditation. All distractions cease, and the mind dwells in uninterrupted contemplation of the chosen focal point. It is a state characterized by a continuous flow of similar thoughts, undisturbed by dissimilar ones.

In essence, meditation unfolds as a journey of inner exploration and connection with the divine. It requires unwavering faith, dedication, and the systematic practice of Ashtanga Yoga to achieve the profound states of consciousness and bliss that meditation promises.

SAVIKALPA AND NIRVIKALPA SAMADHI

In Vedanta, two levels of absorption are delineated, contingent upon the meditator's capacity, termed as savikalpa and nirvikalpa samadhi. In savikalpa samadhi, the meditator's contemplation firmly rests upon Brahman, yet he retains awareness of his ego—the individual self—as distinct from his true Self. Additionally, he remains cognizant of his will and the efforts exerted to attain the state of samadhi. Consequently, a division persists—the meditator perceives himself as the subject, the knower meditating upon the Lord as the object of meditation. Thus, it is aptly named 'objective meditation' (savikalpa samadhi), where the demarcation between subject and object remains evident. In this form of meditation, Brahman is invoked through a 'sound symbol', typically by repeating Vedic mantras with the intent of aligning the mind with the Supreme. Alternatively, a 'form symbol'—such as a sacred image, a candle flame, or any object that symbolizes both the absolute (Brahman) and the relative world—may be used. These symbols serve as external focal points, helping to steady the mind by anchoring awareness to something tangible. This method is commonly adopted by seekers in the early stages of their spiritual journey, as it facilitates concentration and inner connection. However, it is essential to recognize that this is merely a preparatory practice—an aid to focus—not the final or highest state of meditation.

In the second form of samadhi known as nirvikalpa samadhi, the meditator is wholly engrossed in the contemplation of Brahman.

At this stage, the meditator relinquishes his ego and individual self, becoming one with Consciousness—his genuine essence. Here, subject–object differentiation dissolves entirely. The meditator perceives himself as inseparable from Brahman; in essence, he is Brahman. This represents the ultimate culmination of the eight-step path of the Ashtanga Yoga.

The mind can be directed towards the focal point of meditation, fully absorbed in contemplation of Atman, guided by devotion (bhakti) and unwavering determination (vairagya). In Vedantic meditation, devotion is integral to the practice and should encompass contemplation on the nature of Atma. Essentially, the meditator reiterates the teachings concerning Atma, recognizing it as their true nature. Through consistent practice and wholehearted dedication, the flow of contemplative thoughts gains strength, and the process becomes effortless. As a meditator is gradually immersed in this devotion, the *Yoga Shastras* classify the progression into three stages: Dharana, Dhyana, and Samadhi.

In Dharana and Dhyana, the meditator systematically gathers and concentrates the mind, ultimately leading to absorption in Samadhi. In the initial phase of meditation, savikalpa samadhi, absorption is a conscious and deliberate act. However, in the subsequent stage—nirvikalpa samadhi, absorption occurs spontaneously, devoid of any volition. This stage represents the pinnacle of Ashtanga Yoga, marking the culmination of the spiritual journey.

WHAT IS SAMADHI?

It is a state wherein the mind finds complete serenity, similar to the unruffled lake's surface. To attain such a state, one must embark upon the path of Ashtanga Yoga, with its disciplines of yama, niyama, aasana, pranayama, and pratyahara. Through these, the individual soul withdraws from the tumultuous anatma prapancha (world of multiplicity), finding solace in samadhi's tranquil embrace.

In this state, the meditator beholds the Atma, not in the literal sense, but in the profound understanding unveiled by the guru during Shravanam. It is a revelation within the inner recesses of the lower self, the mind itself serving as a conduit. The Atma manifests as the silent observer of one's thoughts, and it is only because the Atma identifies with these thoughts that such realization dawns. Thus, the meditator savours the joy of completeness, while assimilating Vedanta teachings into the silent chambers of the mind.

Samadhi, a realm of boundless bliss, stands apart from the fleeting pleasures of the senses. However, to the true Vedantist, this joy should not be confined to samadhi alone but must permeate every moment. It emanates from wisdom—the realization that one was, is, and shall forever remain replete. It is a ceaseless ecstasy, unshaken by any passing experience.

When one remains absorbed in the contemplation of the Atma, undistracted by the allure of Anatma, it is termed as Sahaja Samadhi. In this state, even amid the daily transitions of life, the person remains steadfast in their true nature, finding harmony in the seamless flow of existence.

ADDITIONAL INSIGHTS FOR MASTERING THE ART OF MEDITATION

Effective Ways to Meditate

1. **Regular practice of Karma Yoga:** Integrate the principles of Karma Yoga in daily interactions to train the conscious mind to act with sensitivity and sensibility, reducing impulsive reactions and fostering mindful decision-making.
2. **Understand the purpose of meditation:** Develop a clear understanding of why you meditate to provide direction and meaning to your practice.
3. **Set a specific goal:** Define a clear purpose for your meditation session, aligning your thoughts with the intended goal to establish focus and intention. Begin by setting this goal, and conclude the session once the mind gains clarity on the actions to take afterwards. This purposeful approach ensures that each session is intentional and outcome-driven rather than arbitrary, fostering meaningful and practical results.
4. **Start with pranayama:** Begin with three to five minutes of alternate nostril breathing to centre your mind and bring awareness to the present moment.
5. **Choose the right time and setting:** Meditate early in the morning before sunrise to harness the tranquillity of dawn. Wear loose, comfortable clothing and, if possible, meditate alone.

6. **Avoid external conditioning:** Do not depend on specific ambience, music, or visualization unless your meditation is goal-oriented for material achievements.
7. **Prepare your body:** Avoid overeating or fasting before meditation, and ensure a restful sleep to maintain focus and avoid drowsiness during the session.
8. **Maintain consistency:** Cultivate a regular meditation practice to experience sustained and lasting benefits.

Addressing Common Concerns

1. **What to do when feet go numb?**
   It's natural to notice sensations like numbness during the early stages of meditation. Allow blood flow to alleviate discomfort without fixating on it. With practice, your focus will stabilize, and such occurrences will diminish.
2. **How to breathe during meditation?**
   Maintain natural breathing throughout the session. Conscious breathing may help manage emotions like anger or reduce distractions, but consult a qualified yoga master to identify suitable techniques.
3. **Is meditation religious?**
   Meditation transcends religion, serving as a tool to calm the mind and reduce mental turbulence caused by external distractions. You can practice meditation within any religious or non-religious framework that aligns with mental tranquillity.
4. **Switching teachers or practices:**
   Transitioning to a new meditation teacher or practice can be beneficial if the teacher is skilled and knowledgeable. For Vedic meditation, ensure the teacher follows traditional methodologies and has a deep understanding of the practice.
5. **Benefits of morning and evening meditation:**
   - Morning Meditation:
     Practising in the morning harnesses the calmness of the 'S' (Sattva) factor after a restful night, fostering introspection and creative thinking with minimal external distractions.
   - Evening Meditation:
     Meditating before bed helps release the day's accumulated stress and turbulence, promoting a peaceful and restorative sleep.

Chapter 29

HOLDING ON TO THE KNOWLEDGE OF SELF

STAYING RESOLUTE WITH WISDOM

Meditation for the mere pursuit of joy conflicts with the primary objective of Vedic meditation: the internalization of the knowledge of Self—imparted by the guru, known as Jnana Nishta Praapti. It is the assimilation of these teachings into our very being, ensuring they remain unwavering even amidst worldly engagements. Clinging to this knowledge signifies a steadfast refusal to revert to the former self. Hence, all external entities—the world, body, mind, and the myriad emotions contained therein—must be negated. Finding delight in meditation poses an obstacle, as proclaimed by Gaudapadacharya in his *Mandukya Karika*; he terms it as 'rasaa swaadhaha', another form of bond.

Knowledge, if it is to hold any worth, must serve a practical purpose in our daily lives; otherwise, knowledge remains but an empty vessel. Thus, it becomes imperative to continually reinforce this knowledge. A swift recollection of these teachings, laid out in three layers:

1. You are not the body–mind complex, but rather, you are the Consciousness. Therefore, embrace your true Self—the Atma.
2. Consciousness resides within every living being. Progress further by recognizing the presence of Atma in every element of the vast universe. Consciousness pervades this universe, and this universe exists in Consciousness.[44]
3. Having claimed your true Self as the Consciousness, not only dwell within every object, but every object resides within you. Extend your perception to encompass every object as existing within your very essence.
   A sage, whose mind is steeped in Self-knowledge attained through Nidhidhaysanam, gazes upon each person with equanimity, perceiving Atma in every human being, as elucidated in the

> Bhagavad Gita: 'sarvatra sama-darshanah' (equanimity towards all). Although distinctions may be observed at physical, emotional, and intellectual levels, the sage never loses sight of Atma's presence within every entity. Revering the Consciousness that stands as the sole force behind the entire creation, the sage holds it in the highest esteem. This veneration plays a pivotal role in Vedic meditation, serving as a direct means to refine one's personality and maintain a tranquil mind at all times.

This realization implies that each time you feel conscious, you are in communion with the divine. There is no necessity to close your eyes in meditation to behold the Lord, for you are perpetually experiencing the divine within yourself and within the life essence animating every living being.

Through unwavering practice, the sage's vision expands to such an extent that he perceives every being as an extension of his self. He understands that he is the Atma not only behind his form, but also behind the bodies of others. This profound realization precludes any inclination to harm another, as he universally identifies with the divine. His empathy knows no bounds, and he remains steadfast at all times. He does not deem his body superior to others, and thus, he exhibits no partiality or selfishness. He is one who, by withdrawing from a few finite relationships, transcends boundaries to unite with the entire world.

THE PATH TO ONENESS

Atman, the all-pervading truth residing within the heart of every individual, eagerly awaits to embrace and merge with the intellect of a sincere devotee who recognizes this innate connection. The initial step, therefore, entails invoking faith in your intimate relationship with Atman, recognizing its support for your very existence and all your endeavours, including meditation. Subsequently, your focus should remain unwaveringly fixed upon Atman throughout the entire duration of your meditation. This, indeed, is the ultimate objective. In the realm of spiritual life, it is not merely the repetition of mantras for divine acknowledgement but the silent communion with the divine principle, bridging the gap between the individual self and the divine.

The meditator's mind must be steadfastly attuned to the Supreme

Consciousness, which presents itself in three distinct aspects of the same divine entity. For beginners, it takes the form of an individual deity with a name and human likeness, providing solace and satisfaction to those immersed in thoughts of their personal God (eka roopa dhyanam). With increasing spiritual wisdom, the same individual recognizes the divine presence in all facets of creation (viswa roopa or aneka roopa dhyanam).

In the ultimate stage, when spiritual seekers attain Self-knowledge, they recognize the formless Lord (aroopa) as their true Self. At this point, a singular thought of Atman consumes their awareness, merging it with the Supreme Consciousness. Meditation reaches its maturity as the non-dual, unchanging reality replaces the illusory, ever-changing duality, eliminating the division between subject and object. In this state, the meditator experiences an esoteric bliss which transcends ordinary comprehension.

OBSTACLES AND SOLUTIONS TO THE PRACTICE OF MEDITATION

Within the sacred texts of Vedanta, one encounters a discourse concerning four distinct impediments, as elucidated by sage Gaudapada in the *Mandukya Karika* under the heading of 'mano nigrahaha'—the mastery of the mind. This wisdom is particularly intended for those who have acquired knowledge and yearn to bask in the tranquillity it brings, emancipating themselves from the shackles of worldly turmoil.

A person who proclaims, 'Aham Brahmasmi' ('I am Brahman'), yet continues to grapple with the repercussions of worldly actions, clearly lacks the mental fortitude required for such a declaration. Vedantic meditation, therefore, becomes essential for individuals who perceive a disconcerting chasm between their acquired knowledge and their lived reality. Typically, those who have not undergone the requisite preparatory stages of 'sadhana chatushtaya' encounter this disjuncture. For such souls, the path of Vedantic meditation beckons.

The four obstacles delineated in the *Mandukya Karika* are as follows:

1. **Layaha:** This manifests as the dullness or somnolence of the mind, like the heavy veil that obscures clarity.
2. **Vikshepaha:** Herein lies the challenge of an overactive, wandering

mind, one that meanders ceaselessly, thwarting the mind's ability to remain steadfast in the embrace of knowledge during Vedic meditation—a practice designed to culminate in the transformation of one's very being.

3. **Kashaayaha:** This obstacle ensues when the mind succumbs to a non-functional state, precipitated by the intensity of likes and dislikes, thereby veering off the path of focused meditation.
4. **Rasaa Swaadhaha:** This state refers to the allure of experiential joy that meditation may provide, enticing the practitioner to revel in its pleasures rather than continuing on the transformative journey.

Recognizing and navigating these obstacles forms an integral part of the meditative voyage, guiding the seeker towards the ultimate goal of self-realization.

The remedies:

1. Sleeping should be avoided by eliminating the cause of sleep, which is engaging in meditation after having a sumptuous meal, indigestion, inadequate and or irregular sleep patterns. Training the mind, making it a habit to meditate is the way out.
2. Handling the wandering mind by training it to stay resolute with the need to accomplish the objective of meditation. The problem of hyper vacillation of the mind is not only turbulence of the mind, but it impacts other organs as well. Together they conquer wisdom too. The only solution is the most difficult act of the reorientation process. It involves sincere practice and dispassionate detachment (vairagya). Patanjali talks of the same in *Yoga Sutras*: 'abhyaasa vairaagya bhayam tannirodha'. Developing interest in the activity of concentration by understanding the value addition through the discrimination process; discriminating between experiencing pleasure and eternal happiness. The second solution is non-attachment to worldly things that do not add any value to one's real nature. Atma that is full.
3. Attaining a desirable focus in meditation involves reminding ourselves of the fundamental truth that every entity in the universe belongs to Atman—our intrinsic reality, when viewed from the perspective of the phenomenal world. Consequently, we cannot harbour likes or dislikes towards different entities, as they are all united by the spirit, the essence of all.

4. Recognizing that even the experiential pleasure derived from the external world is not possible without our cognitive ability, provided by Atman, which, by nature, is blissful, serves as the key to diverting our attention away from objects of the world that lack innate happiness.

THE FOCUS OF VEDIC MEDITATION

Vedic meditation unfolds through two dimensions—Anatma Dhyanam and Atma Dhyanam.

1. **Anatma Dhyanam:** Anatma occupies a lower rung of reality than the true Self. Consider the analogy of a dream: within the dream world, hunger appears real to the dreamer who operates within the dream's confines. Yet, upon awakening, everything within the dream promptly dissolves into unreality. Within the waking and dreaming states, the same individual persists, but only one can be deemed true. Similarly, in deep slumber, the entire world, including one's own body, vanishes into non-existence. The world, therefore, assumes reality solely when perceived from the vantage point of the body–mind complex.

However, when viewed from the standpoint of Consciousness, the entire world, encompassing body and mind, assumes a diminished reality—a mere interplay of names and forms devoid of self-independent existence. The 'I', as Consciousness, bestows existence upon the body–mind complex and the world during the waking state, just as a dreamer imbues existence into the dream body and dream world. Therefore, the dream's subject and object only possess borrowed existence.

Hence, it becomes imperative to meditate upon the unreality of the world, as this meditation takes precedence over meditating on Atma. Even after comprehending various concepts, the world may still disconcert an individual due to the residual sense of reality attached to it. Thus, one must dedicate more meditation to negate Anatma, especially in areas where strong attachments or aversions persist, lest these preoccupations disturb the tranquil state of the mind.

2. **Atma Dhyanam:** In this facet, the individual identifies with the non-dual Atma. Here, one realizes, 'I am the cause of this world, yet I

remain untouched by the world within me, just as space encompasses all but remains unaffected by anything.'

During meditation, individuals should continually remind themselves of the unreality, the 'mythyathvam', of the world. While experiences of the world are not denied, the meditator must assert that the experienced world ultimately lacks inherent existence. It is non-existent because experience alone does not validate its reality.

Just as a dream constitutes an experience, yet we discern its unreality, the world presents a similar reality—a prolonged dream. This truth becomes evident each time one enters the profound realm of deep slumber. The world's existence is the byproduct of a misconceived perception, for only Consciousness stands as the absolute truth. It mirrors the misapprehension of perceiving a rope as a snake. If the mind grapples with unsettling preoccupations, it indicates that the knowledge of the Self has not been wholly internalized.

Chapter 30

BENEFITS AND FUNCTIONAL INSIGHTS OF VEDIC MEDITATION

In the domain of Vedic meditation, an individual who once grappled with the mistaken belief in their inadequacy undergoes a profound realization of inner fullness. With this newfound insight, such an individual understands that fresh desires cannot alleviate the anguish stemming from unfulfilled past cravings. When even life's most splendid pleasures lose their lustre, there is no reason to be perturbed by the deepest falls or enraptured by the loftiest triumphs. One remains serenely poised, whether in the presence or absence of worldly enticements, with the mind under one's control.

Yet, it is imperative not to misconstrue this depiction as a promise that 'knowledge' or the attainment of 'samadhi' shall bestow eternal happiness. All acquisitions, by their very nature, are finite. This is why, despite experiencing the pinnacle of bliss in Nirvikalpa Samadhi, one cannot perpetually sustain such ecstasy once the meditation concludes. Infinite bliss cannot be acquired; it must eternally reside here and now. Therefore, in Vedanta, the pursuit of infinite bliss involves the removal of impediments obscuring the truth, thereby embracing one's inherent nature. Samadhi in Vedanta entails abiding in the natural state of fullness by dissociating from sorrow, an unnatural affliction to humanity.

This accomplishment is realized by redirecting the mind away from worldly thoughts, including our notion about our physical body, and by relinquishing all anticipation of the future along with its attendant expectations. It does not mean forsaking ambition but regarding all aspirations and yearnings as unbinding preferences, freeing oneself from the fixation upon a preordained outcome. The conscious engagement of the mind, infused with intellect and willpower, remains paramount.

The process of withdrawing from the external world to embark on an inner odyssey must unfold gradually. It commences with disengaging from worldly attachments, followed by the negation of the gross body, and ultimately, the mind itself. The crux lies in severing the bonds of attachment by realizing that nothing in this world truly belongs to anyone; nature leases all for our use for a certain period. As we can label things as 'ours' only when they genuinely belong to us, we cannot claim ownership when nothing belongs to us.

Engaging in the contemplation of thoughts centred upon Atma while excluding those of Anatma is termed as dhyana in Vedanta, in contrast to the dhyanam prescribed in Ashtanga Yoga. Dwelling unwaveringly in contemplation of Atma is Nirvikalpa Samadhi. This signifies that within the sanctuary of meditation, dissimilar thoughts shall find no foothold.

Moreover, managing thoughts becomes a crucial aspect of ensuring the support of the mind, which is often disturbed by undesirable thoughts during meditation. The thoughts that stir within our minds at the beginning of mediation possess little potency. Just as ripples upon a tranquil lake become waves only when stirred by the wind's gentle caress, thoughts amass strength only when nurtured through recurrent contemplation. If we quell an undesirable thought as it emerges, the mind becomes receptive to meditation's embrace. To sustain this journey, free from the entanglement of divergent thoughts, one must persistently affirm that thoughts endure solely due to Consciousness that bears witness to all that resides within the mind. It is then that the realization dawns—'Aham Brahmasmi' ('I am that Consciousness').

The process of guiding and redirecting the outwardly oriented mind inward may appear daunting. Yet in truth, we do not compel the mind to embark on this voyage. Atman, being all-pervading, renders nothing truly distant from itself at any moment. Thus, no exertion is required to transport the mind from one place to another and fix it upon Atma. The process entails the deliberate nurturing of thoughts that revolve around Atma, cultivating a continuous, undivided focus.

Vedic meditation does not seek to bestow upon the meditator some rarefied ecstasy, although such bliss naturally emerges each time. Its purpose is to saturate the mind with contemplations of one's genuine essence, uniting with the Atman that observes the mind experiencing bliss. In this state, all passions and desires wane, and the meditator attains pure tranquillity.

How can one practice 'Aham Brahmasmi' while navigating the physical world? Is it necessary to abandon a normal life to embody this profound realization?

The phrase 'Aham Brahmasmi' asserts the true essence of the Self as pure Consciousness. As emphasized in this text, this realization unfolds through the stages of Vedic meditation: Shravanam (listening to spiritual teachings) and Mananam (introspection). The subsequent stage, Nidhidhyasanam (deep contemplation), integrates this understanding into the subconscious mind. While the body–mind complex is essential for navigating the dualistic nature of existence, it often encounters challenges in worldly interactions, leading to numerous human dilemmas. Through profound meditation and contemplation, Nidhidhyasanam offers a sanctuary for mental equilibrium, allowing one to retreat from the clamour of external engagements into inner stillness.

However, mastering the principles of Karma Yoga is crucial to mitigating the turmoil caused by the ever-changing world. Renouncing ordinary life pursuits or material goals is not required. Instead, 'Aham Brahmasmi' serves as a guiding principle that offers two profound benefits.

First, diligent practice of its tenets, coupled with Self-knowledge, can liberate one from the cycle of birth and death. Even for those who do not believe in reincarnation, these principles foster a harmonious balance between intellect and emotions, enabling a fulfilling life.

Second, embracing 'Aham Brahmasmi' dissolves the troublesome 'me' factor—the ego—along with its divisive tendencies and attendant woes. This realization redirects the immense energy previously spent on protecting the ego, enabling acceptance of life's trials, and rejuvenating one's ability to face new challenges with vigour. Thus, 'Aham Brahmasmi' is not about withdrawal from the world but rather about engaging with it more consciously and harmoniously, rooted in the understanding of one's true nature.

SECTION ELEVEN

EXPERIENCE

Chapter 31

DWELLING IN BLISS OF THE ESOTERIC KIND

Every human life unfolds as a chapter of transition, a journey of metamorphosis. The essence of our existence lies in awakening to the purpose of transcending our animal lineage and aspiring towards the divine ideal. Human life has been bestowed upon us for this profound reason. The influence of our innate nature, the reverberations of heredity, and the encompassing environment can only be surmounted by us humans, armed with the fortitude of our will.

Once you've awakened to your inherent higher nature, you must stop meditating as you simply reside in the serene essence of your true Self. You have transcended all consciousness of bondage and freedom, as the Self is eternally liberated. Yet, continued engagement in meditation and other spiritual practices implies an underlying belief in bondage. As long as this perception persists, true freedom remains out of reach.

In reality, you are unattached, devoid of action, radiantly self-illumined, and immaculate. Paradoxically, it is the very act of meditation that will bind you.[45]

Chapter 32

THE FINAL BALANCE

'Control what you cannot eliminate,
Manage what you cannot control,
And if you do not manage your mind, you become a slave.
Your only hope then is to discover your true Self and
realize eternal freedom.'

As you reach the final chapter of this book, allow me a moment to connect with you. If I were to summarize the essence of everything shared within these pages in a single sentence, it would be this: human beings have no right to experience unhappiness.

If the Lord of Lords—Brahman, the Supreme Consciousness and ever-present witness—resides within every object, why do human beings engage in self-deception and suffer its consequences? This is a valid question, and the answer lies in understanding that Brahman is always aware of everything that occurs within it. What Brahman does not know cannot exist as a fact. The law of Karma operates at the phenomenal level, ensuring that actions yield corresponding consequences, even though all such events unfold within Brahman's infinite realm.

Yet, the universe, populated by individuals with active minds, cannot be forcibly controlled, for Brahman is neither a doer nor a dictator capable of preventing all evil actions. Brahman, as the ultimate reality, observes and brings about awareness but does not interfere.

Throughout this treatise, the doctrines of Karma and Karma Phalam have been explored with care and nuance. As we now draw to a close, it is vital to address a commonly misunderstood aspect—one that, if rightly understood, can restore the integrity of this profound teaching. Often, karma from past life is invoked when the cause of present suffering remains unclear. While this notion can offer temporary comfort, it can also serve as a convenient escape, allowing individuals to bypass meaningful reflection on their responsibilities. It discourages proactive engagement with the reality of the present moment. One must be prepared to confront the fact at hand, however obscure the cause may seem. The source of current challenges may lie not in distant lifetimes, but in choices made within this very life.

Such a perspective shifts the emphasis from speculation to sincere introspection. By examining one's past behavior and decisions with honesty, a person may identify attitudes or actions that have contributed to their present state. This discovery is not meant to induce guilt, but to serve as a catalyst for self-awareness and transformation.

Taking responsibility for past misjudgements, and resolving not to repeat them purifies the mind, and renews the spirit. Even a silent inward acknowledgment can bring relief, lightening the emotional burden and creating the conditions for healing. In some cases, this clarity may even soften the severity of physical suffering.

True engagement with karma requires more than theoretical acceptance; it asks us to transform every experience into an opportunity for self-evolution. The journey, then, is not to escape Karma Phalam, but to meet it with awareness, courage, and the will to grow beyond it.

In today's world, where material success and tangible achievements are often admired as the ultimate markers of fulfilment, it can feel challenging—perhaps even impossible—to strike a balance between intellectual growth and emotional well-being. The relentless pursuit of wealth, status, and possessions frequently overshadows the deeper quest for inner peace, leaving us yearning to fill the void within. It can be more formidable than night attempting to witness the day.

Yet, I wholeheartedly believe that achieving a harmonious balance between the mind's demands and the heart's needs is possible and vital for a life of genuine fulfilment. Cultivating the mind while nurturing the emotional core is the cornerstone of this equilibrium, paving the way to embody the profound wisdom of the Gita. This sacred scripture reminds us that we are most suited to pursue inner growth and asceticism while fulfilling the responsibilities of family life, demonstrating that spiritual advancement and worldly duties can co-exist in harmony.

I empathize deeply with the struggles many of you may face when attempting to align with your true identity—the immortal Self. These struggles often arise from deeply ingrained attachments to the body, the mind, and societal expectations. Such attachments, perpetuated by cultural conditioning and conventional worldviews, can make the spiritual journey seem daunting and fraught with barriers. Unraveling these layers and pursuing inner realization takes time, determination, and courage.

Adding to these challenges is the unfortunate misrepresentation of Vedic wisdom by self-proclaimed godmen and gurus. Over time, these individuals have appropriated the sacred knowledge to elevate their status, veiling its simplicity in unnecessary mystique. By presenting the truths of the Upanishads as accessible only to the exceptionally gifted or deeply learned, they have distanced countless seekers from the source of this wisdom. This has tragically led many to believe that spiritual exploration is beyond their reach, leaving them caught in a cycle of struggling first with life and later with the inevitability of death.

But let me assure you that the timeless wisdom of the Vedas is universal. It belongs to no single individual, faith, or group, and it is accessible to all who sincerely seek it. The teachings of the Vedas do not require exceptional intellect but a genuine willingness to embrace the truths they illuminate. Recognizing one's immortality and freeing oneself from fear may seem daunting, but it is far from unattainable. It begins with clarity of purpose, a steadfast commitment to truth, and the courage to let go of societal constructs and false narratives.

It is out of profound desire to see humanity freed from suffering that I undertook the task of writing this treatise. My hope is that this book has offered you clarity and insight, helping to resolve doubts, and inspire deeper exploration. By unveiling the simplicity and universality of Vedic wisdom, my intention is to dispel misconceptions and guide you towards an authentic understanding of your immortal essence.

The spiritual path is not without its challenges, but the rewards—freedom from fear, inner balance, and a harmonious alignment of intellect and emotion—are truly transformative. Remember, the Vedas transcend all barriers of time, space, and belief. They are the eternal voice of Consciousness, calling each of us to discover the profound reality that lies within.

You have a choice—human beings alone possess the remarkable ability to choose: to remain in bondage or to embrace freedom. Yet, choice inherently breeds confusion. Those who truly understand their purpose in life neither deliberate nor decide; they simply act with unwavering clarity and resolve.

Thank you for allowing me to share the knowledge I have gathered during my spiritual odyssey. I hope this book serves as a trusted companion and a source of inspiration as you embark on your unique journey of self-discovery.

ACKNOWLEDGEMENTS

The inception of this literary offering springs not from personal ambition, but from a moment of divine illumination—an inner stirring inspired by the timeless truths of Advaita Vedanta, as expounded by the illustrious sage and philosophical colossus, Param Guru Shri Adi Shankaracharya, and the exalted saints of his lineage. These radiant beings have lit the path of my spiritual journey, and to them, I bow in deepest reverence.

A moment of sacred import is forever etched in the memory of this undertaking: it was at the auspicious hour of 7.20 in the morning, on the 20th day of June in the year 2020, that my most revered Guru, Swami Paramarthananda, bestowed his gracious blessing and gracious approval upon this endeavor.

Its noble aim is none other than to offer to humanity the boundless gift of uninterrupted bliss—through the pursuit and realization of Brahma Vidya, the supreme knowledge of Brahman, the infinite Consciousness—attainable through the time-honored practice of Vedic meditation. For his boundless generosity in imparting this sacred wisdom, I remain forever indebted to my Guru. His penetrating commentaries on the exalted scriptures—such as the Ashtavakra Gita and the Bhagavad Gita—have served as the very foundation upon which this work rests. It is through his luminous guidance that I came to apprehend, with utter clarity, the true meaning of meditation, and more vitally, its power to uproot the fundamental sources of human suffering.

Throughout the shaping of these reflections, one truth remained unshaken: that this composition adds not an iota to the vast treasury of knowledge already held by my venerable master. Any such presumption would be folly. My task has been but to serve as a conduit—to gather inspiration from his teachings and offer them in a form that may speak to seekers as a bridge between comprehension and realization.

This work, then, is no more than a garland strung from the fragrant flowers of his wisdom—an offering of heartfelt gratitude, an acknowledgment of the immense privilege of discipleship, and a modest testament to the peerless light he has kindled within me.

I must also acknowledge the auspicious influence of several erudite scholars whose intellectual brilliance and spiritual clarity have, in no small measure, illumined my path. Among them, I count with deep respect Dr S. Radhakrishnan, Swami Nikhilananda, Shri B. R. Rajam, Swami Tapasyananda, Shri D. S. Sarma, Dr P. Nagaraja Rao, Shri Balasubramanian, and Shri S. Mukerji. Their timely presence in my life proved instrumental in affirming and refining my understanding, deepening my experiential insight, and reaffirming the eternal sanctity of the Self within.

The works authored by these luminaries stand as enduring testaments to their profound erudition and rare ability to distill the subtlest truths into eloquent, accessible prose. Their insights not only provided me with renewed clarity and orientation, but also enriched this present text with refined expressions and luminous thought—some of which have been gratefully included herein.

To these noble souls, I offer my heartfelt gratitude. And to the publishers of their works, whose permission I did not formally obtain before drawing upon these treasures, I extend my sincerest apologies, trusting that the spirit of sincere homage will be rightly understood.

I remain profoundly indebted to all who lent their minds and hearts to the shaping of this humble volume. Foremost among them is Ninupta, a thoughtful and diligent student of law, whose meticulous review of the manuscript yielded numerous invaluable suggestions. Her clarity of mind and sensitivity to language helped refine several passages, particularly those concerning abstract metaphysical ideas, rendering them more accessible to the younger reader.

To Srinath, who not only penned a most precise and thoughtful foreword—distilling the very spirit of the work into a few potent lines—but also stood by this effort from its inception, I owe particular gratitude. His discerning observations and timely interventions, including the restructuring of an entire chapter that had once seemed disjointed, lent cohesion and strength to the final work.

To Neelmani, a nineteen-year-old undergraduate student of finance, I extend warm thanks for his timely and incisive queries urged me to step outside my style and consider the reader's perspective more thoughtfully. His assistance in curating the pictorial representations that accompany the text has also been a contribution of great value.

Lastly, to Pragya, a poised and perceptive young woman with a master's degree in business, I offer my thanks for her graceful touch in the final stages. She undertook the essential task of polishing the prose—correcting both subtle and conspicuous grammatical errors—with patience and precision.

To these kind souls—each of whom played a distinct and irreplaceable role—I offer my heartfelt gratitude for their unwavering support, dedication, and quiet generosity.

I must also acknowledge, with deep appreciation, the discerning contribution of David Davidar—managing director, co-founder, and the guiding force of Aleph Book Company—who, without a moment's hesitation, recommended that the manuscript be reviewed by Aienla Ozukum, publisher at Aleph. That she perceived value in what was, at the time, a loosely formed and unshaped draft, and graciously chose to support its publication—recommending, with quiet wisdom, that it be positioned as a work of self-help—is a gesture I hold in the highest regard.

Thereafter, the refinement of this work was taken up with sincere diligence by Nandini Devdutt Tripathy, Vidisha Ghosh, and finally, my copy editor, Palak Hajela, who carefully incorporated the final changes and refinements, giving the manuscript its finishing touch.

To all of them, I offer my most sincere and enduring gratitude.

ENDNOTES

1 B. R. Rajam Iyer, *Rambles in Vedanta*, Calcutta: The S. P. League, 1946, p. 161.

2 Prakruti P. K. and P. Pavan, 'Berth and death: Seat change proves fatal for TCS techie', in *Bangalore Mirror*, 2 May 2014.

3 See *Brihadaranyaka Upanishad.*

4 Richard B. Chase and Sriram Dasu, 'Want to Perfect Your Company's Service? Use Behavioural Science', *Harvard Business Review,* vol. 79, no. 6, June 2001, pp. 78–84.

5 See *Kaivalya Upanishad.*

6 **Dharma**—embodies righteousness, serving as the guiding light for our actions aligned with our spiritual growth. Embracing dharma propels us towards success in every pursuit, while its abandonment leads to setbacks.

Artha—a legitimate pursuit in certain phases of life, serves as a means for social advancement. It is crucial; however, acquiring wealth must align with dharma, for veering away from it fosters greed and a craving for power, ultimately culminating in chaos.

Kama—indulges our sensual desires, but even this pursuit must heed dharma's guidance, lest it foster excessive sensuality.

Moksha—despite the fleeting contentment offered by Dharma, Artha, and Kama, a more profound and enduring desire lingers; a desire only quenched by freedom. The first three pursuits belong to the material world, providing transient happiness. The genuine essence of freedom, however, resides in the realm of the spirit, where ensuing bliss is eternal.

7 The Ashtavakra Gita, chapter 8, verse 4.

8 Supra-rational: knowledge that stands above reason and logic, but not excluding rational.

9 See *Katha Upanishad.*

10 Consciousness, the enabler of awareness, is often described as 'illumination' due to its inherent ability to unveil everything, much like light.

11 Nicholas Griffin (ed.), *The Selected Letters of Bertrand Russell: The Public Years, 1914–1970*, London and New York: Routledge, p. 215.

12 Extracted from the notification of the United States' Attorney's Office, Northern District of California.

13 See *Chandogya Upanishad.*

14 These encompass mechanical, chemical, electrical, thermal, gravitational, and nuclear energies.

15 'Genetic Mutations in Humans', Cleveland Clinic, available at https://my.clevelandclinic.org/health/body/23095-genetic-mutations-in-humans
16 David Hoinski, '400 years ago, philosopher Blaise Pascal was one of the first to grapple with the role of faith in an age of science and reason', The Conversation, 3 July 2023, available at https://theconversation.com/400-years-ago-philosopher-blaise-pascal-was-one-of-the-first-to-grapple-with-the-role-of-faith-in-an-age-of-science-and-reason-199659
17 See *Isha Upanishad.*
18 'Who created "Nothing" our Universe Formed From', Bright Side on YouTube, uploaded on 1 January 2023, available at https://youtu.be/iugaXcHxY90?si=QJ0PxB209J6IyOlh
19 A thrust fault that does not rupture up to the surface, so there is no evidence of it on the ground. It is buried under the uppermost layers of rock in the crust.
20 See *Aitreya Upanishad.*
21 S. Radhakrishnan, 'Introductory Essay' in *The Bhagavadgita,* London: George Allen & Unwin Ltd, 1963, p. 56.
22 Legitimate desires are meant for personal growth with no malice to others. Illegitimate desires are venomous, and are aimed at harming others.
23 **Mantras**—a collection of hymns recited during rituals and sacrifices to seek favour from, and establish communication with celestial beings. These were employed by the ancient Indo-Aryans as a means of connecting with the divine.

The Brahmanas—they elucidate the significance of these mantras. They also provide comprehensive guidelines for the meticulous execution of rituals and sacrifices (yajna). Both mantras and the Brahmanas were designed for orthodox worship aimed at invoking the presence of deities within the material world.

The Aranyakas—as a subset of the Brahmanas, they propose an alternative approach for those individuals who retired to the forest during the third stage of their life, and were unable to perform traditional sacrifices. It advocates symbolic worship and meditation as substitutes for physical rituals, allowing for spiritual contemplation amidst the serenity of the wilderness.

The Upanishads are the concluding segments of the Aranyakas, primarily intended for those who have renounced worldly desires and seek uninterrupted contemplation of Brahman, the ultimate reality. For individuals on this path, the need for external forms of worship, such as material offerings or idol/symbol worship becomes obsolete as they aspire to directly connect with the transcendent.

24 a) The inherent suffering in achieving something (the pain of acquiring, the stress of preserving, the distress of losing).
b) The constant discontentment that arises, perpetuating ongoing suffering.
c) The inability to pave the path to liberation, which rather binds one further.

25 The Ashtavakra Gita, chapter 2, verse 16.

26 See *Brihadaranyaka Upanishad.*

27 The Bhagavad Gita, chapter 2, verse 40.

28 See *Kena Upanishad.*

29 The Ashtavakra Gita, chapter 3, verses 13 and 14.

30 The Bhagavad Gita, chapter 9, verse 22.

31 The Bhagavad Gita, chapter 2, verse 38.

32 The Bhagavad Gita, chapter 2, verse 47.

33 Perception, inference, comparison, testimony, presumption, and apprehension.

34 See *Brihadaranyaka Upanishad.*

35 The eight malevolent forces are as follows: Kama (desire), Krodha (anger), Moha (delusion), Lobha (greed), Madam (conceit), Matsaryam (jealousy), Raaga (attachment), and Dvesha (aversion).

36 The following are the four phases of human life, which relate to the distinct life stages that humans go through:

a. **Brahmacharya:** This initial phase corresponds to a person's youth, during which they pursue education as a celibate student under the guidance of a teacher. They study various subjects, including the Vedas, and practice values such as chastity, obedience, austerity, and are exposed to the essence of divinity.

b. **Grihastha:** The second stage is when individuals transition into family life. They perform various rituals and follow the Veda Poorva's guidelines for a householder's duties. This is a significant phase when one confronts the impermanence of the material world. Gradually, disillusionment sets in as the allure of the superficial world fades. People seek a more meaningful existence, leading them to the next stage.

c. **Vanaprastha:** At this point, individuals in search of inner peace opt for seclusion, often retreating to forests, away from luxury and the distractions of routine life. Here, they focus on meditation and the pursuit of higher truths and realities.

d. **Sannyasa:** The final stage is for those who choose a monastic life, which is said to be the ideal lifestyle to learn the Upanishads of the Vedanta (last section of Vedas). These individuals, known as bhikshus, travel to spread wisdom and live an exceptionally simple, minimalist, unburdened life, having forsaken material possessions.

37 Noteworthy impacts—thought, speech, and action; intermediate intensity—thought and speech; faint disturbance merely arises within the mind's confines, abstaining from casting its ripples onto speech or action.

38 The Ashtavakra Gita, chapter 2, verse 2.

39 See *Brihadaranyaka Upanishad.*

40 'Ekaagrena chetasaa', as elucidated in the Bhagavad Gita, chapter 7, verse 10.

41 The Bhagavad Gita, chapter 5, verses 27 and 28.

42 See *Kaivalya Upanishad.*

43 The elements of Ashtanga Yoga ('the eight limbs of yoga', as set out in Patanjali's *Yoga Sutras*): Yama (abstinences), Niyama (observances), Asana (yoga posture), Pranayama (regulated breathing), Pratyahara (withdrawal from sense objects), Dharana (concentration), Dhyana (meditation), and Samadhi (absorption).

44 The Ashtavakra Gita, chapter 1, verse 16.

45 The Ashtavakra Gita, chapter 1, verse 15.